D1555133

MASTERS OF PARADISE

MASTERS OF PARADISE

Organized Crime and the Internal Revenue Service in The Bahamas

Alan A. Block

Transaction Publishers
New Brunswick (U.S.A.) & London (U.K.)

Library of Congress Catalog Number: 90-39528
ISBN: 0-88738-382-3
Printed in the United States of America

Library of Congress Cataloging-in-Publication Data

Block, Alan A.
  Masters of paradise : organized crime and the Internal Revenue
Service in the Bahamas / Alan A. Block.
    p. cm.
  Includes index.
  ISBN 0-88738-382-3
  1. Organized crime investigation—United States—Case studies.
2. Money laundering investigation—United States—Case studies.
3. Tax evasion—United States—Case studies.   4. Americans—
Bahamas—Case studies.   5. United States Internal Revenue Service
Intelligence Division—Case studies.   I. Title.
HV6448.B56 1990
364.1'33—dc20   90-39528
                                                            CIP

To Marcia for help and companionship;
and to the memory of Sally

Contents

Acknowledgments

A work such as this could never have been done without the aid and encouragement of many people. First and foremost is Richard E. Jaffe, who spent days answering every question imaginable with quiet poise, who provided entré to Internal Revenue Service (I.R.S.) personnel, including former Tradewinds and Haven agents and operatives, who opened doors without limit, and whose good cheer through adversity is a lesson in humility. My gratitude is also extended to his wife Millie for her patience as I "munched" my way through the interviews. In the category of patient and helpful others, Norman L. Casper, his lovely wife Karen, and attorney Donald E. Van Koughnet stand out for special commendation.

At this juncture I must add that Jaffe, in particular, but also Casper and Von Koughnet insisted on arranging, in one way or another, for me to speak with those whose opinions of past events were often diametrically opposed to their own. Old telephone numbers were "weeded out" of tattered files for my convenience, as well as some very unflattering documents about them, which were passed to me without any hesitation.

I spent about two weeks in The Bahamas reading through the late Sarah Jane (Sally) Woodruff's material, while abusing the kindness of her husband Ed Woodruff. Sally died of cancer in November 1982. I slept in Sally's bed and used her den, which was filled with files from years of quite special investigations. Through this entire research and writing exercise I experienced a growing admiration for her talent and humaneness. She became in my mind an ever more remarkable woman of such keen insight and truly rare abilities, that not actually knowing her still depresses me. She became my greatest inspiration.

From State College, Pennsylvania, I traveled to New York, Washington, DC, The Bahamas, Cayman Islands, Southern California, San Francisco, Denver, and so on, as the research intensified and more and more contacts were made. Often I was accompanied by my wife, Marcia Jenifer Block—a writer and environmental activist in her own right—whose help was also vital to this project. This is not the usual "thanks my dear for keeping things running smoothly while I'm away on yet another adventure." She asked by far better questions, and took finer notes than I in each instance we worked together. Her acuteness was best exemplified while we were in California, where her abilities finally made me understand one of the most complex parts of the Bahamian puzzle. She didn't always go with me, but she always read, with more stamina than I thought possible, the innumerable drafts of this book.

There were times in this research when certain consequential opportunities for data gathering presented themselves, but for which I lacked the wherewithal to afford travel. At critical moments like this my friend Jeremiah McKenna (former counsel of the New York State Senate Select Committee on Crime) stepped in and helped. I have always owed a great deal to Jerry and his family's generosity. They treated me with kindness and dignity, and usually to the most illuminating conversation one can find in New York. Jerry's closest counterpart is Carl Shoffler, recently retired from the Washington DC police. Although he always really wanted to coach women's basketball, Shoffler instead arrested the Watergate burglars, and turned out to be among Washington's finest detectives for two decades.

There are many others who took the time and trouble to help. One who stands out is Jim Drinkhall, formerly of the *Wall Street Journal*; another is John Daley, retired narcotics officer and I.R.S. Special Agent. In this same category are Robert Grant and Nick Tsotsos, I.R.S. Special Agents of unusual skill and courage.

I also am grateful for those who allowed me to interview them, either in person or on the telephone. Although many may disagree with my conclusions and interpretations, I nonetheless thank Ber-

nard Bailor, Burton Kanter, C. Carr Ferguson, Columbus O'Donnell, Colonel Gregory D. Stampados, Lawrence Freeman, Ian
Paget-Brown, Edwin Cohen, Jerome Kurtz, Ritas Smith, Dora
Saharuni Welch, William Wyatt, Scott Pratt, Nelson Barry, Sam
Pierson, Eugene H. Ciranni, and John Ehrlichman, who, like
some of the above, was candid and extremely helpful. I talked
several times with attorney Bill Metz in New York, whose knowledge of Robert Vesco's affairs is singular. In fact, these meetings
encouraged me to journey to Cuba in February 1988 in a vain
attempt to find and interview the slippery financier. I did meet
and talk with some Cubans who seemed to know Vesco, and what
he was doing on that magnificent island. But in all candor I spent
more time eating, drinking, and swimming with my friend, crim-
inologist William J. Chambliss (who helped arrange this most
curious expedition), than I did with Vesco confidantes. Lately, I
have been corresponding with Rebecca Sims, a fabulous re-
searcher currently working to unravel the savings and loan (S&L)
scandal, possibly this nation's most expensive "serious crime."
Her research is proving exceedingly fruitful, as some of the S&L
"players" were long at work in The Bahamas. Also very cooperative and kind has been *Forbes* reporter Graham Button.

I began this project while at the University of Delaware where
Professor Frank Scarpitti, my former chairman, supported this
research. In fact, the earliest stages of this project were done
together. On one trip to Florida to interview several principals,
Frank and I stayed at my cousin Andrew Block's house in Coconut
Grove. I woke the second morning to see Frank nearly smothered
by one of my cousin's huge Samoyed dogs, while another (called
Bear) was busy going through Frank's wardrobe. This may well
explain why Frank moved into more civilized research endeavors.

Cousins Andy and Yvette Block were not my only Florida
relatives to find me unannounced on their doorsteps. Bruce and
Bonnie Gaines, Celeste and Gerry Doliner, and Susan Shifrin
were all just as lucky. So too was my old high school chum Tony
Cutler and his wife Sarah. To all of them I am indebted. Out
west my sister-in-law Stephanie Abronson and her husband Chuck
provided food and lodging at their Malibu ranch. Their kindness
was not matched, even by the magnificent surroundings.

This kind of list, as most authors know, could drag on forever, so I will try and get to the end as quickly as possible. I started working on *Masters of Paradise* at the University of Delaware, and finished it at The Pennsylvania State University. The bulk of research, writing, rewriting, etc., were accomplished while going through my "breaking-in" period at University Park. I can say without hesitation that my new chairman, Daniel Maier-Katkin, created the ideal work environment. On many occasions Dan asked "what can I do to enhance your ability to work; what equipment do you need; what funds do you require? And no matter how outrageous my response, he always came through. I must add that I am not the only member of the Administration of Justice Department to experience this gentle man's dedication to our individual and collective well-being. Daniel's outstanding care is enhanced by several department secretaries who are friends as well as coworkers. Melody Lane is Daniel's secret weapon, a woman capable of amazing miracles on a daily basis. Tracey Melnick, the department's undergraduate adviser, is my other indispensable associate. Tracey works as the editorial assistant and general factotum for the journal I edit, once known as *Contemporary Crises*, and now titled *Crime, Law and Social Change: An International Journal*. Jennifer Morris, who sadly for the Administration of Justice Department moved to the dean of liberal arts' office, was yet another of the very bright women who diligently labored on this and other of my projects. Many others played one role or another in the production of this book. My youngest daughter Hallie Lorraine Block, now a sophomore at Penn State, for instance, computerized extensive news clips on Bahamian issues, thus considerably easing the research burden.

When I think back on all those who helped in some way, I wonder why they should not at least share responsibility for any serious errors of fact or interpretation there might be in this book. But custom will not allow this, and I thus absolve them of whatever is erroneous in what follows.

Introduction

The Serious Crime Community

Masters of Paradise is an account of this nation's most "serious crime community" at work in The Bahamas, and at home, from roughly the mid-1950s to 1980. During this time, the Internal Revenue Service (I.R.S.) had an unparalleled opportunity to strike at this community in a way not available before, and probably not since. How this came about, and why this chance was lost in the 1970s, is the heart of this work. American criminal activity in The Bahamas, and the contemporary history of the I.R.S., particularly that of its Intelligence Division (the service's renowned criminal investigative branch created in July 1919 and since 1978 called the Criminal Investigation Division), are completely interwoven; they are inseparable occurrences.

Writing about the serious crime community places one at the crossroads of several criminological subjects. It is a juncture, because the community's population is composed of those conventionally characterized as either organized criminals, or white-collar criminals. These types of criminals are regularly considered unique, and are studied in isolation from one another. There are many fine accomplishments in the study of white-collar crime; one thinks, for instance, of Michael Levi's analyses of fraud in Great Britain, and Susan P. Shapiro's 1984 study of white-collar crime and the Securities and Exchange Commission.[1]

Masters of Paradise, however, seeks to produce a unification, to draw categories together, to bridge a gap between our ideas about white-collar and organized crime. The term *"white-collar criminal"* was created by Edwin H. Sutherland and presented in

1

his presidential address at the thirty-fourth annual meeting of the American Sociological Association in 1939.[2] By bringing the " 'upper-world' " crimes of business and government into a field of study that traditionally focused on the crimes of the poor and the underprivileged " 'underworld,' " Sutherland creatively enlarged the breadth of his discipline.[3] Almost from the moment he spoke, however, there have been sharp and serious debates over his definition of white-collar crime. Sutherland held it was crime "committed by a person of respectability and high social status in the course of his occupation."[4] However, disputes over the meaning of "high social status" and the "course of his occupation" fostered attempts by many to replace Sutherland's term with others thought more precise. Corporate crime, organizational deviance, elite deviance, and so on, have their advocates.[5]

My quarrel with the term lies in its imprecision when differentiating white-collar crime and criminals from organized crime of the so-called Mafia type. Let me quickly point out this does not mean support for claims about an overarching American Mafia of La Cosa Nostra (LCN). Most analyses of LCN are built upon demonstrably false historical grounds. For example, the Justice Department's Organized Crime Intelligence and Analysis Unit, which operates within the criminal investigative division's Organized Crime Section, recently testified that the history of LCN began with the 1890 murder of David Hennessey the superintendent of police in New Orleans.[6] It thus fell immediately into the error of "prolepsis," which describes an event as happening before it could have done so.[7] It is simply not true that the Hennessey murder made anyone aware of La Cosa Nostra as a term signifying organized crime, for it was not invented, and certainly not popularized for another seventy-three years.[8] The burden of presenting a credible historical account of its supposed rise has exceeded the grasp of those who accept the organization as a fact.[9]

Still, it is the separation between organized and white-collar crime that most often puzzles me. I wonder which category to invoke when considering crimes such as loan sharking committed in tandem by racketeers and bankers;[10] or how to define criminality associated with the looting of union pension and welfare funds, in which cabals of organized criminals, government and private lawyers, and accountants are prominent?[11] Which term is appropriate when analyzing financial schemes designed to evade taxes and "launder" money for corporate executives, mobsters, drug smugglers, politicians, attorneys, etc., carried out in offshore banks in tax-haven countries such as The Bahamas, the Netherlands Antilles, Panama, and the Cayman Islands?[12] Clearly such situations involve organized criminals often doing white-collar-type crimes, and white collar criminals frequently acting like racketeers.

Many of these same questions earlier confounded certain critical areas of federal law enforcement as a United States Attorney's Advisory Committee remarked in the winter of 1974.[13] Brought together because of turf battles between U.S. Attorneys and the Strike Forces (special amalgams of federal agents from Justice, Treasury, etc., created to specifically target organized crime) operating within their jurisdiction, the Committee felt "the most serious roadblock to effective cooperation" was confusion over the meaning of organized crime.[14] Many U.S. Attorneys thought of organized crime as the "Mafia or La Cosa Nostra" despite "those terms falling into official disuse" following Attorney General John Mitchell's order on 21 July 1969. Mitchell's guidelines for the relationships between Strike Forces and U.S. Attorneys' Offices, issued 20 April 1970, defined organized crime as "all illegal activities engaged in by members of criminal syndicates operative throughout the United States, and all illegal activities engaged in by known associates and confederates of such members."[15] However, there was no further explanation of "criminal syndicates" and "associates and confederates," and thus U.S. Attorneys still felt somewhat "at sea." Many, therefore, continued to believe that without a Mafia there was no organized crime, and hence no need for competing Strike Force field offices. U.S. attorneys, nevertheless, did acknowledge districts lacking the "Mafia" still had widespread organized gambling operations and narcotics trafficking.

One partial answer to this always prickly discussion was offered by two high officials from the Justice Department. They "described the existence of 'Jewish syndicates,' 'Syrian syndicates,' 'Chinese syndicates,' etc.," and stated that they regarded them "as of equal 'syndicate' stature within a particular district as the classic 'family' of the 'Mafia' or 'La Cosa Nostra.' " [16] Organized crime was not ethnically exclusive, they argued, although it was still quite ethnically oriented. This, as one might expect, did not settle the dispute.

In fact, the way out of the conundrum for several U.S. Attorneys was to include within organized crime "extensive security theft . . . and other high-powered and continuing frauds and swindles." [17] This meant that U.S. Attorney James Thompson from northern Illinois would likely claim Mike Levi's white-collar criminals as organized criminals. So too would Gerald Gallinghouse, the U.S. Attorney from eastern Louisiana. Gallinghouse argued for a broader definition based upon the *type of crime* committed. Gallinghouse wanted the following

> to include continuing criminals conspiracies . . . involving illegal goods and services, including but not limited to narcotics, gambling, prostitution, interstate theft, loan-sharking, labor-management racketeering, public bribery, corrupt influencing, obstruction of justice, security frauds, and other similar or related offenses. [18]

This debate had some impact on studies of organized crime, particularly among revisionist criminologists, but failed to have much effect on academic research into white-collar crimes. For those sensitive to definitional problems with organized crime as commonly understood, there was a developing way out. Indeed, it has been argued that this amalgam of different-collared crooks affirms organized crime as the expression of a particular social system. [19] Formulated through patron-client cliques and coalitions, organized crime is a system composed of under- and upperworld individuals in complicated relations of reciprocity. [20] One thinks in this regard of the implicit reciprocal relations when gamblers operate from political clubhouses, or when criminal justice agents take money from vice entrepreneurs, or when shipping companies hire gunmen to break strikes. [21]

Unlike the bogus historical material offered to explain the evolution of LCN, the historical development of organized crime as a social system is fairly well known. In the United States it was created from the entrepreneurial politics of the nineteenth century, which through patronage, controlled criminal justice institutions; from the actions and activities of industrial "Robber Barons" fearful of labor agitators; and from the successful agitations of Temperance groups. Professional criminals provided services for politicians, particularly at election time, and for Robber Barons as "agent provocateurs" and strikebreakers. They also manufactured and/or distributed commodities outlawed by moral reformers. Naturally they received protection from criminal justice, and often a great deal of money in return.[22]

Some criminals tended to specialize, although others were active in many spheres. Over time, some founded large and relatively stable gangs which pursued alliances with other criminals. Other organized criminals preferred the efficiency of small groups quickly brought together and speedily scattered.[23] All sorts of events from successful, ephemeral, reform campaigns to murderous competition among criminals for territories and status, worked to diminish the size and stability of criminal organizations.[24] For scores of particular personal reasons, alliances came and went.

In sum, professional criminals were those who took it upon themselves to organize crime. Their true work was the process of organizing crime itself. Organizing crime demands ceaseless self-affirming activity and professional or organized criminals were, and remain an anxious, worried lot similar to the most Weberian Protestant/capitalists.[25] Forms of "clientelism" bind the system together, and it surprises no one to find "bent" lawyers and gangsters working to satisfy demands for illicit goods and services, or plundering a host of victims.[26]

The serious crime community seems an equivalent, but more evocative way to describe the social system of organized crime. It is particularly useful if there are no quibbles about "what is serious," which in this context means the illegal concentration of power. This responds to quite an important suggestion made by the chief of a Rackets Bureau not long ago. He proclaimed the necessity for "a reconceptualization of the basis for racketeering work: one which would focus resources upon situations where economic analysis indicated illegal concentrations of power."[27] The crime community, on the other hand, indicates the participants in "private criminal orders" (which have some organizational scheme, and most importantly the power to overcome public order), and who are separated from others by some unquantifiable ratio between "wiseguy" and "chump." In searching for a way to describe organized criminal activity in the Brooklyn, New York, inner city neighborhood of Bedford-Stuyvesant, Harold Laswell and Jeremiah McKenna of the Policy Sciences Center coined the phrase "private criminal order." They judged that organized crime was the most powerful force in the community for many reasons, including the following: it grossed more revenue from its drug operations and gambling activities than the federal government collected in income taxes; was the largest employer of Bedford-Stuyvesant residents; and had effectively nullified every counterattack government mounted against it. Constructing their theoretical position around a policy sciences approach, Lasswell and McKenna noted that organized crime "participates in the official decision process of the community."[28] Organized crime, "a ruthless private monopoly of power," through its demonstrable ability to overwhelm "official decision processes of community," causing the "confusion and demoralization of the processes of law and government," is thus responsible for a "public order problem" of great magnitude. They judged organized crime was therefore "*non-ideological, concerted criminality of sufficient weight and scope of power to inhibit public control*" (emphasis added)—it was, in their estimation, a private criminal order.[29]

The expression, the "serious crime community," was created by an undercover operative working for the Intelligence Division of the I.R.S. in a secret project whose purpose was to gather relevant information about American criminals' illicit activities in The Bahamas. Called Operation Tradewinds (TW), the project was conceived and placed in motion in the period 1963–1965. The founder was Richard E. Jaffe, an Intelligence Division Special Agent working in Miami. Jaffe's agents were initially drawn from an expatriate American family of four living in Nassau. In time, one family member in particular stood out. Sally Woodruff, the married daughter of John Davis, the first TW agent, became agent TW–5, and was transformed by the experience. She found her natural metier working as a confidential informant for the I.R.S. At many points in her clandestine career, which was covered by a small public relations firm specializing in company and real estate searches, she pondered its general significance. In a reflective frame of mind in 1973, she sent Jaffe a long letter summarizing her agent's creed, providing an analysis and justification for overseas clandestine I.R.S. operations. The letter contains the phrase "the serious crime community," and her good sense is reason enough to borrow it.

"Am I correct," she asked Jaffe, "in assuming that you are not supposed to have permanent establishments overseas? I can see that an office that interferes with the internal operations of a foreign country would definitely be against the interests of the United States as well; but the U.S. Congress has written and passed tax laws, which require all working citizens with incomes of any kind, to report their income to the U.S. Government NO MATTER WHERE THEY RESIDE." Therefore, she argued, "The U.S. Congress moved its arm of authority into every country of the globe." And, "if the U.S. Government is to have an interest in individual citizens to the extent that it requires the filing of an annual tax return," then it must follow that "some means must be made to see that such returns are indeed completed." That wasn't a problem with the thousands who live on Social Security or small annuities. Sally thought these people are probably honest and likely overpay their tax.

The people who concerned her, she told Jaffe, were "of world-wide interest because we find that it is the sophisticated person who is most likely to be the tax evader." Sally was certain that in the past half century or so, organized crime had moved heavily into legitimate businesses. She wrote "the money generated has been fantastic," then added, "no one knows better than those entrepreneurs that money generates money and that money under the bed is money lost. They put their money to work." Experience in The Bahamas had convinced her "that most of the money that we have seen working overseas in the areas where we have been living has filtered down through or is directly traceable to organized crime or to some U.S.-based illegal operation."

Sally and her family of Tradewinds agents were not interested in harassing "the person of modest means," but looked instead for the "corrupt U.S. lawyer who comes to a foreign country to establish and direct a bank and numerous low-profile companies, which are then utilized to launder unreported state-side income through land companies and other development agencies." She knew such individuals were not in these operations for the paltry sum in legal fees collected for forming such companies.

People like that are never picked up in general I.R.S. audits because they have skillfully hidden their interests and assets in an offshore tax haven. To find these people "takes an intimate knowledge of the country or countries in which the income has been hidden." Such knowledge requires a continuing look at the actions of companies in places like The Bahamas. Of equal concern was the "growing use of foreign companies in name only by U.S. companies." Sally explained "the companies are formed as subsidiaries or as undeclared offshoots of the parent company, using the parent company funds, but in fact the profits are never returned to the U.S. company books." Once again, she stated that without overseas clandestine operations like Tradewinds, there was no way such companies could be spotted. "We know the area," she remarked, and "the types and kinds of companies, what they do and how they do it." Agents also know the important foreign and local residents.

Sally continued with a recommendation for operations like Tradewinds in other locations. There should be an undercover team of at least four people in the capitals of every tax haven country, those nations which encourage foreigners to conduct certain businesses anonymously with incomes untaxed. Furthermore, members of the team must be long-time residents of the area familiar with the government's official "Gazette," and the local and important world newspapers. They also have to know the company and real estate registries, plus the significant legislation dealing with banks and trusts in their respective countries. Fiscally conservative, Sally noted the value of these teams would far exceed their expense, if for no other reason than the recovery of tax monies. In the case of Tradewinds, she was absolutely correct.

There was another, even more important advantage to these operations. Teams "would spot correlated activities such as those related to large-scale monetary manipulations, bank frauds involving U.S. subsidiary banks, U.S. companies involved in S.E.C. violations; as well, of course, as those members of the *serious crime community* who have taken money overseas and have moved into legitimate looking operations there" (emphasis added). For Sally, outwitting the serious crime community was her true passion.

Operation Tradewinds was probably the first, and certainly the longest investigation of a sector of the "underground economy," which is most fruitfully thought of as the aggregate worth of financial crimes undertaken by the serious crime community. There are some, though, who insist the it represents the sum of all monies unreported to revenue agents—from drug profits to waitresses' tips. No one knows the extent of these funds, though ten years ago the I.R.S. guessed it might be about \$134 billion.[30]

The impact of the underground economy is a serious worldwide problem. In 1981, for instance, S. K. Ray, an Indian economist, wrote it had become so integral to the Indian economy that it represented a "definite branch of applied economics."[31] He added the possible conversion of unearthed "black money and evaded income" could represent a serious state investment for development programs. There were a few examples in India where this was done on a small scale, and Ray proposed a long-term government effort against the underground economy.[32] British economist, K. G. P. Matthews, from the University of Liverpool, after studying the United Kingdom's underground economy, found strong evidence "the informal economy is a growing phenomenon" with serious implications for the "integrity of the tax system." Moreover, Matthews held "the implications for the macro economy and macro economic variables are such that output and unemployment figures require major revision."[33]

While scholars in India and the United Kingdom are worried about the underground economy, the apprehension in Italy over it, and thus the impact of organized crime upon the nation's financial institutions, is far deeper and more broadly based. One of the major reasons for this is the intimate connection between the drug trade and Italian financial institutions. Italian journalist Ezio Mauro noted in 1982 that the Sicilian Mafia controlled so much money that its relationship with politicians was radically altered, as well as its ability to "negotiate with the national and international financial world."[34] The Mafia faced the problem of "allocating this large 'surplus value' from heroin, sums of money vast enough to upset the economy of one of our Regions," Mauro added. This brought about new and extremely dangerous connections between the Mafia and the Sicilian banking world. Mauro cites the rapid growth of Sicilian banking in comparison to Italian banking, in general, during the critical years of Mafia drug trafficking (beginning in the 1970s), and quotes part of a report by the Sicilian branch of Magistura Democratica (a Judges' and Magistrates' Association), which stated the subsequent proposition:

> the growing weight of banks in the Sicilian economy, the common interests shared by banks and Mafia businesses, the selection banks make in granting credits or in financing the strangest and unknown organizations, places the Banking System itself at the centre of financial manoeuvres, making them the load bearing pillar of the entrepreneurial activities of political-Mafia groups.[35]

Of course the full measure of the underground economy in Italy was only revealed in the unfolding stories of bankers Michele Sindona and Roberto Calvi. In the 1970s they conspired with various Sicilian Mafia bosses, Vatican Church leaders, American organized crime figures, international drug smugglers, and right-wing Italian politicians, in order to loot several major financial institutions, and to help their friends in the serious crime community. Although their criminality overlapped, Sindona's primarily centered on draining the Franklin National Bank, headquartered on Long Island, while Calvi worked to steal perhaps $200 million from the Vatican Bank, "Institute per le Opere di Religione."[36] In these extraordinarily complex crimes, the use of tax haven countries which guarantee bank secrecy was of absolute paramount importance.[37] And although The Bahamas was not central to the Sindona and Calvi conspiracies, it was utilized; in fact, the two men (and many of their associates) routed millions through Bahamian companies.

Using The Bahamas for international criminal activities is a relatively recent development. For American criminals in particular, The Bahamas' prominence was related to Cuban developments. Almost as close to Cuba, as it is to Florida, The Bahamas was at most an underdeveloped criminal entrepôt until Castro and his revolution succeeded. Castro's triumph in January 1959 marked the end for American organized criminals on the Caribbean's largest island. Havana has been characterized as "the place for the good time, the prostitute, and the cigar, the blue film, the daiquiri at Sloppy Joe's or the Florida Bar, the quick win at the roulette table."[38] A fair amount of Havana's organized crime was controlled by American criminals, who were as displeased with socialism's conquest as were the American sugar companies. American organized crime boss Meyer Lansky was by far the most important. In partnership with dictator Fulgencio Batista, Lansky has been credited for helping turn Cuba into "the whorehouse of the Western Hemisphere."[39] Lansky and associates turned to The Bahamas when they were driven from Cuba.

Their initial move took place in Freeport, Grand Bahama Island.[40] Freeport was a brand new urban and resort complex dreamt out of whole cloth in the mid-1950s by former swindler Wallace Groves. By the turn of the decade, the project seemed to be foundering for the lack of a suitable attraction sufficient to pull in tourists, residents and investors. Lansky and his men took care of that problem, building and managing The Bahamas first licensed casino.

Bahamian development in general took off during the 1960s once legalized casino gambling, and refined bank secrecy and company laws were in place. Between 1960 and the end of the decade, a plethora of U.S. and British bank subsidiaries arrived, joining the expanding number of local merchant banks, often little more than tiny offices with a brass plate on the door, with a telephone and telex inside. There were Bahamian counterparts of banks from Boston, Philadelphia, Cleveland, Chicago, New York, Dallas, Seattle, and Grand Rapids, Michigan. Bahamian financial operations grew, becoming increasingly sophisticated. In a relatively short time, The Bahamas was an international banking center with almost 350 banks and trust companies headquartered there. By the early 1980s, the little island nation was a principal Eurobanking hub, with Eurodollar assets totalling more than $100 *billion*. The Bahamas serves as a locus for either booked or actual interbank exchanges by the offices of the 189 American bank branches there. Estimates published in 1984 of the dollar volume in trust businesses managed in Nassau run between $2 and $5 billion. Approximately 95 percent of the trust accounts were for people living abroad.[41]

This startling financial development has both contributed to and taken place within a political climate of unbounded corruption. Bahamian politicians provide protection for international criminals, including the world's largest drug smugglers and just plain tax evaders in return for a significant part of the action.[42] Poor countries which live on the proceeds of parasitic industries, such as casino gambling, offshore banking, and drug smuggling often seem on the verge of totally submitting to illicit interests.[43] In The Bahamas it happened. A process of criminalization that started with the building of Freeport undermined every important political modification in recent Bahamian history. These included the end of colonialism and white rule. Crime trivialized this reformation.[44] White rule ended in 1966 and independence from British rule in 1973. The revolution that both events portended never took place. The Black government, in power since 1966, was eager to claim its rights to illicit profits that were greatly heightened with the rise in cocaine trafficking during the 1970s, which made The Bahamas a world drug smuggling center.[45]

Tax haven banking for the purposes of tax evasion and the laundering of illicit monies; resorts featuring casino gambling, apparently owned or managed by organized criminals; and the international traffic in cocaine and marijuana, all grew like "topsy" in The Bahamas. Jaffe's Operation Tradewinds was on hand for much of this action. Among its first major targets was a new resort and casino company called Resorts International. Tradewinds' interest was peaked because Resorts appeared to have suspicious connections to the Lansky syndicate, plus a financial package put together by scads of "funny-money" types, some clearly connected to organized crime. Moreover, the head of Resorts International was a close friend of President Richard M. Nixon and Charles "Bebe" Rebozo, his most intimate associate. This raised in the minds of congressional staffers the possibility of the President's association with organized crime.

The issue of Resorts International became a kind of leitmotif, appearing, in one guise or another, in a very large number of Tradewinds' reports. There was so much suspected criminality, so many high rollers passing through, so many outrageous characters at one time vying to buy the complex, that Tradewinds' concentration on Resorts International was unrelenting and paid off. Watching Resorts International, for instance, brought into focus some of the affairs of Howard Hughes right around the time Watergate began its steamy path through Washington. The same watch settled on Robert Vesco, whose presence in the Watergate affair was, if anything, more disturbing than Hughes' presence. Vesco also had his "hooks" into Nixon family members. The President's brother Ed was a Vesco money courier, and that wasn't all. Nixon's nephew, Donald's son, who seemed destined for the hippie life in a California commune, was convinced by John Ehrlichman to work for Vesco, preferably in Switzerland outside the range of public notice.

For as long as Tradewinds existed, it kept tabs on the Resorts International crowd. While doing that, it chanced upon a private bank suspected of doing business with American drug smugglers. Jaffe and his team of undercover operatives turned their attention toward Castle Bank, a tireless engine of financial criminality secretly owned and run by American attorneys from Chicago and Miami. And like Resorts International, Hughes, and Vesco, Castle Bank had possible connections to President Nixon. According to a Tradewinds agent in 1972, the President's name was spotted on the Castle Bank account list. In January 1973, the account list was purloined from a Castle officer's briefcase while he was in Miami. The contents were photographed, and then the documents and briefcase returned. The bank officer was none the wiser.

Two and a half years later, this action became the centerpiece in an internal struggle over the destiny of the I.R.S. Intelligence Division itself. Questions were raised, and continue to surface about the Intelligence Division's Miami and Bahamian operations as examples of political spying. They were not, as we will see.[46] This internal I.R.S. conflict had actually begun with the appointment of Donald C. Alexander as Commissioner in the spring of 1973. He was openly critical of all criminal investigative work done by the I.R.S. Alexander's views prevailed, and the Intelligence Division was gutted.

With each passing day, beginning with Wallace Groves' Freeport development, The Bahamas moved along the dangerous road from a nation to a racket, with no hope in sight. The I.R.S. investigation was shut down at the worst possible time; it was uncanny.

The I.R.S. retreat from effective criminal law enforcement during the 1970s was of momentous significance, as this was the decade which experienced the related world-wide explosions in drug smuggling and money laundering. Operation Tradewinds was discontinued, for example, around the time Colombian drug smuggler Carlos Lehder bought most of a Bahamian island called Norman's Cay, which was the Medellin cartel's primary cocaine transshipment point. Stephen S. Trott, an assistant attorney general from the Justice Department's Criminal Division, stated in the summer of 1986, "it is absolutely true that the seeds of the problem [cocaine trafficking] were sown during the late 1960's and 1970's."[47] It was also Trott's position, and no one disputed it at the 1986 House Hearing to consider providing for a White House Conference on Narcotics Abuse and Control, that the Federal effort against narcotics actually "lost ground between 1975 and 1981.[48] Far from vigorously attacking money laundering, especially in relation to drug profits, those years witnessed a general I.R.S. withdrawal from tackling these issues, as well as the Intelligence Division's debacle, over the Bahamian investigations.

Confirmation of the Internal Revenue Service's rather suspicious policy under Alexander of pulling back from working cases against organized criminals and drug traffickers, came from the Senate's Permanent Subcommittee on Investigations (PSI). Alexander was helped in hamstringing the Intelligence Division by passage of the Tax Reform Act of 1976. Signed by President Ford in the fall, the new law had a key section which restricted "what information Federal law enforcement agencies could request access to from IRS."[49] Clearly pleased with the legislation, I.R.S. management strictly interpreted the Act. This led some agents to believe "that if they were to come upon information indicating that a major non-tax crime was being planned, they were prohibited from reporting that information outside their own service."[50]

The year before the PSI report, the General Accounting Office (G.A.O.) reviewed federal progress in controlling illegal drugs, and had commented on the problems brought about by the Tax Reform Act. In addition, the G.A.O. commented that the Bank Secrecy Act passed in 1970 to combat "organized and white-collar crime, including the drug traffic," was not working very well. It required the following: domestic banks had to file a report with the I.R.S. on each currency transaction of $10,000 or more; individuals who transport in excess of $5,000 into or outside the United States must report this to the Customs Service; and lastly, people subject to U.S. jurisdictions who have "interests in foreign financial accounts must disclose this by filing a financial statement with the Treasury Department."[51] The G.A.O. concluded that the intent of the act, which was the collection and dissemination of information pertinent to investigating organized crime and drug smuggling, was subverted by "the minimal dissemination of the information collected." A House Government Operations Committee study in 1977 determined the exchange of currency information outside Treasury was "nonexistent." In fact, information exchange within Treasury was at best "minimal."[52]

Further Congressional hearings during the 1980s continued to highlight I.R.S. retrenchment in the past decade, which they coupled with the simultaneous expansion of drug trafficking and money laundering. The PSI's 1981 hearing on *International Narcotics Trafficking* was concerned with the need to get the I.R.S. more involved in anti-drug syndicate work, while its 1983 hearing, *Crime and Secrecy: The Use of Offshore Banks and Companies*, provided several examples of how this aspect of the underground economy worked and, by implication, how poorly the I.R.S. had functioned in combating drugs and money laundering over the past decade. The following year President Reagan's Commission on Organized Crime published an "Interim Report" called *The Cash Connection: Organized Crime, Financial Institutions, and Money Laundering*, which ended with this peroration: the federal government "must strike directly at the heart of the problem by making the use of financial institutions by money launderers a criminal offense."[53]

It would be a mistake to leave the impression that the I.R.S. did not perceive the underground economy as a problem. It did, both before and after the Castle Bank episode, which spanned the careers of Donald Alexander and his successor Jerome Kurtz. The earliest indication of concern surfaced in 1961. That year the I.R.S. Audit Division prepared a pamphlet for in-house use, prompted by many signs that schemes for the evasion of taxes were multiplying. These schemes depended for the most part on the use of controlled foreign corporations, partnerships, or trusts.[54] It was becoming clear that money was being funneled at an increasing pace to offshore countries, and newly formed companies in order to beat domestic taxes. The pamphlet's first example dealt with currency moving through Panama and the Netherlands Antilles. Another illustration featured The Bahamas. In this case the culprit was quaintly described as "Mr. X, the cunning taxpayer." The Internal Revenue Service calculated he owed about $10 million in taxes and penalties.

Interest in this area was so new, however, that the Internal Revenue Service felt the need to provide fifteen "clues" for agents to alert them to these plots. "Keep watch," agents were informed, for telltale signs such as a license to operate in a foreign country; a domestic corporation borrowing from a foreign corporation; the liquidation of foreign corporations; and the transfer of assets to a foreign corporation. At this early point no mention was made of organized crime or foreign banks. The reason for this is not hard to find and needs comment.

Prior to the mid-1950s at least, the serious crime community at work in the underground economy was of little consequence.[55] Those traditionally involved were international corporations, and the very wealthy with homes in America and also in places like the French Riviera, the Balearic Islands, London, and Rome. But something was clearly brewing during the postwar decades, which would create new customers eager for a chance to participate.

After World War II Americans, who had more disposable income than ever before imagined, went travelling. Pensions, retirement plans, smaller families, larger salaries, and paid vacations, enabled many Americans finally to see the world. And the more Americans wished to travel, the easier and cheaper it became. Airlines were themselves transformed by the boom in travel. The passenger jet age took off on 15 July 1954 when the prototype of Boeing's 707 aircraft first flew. That year airlines carried approximately 37 million passengers.[56]

This "crush" of new people (who so annoyed the wealthy, as one exclusive spa after another was invaded) was welcomed by entrepreneurs and promoters of one kind or another. For them the middle-class tourist represented an untapped and untouched market. Tax havens popped up around the world, and in them a variety of trusts, savings and loans, and banks. The imperative point was to get a foreign company (bank or trust) formed and operating in one of the new tourist spots. On vacation, people were uninhibited and often did the unusual with their money. Enticed by interest rates on deposits, always a point or two above U.S. domestic bank rates, they actually deposited funds into foreign banks with imposing names and little else. There were certain things the new investors wished to know. Could they get their money on demand? What was the schedule on interest payments? Would such payments and any withdrawals be in U.S. currency? And perhaps most importantly, was the interest reported to the I.R.S.? No, was the answer to the last question, and it was especially reassuring. This was the early pattern as the underground economy expanded, reshaping itself for many small investors.

In just a few years the pattern altered slightly as depositors themselves became more sophisticated, forming their own foreign-based companies. These firms were used as real estate fronts and investment vehicles in the trading of stocks, bonds, and other commodities. It became increasingly difficult to tell the sharp entrepreneur from the cunning depositor. More and more they were one and the same. Indeed, the most astute put their resources in foreign trusts run by foreign companies and nominees. For all intents and purposes, their money vanished.

The structural changes in the decades after World War II naturally attracted corporate directors and other company officers, particularly those with law and accounting backgrounds. They plunged into the game, many funding their action with money "skimmed" from their firms. Embezzled corporate monies were used to start foreign investment companies, or best of all, private merchant banks. These did no business with the general public, operating exclusively for anonymous owners and their friends.

Organized criminals, who must operate in the underground economy, were more eager than most to reap the advantages offered by such helpful institutional growth. Their natural allies in banking, law, and accounting not only served their financial needs in the traditional onshore sense, but offshore became partners with them in the absolute sense. And that made a difference. So long as their banks and trusts engaged in financial crimes, including massive tax evasion and the laundering of illegal monies for organized crime, the owners and depositors were confederates; this bound the serious crime community more securely than otherwise would have been the case. It was one thing to professionally represent racketeers in stateside litigation, and another to create and manage offshore institutions in their interests.

The I.R.S. Audit Division's 1961 pamphlet is naturally light years behind later concerns. In fact, by 1979 the Treasury Department (home of the Internal Revenue Service) was clearly alarmed. Perhaps the six preceding years of retreat and retrenchment had given Treasury pause. In any case, that year Deputy Secretary Robert Carwell requested Assistant Secretary (Enforcement and Operations) Richard J. Davis to conduct an analysis of unusual flows of U.S. currency.[57] A report was submitted in August 1979, which noted that the Treasury was responsible for the administration of the (Foreign) Bank Secrecy Act discussed earlier.[58] A section of the analysis dealt with "an historical perspective of the volume of currency handled in the FRS [Federal Reserve System] offices in Florida from 1970 through 1978." It determined "the annual surplus of currency in Florida increased by nearly 500% from 1970 to 1978." The most startling changes occurred since 1975, when surplus currency figures started to accelerate at an ever quicker rate. It was estimated the surplus for 1979 might be $4.5 billion, and appeared to represent, to a large degree, a remarkable flow of illegal monies into Florida. There was little doubt that it was a portion of the immense wealth garnered by drug racketeers. Moreover, this was money virtually untraceable, particularly if first laundered through foreign banks. Speaking about this the analysts said: ". . . it is possible that the transactions are with foreign financial institutions and are not required to be reported or have been exempted from the reporting provisions by the commercial banks."[59] Although this was by no means the start of a correction of past policy, when it came to either The Bahamas or Castle Bank, it does point ineluctably to the heart of the problem and the subject of this book.

Masters of Paradise follows the history of contemporary Bahamian development beginning with Freeport, then Nassau's Paradise Island and the creation of Resorts International, next the origins of Operation Tradewinds, the criminality of Robert Vesco, and subsequently the entire Castle Bank affair. All the relevant I.R.S. files have been located and examined, and many of the principals interviewed. The records reviewed include approximately eleven large file boxes crammed with documents mostly collected by Sally Woodruff. These documents were otherwise purchased in Nassau and flown to the United States.

It has taken about four years to find and analyze the material used in this study. It has hardly been dreary research, however. The search has taken me to Washington, DC, New York, Philadelphia, Miami, Orlando, Long Beach, Los Angeles, San Francisco, Denver, the Grand Cayman Islands, and lastly The Bahamas on several occasions.

All relevant documents used in *Masters of Paradise* are available for scholars by appointment with the Administration of Justice Department's Research Resource Center at The Pennsylvania State University, State College, PA.

Notes

1. Michael Levi, *The Phantom Capitalist: The Organisation and Control of Long Firm Fraud* (Gower 1981); Michael Levi, *Regulating Fraud: White-Collar Crime and the Criminal Process* (Tavistock 1987); and Susan P. Shapiro, *Wayward Capitalists: Target of the Securities and Exchange Commission* (Yale University Press, 1984).
2. See the "Introduction" by Gilbert Geis and Colin Goff to Edwin H. Sutherland, *White Collar Crime: The Uncut Version* (Yale University Press, 1983), p. ix.
3. James W. Coleman, *The Criminal Elite: The Sociology of White Collar Crime* (St. Martin's Press, 1985), p. 2.
4. Coleman, *The Criminal Elite*, p. 2.
5. Ibid., p. 3. Also consult M. David Ermann and Richard J. Lundman, *Corporate and Governmental Deviance: Problems of Organizational Behavior in Contemporary Society* (Oxford University Press, 1978). Ermann and Lundman note that since Sutherland other significant sociologists have called for shifting or refining the concept. They cite Albert Reiss, Jr.'s 1966 declaration that sociologists concentrate on organizational deviance, and Stanton Wheeler's 1976 article reiterating that theme. Ibid., pp. 5–6.

   An illuminating discussion of the theoretical issues embedded in many works on white-collar crime is Kelvin Jones, *Law and Econ-*

omy: The Legal Regulation of Corporate Capital (London: Academic Press, 1982), pp. 1–17.

6. U.S. Department of Justice, Criminal Investigation Division, Organized Crime Section, Organized Crime Intelligence and Analysis Unit, "Chronological history of La Cosa Nostra in the United States, January 1920–August 1987," (October 1987) included in U.S. Senate, Committee on Governmental Affairs, Permanent Subcommittee on Investigations, *Hearings, Organized Crime: 25 Years After Valachi,* (Government Printing Office, 1988), p. 294.

7. See David Hackett Fischer, *Historians' Fallacies: Toward a Logic of Historical Thought* (Harper & Row, 1970), p. 270.

8. See the interrogations of crime informant Joe Valachi, properly credited with first uttering the term. U.S. Department of Justice, Federal Bureau of Investigation, File No. NY 92–1459, "Interrogation of Joe Valachi," by special agents (SAS) Patrick J. Moynihan and James P. Flynn at Westchester County Jail, 14 December 1962.

9. No one better analyzes these failures than Joseph Albini, *The American Mafia: Genesis of a Legend* (Appleton–Century–Crofts, 1971); and Dwight C. Smith, Jr., *The Mafia Mystique* (Basic Books, 1975). On the government's most recent attempts to create a history for La Cosa Nostra see my "Clio and the Mob: Historical Assumptions in the Federal Assault on Racketeering," paper presented at the annual meeting of the American Society of Criminology, 1989, which is forthcoming in *Organizing Crime: Essays in Opposition* (Kluwer Academic Press, 1991).

10. Robert Windrem, "Portrait of a Corrupt Union—Teamster Local 945," in U.S. House of Representatives, Subcommittee on Oversight and Investigations of the Committee on Energy and Commerce, *Organized Crime Links to the Waste Disposal Industry* (Government Printing Office, 1981), pp. 185–188.

    Windrem describes loan sharking schemes between the president of New Jersey's Bank of Bloomfield, who also embezzled bank funds, and organized criminals.

11. In this matter consider the findings of the U.S. Senate, Permanent Subcommittee on Investigations of the Committee on Governmental Affairs, *Oversight Inquiry of the Department of Labor's Investigation of the Teamsters Central States Pension Fund* (Government Printing Office, 1981).

12. U.S. Senate, Permanent Subcommittee on Investigations, *Crime and Secrecy: The Use of Offshore Banks and Companies* (Government Printing Office, 1983), especially pp. 142–146.

13. United States Attorney's Advisory Committee to the Attorney General of the United States, "Report on Department of Justice Field Office Operations: Organizational Concepts and Relationships With United States Attorneys, 25 February 1974.

14. Ibid., pp. 16, 18.

15. Ibid., Appendix A, Office of the Attorney General, Order No. 431–70, 20 April 1970.
16. Ibid., p. 17.
17. U.S. Attorneys' Advisory Committee, Subcommittee on Department of Justice Field Operations, James L. Browning, Jr., United States Attorney Northern District of California, Subcommittee Co-Chairman, "Report to the Subcommittee on U.S. Attorneys' Statistical *Survey—Organized Crime Strike Forces*," 6 February 1974, pp. 2–3.
18. Ibid., p. 7. This was persuasive, and among the recommendations the Committee offered to the Attorney General was the expansion of Strike Forces "into other areas, e.g., SEC violations, housing fraud, etc." See United States Attorneys, 25 February 1974, p. 30.
19. Alan A. Block, *East Side—West Side: Organizing Crime in New York, 1930–1950* (Transaction, 1983), pp. 10–12.
20. The line of this argument that American organized crime is composed of patron–client cliques, etc., rests heavily upon the insights on the structure of organized crime and its interaction with national political parties in Italy found in the following work: Jane Catherine Schneider, "Family Patrimonies and Economic Behavior in Western Sicily," *Anthropological Quarterly*, 42 (1969), and continues with Peter Schneider, Jane Catherine Schneider, and Edward C. Hansen, "Modernization and Development: The Role of Regional Elites and Non-corporate Groups in the European Mediterranean," *Comparative Studies in Society and History*, 14 (1972); Henner Hess, *Mafia: Zentrale Herrschaft und lokale Gegenmacht* (Tubingen, 1970); Jeremy Boissevain, *Friends of Friends: Networks, Manipulators and Coalitions*, (Oxford, 1973); Anton Blok, *The Mafia of a Sicilian Village, 1860–1960: A Study of Violent Peasant Entrepreneurs* (Harper and Row, 1974); Pino Arlacchi, *Mafia Business: The Mafia Ethic and the Spirit of Capitalism* (Verso, 1986); and James Walston, *The Mafia and Clientelism* (Croom Helm, 1988).
21. On the first two issues see New York State Supreme Court, Appellate Division—First Judicial Department, In the Matter of the Investigation of the Magistrates' Courts in the First Judicial Department and the Magistrates Thereof and of Attorneys-at-Law Practicing in Said Courts, *Final Report of Samuel Seabury, Referee* (New York, 1932); and Samuel Seabury, Counsel to the Legislative Committee, In the Matter of the Departments of the Government of the City of New York, etc., pursuant to Joint Resolution adopted by the Legislature of the State of New York, March 23, *Intermediate Report* (New York, 25 January 1932).
    Concerning the waterfront, check the District Attorney of Kings County and the December 1949 Grand Jury, *Report of Special Investigation, December 1949 to April 1954* (New York, 1 February 1955); and, Waterfront Commission of New York Harbor, "Pro-

ceedings in the Matter of an Investigation Under Article IV of the Waterfront Commission Compact," 9 January 1967.

22. See David R. Johnson, *Policing the Urban Underworld: The Impact of Crime on the Development of the American Police* (Temple University Press, 1979; Alan A. Block and William J. Chambliss, *Organizing Crime* (Elsevier, 1981); and Robert Smith Bader, *Prohibition in Kansas: A History* (University of Kansas Press, 1986), pp. 181–83.

23. On the propensity for small informal gangs see my, "The Snowman Cometh: Coke in Progressive New York," *Criminology* 17(1) (May 1979), pp. 75–99. For more extensive criminal organizations consult Herbert Asbury, *The Gangs of New York: An Informal History of the Underworld* (Alfred A. Knopf, 1927).

24. Consider the "Memorandum of Information given by Albert Tannenbaum, Re: Lepke and Gurrah hideouts, etc.," in William O'Dwyer, *Personal Papers: Murder, Inc.*, which used to be somewhere in boxes 9239–9252 at New York's Municipal Archives. The Archives when I used them had not yet catalogued the material, which was placed randomly in boxes. I understand the situation is no better today.

25. It seems that even a casual reading of electronically recorded conversations among organized criminals reveals the constant anxiety and continuous plotting of new crimes. For example, Supreme Court of the State of New York, County of Bronx, *The People of the State of New York against Schiavone Construction Company, Raymond J. Donovan, Ronald A. Schiavone, Richard C. Callaghan, Joseph A. DiCarolis, Morris J. Levin, Albert Magrini, Gennaro Liquori, Robert Genuario, Jopel Contracting and Trucking Corporation, Joseph L. Galiber and William P. Masselli, Defendants* Indictment No. 3571/84, "Exhibits in Support of Affirmation in Opposition," Volume I, "Application for Order Authorizing Interception of Oral Communications," by U.S. Attorney, Southern District New York, 4 January 1979, approximately 210 pages.

26. Valuable work on "clientelism" is Judith Chubb's, *Patronage and Power in Southern Italy: A Tale of Two Cities* (Cambridge: Cambridge University Press, 1982); and James Walston, *The Mafia and Clientelism* (Croom Helm, 1988).

   In a study of political assassinations I have argued that clientelism, which "is at the root of the Mafia phenomena in Sicily and Calabria, is also found in the international relations between superpowers and Third World states, which are linked together in the world military order. In the asymmetrical exchange relations characteristic at this level, the superpower trains and arms the local military; the latter's job is domestic stability, which normally means the rooting out of all left-wing subversives. This is done to shore up traditional forms of economic exploitation, which are themselves another vast ocean of violence and inequality that link foreign economic interests and local notables in still other asymmetrical relations." See my essay, "Violence, Corruption and Clientelism: The Assassination of Jesus de Galindez, 1956," *Social Justice* 16(2) (Summer 1989), p. 71.

27. Quoted in Robert Blakey, Ronald Goldstock, and Charles Rogovin, *Rackets Bureaus: Investigation and Prosecution of Organized Crime* (Government Printing Office, March 1978), p. 4.

28. Harold D. Lasswell and Jeremiah B. Mckenna, *The Impact of Organized Crime On An Inner City Community*, (U.S. Department of Commerce, 1971), pp. 10, 25.

29. Ibid., p. 26.

30. Richard H. Blum and John Kaplan, "Offshore Banking: Issues With Respect to Criminal Use," a report submitted to Center for Research in Social Policy, November 1979, p. 1.

31. S. K. Ray, *Economics of the Black Market* (Westview Press, 1981), p. xix.

32. Ibid., p. 146.

33. K. G. P. Matthews, "Demand for Currency and the Black Economy in the UK," *Journal of Economic Studies*, 9(2), p. 20.

34. Ezio Mauro, "A New Mafia," in *Notizie Dal'Italia*, 8, November 1982, p. 5.

35. Ibid., p. 6.

36. See Nick Tosches, *Power On Earth* (New York: Arbor House, 1986), and Luigi DiFonzo, *St. Peter's Banker: Michele Sindona* (New York: Franklin Watts, 1983).

37. A tax haven was defined by an I.R.S. consultant, Richard A. Gordon in a 1981 study entitled "Tax Havens and Their Use by United States Taxpayers," as an area with little or no income tax, and high levels of bank or commercial secrecy." Quoted in U.S. Senate, Permanent Subcommittee on Investigations, *Crime and Secrecy*, p. 11.

38. Hugh Thomas, *The Cuban Revolution* (Harper and Row, 1977), p. 280.

39. Peter Wyden, *Bay of Pigs: The Untold Story* (Simon and Schuster, 1979), p. 124; the statement was made by Professor John Plank.

40. American organized criminals have always contributed to the forms of sophisticated criminality rampant in The Bahamas. In the 1920s, American bootleggers brought prosperity to The Bahamas, using it as a base to store and then illegally move alcohol into the United States. This repeated a pattern established during the American Civil War when munitions and supplies destined for the Confederacy were smuggled into southern ports through The Bahamas. Both activities foreshadowed the contemporary drug smuggling scene.

41. Richard H. Blum, *Offshore Haven Banks, Trusts, and Companies: The Business of Crime in the Euromarket* (Praeger, 1984), p. 135.

42. On the question of narcotics see the London *Sunday Times*, Insight

Section, 29 September 1985; the *Miami Herald*'s Special Supplement on Drugs in The Bahamas distributed as a booklet in 1984; Bahamas Commission Of Inquiry Appointed To Inquire Into The Use Of The Bahamas For The Transshipment Of Dangerous Drugs Destined For The United States Of America, November 1983–December 1984, *Report* (Nassau, Bahamas, 1984); and U.S. Senate Subcommittee on Terrorism, Narcotics and International Communications and International Economic Policy, Trade, Oceans and Environment of the Committee on Foreign Relations, *Hearings: Drugs, Law Enforcement and Foreign Policy—The Bahamas* (Government Printing Office, 1988).

A denial that the Prime Minister was a drug racketeer can be found in a thick response entitled "A Call for Action, a Plea for Justice: A Personal Rebuttal and Request for Investigation from the Prime Minister of The Bahamas to the U.S. Attorney General," (1988). This strange document very likely was constructed with help from a former high ranking D.E.A. officer who later became a consultant for the House Narcotics Committee.

43. Poor countries do not, of course, have to develop in the way The Bahamas did. Socialists argue, for instance, for a measured "withdrawal from the capitalist world system." Until that can be done their participation must be an "oppositional" one. They must aim to "change an exclusive *economic* world order into a *social* order. See Gerald J. Kruijer, *Development Through Liberation: Third World Problems and Solutions* (MacMillan Education, 1987), p. 193.

44. This exemplifies one of the real tragedies of the past several decades, not by any means limited to The Bahamas. The demise of European political colonialism marked by the extension of suffrage to long abused populations, and the natural and inevitable emergence of local leaders, has not stemmed the tide of exploitation as we have seen in many post-colonial regimes.

45. In 1986 Congress passed legislation mandating the President must yearly "certify" whether or not "major drug producing and transit countries" are at last working with the United States to curtail their illicit activities. If not certified, a number of sanctions follow, including the curtailment of foreign aid. In the spring of 1988 President Reagan's certification of five nations—Mexico, Bolivia, Peru, Paraguay, and The Bahamas—brought forth a "resolution of disapproval from Congressman Larry Smith of Florida. Chairman of the House Foreign Affairs Committee Task Force on International Narcotics Control, Smith urged his congressional colleagues to find, as he had, that the five countries were doing virtually nothing to stem the flood of drugs into America. The Bahamas was characterized as massively corrupt, providing a "low-risk environment for drug smugglers." U.S. House of Representatives, *Congressional Record*, 134(42), 30 March 1988, p. 2.

46. On political policing, see Frank J. Donner, *The Age of Surveillance:*

The Aims and Methods of America's Political Intelligence System (Vintage Books, 1981); and Gary T. Marx, *Undercover: Police Surveillance in America* (University of California Press, 1988).

47. House of Representatives, Committee on the Judiciary, Subcommittee on Crime, *Hearing: White House Conference on Narcotics Abuse and Control*, 24 July 1986 (Government Printing Office, 1987), p. 14.

48. Ibid., p. 58; statement by William J. Hughes, the Subcommittee's Chair.

49. U.S. Senate, Permanent Subcommittee on Investigations, *Report: Illegal Narcotics Profits* (Government Printing Office, 1980), p. 3.

50. Ibid., p. 4.

51. U.S. Government Accounting Office, *Gains Made in Controlling Illegal Drugs, Yet the Drug Trade Flourishes*, 25 October 1979, p. 99.

52. Ibid., p. 100.

53. See the President's Commission on Organized Crime, "Interim Report to the President and the Attorney General," *The Cash Connection: Organized Crime, Financial Institutions, and Money Laundering* (Government Printing Office, 1984), which discussed organized criminals Anthony Scotto from New York, Carlos Marcello out of New Orleans, and the infamous Sicilian/American heroin racketeers.

Just a few years later, however, the question of drug smuggling and money laundering entered a new more difficult phase as details of the Iran/Contra scandal emerged. These details strongly intimated the Administration's intelligence services were supporting certain smugglers, and utilizing offshore institutions in the interests of regional anticommunism. See the National Security Archive, *The Chronology: The Documented Day-by-Day Account of the Secret Military Assistance to Iran and the Contras* (Warner Books, 1987); and Theodore Draper, "The Rise of the American Junta," *New York Review of Books* (8 October 1987), pp. 47–58.

Even the indictment of Panamanian strongman, Manuel Noriega, cannot quite establish the Administration's anti-drug credentials. First of all, the indictment was bitterly opposed by the State Department and many within the Administration. It was unsealed only through the determination and pluck of the U.S. Attorney in South Florida. This official reticence to indict Noriega had nothing to do with his notorious drug activities, which were so well known that in 1975 two D.E.A. agents allegedly proposed assassinating him. See Mark L. Wolf, Special Assistant to the Attorney General to Peter Bensinger, Administrator Drug Enforcement Administration, "MEMORANDUM: *DeFeo Report*," 26 March 1976, p. 11.

54. U.S. Department of the Treasury, Internal Revenue Service, Audit Division, "Tax Devices of U.S. Taxpayers and Their Foreign Entities," Document No. 5298 (1961), 1.01.

55. I have borrowed this argument from the late Sarah Jane (Sally)

Woodruff, an I.R.S. operative in The Bahamas. It was Sally who also happily invented the phrase, the serious crime community. There is much more about her in the chapters to come.

56. The data came from *American Heritage*, December 1989, pp. 72–3.

57. U.S. Department of the Treasury, Richard J. Davis, Assistant Secretary, to Robert Carwell, Deputy Secretary, "MEMORANDUM: Analysis of Unusual Flows of U.S. Currency in 1978," 5 September 1979.

58. U.S. Department of the Treasury, Office of the Assistant Secretary (Enforcement and Operations), "Currency Flows in the United States in 1978," August 1979, p. 1.

59. Ibid., pp. 10–11.

1

The Dream Town of Freeport

Grand Bahama Island's future belonged to Wallace Groves, once considered one of Wall Street's bright young men, until he took a fall for various frauds and embezzlement. Later, in attempting to fulfill his plans for the island's development, Groves didn't hesitate in mortgaging a portion of that future to organized crime.

Groves started out in Baltimore as a bond salesman, and then attended Georgetown University Law School. While still a student he acquired several small-loan companies in and around Washington, DC. In this he was helped by his brother, who had been in the loan business, and by his sister, who partially bankrolled the enterprises. His method was to buy the companies, "puff" them up with some capital, merge them with a Chicago firm, and quickly sell out his interest. The method was repeated with the purchase of a fistfull of broken-down investment trusts, which he transformed into the Equity Corporation, and then sold at a profit of about $750,000. Next, he affiliated with the General Investment Corporation (an investment firm) in collaboration with the president of a shaky business called Phoenix Securities.[1]

These were the Depression years, and Groves had done exceptionally well. Feeling "flush," he sailed to The Bahamas and bought an island, Little Whale Cay, located approximately 35 miles from Nassau. He also started two Bahamian companies and became friendly with some of the local power brokers, especially attorney Stafford Sands.

But in the late fall of 1938, Groves' modest financial empire

27

crashed, and he was charged with defrauding the General Investment Corporation. Groves and several others had sold the company some of its own stock, and collected rather large fees and commissions for this dubious assistance. Also indicted were Groves' other companies, including the Bahamian ones. Three years later, in February 1941, Groves was convicted and sent to prison. He was released in 1944.

When Groves emerged from prison, he returned to Little Whale Cay and tried to resume business. By this time he and his first wife, the former actress Monaei Lindley, had divorced. He subsequently married Canadian-born Georgette Cusson, who had been his first wife's hairdresser.[2] She would become his business partner in Freeport's development, and later in further development of Nassau's Paradise Island. They made an interesting pair; Wallace was heavy and tall, resembling Sydney Greenstreet with a moustache; Georgette was a lovely, elegant-looking woman of striking taste. Despite Groves' prison record and Georgette's humble background, they both appeared urbane and sophisticated.

Just before the visionary Groves arrived on the scene, Grand Bahama Island barely supported 5,000 people, and some fishing and some farming.[3] It was little more than a very large pine barren. But there was no denying Grand Bahama Island had potentially important features, which caught the eye of resort developers. Its proximity to Florida, fabulous weather, and shimmering beaches were obvious advantages, which attracted Englishman Billy Butlin in the latter 1940s. He was fast becoming the travel and vacation "czar" for the British working and lower middle classes. Butlin's experience was in constructing modest vacation villages for retired pensioners; those with little money and a desire for the seaside. His Grand Bahama scheme to construct a "Vacation Village" at the west end of the island ended in failure by 1950. It was the victim of conflicting cross purposes— retired English workers didn't fancy being so far from home, and couldn't afford it anyway.

No two developers were further apart in styles and concerns than Butlin and Groves. Two years after his release from prison, Groves bought the unsuccessful Abaco Lumber Company, which had transferred part of its activities from Abaco Island to Grand Bahama. The island of Grand Bahama was heavily forested and logging operations started immediately. Groves turned the failing enterprise around, and with it as a base of financial security he enjoyed the luxury of the "big dream." It took almost a decade before it matured. Meanwhile, as a consequence of heavy logging, the island was transformed to mostly scrub and brush. The most fertile soil leached out to sea during the summer rains without the pines to serve as its anchor. It was clear why old-timers called it the "Rock."

Groves' notion was to build a free port and an industrial complex in the vicinity of Hawksbill Creek, located on the southern shore of Grand Bahama about 20 miles from the western end of the island. The creek, named after a particular type of turtle once abundant in the area's marshy water, almost bisected the island, running north to south, with its southern terminus ending in a shallow harbor. Inadequate for a deep water port, the harbor would have to be dredged.

It is expensive to build a working harbor and supporting facilities, let alone an industrial complex with factories. Without government backing, no one would have risked the Freeport venture. Government support was crucial, and by the time the plan took shape, it was evident that Groves and Stafford Sands, his political friend from the 1930s, had an intriguing deal. In the intervening years, Sands had become chairman of the Bahamas Development Board, roughly equivalent to a Ministry of Tourism. For his part, Groves would organize the Grand Bahamas Port Authority Limited (called by everyone the Port Authority) to do the initial dredging and construction work, while Sands would persuade the Bahamian government to provide over 50,000 acres of Crown land at $2.80 an acre. The entire area, including land thought eventually necessary for development, was officially designated "The Port Area."

Most importantly, within the port area the government granted certain rights and privileges to the Port Authority, including the prerogative to license others wishing to conduct business within the port area. This was an extraordinary grant of power, putting what is often labeled the "new property" by political scientists (licenses which create semimonopolies in affected occupations) into the hands of private entrepreneurs. The government relinquished all custom duties, emergency taxes, and all other duties and taxes upon everything needed to construct the port, including all buildings and accommodations of every kind, all roads and bridges, and all utility undertakings. In fact, as the agreement put it, there would be no custom duty or tax upon "any other undertaking or thing within the port area constructed, erected, or operated by the Port Authority, or by any person or company licensed by the Port Authority." The government agreed to neither charge nor collect any revenue on real property in the port area, on personal income, capital gains, capital appreciation on any individual or company within the port area, including companies incorporated outside The Bahamas, but having their registered office and principal place of business in Freeport. Additionally, there would be no excise, export, or stamp taxes imposed by the government on goods flowing in and out of the port area.

Wallace Groves and Stafford Sands negotiated the transfer of governmental power and authority to the company as the necessary condition for building Freeport. The Hawksbill Creek agreement stated it was a private port under the administrative control and authority of the firm known as the Port Authority. This company not only had the authority to license businesses, it had the right and power to levy, charge and collect harbour dues and other fees considered reasonable by the company, and the absolute right to exclude any person and vehicle from the port area. The Port Authority was also put in charge of immigration into its private zone, enjoying the right to bring in and employ anyone the company or its licensees thought necessary—"the Government will not withhold permission for the entry of such key, trained, and/or skilled personnel into the Colony," and their families the agreement stated.

This initial transfer of public authority to private power set the process in motion by which organized criminals would inevitably increase their sway over Bahamian affairs. For as long as it lasted, this grant made the company a government, and soon gave Meyer Lansky, his associates and affiliates, an "open door." It was reminiscent, although on a vastly smaller scale, of China's territorial concessions to British opium merchants in the nineteenth century.

Stafford Sands had come a long way since his 1930s meeting

with Groves. Then he was just another member of the local elite composed of wealthy merchants and attorneys. By the standards of The Bahamas, these men were wealthy and influential. They were called the "Bay Street Boys," because they regularly met at a club on Bay and Charlotte Streets in downtown Nassau to discuss politics and business over pints of dark beer. The Bay Street Boys controlled The Bahamas until the rise of local black power in the mid-1960s. Their rule was so complete they never bothered to form a political party until the challenge of the black-led Progressive Liberal Party (P.L.P.) moved them to organize. They then formed the United Bahamian Party (U.B.P.), but its rule lasted just a few years.

Stafford Sands was always interested in Bahamian development, which meant for him resorts and casinos. Starting in the early 1930s, he was busy attempting to work out a way to legalize casinos. There had been several small private clubs and casinos in Nassau since around 1920, which catered to wealthy tourists during the short "season" (December, January, and February). Although illegal, the clubs had little to fear from local authorities. One of these was the Bahamian Club situated on West Bay Street, owned by an American named McKenzie from Rhode Island. Collaborating with him in this casino was Bahamian barrister Kenneth Solomon, a prominent Bay Street Boy (whose son, Norman Solomon, would become the leader of the political opposition in The Bahamas, especially concerned with drug corruption in the 1980s). A member of the Bahamian House of Assembly and a merchant, Solomon protected the former owner's interests, which included entertaining Gloria Vanderbilt, the Duke of Kent, the Governor-General of Canada, and Al Capone.

Toward the end of the 1930s Sands found the necessary procedure, and successfully sponsored a bill in the Assembly that allowed casinos to operate under certain circumstances. By securing a Certificate of Exemption (exempt from laws prohibiting gambling) from the local government, a gambling casino could legally operate under what was, in effect, a government license. The bill passed in 1939 and a certificate was quickly granted to the Bahamian Club.

Before the benefit of a government gambling license would bolster Freeport's allegedly lagging development, Groves was busy with ideas for his port. The first and most basic move was to get the harbor constructed by dredging a 200 foot wide, 30 foot deep channel, and a turning basin with at least a 600 foot radius, and a long and wide wharf.[4] For this, he turned to the mysterious Daniel Keith Ludwig, who was on his way to owning the largest private shipping fleet in the world.[5] A quiet and self-effacing man, Ludwig hardly ever granted interviews, and during the 1960s employed a small and extremely loyal staff marked by its efficiency and silence on company matters. He had around 55 huge tankers and bulk carriers, a few sailing under the American flag, and operated by a Ludwig firm called National Bulk Carriers, Inc. The majority of his fleet was registered in Liberia, West Africa, and was managed through a complex chain of holding companies located in Liberia and Panama, and probably several other offshore havens as well.

From his modest headquarters in New York, Ludwig ran a diversified world-wide industrial and financial empire. His project with Groves metamorphosed into other major concerns in The Bahamas and elsewhere. Within just a few years Ludwig's known holdings included coal mines, oil wells, shipyards, a harbor construction and dredging company that cleared the mire from Hawksbill Creek, and soon was working on an $80 million project to dredge the Hooghly River in India to permit iron ore exports. He had real estate interests embracing an estimated $40 million in Common Market countries, and some of the largest private holdings in the world, including an immense section of Amazonian Brazil. In addition, Ludwig owned over $100 million of Union Oil stock, two hotels in Bermuda, and plans for others in Freeport, Nassau, and Paradise Island in The Bahamas, and still others in Mexico and San Francisco, which became part of Ludwig's Princess Hotel chain. He also had a deep water cargo transfer complex on an island near Japan, and about 33 percent of the Maruzen Oil Co., and a myriad of other enterprises involving almost everything under the sun. Eventually, Ludwig constructed a couple of hotels in Freeport and leased them to Morris Lansburgh, a Lansky confederate and Miami Beach hotel owner.[6]

Ludwig built the port facility because he needed an offshore oil bunkering (fuel depot) operation close to the east coast. This was necessary for his own fleet of oil tankers as well as others, which were already too large for most ports to handle. He also prudently desired to avoid steep harbor costs for fueling. Ludwig's bill for constructing the harbor was $5,600,000. While this operation took place, Groves sought additional financing. Even though some potential developers were intrigued by the investment possibilities, especially the tax breaks, many were repelled by the barren, white limestone land and clouds of sand flies and mosquitos. They lacked the vision to match Groves', and the particular need for an oil bunkering facility which prompted Ludwig. It wasn't too long, however, before Groves found people with imperial ambitions and lots of capital. He secured funding from the exceptionally wealthy Charles Allen, the leader of a family-centered investment banking house (Allen & Co.) with major interests in Hollywood, and from Charles W. Hayward, an English entrepreneur who also commanded a substantial fortune.

There were several others besides Allen and Hayward who joined forces with Groves to bankroll the Port Authority in those first years. Some comprised a consortium with Allen, which owned 25 percent of the Port Authority, as did Hayward. Groves and his wife owned the rest.[7] There was now substantial capital invested in the Port Authority, but still few individuals who were willing to actually create businesses on Grand Bahama and fulfill Groves' desire to merge the free port with industry. After more than four years of work, the primary firms in Freeport were the Port Authority itself, Freeport Bunkering (Ludwig's petroleum facility), Freeport Construction Company Limited, Freeport Stores Limited, Freeport Medical Services Limited, and Freeport Educational Services Limited.

Freeport Bunkering was the only business that made money. Fuel pipelines were laid, allowing the company to fuel simultaneously five ships anchored offshore. Shippers enjoyed substantial savings from this operation, with the result that Ludwig's enterprise became one of the largest in the world. At its peak, it was moving over a million barrels of fuel each month. This must have cut sharply into the business of domestic American suppliers, because a British Government report laconically noted that, after some time the United States government took steps which effectively reversed the trend.[8] Freeport Construction, which was created in the summer of 1956 by Groves and Sands, and capitalized with 100 pounds, had precious little business for the first few years. The other companies, Freeport Stores, Medical, and Educational Services, were "shells" set up to satisfy certain requirements of the Hawksbill Creek Agreement, which envisioned the necessity for social services as the town grew. But it didn't grow, and thus didn't need such agencies. Plainly, something had to be done.

Groves and the compliant government, which had a considerable political investment in Freeport, turned from industrial to resort development. The Hawksbill Creek Agreement was amended through Sands' influence on July 11, 1960, in order to allow the Port Authority to build a "first-class de luxe resort hotel," as the amendment quaintly stated. To accomplish this, and to take advantage of the area's resort potential, the Grand Bahama Development Company (DEVCO) was formed in 1961. DEVCO was the creation of Groves and Louis Arthur Chesler of Toronto, Canada. It would prove to be a consequential company in the life of Freeport in particular, and The Bahamas in general.

Groves' new partner, the three-hundred-pound Chesler (called Uncle Lou, Big Lou, and The Moose) was born in Belleville, Ontario, in 1913. He was a sometime student and athlete at the University of Toronto, and then became active in various Canadian mining ventures. Chesler made his first million by 1946 trading in mining stocks, and subsequently in land development in Florida. In 1959 his Florida real estate firm, the General Development Company, was reportedly worth $50 million.[9]

Big Lou had an intriguing range of associates, including several of the financiers backing the Port Authority and most of the Lansky syndicate. He was very closely aligned with the Allen family, thereby bringing them into the orbit of organized crime. Additionally, the vulgar Chesler (he once urinated in public at a posh New Year's Eve party in Freeport) served as Lansky's Bahamian point man. Indeed, in the genesis of Chesler's relationships with the Allens lies one of the paths used by organized criminals into The Bahamas.

The Chesler and Allen association was formed in Hollywood, and prospered when Warner Brothers pictures was coming apart at its financial seams. It happened in the following way. Charles Allen decided to get involved in the risky business of motion picture production. His interest in show business had been sparked by his first wife, who was a Broadway producer. In time, he became friends with several studio heads including Jack Warner of Warner Brothers.[10] Allen also got to know and like Ray Stark, a legendary literary and film agent who represented Marilyn Monroe, Ava Gardner, Lana Turner, Kirk Douglas, and William Holden. Lastly, Allen formed an association with banker Serge Semenenko from the First National Bank of Boston, who was an active and innovative film financier.

Semenenko was characterized as "The Mystery Man of Banking" by reporters, when he finally granted them a long sought interview in the spring of 1964. At that time he was riding the crest of a wave highlighted by his managing to arrange loans in excess of $5 billion without a loss. Among his clients were Warner Brothers, the International Paper Company, Conrad Hilton and the Statler Hotel chain, and the Hearst publishing conglomerate. Semenenko was born in Odessa, Russia in 1903, into a very well-to-do family. Before the Russian Revolution in 1917, which forced his family to flee to Constantinople (now Istanbul) Turkey, his father had been a wealthy banker and philanthropist. Serge started his education in Odessa, continued it at Roberts College in Constantinople, receiving a B.S. degree, and finished it at the Harvard Graduate School of Business Administration. From Harvard, he went to the First National Bank of Boston as a credit clerk and stayed there for five decades, eventually becoming a vice chairman with unique authority—he was something of a "bank within a bank," making his own deals, collecting million dollar fees that, contrary to bank policy, may not have been turned over to the bank. Semenenko was gently forced out of First National when it became known he bought shares in the same companies he financed as a banker. He retired on 17 July 1967, the day the *Wall Street Journal* carried a page one story headlined "Unorthodox Banker" and subtitled "Swinging With the Jet Set."

While billionaire D. K. Ludwig was dredging Freeport's harbor, Allen and Semenenko were restructuring the dismal finances of Warner Brothers. The film company was in desperate condition with little cash on hand in 1956. Because of an antitrust action three years earlier, Warner Brothers had been split, with part of it becoming the Stanley Warner Corporation (Stanley and Jack

Warner were, of course, the Warner brothers), a movie theater operating company. Unlike his brother's company, which did very well, Warner Brothers, run by Jack was a failure. Allen and Semenenko were called in to help out.

Their first move to raise some working capital for the business was to sell all of Warner Brothers, pre-1948 films to a new company called Associated Artists. The Board Chairman of Associated Artists was Lou Chesler. One year later Ray Stark joined Chesler. Shortly after, Stark and another Associated Artist officer, Eliot Hyman, left to form a production company called Seven Arts, which also bought and sold films for television. Chesler was close on their heels, and before much time had passed he was the head of Seven Arts. Now, when DEVCO was formed in The Bahamas, among the investors were Allen, Stark, and Hyman. In addition, the Seven Arts corporation purchased 21 percent of DEVCO for $5 million. Chesler was made DEVCO's president while he was Chairman of Seven Arts. Not to be left out was Semenenko, who was installed as DEVCO's own banker.

By the time Chesler was chairman at Associated Artists, he was known as a stock promoter who worked from time to time with organized crime boss Meyer Lansky and various other mob gamblers and racketeers.[11] Among Chesler's criminal specialties was the handling of stolen securities, which he moved through both Switzerland and The Bahamas.[12] The rotund Chesler had a coterie of crooked friends and questionable associates, some of whom merely invested in his enterprises, although others enjoyed company positions that covered either part-time criminal activities, or masked full-time criminal careers. An example of the second category was New York attorney Morris Mac Schwebel, an officer and director of Chesler's Florida firm, General Development, and a vice president at Associated Artists. While at the latter firm, he was busy working a securities fraud for which he was later convicted.[13]

Chesler's involvement with gangsters stretched back to at least 1942, when he was a partner in various ventures with racketeer John Pullman and Pullman's brother-in-law, Alfred C. Cowan. Pullman had been a bootlegger who served time in 1931 for prohibition violations. In prison, Pullman became friendly with "Yiddy"

Bloom, a notorious bootlegger from Minneapolis, Minnesota. Bloom's real name was Isadore Blumenfeld, and he and his two brothers (known as Kid Cann and Harry Bloom) led an exceptionally violent band of midwestern mobsters. "Yiddy" was a long-time confederate of Lansky's. The bootlegging and gambling underworlds of New York, and various midwestern cities such as Minneapolis and St. Paul, were bridged by Lansky and many of his racketeer friends. These included Charles Ward from New York, also involved in Reno gambling establishments in the 1930s, Dave Berman, a leader of Detroit's infamous "Purple Gang," and Michael "Trigger Mike" Coppola, who frequently booked Chesler's high rolling sports bets.[14] Pullman's introduction to Lansky came by way of Bloom, whereas Chesler's was likely arranged by Pullman. To make sure Pullman and Lansky were ably represented in Freeport, Chesler appointed Al Cowan, a DEVCO executive vice president and paid him $60,000 a year.

In the mid-1950s, Pullman became a Canadian and moved to Toronto, Chesler's old bailiwick. At the same time, Chesler teamed up with Schwebel and others in California and Florida. In addition to his Hollywood partners, others toiling with him were Max Orovitz, later indicted for stock fraud and a member of Lansky's Miami Beach crowd, John Reagan "Tex" McCrary, a well known radio personality and public relations officer for Seven Arts, who was characterized by a British Commission as "an irresponsible and meddlesome person,"[15] and the politically important Maxwell M. Rabb. Under Eisenhower, Rabb was both the Cabinet Secretary, and a special assistant to Sherman Adams, Ike's White House chief of staff. Most recently, Rabb was appointed ambassador to Italy by President Reagan.

Chesler and Lansky (and their associates) were intertwined in many endeavors. For instance, Lansky men provided much of the investment capital for Miami's International Airport Hotel started in 1958.[16] Two years later Rabb was chairman of the board and a member of the stock option committee. Other project investors included Bryant R. Burton, a Los Angeles attorney connected to the mobster dominated Sands and Fremont hotels in Las Vegas, who served as vice president and a director for the Airport Hotel, and Jack Cooper, who also owned a substantial interest in the West Flagler dog track in Miami.

Cooper was more than he appeared in the Airport Hotel prospectus filed with the Securities and Exchange Commission. A major shareholder in the West Flagler Kennel Club and of the minor league baseball team, the Miami Marlins, he also sold munitions. One deal involved a squadron of supposedly inoperative P–51 fighters sold to Rafael Trujillo, the dictator of the Dominican Republic. This 1953 transaction led, nine years later, to Cooper's conviction for tax evasion.[17] Cooper was also close to Lyndon Johnson's notorious aide Bobby Baker. They often travelled together, for example, to the Dominican Republic working various deals. They were joined in these ventures by gambler Ed Levinson, born in Chicago and weaned in gambling clubs in Detroit, Newport, Kentucky, Miami Beach, and Las Vegas.[18] In Vegas, Levinson was associated with the Sands Casino, then the Flamingo, and finally the Fremont, which he refurbished with the help of a friendly loan from the racketeer-controlled Teamsters Union. These relationships between Lyndon Johnson's intimate associate, and organized criminals from Miami Beach and Las Vegas, confirmed the mob's continuing influence in the White House after the assassination of President John Kennedy.

Chesler's connections to Meyer Lansky became more explicit in the 1950s. He hired Michael McClaney, one of Lansky's Cuban casino directors, to manage a Miami Beach dinner club Chesler owned. This was an important period for the mob bosses of Las Vegas and Cuba, too, as they sought legitimate businesses in which they could safely invest "skim" money coming out of their casinos, as well as profits from other illicit activities. They needed new capital investments for the obvious reasons, and because they were always in a fever of speculation, spending their days and nights talking deals, making deals, and dreaming deals that crisscrossed the boundaries between legal and illegal. To deal was to live.

Individuals like Chesler and some of his partners played a middle role in this financial whirl, founding and directing companies, then folding them into other companies, and so on, with illicit capital the fixed point around which dozens, perhaps hundreds of interwoven firms pivoted. They created ventures, some chancy, others blue chip, for themselves and their underworld colleagues. Although deeply involved in organized crime, Chesler was not a gunman associated with violence. He was a thief, swindler, money maker, and mover with enough respectability to provide a cover for the myriad deals linking racketeers and upperworld notables.

In 1960 the two peripatetic Canadians, Chesler and Pullman, left continental North America for new pastures. Chesler moved to Freeport, while Pullman went to Switzerland. The result of Pullman's relocation was the founding of a Swiss bank in Geneva called The International Credit Bank, another step in safeguarding mob money; the consequence of Chesler's migration was DEVCO.

To get the development company moving, it purchased a bit more than 100,000 acres from the Port Authority by trading DEVCO stock for the acreage. In a further series of predictably complicated moves, Chesler and two of his Canadian companies (Lorado of Bahamas Limited and Canadian Dyno Mines Ltd.) acquired most of the rest of DEVCO's stock. DEVCO was now almost totally a Chesler and Port Authority company. The land bought by DEVCO was named Lucaya, and along one of its beaches the "de luxe" hotel called for in the Hawksbill amendment was built.

Even before the Lucayan Beach Hotel was finished, it was apparent to some that the development of Freeport would still lag. The hotel alone would not be the necessary spur after all. A British inquiry found Freeport's growth had not made any significant headway by 1962, and the developers were desperate for a solution. The Port Authority and its offshoot DEVCO were described as losers, despite having spent vast sums to promote Freeport/Lucaya.[19] Casino gambling was supposedly the only resolution to Freeport's perennial problem of intractable underdevelopment, according to a 1970 British Royal Commission looking into Freeport's history. This, however, may not have been accurate. Underdevelopment may at this time have become a ploy to achieve casino gambling. Certainly, those most interested in this knew how to "cook" the books and make any venture appear impoverished.

In response to the reportedly deteriorating situation, a new company, Bahamas Amusements Limited, was formed on March 20, 1963, by Stafford Sands, for Groves and Chesler. Within just a week or so the company was granted a Certificate of Exemption giving it the exclusive authority to operate casinos on Grand Bahama for ten years. Other conditions of the certificate, such as the total prohibition of all Bahamians from casino gambling, were as socially retrogressive as anything imaginable. Another provision of the certificate was designed to curb American involvement. Under Clause 7, that dealt with croupiers and dealers, Americans were precluded from employment. Personnel for these important jobs were to come from the United Kingdom, the Republic of Ireland, or Western Europe. The clause did, however, allow Americans to work as casino credit managers, one to each casino, and as supervisors of dice or "craps" tables, but only for the initial three years of a casino's operation. Also of interest, the casinos were not to be exempt from taxation, and the government passed two casino tax acts. With the certificate in hand, and the various restrictions and conditions in place, it was at last possible to add a casino to DEVCO's hotel project, which itself had been formed to rescue the investment in the Port Authority.

The grant of the certificate did not come easy or inexpensively. In the period just prior to passage, there was some noticeable fear over the matter on the part of Sands, Wallace Groves, and Chesler. Their misgivings were centered on whether or not the Executive Council (composed of Sir Roland Symonette, Leader for the Government, Eugene A. P. Dupuch, Sir Stafford Sands (recently knighted by the Queen), and chairman of the Development Board, Dr. R. W. Sawyer, a member of the Health Board and its former Chairman, D. E. d'Albenas, and C. Trevor Kelly) would vote a positive recommendation to the governor. Sands, Groves, and Chesler were well aware that a large and influential section of the community had openly expressed hostility to the extension of casino gambling in The Bahamas. The Executive Council vote was critical and still uncertain.

To grease the wheel of Bahamian progress, Sands was paid anywhere from $519,000 to $1,090,000 for legal services. With Sands taken care of, he, Groves, and Chesler next worked out "consultancy" agreements with Symonette, Dr. Sawyer, and several others with influence in the Executive Council, and entered into transactions designed to fill the coffers of the newly formed United Bahamian Party. On this last point, DEVCO was obliged to pay the U.B.P. $10,000 per month and covered the payment by listing it as Sands' monthly legal retainer. As it turned out, most, if not all, the financial arrangements with the politicians were paid by DEVCO or the Port Authority. Sometimes the payments were reimbursed by other Chesler creations, such as the Grand Bahama Service Company Limited, owned by the Port Authority and DEVCO, which was formed to collect license fees and work on land development. The payback to DEVCO and the Port Authority would come from the brand new Amusements Company's profits.

On the morning of 28 March 1964, Sands phoned Groves with the news that the certificate had been approved by the Executive Council. Groves then wrote the following letter to Chesler:

> Dear Lou,
> Stafford called me this A.M. The news is of course grand and definitive. Vote 5/3. I do not know full details but gather RTS [Sir Roland Symonette] voted No.
>
> Stafford is *really* concerned over leaks, rumours, etc. and says that the matter can still be defeated. It will take two weeks more or less for certificate of exp. to be signed and in addition he has *promised* no publicity until after return from England. Stafford blames S. Kelly and us (He thinks you). Please, please, be careful.
>
> Ellis of Freeport News (and one other) say *you* laid at Caravel Bar 50 to 1 bet that there would be gambling in Freeport before end of year and Frank Stream told all over that Wednesday was D Day — and you did. We are being flooded with requests for information. Too bad.
>
> Do hope you feel better. I am now *most concerned* over *money* and think a meeting must held on that soon.[20]

Of those on the executive council who were lobbied so intensively and expensively, Sir Roland Symonette was the most reluctant and disturbed. Soon to become the first premier of The Bahamas, with the passage of a new constitution in 1964, Sir Roland was morally opposed to gambling. And even though he finally accepted a modest consultancy arrangement with DEVCO, he still could not bring himself to vote for the certificate. Shortly after this difficult and morally ambiguous period, Symonette became Premier and resigned his consultancy, having collected only 5,000 pounds.[21] It also appears that Eugene Dupuch was hesitant about the arrangement and gave most of his fees to charity. The only member of the council not even approached was d'Albenas, who suffered no pangs of a divided conscience. He was unalterably opposed to gambling and no one thought he could be persuaded otherwise.

The relationship between DEVCO and Bahamas Amusements was very close, with the development company scheduled to receive the net profits earned by the Amusements Company in return for financing it. This was a rather oblique way of referring to the payments of the huge legal fees required by Sands, and the so-called consultancy fees and political contributions needed to secure the certificate. Certainly the Amusements Company, capitalized at a modest 1,000 pounds, required relatively little money as it was merely a license holder not a developer.

DEVCO and Bahamas Amusements enjoyed a unique arrangement that produced for the former about $317,000 in cash in two and a half years. In the same time period Amusements also absorbed hotel and airline subsidies of $2,200,000 and so-called management fees of over $600,000 that emanated from DEVCO. Clearly, all the sums represent the distribution of profits assigned to DEVCO. Just as clearly, no one really knows how much money Amusements made through its first casino, nor exactly all those who received a cut. The accounting procedures were remarkably primitive; some casino officers simply grabbed fistfuls of cash from the tables ostensibly for distribution to casino employees as either salary or a bonus. Large amounts of cash were also being flown to the United States by the Amusements Company, some of it packed in St. Pauli Girl beer cartons as a disguise.[22]

Although several experienced onlookers contended casino gambling on Grand Bahama evolved from the failure to develop Freeport in other ways, and followed DEVCO's inability to do much better than the Port Authority, there is reason to believe otherwise. The problems DEVCO was experiencing were either fairly insubstantial or the direct result of paying such heavy bribes to win casino gambling rights. They certainly could not have stemmed from the Lucayan Beach Hotel, because it wasn't built yet, and besides it was being constructed with money drained from a Canadian investment firm. DEVCO had over 100,000 acres (only a small part was destined for the hotel complex) and its mission was to stimulate residential and commercial invest-ments *after* the hotel was built. The DEVCO capital crisis was either manufactured to provide an excuse for casino development, or came about from the questionable process of acquiring the gambling license.

In addition, plans for a Freeport casino had been in the wings before DEVCO was itself formed. Discussions about setting up a casino in Freeport were held in Miami in 1960 among Lansky, Chesler, Max Orovitz (mentioned earlier as a Chesler and Lansky subordinate who became a DEVCO director through Chesler's influence), and Dino Cellini, one of Lansky's most important confederates. The formation of Bahamas Amusements occurred about midpoint in the building of the Lucayan Beach, thus making the construction and integration of a casino quite easy. It wasn't entirely luck, however. The original hotel design had included room for indoor squash courts. There was never any intention of constructing the courts, which were instead an architectural cover for the casino. It was planned long before the creation of the Amusements Company and the granting of the certificate of ex-emption.

The hotel and its Monte Carlo Casino opened on 11 January 1964, and finally Freeport's prospects seemed to improve. This was reflected in the city's population growth and other indicators showing Freeport was turning the developmental corner. From 1963 to 1966, for instance, aircraft arrivals in Freeport went from 13,000 to 52,000. In the same spirit, Bahamas Amusements re-ported an inflow of 100,000 tourists in its first year of operation. It isn't quite clear what they meant by inflow, because, surpris-ingly, the Lucayan Beach Hotel lost money that year. The primary reason for this was attributed to the extremely high cost of the hotel's construction, amounting to around $8 million. With 250 rooms, the cost per room was $32,000.

The Lucayan Beach Hotel and Monte Carlo Casino were built by another Chesler company named Lucayan Beach Hotel and Development. Most of the approximately four million shares were held by Canadian firms, such as the Montreal Trust Co. which had 2,626,667 shares. A minority were sold to individuals includ-ing the family of Frank Nitti, Chicago's former crime boss. Con-struction funds totalling $11 million were borrowed from the Atlantic Acceptance Corporation, a finance company based in Toronto and Hamilton, Canada. In return, Atlantic received 850,000 shares of Chesler's new company. It was not a very good deal for Atlantic. Simply put, Chesler, who was associated with one of the small groups controlling Atlantic, drained the company of cash.[23]

Advancing Chesler so many millions for his unprofitable hotel project meant Atlantic would be unable to pay investors' maturing notes. Atlantic Acceptance, one of Canada's largest financial businesses, went under on 15 June 1965. As one accountant investigating its downfall (costing investors $50 to $70 million) concluded, the loans to Chesler were really gifts. It was no wonder the Lucayan cost so much to construct; Chesler was undoubtedly pocketing vast sums of the money by inflating construction costs. The inflation and corruption were visually obvious in just a few years; construction quality was quite shoddy and soon the hotel had the tinge of real squalor. Atlantic's stock in the Lucayan development company wasn't worth very much after all. It was another in a long line of Chesler scams, which call into question any official estimates of DEVCO's or the Port Authority's real worth.

In the second week of January 1964 the hotel and casino opened, although some of the rooms weren't finished and much of the paint was still wet. The grand opening came on 22 January, and was reportedly attended by "High Society" free loaders, faded debutantes, and jaded gigolos from the Florida Gold Coast. The seaminess of the affair was caught by a Miami *Herald* reporter in attendance, who noted the casino was in "the hands of a dozen or more men long associated with gambling in Las Vegas, Havana, New York, Washington, and Miami."[24] He identified the professional gamblers and racketeers staffing the Monte Carlo beginning with Frank Ritter, better known as Reed, the casino's general manager. Ritter was then banned from several American race tracks including Florida's Hialeah. The credit manager was an old-time gambler and bookmaker with a record dating back to the 1920s, when he ran an illegal casino in Saratoga, New York. He was called Max Courtney, born Morris Schmertzler. The cashier, Max Brudner, was a bookmaker from Miami Beach with a record of gambling arrests, and the "towerman" (who watches the entire casino floor from a hidden perch) was currently out on bond from Miami Beach. Dino Cellini, a confederate of Meyer Lansky, was the supervisor.

Chesler claimed he hired the American bookmakers because of their experience. That was partially true; but they also worked for his partner Lansky and thus there wasn't much choice. Chesler also claimed to have provided the casino's bankroll for the opening—$600,000. He didn't; it was organized crime money put up by Lansky.[25] Clause 7 was an annoyance not a bar, and it was rewritten in the summer of 1966.

Public disclosure that American gangsters were in charge of the casino produced a crisis for the Symonette government. In a letter sent on 3 February 1964, Sir Roland told Sir Stafford Sands that everyone knew mobsters were running the casino. He himself was told on Christmas day. Symonette was disturbed with Sands for not providing the names of casino employees long before the opening. This would have given Bahamian officials time to examine the proposed employees and saved the government from current embarrassment, which is precisely why no one was told. Although Premier Symonette could deport the racketeers, he agreed not to on condition they would leave within twenty-four hours of a governmental request.[26]

The government's feeling of crisis was also reflected in a meeting called that same day (3 February) in Nassau by the Commissioner of Police and certain American authorities. The Commissioner had decided the "American personnel being recruited for the casino should be vetted by the United States authorities."[27] The Commissioner stated the following Americans were undesirable: Frank Ritter, Max Courtney, Max Brudner, Dino Cellini, George Saldo, James Baker, Roy Bell, David Geiger, Howard Kamm, Al Jacobs, and Anthony Tabasso.

Faced with a difficult problem brought about by Sands and his "bent" associates, who had involved high government officials in bribery, the government squirmed under the light of unfavorable publicity. Symonette angrily wrote Sands that "it should not be the duty or responsibility of our police to run down reports made by the Miami Herald on employees at the casino after they are already there." When the immediate shouting was over the Amusements Company reached an agreement with the commissioner. Dino Cellini, the individual most closely identified with Lansky would leave along with three or four others. Once out of the colony these men were to be placed on an immigration "Stop List" preventing them from ever returning. The system, however, broke down and this particular list or notice never reached any immigration or police officer on Grand Bahama Island, the very place where it was most needed.[28] The notice was found languishing in a box in the Chief Immigration Officer's office in Nassau.

Ritter, Courtney, Brudner, and Geiger were allowed to stay until the casino could find suitable replacements. The Monte Carlo worked slowly and thoroughly, and it was three years before the four undesirables finally left.[29] During that time the first three each received around $400,000 in bonus money, $110,000 in salary, and paid not a nickel for room and board. These figures disclosed in a 1967 investigation failed to represent other monies paid to the trio which will be discussed in the following chapter.

Their sojourn in The Bahamas was all the more telling because Ritter, Courtney, and Brudner had been named in a secret Federal Grand Jury indictment handed down in Manhattan sometime in the summer of 1964.[30] They were described as participating in the largest layoff gambling operation in the United States. Arrest warrants were issued, but nothing seems to have subsequently occurred.[31] They continued working for the Amusements Company while the warrants aged and the case became stale.

Dino Vincent Cellini was the man on the spot. Born in Steubenville, Ohio in 1914, Dino was among Lansky's most prominent criminal confederates, working closely with him in Cuban casinos. In Havana, Cellini's primary responsibility was managing the casino in the Tropicana. At the same time, two of his younger brothers, Edward and Goffredo, ran Lansky's casino in the Hotel Internacional. One brother handled things in the afternoon, the other in the evening.[32] Dino's Bahamian significance is underscored by the fact that although he left the Monte Carlo Casino, and for the most part Freeport, he didn't leave the employ of Bahamas Amusements. He was sent to London where Bahamas Amusements opened a croupier school to train the European staff of dealers made necessary by the much abused Clause 7. The school was important, and Bahamas Amusements vigorously defended their choice of Cellini when later questioned about this by Bahamian officials. His tenure in London ended in 1967 when British authorities deported him as an undesirable alien.

One cannot leave this group of racketeers without commenting upon their geographical and generational extensions. While in London, Cellini worked with Robert Edward Ayoub, who preferred, however, to be called Fred. He was also a native of Steubenville, Ohio with an extensive gambling background in Las Vegas, including a minority interest in one of Ed Levinson's clubs. The Cellini brothers and Fred Ayoub also teamed up with Washington, DC's most important crime leader, Joseph Francis Nesline, and Nesline's close friend and business partner Charles Tourine. This indicated another segment or part of the phenomenal Lansky syndicate that, with the exception of Tourine, somewhat inexplicably emerged from the Steubenville underworld.

Nesline was born in Washington in 1913, but grew up in that Ohio River town. Later when Nesline was running illegal gambling casinos in Washington, including one called the Amber Club, his "strongarm man" was Ralph "Dum Dum" De Mark, yet another gangster from Steubenville. Nesline had been a bootlegger during Prohibition and was subsequently known primarily as a gambler. He had one homicide on his record. During a dispute in a gambling club on K Street in the Northwest section of Washington, Nesline shot and killed his rival George Harding. The fight took place in the winter of 1951 and established Nesline's reputation in the District.[33] From then on he was Washington's most menacing organized criminal.

Charles Tourine, variously known as Charles White and "The Blade," was born in 1906, and hailed from Matawan, New Jersey.[34] A formidable organized crime figure in his own right, Tourine was part of a gang of New Jersey racketeers led by Ruggiero Boiardo that was affiliated with the New York Genovese crime syndicate. Like Vincent Alo, Joe Adonis, and many others mentioned so far, Tourine was a member of a very powerful so-called "Mafia" syndicate, although at the same time working with organizations and businesses run by Lansky and his crowd.

Important racketeers, of course, had pieces of the action in many locales, and this particular cabal of Lansky associates had gambling interests ranging from central and western Europe, through the Caribbean to Washington, DC and Las Vegas. Moreover, they all had been involved in Cuban casinos. Tourine operated several casinos in Havana, including the Havana Casino de Capri that he ran for at least three years. Among those reputed to either own or have a weighty piece of these casinos were Tourine's New Jersey crime boss, Boiardo, and Anthony Salerno from East Harlem. When Castro took control, Tourine reportedly escaped just in time carrying three suitcases filled with cash that belonged to him and his sponsors.

Tourine was more than an organized crime gambler. As early as 1945, the New Jersey State Police believed he was a mob killer. In 1961 he was the primary suspect in the gang slaying of racketeer Frank "Buster" Wortman in St. Louis. The murder resulted from a vending machine "war" between Wortman's gang and another from New York.[35] Tourine, like Nesline, and others associated with Lansky found opportunity everywhere. In 1976 Tourine, along with the former U.S. Attorney in Anchorage, Alaska, a former Assistant to Alaska's Governor, and a former Nevada casino owner were all charged with conspiring to establish organized prostitution and gambling for Alaska's pipeline workers.[36]

During the early 1960s, law enforcement agencies were closely monitoring the activities of Tourine, Nesline, and others in criminal partnerships with Lansky. One of the reasons for this intense interest concerned narcotics, and the belief that Lansky and his friends were financing and managing a large part of the West's heroin trade. In 1962, narcotics officers carefully kept tabs on the group, noting that Nesline's wife and Tourine left together for Paris; later that year Nesline and Lansky were followed in England; and on 25 July it was duly noted that Nesline and Tourine had turned up in Bermuda. American narcotics officials enlisted the help of their foreign counterparts, and the Central Office for the Repression of the Illicit Narcotics Traffic (a division of the French Sureté) watched Lansky and his wife during a ten day trip they made to Paris in the fall of 1962.[37]

American narcotics agents resident abroad also surveilled Lansky whenever he travelled overseas. In 1965 Agent Albert Garofalo, working out of Marseilles, then Europe's most notorious heroin center, reported on Lansky associates in Nice. Another agent then conducted a review of those named, as well as Frank Ritter, Ed Levinson, Charles Turner, connected to the Sands Hotel in Las Vegas, and Miami Beach hotel owner Benjamin Bernard Gaines. The Federal Bureau of Narcotics suspected that they travelled the world on behalf of Lansky in order to purchase drugs and arrange smuggling.[38]

The criminality of the Lansky syndicate was not yet exhausted. When Dino Cellini moved to England to set up the gambling school for Bahamas Amusements, he and Fred Ayoub had additional ventures in mind, which were not thwarted by Cellini's deportation. They opened shop in Amsterdam, the Netherlands, and soon were running the Casso Rosso Club, which owned a large number of sex businesses in Amsterdam, and an illegal gambling casino operating under the name Club Caballa. Joe Nesline was a partner with them in their Dutch enterprises, as were Cellini's brother Goffredo and Ayoub's son. By 1972 Nesline and Ayoub (and Lansky and perhaps Tourine) also had an interest in a gambling casino in the Hotel Lav, located in Split, Yugoslavia.[39]

The Amsterdam projects of Lansky's henchmen reportedly involved narcotics, along with prostitution, pornography, and gambling. INTERPOL in Washington, working with the German police, had traced certain Nesline contacts to the German underworld. In particular, Nesline was thought to be in communication with Wilfried Schulz, an entrepreneur in the Hamburg red-light district and a former fight manager and suspected thief and pimp, and Daviad Dargahi, an Iranian national living in Hamburg, with a background in drug smuggling, gambling, and international prostitution in Germany and Northern Italy.[40]

Around the same time that Nesline was talking with Schultz, Fred Ayoub, using his given name, Robert, became the director of the New York School of Gambling located in Manhattan. The New York venture trained dealers for the new Atlantic City casinos. Ayoub sought to expand this undertaking in either late 1977 or early 1978, and applied for permission to open a branch of his school in New Jersey for members of the New Jersey Gaming Bureau.[41] There truly was much he could teach them.

And on it went, a seemingly unending series of criminal enterprises and activities staffed, however, by aging mobsters. Indeed, many members of the Lansky syndicate by the 1960s could have qualified as senior citizens. It is only natural that a new generation of "wiseguys" was being groomed. For this syndicate, the most important youngster (born in 1933) was Alvin Ira Malnik. He was educated, earning a B.A. from Washington University in St. Louis, and a law degree from the University of Miami in 1959, and sophisticated. While in law school Malnik worked in a fraudulent second mortgage business.[42] Just out of school he was employed by Alfred Mones, a major layoff bookmaker on Miami Beach, who had investments in the Casino de Capri in Havana and several Las Vegas casinos. Mones was also a "loanshark's loanshark," lending money at reduced rates to retail level "sharks."

In 1964 Malnik lived in the same lavish Miami Beach apartment house as did Tourine and Nesline. His previous residence was transferred to the mistress of another older organized crime associate, gangster Anthony "Fat Tony" Salerno. Malnik conducted a fair amount of business in southern California, and had a second home in west Los Angeles. In California he was the general counsel to the Allied Empire Corporation, a major stockholder in a secret Bahamian bank of prime importance for the syndicate's gambling operations. This was the Bank of World Commerce whose discovery led to Operation Tradewinds.[43]

Barely four years out of law school, and Malnik was recognized by the F.B.I. as a major organized criminal. The bureau bugged his office in the summer of 1963 and discovered his close relationship with Richard Gerstein, a Florida state attorney, overheard conversations with a local judge about buying some of Lou Chesler's Freeport land, noted that "Fat Tony" Salerno's mortgage was secured through a loan from John Pullman, listened to discussions about a deal on a juke box video machine manufactured in Paris, in which many racketeers and State Attorney Gerstein eventually invested, and finally recorded several conversations between Malnik and Jake Kossman, another mob attorney. The F.B.I. was very interested in Kossman, because he was Jimmy Hoffa's attorney, and those were the days when Attorney General Robert Kennedy was determined to send the Teamsters Union boss to prison. Malnik and Kossman talked about Hoffa, fixing juries, and general mob business. Later, the F.B.I. recorded Malnik talking with another Lansky associate, who had obtained a top-secret intelligence report from the Department of Justice concerning the mob's Bahamian operations.[44]

By 1964 many important syndicate criminals from America were at work in Freeport, enjoying the fruits of their past labors in pulling together the Monte Carlo Casino, and making land and other investment deals available for judges and public officials from Dade and Broward Counties in South Florida. They were also busily concocting schemes to further their criminal enterprises, to enlarge their already vast domain, and to handle the huge amounts of money pouring in. Increasing attention was turned to offshore banking, and it was correspondingly complex enough to make it exceedingly difficult to find and follow mob businesses.

The Bank of World Commerce, for example, was established in Nassau to handle the "skim" from two Vegas casinos. Joining it were several others, including John Pullman's International Credit Bank (ICB) in Switzerland, which opened a branch in Freeport to handle the skim from the Monte Carlo. Pullman's bank had several Bahamian subsidiaries including one called Atlas Bank (later Atlas Trust). Atlas, in turn, was united in some shadowy way with Intra Bank in Beirut, Lebanon, which also had a Bahamian branch named Intra Bahamas Trust Ltd. opened by Stafford Sands on 7 December 1963.[45] This Beirut bank was heavily financed by the governments of several Arab nations, including Saudi Arabia and Kuwait. Running many of its operations was the former Saudi Arabian finance minister and munitions trader, Sheikh Suleiman. As part of its Lebanese holdings in the early 1960s, the bank owned a casino whose gambling concession was controlled by Marcel Paul Francisi, France's top heroin dealer.[46] Some investigators were convinced that Lansky and Francisi were partners in heroin racketeering, and that Lansky and his associates had a piece of the casino as well. Intra Bank Beirut ran into financial difficulties and was closed in the fall of 1965. It is unclear, however, exactly when and if its Bahamian operations closed. As late as 31 May 1974, it was reported that the "company remains paid-up; though one could not exactly say it is in good order or good standing."

The Bahamas had been infiltrated by the most sophisticated

band of professional criminals this century has produced. They were at the pinnacle of their power and Freeport was a suitable accomplishment. But Freeport was not the whole game in The Bahamas; there were other tempting Bahamian projects that could be just as secretly lucrative as Freeport was, profits hidden by a banking system devoted to depositor anonymity and a government so ultimately pliable.

But as happened to other colonial nations in the early 1960s, long overdue political change was brewing. The Bahamas was in a state of flux, its old-fashioned political foundation under siege, although there was little doubt of the country's direction. A kind of restless worry, or vague misgiving, over the political future of The Bahamas settled in. The Bahamas seemed an unlikely setting for anything more heated than temporary low-scale turmoil. There was no revolutionary tradition and no known local interest in starting one. Although the future was clouded, there was more than enough confidence for money to flow in, so the deals could be made. And the pressure to move ahead was relentless. Attention had already turned from Freeport to Nassau, where the next phase of casino gambling would take place. There the developers gazed upon a little island in the harbor, and let their imaginations again take over. When that happened, an audacious political plan was employed, which placed the racketeers firmly behind new Black political leaders. Lansky's men provided campaign financing and a strategy that made crime and corruption, ironically, their theme.

Notes

1. Hank Messick, *Syndicate Abroad* (MacMillan, 1969), pp. 49–50.
2. Central Intelligence Agency, File No. 473 865, *Synopsis: Wallace Groves*, 26 January 1966.
3. The material which follows on Groves and Freeport comes from United Kingdom, *Report of the Royal Commission Appointed on the Recommendation of the Bahamas Government to Review the Hawksbill Creek Agreement* (Her Majesty's Stationary Office, 1971), Vols. 1 and 2; files collected and collated by Sally Woodruff and Hank Messick, *Syndicate Abroad*, and *Syndicate in the Sun* (MacMillan, 1968).
4. U.K., *Report . . . Hawksbill Creek*, p. 16.

5. Material on Ludwig from *The Bahamian Review*, July 1964, pp. 26–29.

6. "King's Tower Hotel, due for completion in 1971," Nassau *Tribune*, July 1969; and Sally's folder "Port Authority," p. 5.

7. Although many of the original documents are lost, the first company Annual Return dated 1 December 1959 shows the following shareholders in the venture:

Shareholders	Shares	Description
Wallace Groves	96	Dir. & Chair of Board
Georgette Groves	35,001	
Abaco Lumber Co.	964,900	A Groves company
Variant Industries, Ltd.	505,000	A Hayward company
Charles Allen	252,500	
Arthur Rubloff	71,428	A Chicago based real estate agent
C. Gerald Goldsmith	85,822	An officer in the New York Cosmos Bank
Evelyn J. Lubin, Trustee for Barbara Lubin Goldsmith	31,750	
Evelyn J. Lubin, Trustee for Ann Lubin Goldstein	31,750	
Alfred R. Goldstein	31,750	Engineer

8. U.K., *Report . . . Hawksbill Creek*, p. 23.

9. Messick, *Syndicate Abroad*, p. 64.

10. Material on Allen and Hollywood is from David McClintick, *Indecent Exposure: A True Story of Hollywood and Wall Street* (Dell, 1983), p. 87 et passim.

11. McClintick, *Indecent Exposure*, p. 88; Messick, *Syndicate Abroad*, p. 64.

12. U.S. Senate, Permanent Subcommittee on Investigations, *Hearing: Organized Crime, Stolen Securities*, 28 July 1971, p. 857.

13. McClintick, p. 88.

14. New York City Municipal Archives, Papers of William O'Dwyer,

Murder Inc., "Memorandum in Reference to Charlie Ward," 21 March 1941.

15. The description of "Tex" McCrary in Nassau *Guardian, Report of the Commission . . . Casinos*, par. 282.
16. Securities and Exchange Commission, Division of Corporation Finance, "Prospectus International Airport Hotel System, Inc.," 25 April 1962.
17. *Miami News*, 12 February 1962.
18. G. R. Schreiber, *The Bobby Baker Affair* (Henry Regnery, 1964), pp. 87–88.
19. U.K., *Report of the Royal Commission . . . Hawksbill*, p. 8.
20. Nassau *Guardian, Report of the Commission of Inquiry . . . Casinos*, par. 83.
21. Nassau *Guardian*, pars. 107–112.
22. Ibid., par. 272.
23. Catherine Wismer, *Sweethearts* (James Lorimer and Co.), p. 112.
24. Quoted in Messick, *Syndicate Abroad*, p. 155.
25. Messick, *Syndicate Abroad*, p. 154.
26. Nassau *Guardian, Report of the Commission . . . Casinos*, par. 177.
27. Nassau *Guardian, Report of the Commission . . . Casinos*, par. 176.
28. Nassau *Guardian*, par. 184.
29. Ibid., par. 184.
30. U.S. Department of the Treasury, Federal Bureau of Narcotics, "In Re: Meyer Lansky," 4 November 1965, p. 2.
31. Ritter's warrants were Docket numbers 64CR829 and 65CR238, U.S. District Court, Southern District of New York.
32. Central Intelligence Agency, "Letter from John Edgar Hoover, Director of the F.B.I. to Director C.I.A., Re: INTERNAL SECURITY—CUBA," 18 January 1961.
33. Washington, DC, Metropolitan Police Department, "Statement of Facts in Case of Prisoner Joseph Francis Nesline," taken by Detective R. G. Kirby, D.C.P.D. 74798.
34. Federal Bureau of Narcotics, "Examination of Passport Office File of Charles Tourine, Sr.," 6 December 1961.
35. New York County, District Attorney's Office Squad, "Letter Re: Charlie Tourine and His Associates," 30 November 1961.
36. "Ex-U.S. Attorney and 8 Others Indicted in Alaska Prostitution," *New York Times*, 9 August 1976.
37. Federal Bureau of Narcotics, "Translation of report, in Re: Meyer Lansky," Letter #1395, 11 December 1962.
38. Federal Bureau of Narcotics, District No. 5, "File Title—Meyer Lansky," 4 November 1965.
39. Montgomery County, Maryland, Police Department, Office of Criminal Intelligence, Organized Crime Unit, "Letter to Interpol," 2 March 1978.

40. Interpol Weisbaden Bundeskriminalamt, "Investigation Reports submitted by the Landeskriminalamt Hamburg and Kiel, Re: Joseph Nesline," variously dated in 1977, 1978, and 1979.

41. State of New Jersey, Department of Law and Public Safety, Division of the State Police, "Letter from Captain Justin J. Dintino, Re: Robert Ayoub," 28 February 1978; and State of Maryland, Montgomery County, Department of Police, Office of Criminal Intelligence, Organized Crime Unit, "Re: Joseph Nesline," File No. OCR 75–12, 13 August 1978.

42. Hank Messick, Special Consultant to Florida Governor Claude R. Kirk, Jr., "A Report on Crime and Corruption in South Florida," 16 November 1970, p. 7.

43. Internal Revenue Service, Intelligence Division, "Intelligence Report, Alvin I. Malnik and Bank of World Commerce," 12 February 1964.

44. Messick, "A Report . . . ," p. 40. Nothing came of this particular information about Malnik and his role in the Lansky crime syndicate, and the stunning political corruption in South Florida, until later in the decade. After a number of years of investigation Malnik was finally charged with income tax evasion. He was, however, acquitted in 1970 when government prosecutors were unable to challenge his numerous perjuries, as they would have had to disclose valuable Bahamian banking sources.

45. Sally Woodruff, "Intra Bank Folder #6242."

46. Staff and Editors of *Newsday, The Heroin Trail* (New American Library, 1973), pp. 135–142.

2

Paradise Island

The development of Paradise Island was quite different than that of Freeport, although the end result was quite similar. Freeport was wilderness until Wallace Groves put his stamp on it. Industrial development was his first thought, with casino gambling in partnership with the Lansky syndicate a late, and for Groves, perhaps bitter outcome. Freeport's uniqueness was based on the incredibly generous Hawksbill Creek Agreement, which granted political and economic autonomy to Groves, Lou Chesler, and their associates. Paradise Island, on the other hand, was a private preserve for the extraordinarily wealthy. Its owner in the postwar period was a Swedish billionaire, Axel Wenner-Gren, with ties to the Nazi party. Toward the end of his life, he gave some thought to developing it, but sold it instead to an American millionaire with a yen for art and unorthodox sex. The second owner tried to turn the island into the kind of place he himself would visit, and thus spent most of his fortune building an exquisite "white elephant" resort. In desperation he turned to Lansky, hoping he would help him recoup his millions by getting him a certificate of exemption. It didn't work out for him in the end, but the course for Paradise Island was set.

The little island is four miles long and at most two-thirds of a mile wide. Called Hog Island for centuries, it forms one side of a channel somewhat less than one-half mile in width. Bordering the channel on the south is a part of Nassau city. The sheltered waterway forms Nassau's harbor, and a lighthouse on the island's western tip marked the harbor's entrance. Along the eastern edge and northern shore were sandy beaches, two of which, Pirate Cove and Paradise Beach, were on either side of Hog Point, which jutted out to sea, resembling in its configuration the odd face of the hammerhead shark. The southern shore line was rocky and dotted with numerous coves. Low growing shrub and Australian pine trees covered the island. In 1956, Hog Island was a pleasant ten minute boat ride from the Nassau waterfront.

Eighty percent of the island was then owned by the extraordinarily rich and controversial Wenner-Gren. His home, Shangri-La, sat on 30 flowered acres near a small lake, which connected to a canal running the width of the island. Shangri-La was a famous estate and Wenner-Gren entertained numerous well-known and powerful industrial, financial and political figures including, in 1960, United Nations Secretary General Dag Hammersjkold. Wenner-Gren had invited the secretary to his home to discuss United Nations support for a University of Human Values that Wenner-Gren wished to establish in Cuernavaca, Mexico. There was something ironic about this, however. Wenner-Gren was suspected by many to be a long-term Nazi and so-called Aryan idealist.

Born in Uddevalla, Sweden, in 1881, Wenner-Gren made a fortune estimated in the late 1950s to be worth well over a billion dollars.[1] His money derived from the Electrolux vacuum cleaner, developed by Swedish engineers (from an American model) for Wenner-Gren, and aggressively marketed world wide. Wenner-Gren was as industrially expansive as D. K. Ludwig. At the opening of the 1960s he owned transportation companies in West Germany and the United States, finance and real estate firms in Mexico, harbor and road construction enterprises in The Bahamas, electronic factories and firms in Sweden, and one of the world's largest electric power ventures, located on 40,000 square miles of British Columbian territory to be developed at a reported cost of $611 million.[2] Wenner-Gren was unlike the private Ludwig. He was outgoing, gregarious, and exceptionally philanthropic.

Wenner-Gren stepped down as the head of Electrolux in 1939, with the outbreak of war in Europe, and sailed off to The Bahamas on his yacht, the 335 foot, 1,800 ton, *Southern Cross* purchased from Howard Hughes. On the way, he rescued some 400 passengers from the torpedoed British liner *Athenia*.[3]

His lifesaving action in the Athenia case, as well as numerous philanthropic endeavors, and his later work to create a University of Human Values, stand in stark contrast to his involvement with and support for German militarism. Just a few years after the *Athenia* went down, and only months after the United States officially declared war on Germany, Wenner-Gren was "blacklisted" by the United States. He was placed on the "Proclaimed List" on January 14, 1942, in order to limit his financial activities in the western hemisphere. There was concern he was able to "penetrate" the economies of countries like Mexico, and would use his considerable influence for the Axis.[4]

There was ample reason to suspect Wenner-Gren of Axis sympathies. He had been one of Herman Goering's close confidantes before and during the war, working with him to secure a steady oil supply for the German navy and, more importantly, helping "to render Mexico a debtor republic that could be relied upon to be an ally in time of war," through the mechanism of the German Import-Export Corporation in Mexico City.[5] Additionally, Wenner-Gren was involved in various pro-Nazi schemes with an American collaborator, the oil magnate William Rhodes Davis who was in the thick of Nazi petroleum ventures.[6]

After the war, from the splendid comfort of Shangri-La, Wenner-Gren labored to economically and socially rehabilitate the notorious Alfried Von Krupp, Germany's munitions master. In the mid-1950s Von Krupp and his wife Vera were guests at the Bahamian estate, and there planned the family's rebirth. Wenner-Gren "had sworn that he was ready for one more mighty lunge toward the grail which had fascinated him since youth—a German Europe." He became the key conspirator in a complicated plan to enable Krupp to reacquire the family's munitions empire seized following Germany's defeat.[7]

It was in the midst of his plotting the restoration of the Krupp empire that Wenner-Gren and one of his associates, Arne Lindroth, thought about developing Hog Island. They contacted the New York accounting firm of Horwath & Horwath, hiring it to work up a feasibility study on resort development. The report had several development options from the simple to the grand. For unknown reasons, Wenner-Gren decided not to proceed. A few years later, in 1960, he sold his portion of Hog Island for $14 million to American millionaire George Huntington Hartford II (better known as Huntington Hartford), heir to the Great Atlantic and Pacific Tea Company (the A & P grocery chain) fortune. The following year Wenner-Gren died. His death produced a great mystery; his vast estate had been looted. One result was the curious spectacle in The Bahamas of his widow selling her furniture and paintings at auction to raise needed cash.

Huntington Hartford, grandson of the founder of the A & P chain, changed the name of the island to Paradise, and then transformed it into a resort for the wealthy. He was an educated and aesthetically minded man. He graduated from Harvard College in 1934, and spent a considerable part of his fortune and time on artistic matters, acquiring a fine collection of contemporary art and a commitment to the theater. In the summer of 1948, he formed a company to bankroll theatrical productions. Later, he became a member of the National Council of the Arts in Washington, and owner of a well known modern art gallery in New York which he built to house and exhibit his private collection.[8]

Working with Hartford on all his projects since 1945, as a general assistant and factotum, was Seymour Alter from New York.[9] They were very close friends but markedly different in taste and temperament. Hartford was elegant and refined, Alter was coarse, vulgar, and gruff. Hartford's factotum was born in 1922 and served in the military during World War II. Following the war, while his relationship with Hartford deepened, he worked as a private investigator, garage manager, and garment manufacturer. Finally, he co-managed a liquor store called Bermuda Wines, which was owned by Hartford. Licensed in the winter of 1958, Bermuda Wines would shortly embroil Alter in a New York corruption scandal.[10]

Such close, but diverse personalities sparked vivid speculation about the bond between them, once they arrived together in The Bahamas. It was widely believed, and often stated that Alter helped arrange sexual liaisons for Hartford, whose tastes were considered somewhat peculiar. Those convinced of this arrangement (which would have an impact on Hartford's future in The Bahamas), thought it started in New York when Alter was in the detective business and Hartford owned a modeling agency.[11] Alter controlled much of Hartford's life, screening all of his visitors. Hartford told people in The Bahamas that Alter was his bodyguard, and let it go at that. Few believed him; most thought Alter was blackmailing him—a classic case of a pimp's rise to power.

Alter had a deserved reputation as a corrupter. In fact, while Hartford's development of Paradise Island was proceeding, Alter, as the manager of Bermuda Wines, was called before a New York State Grand Jury investigating corruption in the State Liquor Authority. Granted immunity from prosecution, he testified about graft offered to S.L.A. officials in order to stop them from closing the store for several violations of the State liquor code. Alter tried to "fix" the problem by calling upon a politically connected attorney. A few days later his lawyer said $25,000 would take care of everything. Alter contacted others with influence and arranged to fly S.L.A. people (including the commissioner) to Paradise Island as his guest. But before the deal was finalized, the investigation became public and the scheme fell apart. The worried S.L.A. commissioner told him that he could no longer help; he even asked Alter if he could get him a job in The Bahamas.[12]

Hartford spent millions on a small and lovely hotel (the Ocean Club), an expensive nightclub, and roads, sewerage, water facilities, and street lighting. He rebuilt and remodelled the Wenner-Gren estate. The attractive nightclub had been the caretaker's house. Another part of the hotel was constructed from Wenner-Gren's own home. The Ocean Club was then painted the color of luscious "strawberry ice cream"; it was surrounded by palm trees interspersed with exquisite fish ponds. On the grounds Hartford used imported stone from a Spanish cloister built in the early Middle Ages, and reassembled in a magnificent formal garden. Dotting the garden were wonderful statues culled from his private collection.[13] Hartford's dream resort devoured money much like Groves' initially did. Groves, however, was a master at using other people's money; Hartford wasn't. The A & P heir spent his own, thus by 1963 he had gone through about $24 million.[14]

All the work was exquisitely done, and the final product was truly beautiful, but the resort couldn't make it. It was expensive, small, remote; just the ticket for the very rich, but Hartford's investment required a volume trade. The Ocean Club had only 50 rooms, so there was simply not enough business to break even.

Hartford, again like Groves, sought financial salvation through casino gambling. He vainly tried to secure a certificate of exemption.[15] In preparation for this he turned to the Lansky mob, using Al Malnik as one of the principal intermediaries.[16] The effort was wasted. Hartford applied for a casino license on 17 April 1963, only a couple of weeks after Groves received his for Bahama Amusements. His application was summarily turned down, rejected the very next day. Mindful of Groves' recent good fortune, Hartford referred to it in his petition. On that issue the Colonial Secretary dryly replied the certificate recently granted to Grand Bahama Amusements set no precedent, it was experimental.[17]

As far as casino gambling was concerned, Hartford was out. There seemed nothing to be done, no way for him to rectify what turned out to have been major political gaffes, which were the cause of the government's enmity. First of all, his unusual sexual proclivities were rumored to have disgusted and angered Sir Stafford Sands.[18] Second, disgusted or not, Sands was still the man to "consult" over the delicate issue of a Certificate of Exemption. Instead, Hartford had retained the firm of Higgs & Johnson who were capable attorneys but not in the same league as Sands.[19] His final mistake was perhaps the most serious. He supported the Progressive Liberal Party in its 1962 run against the Bay Street Boys and their newly formed United Bahamian Party. Out of a sense of idealism he donated $15,000 to the Black P.L.P. for the 1962 election. Such virtue was perceived by the Bay Street Boys as little short of racial and political treason.[20]

In the evolution of Bahamian politics, 1962 was the end of a long historical era. It was the final year in which national elections were held under a constitution virtually unchanged since 1728. Among its most anachronistic features were those governing the franchise. It was based upon race, gender, residence, and property. Voting had been restricted to men (white men for the longest section of this history), and plural voting was allowed for those who owned or rented real estate in constituencies other than their primary residence. This last was seen as a substantial, perhaps radical advance over the past when the ownership of property was a necessary condition for voting, and companies were allowed to, and did vote.[21]

All constitutional power resided in the hands of the Governor, who was advised by an Executive Council made up of the Colonial Secretary, the Registrar General, the Attorney General and six other persons chosen by him, usually from the membership of the House. The Governor had almost unlimited discretion in many areas, and the fundamental right to appoint public boards to deal with public works, health, education, pilotage, agriculture and marine products, telephones, oil exploration, etc.[22] The only real limitations on the Governor's power were those which were self imposed. The prime example was found in the Hawksbill Creek Agreement, in which national supremacy was purposely circumscribed. In addition to the Governor and his Executive Council, there was a Legislative Council totally under the Governor's control. The last segment of the government was an elected General Assembly sometimes called the House.[23] This structure guaranteed that real power was in the hands of the white oligarchy. "Property and privilege," as an investigative commission called it, were "entrenched in both legislative chambers, in the Executive Council and in the body politic generally."[24]

The political framework was clearly untenable in a world increasingly marked by the demise of imperialism, and the emergence of anti-colonialism. Neither brutal nor subtle race regimes, characterized by tiny white ruling oligarchies set in the midst of comparatively huge "colored" populations, could confidently face the future. The first contemporary attempt to change the structure of power in The Bahamas came in 1953 with the formation of the Progressive Liberal Party (P.L.P.). Three years later the party entered the election, and surprisingly managed to win six of the 29 General Assembly seats. Continued organization and agitation by the P.L.P. caused the ruling oligarchy to organize the United Bahamian Party (U.B.P.) in 1962.

Given the perspective of centuries-old encrusted power, Huntington Hartford's $15,000 contribution to the P.L.P., in the very year whites felt threatened enough to form their own party, cost him far more than he realized. Moreover, Hartford's generosity to the emergent black leadership ran directly counter to the political intent of the Freeport developers' payoffs. The notorious "consultancy contracts" worked out by Stafford Sands and the others were partially used for the 1962 campaign. As mentioned before, some of the Freeport payoffs were put together in such a way that DEVCO was obligated to pay the brand new U.B.P. $10,000 per month. Hartford's political liberality had tremendous repercussions that were, unfortunately for him, not even dimly perceived. And it didn't matter that the P.L.P.'s 1962 share of the General Assembly only marginally surpassed its 1956 total (*1956*:6 of 29; *1962*:8 of 33). The impact of the P.L.P. was far greater than could be determined by election totals.

The presence of a black political party had created and shaped a demand for political and social change that would be reflected by changes in the structure of the government. In 1962 the P.L.P. and its supporters pushed for a constitutional conference to alter the administration of government. So obviously timely was this call, even the "Bay Street Boys," couldn't stand in opposition. The 1962 campaign found both parties in agreement then "that they would seek for some constitutional advance towards internal self-government." The conference was set for London in 1963, and during that year details of the new Bahamian constitution were hammered out. The British Parliament passed The Bahama Islands (Constitution) Act on 20 December 1963, to take effect in The Bahamas on 7 January 1964.

Hartford had stepped over a dangerous political and social line in The Bahamas, and thus was shut out of the other political games. There was nothing he could do to get his certificate, although he tried several times. Having failed in the spring of 1963, he returned with another application one year later. Again represented by Higgs & Johnson, the artistic millionaire's plan had merit. The certificate would be for ten years, during which time Hartford would first build a 500-room hotel with a casino and convention center. Once that was done, he pledged to construct another 1,000 rooms within five years. And if the Government thought he was incapable of running this complex resort, he further offered to have Hilton Hotels International operate the hotel and the casino.[25] The Government flatly denied the application knowing "that there was a continuing yearly loss in substantial figures for operating the existing facilities at Paradise Island."[26] He was trapped in Paradise.

While Hartford was left to stew and spend, others interested in Paradise Island came forward. Within fourteen months one particular group, an amalgam of new players from the Mary Carter Paint Company, joined by Groves and other Freeport veterans, was easily able to secure a certificate of exemption for a new casino on Paradise Island. What Hartford could never accomplish was done with ease. Hartford, however, still had to be dealt with, as he owned most of the island. Therefore, he was cut in at the start of the deal, and for a few years after. It was not a relationship he relished, especially after he discovered that his new partners were cheating him. Eventually, he was left in the cold.

In pre-Bahama days, Mary Carter Paint was a small New Jersey paint company which displayed slow but steady growth.[27] Beginning in about 1950 the company expanded sales and manufacturing operations into Florida.[28] New retail outlets were opened in several deep south states, and the firm began franchise paint stores. They were successful enough in 1957 to open a manufacturing plant in Tampa. Two years later they ran 63 stores, while franchising 165 others.

Mary Carter's earning potential attracted the interest of James M. Crosby, a young investment banker and former stockbroker. Crosby was then working for financier Gustav Ring, a one-time construction magnate in Washington DC. One of Crosby's first jobs for Ring was the acquisition of the Unexcelled Chemical Company. Ring rewarded Crosby's success by making him the chemical firm's president. Crosby tried to interest his boss in the paint company, but was turned down. He looked elsewhere for the capital, contacting his father, John M. Crosby, a lawyer (once an Assistant Attorney General in the administration of Woodrow Wilson) and major Wall Street trader.

The idea appealed to John Crosby, who used a firm called Crosby-Miller to work the arrangement. Crosby-Miller had developed over the years from the Schaefer Manufacturing Company of Wisconsin, a manufacturing, foundry, and metal working business which started in 1908.[29] John Crosby bought half of the firm in 1955; shortly, thereafter, Crosby-Miller appeared.

In anticipation of the purchase of Mary Carter Paint, Crosby-Miller authorized a large increase in shares. Most of the subscribers were members of the Crosby family. Outside investors included the famous writer and commentator Lowell Thomas, who bought about five percent, and former New York State governor and Republican presidential candidate Thomas E. Dewey, who held less than three percent. Dewey was brought into Crosby-Miller by stockbroker Richard C. Pistell, later sanctioned by the Securities and Exchange Commission for violations. Pistell was close to Jim Crosby (and in time with Robert Vesco), working on many of his ventures beginning with Unexcelled Chemical. In fact, this early association produced a momentary rift between Dewey and broker Pistell, which provides some insight into the character of both men.

Pistell sold Dewey and several of his friends stock in a firm called R. R. Williams in 1959. Dewey thought it was a straightforward investment, and became angry when he learned he was being used. The plan, unknown to Dewey and many of the other subscribers, involved merging the newly acquired shares into Crosby's Unexcelled Chemical. Dewey was irate, believing the deal unfair and improvident for the Williams' stockholders, particularly in light of a recent rise in the price of Unexcelled's stock.[30] He took his Williams' stock out of Pistell's firm, writing a heated note to other affected investors. What specifically galled him was the belief the merger was "up their sleeve when we bought the stock"; they "were all ready to call an emergency meeting and jam it through," he wrote.[31]

Dewey and Pistell managed to patch up their differences. They resumed their "brokerage" relationship, which also included sharing political jokes, no matter how turgid. Around the time of the 1962 U.S. Congressional elections, Pistell sent Dewey a crude political joke in the form of a mock press release dated 5 June 1985, which Governor Dewey thoroughly enjoyed:

> President Ted Kennedy, commenting today on the Russian occupation and fortification of Long Island, the Panama Canal and the southern tip of Florida, said "We are watching these developments carefully and have sent a stiff note of protest to Moscow."

Congresswoman Caroline Kennedy (Dem. Mass.) and Richard King, son of evangelist Martin Luther King, were married today. The ceremony was performed by Chief Justice of the Supreme Court Frank Sinatra. . . . The happy couple will leave tomorrow on a six-month honey-moon in the Congo.

. . . Secretary of Labor Mike Quill announced his retirement today and will be replaced by Teamsters president Jimmy Hoffa . . .[32]

With the infusion of new capital in Crosby-Miller it was time to act. One week after the investment, on 5 December 1958, Crosby-Miller bought 80 percent of Mary Carter for $2,480,000. When all the various details were settled Crosby-Miller had become the Mary Carter Paint Company.

However desirable and robust the paint company looked in the late 1950s to the Crosbys and Pistell, it soon must have appeared slightly anemic. According to Mary Carter attorney Richard Olsen, the market share of Mary Carter was eroding. As a consequence, the officers looked for new investments.[33] The watchword was diversification. After some discussion about buying Kentucky Fried Chicken, the paint company entered the fast food market, buying the assets of the "Biff-Burger" chain.[34] Mary Carter Paint next determined to get into the land development business. It was intrigued by Bahamas Developers Ltd., which owned property in the Freeport area. This firm had a serious cash flow problem in 1962, and was afraid it couldn't meet the first mortgage payments on the land. It was looking for help. Attorney Olsen passed the word to Jim Crosby; before long Mary Carter acquired the development company through an exchange of stock.[35]

The exchange took place in May, 1963, and when completed Mary Carter owned 1,300 acres (with an option on 2,200 more which was rapidly exercised) near Freeport. The paint company ended up with two sites called King's and Queen's Cove. Situated on the northeast bank of the Hawksbill River (a continuation of Hawksbill Creek), Queen's Cove was next to the Freeport International Airport. King's Cove was on the other side of the river.[36] Both developments faced the less desirable north coast of Grand Bahama Island. The most beautiful and popular beaches are on the south side, as far away as possible from the Hawksbill Creek and River, and the Freeport Harbour, which featured the area's only significant industrial activity. When Mary Carter bought

Queen's Cove, over 1,500 building sites had already been platted, and many sold. But the development never really took off. Fifteen years later the site was almost as barren as when it was bought.

Once bitten by the Bahamian real estate bug, Mary Carter was in for more. About a year later, Attorney Olsen had another deal. His friend and past client Huntington Hartford wanted to sell three-quarters of Paradise Island. Olsen called Crosby with the news, which aroused his interest. A meeting was held among Olsen (representing Mary Carter Paint), the desperate Hartford, Cabinet Minister Robert Symonette, and Stafford Sands. During this meeting Sands suggested a gambling license could be had for Paradise Island. It must have infuriated Hartford to hear this, for Sands described Hartford's last proposal with a few important additions. For one, a bridge would have to be built connecting Paradise Island and Nassau. Also, the Freeport "group" would have to be given minority interests in the new venture.[37] One final condition (galling for Hartford) held the buyer was required to retain the services of Sands in its attempt to obtain a certificate of exemption.[38]

The paint company agreed, and in 1965 placed Sands on the payroll. It then applied for a gambling license, and got the bridge financing moving through a private company headed by Crosby. In January 1966 it bought a 75 percent interest in Paradise Island from Hartford for $12,500,000. Mary Carter gave him $3.5 million in cash and picked up a $9 million mortgage held by the Bank of Nova Scotia. Sands created the companies to take over Paradise. He put together three interlocking firms—Paradise Island, Ltd., formed to acquire and lease the land for the casino; Paradise Realty, Ltd., which was to build the casino; and Paradise Enterprises, Ltd., whose function was the management of the casino.[39] This placed Mary Carter Paint and Wallace Groves together. Groves would control four-ninths of the Paradise Island operations, Mary Carter the rest.

Huntington Hartford, who still retained 25 percent of the island, was effectively isolated with a minority interest in one of the three companies established by Sands. He also had a very insecure entitlement of 12½ percent of casino profits. There was another turn in the complex of companies that brought Bahamas Amusements very close to Paradise Island. Groves gave the

Amusements Company responsibility for financing Paradise Realty and for managing Paradise Enterprises.[40]

In the late summer and early fall of 1965 the transformation of Paradise Island was well on its way. Mary Carter Paint had made rapid strides into the power center of Bahamian life since acquiring Bahamas Developers. It was a partner with both Groves and Lou Chesler in one of the largest resort complexes yet contemplated for The Bahamas. The agreements leading to the development of Paradise Island continued. Among the most fascinating was one with the old Bahamian Club. While waiting for the completion of the "new" Paradise Island, Mary Carter Paint and Bahamas Amusements formed a new company and bought the old Bahamian Club and casino, the first licensed gambling club in The Bahamas. Sands had the certificate of exemption, granted in 1939, transferred to Paradise Enterprises in 1966. Jim Crosby felt the price was steep, remarking that the owner, an American named MacKenzie from Providence, Rhode Island, was paid $750,000 for the club.[41]

This slick arrangement closely followed the government's denial of a far different offer to buy the Bahamian Club. The prominent Mrs. Shirley Oakes Butler bid $2,700,000 for the club and its certificate, and most importantly planned to donate a substantial portion of the casino's profits to local charities. Her proposal was submitted on 4 December 1964, and turned down by the government several months later with no explanation.[42] Shirley Butler knew nothing of Sands' machinations with the Amusements Company and the new player in town, Mary Carter Paint, concerning the Bahamian Club. She was left unenlightened, although it was already apparent to Premier Roland Symonette that Sands and the others who had the inside track for the old club had far less charitable plans than hers in mind. Also, the scheme to transfer the Bahamian Club's casino license to Paradise Island was public knowledge by May 1965, and thus had to have originated months earlier.[43] Most likely the Bahamian Club buyout and license transfer were tactics used to freeze out any potential Nassau competitor, no matter how civic minded, as well as to guarantee Sands his profitable participation.

The government's desire to sell the Bahamian Club to Paradise Enterprises was resisted by its long-time proprietor W. D.

MacKenzie, the American from New England. In July 1965, however, it was clear MacKenzie was forced to sell out, pressured by Sands and joined by other interested parties. "He was bluntly told," one commentator noted, "that his casino license would not be renewed and that he had better sell his club." Quite angry, MacKenzie grumbled the real powers behind the deal were the Las Vegas gamblers who will control the new Paradise Island casino.[44] MacKenzie was familiar with Nevada gambling, supposedly having an interest in a club at Lake Tahoe.

MacKenzie was not far off when it came to the new faces at the Bahamian Club. Those who ran the casino were primarily from the gangster-plagued Monte Carlo casino. Eddie Cellini was the assistant manager and others on staff came from the London croupier school set up by his brother Dino. It was to be business as usual in the Bahamian Club, and probably its fancy successor, too, as far as the mob was concerned. That was the opinion of Department of Justice attorney Robert D. Peloquin, sent to The Bahamas in order to investigate "rumors" of the mob's infiltration. Peloquin wrote a memorandum on the subject, which contained these famous lines: "Mary Carter Paints will be in control of Paradise Island, with the exception of the Casino, which Groves will control. The atmosphere seems ripe for a Lansky skim."[45]

A reasonable presumption in January 1966, when the memorandum was written, it would later prove embarrassing to Peloquin and Mary Carter's successor corporation, Resorts International. After his investigation, Peloquin resigned from the Justice Department to head Intertel, a private security outfit owned by Resorts. The Paradise Island company would be asked numerous times in different forums to explain Peloquin's statement and subsequent new post; and its alleged connections to Lansky and his mob.

When Sands turned the deal for Mary Carter Paint and his associates from Freeport, he must have felt smug, although it was nearly the end of the line for him and some of the older power brokers. Bahamian politics were about to heat up once again. What had started in the 1950s with the formation of the Progressive Liberal Party, found encouragement in the 1962 election. More inspiration came the following year when the constitutional

conference mandated important changes in politics and government. In 1966, significant pressure was built as the P.L.P. and its
leader, attorney Lynden O. Pindling, discovered new friends and
an issue which would carry him and the party to real power in
1967.

The mid-1960s were a time of both consolidation and innovation
in Bahamian life. Freeport had, in a sense, grown up; no longer
about to make it, Groves' dream city had arrived. Even the revelations about the staff at the Monte Carlo, people thought, could
not substantially tarnish the town's new image. Casinos are always
in a constant struggle to either keep racketeers out, or to convince
gaming authorities that they are clean. Tension over the organized
crime issue comes with the territory, and through 1965 it wasn't
too difficult to weather the sporadic squalls washing over Freeport.

As a mark of the new dignity, the brassy Lou Chesler had been
taken down a notch or two, or so it was rumored. In 1964 there
had been a public falling out between Groves and Chesler, leading
some to believe that Chesler either had pulled up stakes, or been
driven out of Freeport by Groves. One report had it that Chesler
was finished on Grand Bahama Island by the end of 1966, having
earlier sold off his interest in the Lucayan Beach Hotel to Allen
Manus, a Canadian financier. Shortly thereafter, the hotel went
into receivership.[46] Chesler did sell the hotel, but was hardly
washed up. He just moved more quietly, trying to hide his weighty
presence and assets behind several real estate and development
companies. One of his new primary enterprises was in the Berry
Islands, lying between Grand Bahama Island and Nassau on New
Providence Island. He began developing a project there called
Great Harbour Cay.

With the government-backed arrangements between Mary Carter
Paint and the Freeport developers to open up Paradise Island,
Groves was surely riding high. In addition, he was strategically
placed and important enough to be contacted by the Central
Intelligence Agency which needed his help. This must have been
quite flattering for the ex-con. On 30 December 1965, there was
an internal C.I.A. request "for a Covert Security Approval" to
allow Groves to work as "an advisor" or "possible officer" for a
project probably involving Cuba.[47] This was approved on 11 April

1966 and Groves worked for the Agency for the next six years. His operational interest to the Investigations and Support Division of the C.I.A. ended in the spring of 1972.[48]

Conquering the wilderness of Grand Bahama Island and actually building Freeport, preparing to enter Nassau and Paradise Island, and working in covert operations with the C.I.A. were milestones of achievement for Groves, each marking, in its way, the distance covered from his swindling and prison days. There was "clear evidence that the period of disgrace in his life had a haunting quality which," it was stated, "was of real and constant concern."[49] Every step into respectability helped him minimize his painful past.

Within the year, however, he would face a publicity barrage, which had the potential to undermine much that he had accomplished, and to bring back the troubling memories of the past. It was a tough development for Groves, not helped by the fact that part of it had been set in motion by members of the Freeport gambling confraternity and their associates. Many of Pindling's new friends were Groves' old ones. The issue they would masterfully play together was public corruption.

The times had changed and none recognized this more completely, argued crime writer Hank Messick, than Meyer Lansky.[50] He and his associates set out to capture Pindling, thereby recovering from the financial consequences of the Cuban debacle. They knew what it meant to be on the wrong side of "history," and were not about to sit back and lose out as political change swept the nation. Far better to cut new deals with Pindling and the Progressive Liberal Party (P.L.P.) crowd, helping sweep the Bay Street Boys out, than to be forced out themselves. It was chancy and dangerous, but eventually it would be done.

Pindling's capture came first. Subsequently, the use of incriminating material to unnerve, then destroy the United Bahamian Party (U.B.P.) was orchestrated. Pindling was inexpensive in those early days. He needed money for political work, and there was precious little of that in The Bahamas for a black candidate with an undeserved radical reputation. Pindling found backing from gambler Mike McLaney and Chesler. McLaney helped Pindling in many ways. He paid his printing bills and provided rent free office space (worth $1,100 per month) to two members of the

P.L.P. One of them was the editor of *The Bahamian Times*, partially owned by Pindling.[51]

McLaney and another of his partners, Louis Colasurdo, supplied Pindling with the air transport necessary for him to campaign around the widely scattered Bahamian out islands. McLaney, Colasurdo, and Pindling were also business associates. In 1965 they were involved in highly questionable financial manipulations affecting several related companies called Caletta Blueberry, Makepeace, Crescent Corp., and Six M Ltd. Joining them in this scheme was Pedro Torres, a major securities swindler working with Lansky.

Another new Pindling political adviser active in 1965 was David Probinsky, out of New Jersey. Probinsky had managed the Sir John Hotel in Miami, a well-known inn catering to Blacks in those days of segregation. According to various insiders, there were several important political meetings dealing with campaign financing and similar matters held at the Sir John. Pindling and Probinsky became close associates which would eventually prove helpful, but later disconcerting to Resorts International, Probinsky's future employer. Using a consulting firm called Diversified Services as a cover, Probinsky was one of Pindling's major bag men.[52]

Pindling's political strategy since the opening of the Monte Carlo casino, with the attendant publicity about organized crime, was to portray the ruling clique as corrupt lackeys of the mob. In 1965 this claim was enhanced by the judicious leaking of incriminating material about crime and corruption in Freeport to influential reporters. Odd as it may seem on the face of it, this was done by those very close to the gamblers. For instance, the "irresponsible and meddlesome" Tex McCrary, who had excellent contacts with the national press, began leaking stories, as did others associated with Lansky. This was a risky gambit because it was impossible to predict just where reporters with McCrary's leads might go.

The plan, or its unforseen consequences, came together on 5 October 1966, when the story of organized crime and corruption in Freeport broke on the front page of the *Wall Street Journal*. Brilliantly researched and written by Stanley Penn (assisted by Monroe W. Karmin), it laid out the seamy history of casino gambling in The Bahamas. Penn's prize-winning account mentioned Groves' 1941 conviction; the consultancy contracts worked out by Sands; the Lansky presence; the mobsters staffing the Monte Carlo; and the "Bay Street Boys," characterized as that "powerful group of merchant-politicians who dominate the colony." He quoted Pindling saying that his policy would be to renegotiate the casino license to drive out the mob. Penn noted that Bahamian "upper-crust" wrath had turned on Stafford Sands. He was described by his new critics as a huge man living like an emperor in his Nassau estate, Waterloo, which had a private lake.[53]

As for Pindling's future, the *Journal* wrongly thought that he wouldn't have enough support to win in the next election, which had to be held by the end of 1967. He is bold, it was added, having brought "conflict-of-interest" charges before the United Nations the past year. The core of this indictment was that gov-ernment ministers owned businesses that did business with the government. He angrily stated they were awarding themselves substantial government contracts. Pindling kept the pressure on, returning to the U.N. just weeks before the *Journal* story broke. He claimed The Bahamas was "being sold out to 'gangsterism' by his political opponents."[54]

A week after the *Journal* exposé, it was announced that three of the most notorious underworld characters working at the Monte Carlo, Ritter, Courtney, and Brudner, would be leaving the ca-sino by mid-January. What wasn't announced, however, was the special contract they had signed with the Amusements Company. They leased their credit files on known gamblers to the company for ten years at a price of $70,000 per year per man.[55]

Allegedly cleaning up the Monte Carlo, by finally dumping the three well-known (and now very well-heeled) racketeers, was hardly a sufficient response on the part of Bahamian officials, Pindling said, as he pressed his attack. In meetings in both Miami and New York, where he was briefed by Tex McCrary among others, his next move was discussed—the P.L.P. would demand a national election as soon as legally possible. Following that, they would forcefully request the British to establish a royal com-mission to investigate public corruption in The Bahamas. Both tactics were used and national elections were set for 10 January 1967. The Commission would sit after the election.

A P.L.P. victory was by no means assured. The white oligarchy was still powerful and the franchise still skewed in favor of property owners. In was a very tight election. When the votes were in, the P.L.P. and U.B.P. were dead even. Each had eighteen representatives in the General Assembly. The tense outcome was finally decided by Randol Fawkes, the lone Labor party representative, after a week of constitutional crisis and bargaining. He gave his support to Pindling in return for the post of minister of labour. The *New York Times* headline on 17 January 1967, bannered the change: ALL-NEGRO REGIME RULES IN BAHAMAS. A 300-year colonial tradition had been shattered.[56] One hour after being sworn in as prime minister, Pindling announced his cabinet, and the reins of government were passed from the white administration of Sir Roland Symonette, which had held power for the last nine years. Stafford Sands must have been singularly upset when Prime Minister Pindling took the major government portfolio of tourism and development.

Events were moving very rapidly. Hardly had the new government taken over when *Life* Magazine published "The Scandal in The Bahamas," the story of Freeport and the mob. Caption writers characterized Wallace Groves as "The 'Big Daddy' of Free-Wheeling Freeport," portraying him as though he was a ludicrous Tennessee Williams character. The article's writers noted the speculation that infamous gangsters from New York, Buffalo, Philadelphia, and Tampa were getting a cut of the Monte Carlo's profits.[57] Another sensational story on Bahamian corruption appeared at the end of February in the *Saturday Evening Post* and was luridly titled "The Mafia: Shadow Of Evil On An Island In The Sun." *Post* writer Bill Davidson claimed federal authorities strongly believe that in 1966 Lansky funneled around $6 million from the Monte Carlo to several crime syndicates.[58] Concerning Sands, Davidson wryly stated "Sir Stafford Sands as attorney for Bahamas Amusements Ltd. negotiated a license fee for the casinos with Sir Stafford Sands, the minister of finance."

Three days after the *Post* story Pindling was in New York announcing he was going to make it more difficult for racketeers to use The Bahamas as a haven for illegal business. But a new note of discord had crept into the proceedings. Reporters wanted to know if he had any business connections or links with Representative Adam Clayton Powell, the tarnished New York Democrat, then living on Bimini island in the Bahamas.[59] At that moment, Powell was under investigation by a congressional committee for various misdeeds. Pindling said he had no significant business connections with Powell. He did admit when pressed, though, to a minor and meaningless exception. The prime minister owned a share in Huff Enterprises, a Bahamian corporation set up by some of Powell's associates and headed by Corrine Huff, a former beauty queen and Powell's mistress who appeared on his congressional payroll as a secretary. The company had been organized to secretly funnel money from the States into Bahamian ventures.[60]

Stories on organized crime, casino gambling, and Bahamian corruption were almost daily occurrences. The day before Pindling's press conference, British authorities notified Dino Cellini his work permit would not be renewed and he must leave Britain by 21 March. The Associated Press reported Cellini was the gambling adviser for a London casino, but made no mention of the croupier school.[61]

All the attention was finally focused on the royal commission that was formed on 4 March. Every few days brought new revelations that confirmed the investigative reports, adding only a few details here and there. The mere fact of the inquiry, let alone the particular findings, had a discernible impact on Bahamian affairs. Several developments followed, and one in particular concerned Paradise Island. With the Freeport developers branded as buccaneers or worse, Wallace Groves now appeared as a liability to those counting on turning Paradise Island into a gambler's haven.

Mary Carter Paint bought out Groves to protect itself from the broadening scandal. The royal commission and news stories convinced Crosby and Mary Carter's management that they had to appear without a taint of organized crime. Yet the firm was in the organized gambling business, and found it burdensome to operate without the services and expertise of numerous tainted individuals. That would pose one dilemma, which had its own interesting history, particularly affecting the Cellini family. It was, however, only one segment of the organized crime issue. Another more serious part concerned the function organized criminals and their associates in finance performed in transforming the paint company into Resorts International, the gambling kingpin of The Bahamas with interests in other casino projects from the Dutch West Indies to Atlantic City.

Notes

1. The *New York Times*, 25 November 1961.
2. The *New York Times*, 25 November 1961. See also AmEmbassy MEXICO, D.F., FOREIGN SERVICE DESPATCH No. 1526 to Department of State, "Re: Axel Leonard Wenner-Gren, Swedish Industrialist and International Financier," 27 June 1960, Enclosure #2.
3. Ibid., Enclosure #2.
4. H. Freeman Matthews, Deputy Under Secretary, Department of State, "Letter: *Secret Security Information*," to R. L. Gilpatric, Under Secretary of the Air Force, 22 May 1952. Wenner-Gren complained often about his unfair treatment.
5. Charles Higham, *Trading With The Enemy: An Exposé of the Nazi-American Money Plot, 1933–1949* (Dell, 1983), p. 87.
6. When Davis died in 1941, either of natural causes according to the F.B.I., or murdered by British Intelligence agents, as reported by spymaster Sir William Stevenson, the chief of British security operations in the United States, his firm was quickly sold to Wenner-Gren, among others, in order to protect its real purpose of supplying the German war machine. Virtually all of Wenner-Gren's enterprises served the Nazi cause during World War II, including the Bofors munitions firm, which he partially owned. Headquartered in Sweden, it provided Germany with a significant part of its steel production. Ibid., pp. 93–94, p. 138.
7. Plotting with the Krupps was "old hat" for Wenner-Gren. From 1914 to 1918 he had cloaked the Krupp's foreign businesses to allow them to operate and profit, no matter what the war's outcome. And in the 1920s he aided Gustav Von Krupp on clandestine projects of German rearmament in violation of the Versailles Treaty. See William Manchester, *The Arms of Krupp, 1587–1968* (Bantam Edition, 10th printing, 1981), pp. 866–67.
8. Resorts International, "Report to Stockholders," 26 May 1968 in TW5 folder "IOS/Vesco/Resorts."
9. New York State Grand Jury, "Testimony of Seymour Alter," 13 April 1963, 3243–3283.
10. State of New York Liquor Authority and State of New York Executive Department, Division of Alcoholic Beverage Control, "Documents on File, Re: Bermuda Sales Corporation," 31 January 1958 through 13 June 1963.

11. TW5 folder, "Seymour Alter," report on 19 April 1975.
12. New York State Grand Jury, 3243–3283.
13. Gigi Mahon, *The Company that Bought the Boardwalk: A Reporter's Story of How Resorts International Came to Atlantic City* (Random House, 1980), p. 27.
14. See Nassau *Guardian, Report of the Commission . . . Casinos*; and Messick, *Syndicate Abroad*, p. 178.
15. Nassau *Guardian, Report of the Commission . . . Casinos.*
16. There are two accounts of how Hartford and the mob came together. One was constructed by two U.S. Justice Department attorneys, Robert D. Peloquin and David P. Bancroft, who had been assigned to investigate rumors of organized crime's move into The Bahamas. Reporting to William G. Hundley, head of the Organized Crime and Racketeering Section of the Department of Justice, Peloquin and Bancroft wrote that Hartford "through the Braganini (PH) Research Bureau, Time/Life Building, New York City was introduced to Sam Golub of Miami, Florida." Golub had the reputation of a "fixer" with connections to Stafford Sands. This version adds that Hartford met Golub at the Fountainbleu Hotel and was there introduced to Alvin Malnik. The three struck a deal calling for Hartford to pay a substantial finder's fee if Golub and Malnik were able to get him a gambling license. Hartford signed a contract with Golub and Malnik on 15 October 1962. U.S. Department of Justice, "Memorandum, Re: Bahamas Inquiry; interview of Huntington Hartford," 18 January 1966.
    The second account places Sy Alter at the center. Alter himself stated in 1974 (during discovery proceedings in a civil suit) that he and Malnik talked about Hartford's financial dilemma and Malnik offered his assistance. Alter flew to Miami and Malnik introduced him to Lansky, who asked if he was interested in a casino license. Alter supposedly respectfully responded, "no thank you." He claimed to have told Lansky "I don't think Mr. Hartford nor his lawyers would allow any sort of negotiation with you in any manner or form, and I hope you are not taking it personally." In 1976 Alter tried to repudiate his testimony, no doubt at Malnik's request. See James Savage, "Nevada Orders Casino to Stop Dealing with Malnik," *Miami Herald*, 20 March 1976.
17. Ibid., 20 March 1976.
18. *The Company that Bought the Boardwalk*, p. 29.
19. Nassau *Guardian, Report of the Commission . . . Casinos*, par. 224, p. 21.
20. Messick, *Syndicate Abroad*, p. 179.
21. U.K., *Report . . . Hawksbill Creek*, Vol. I.
22. U.K., *Report*, Vol. I.
23. Ibid., pp. 34–5.
24. Ibid., p. 35.

25. Nassau *Guardian, Report of the Commission . . . Casinos*, par. 226.

26. Nassau *Guardian*, Report, par. 227.

27. Bruce Locklin and Vinny Byrne, "Behind the Casino Push: A Look At Resorts International," in New Jersey *Bergen Record*, 14 October 1976.

28. New Jersey Department of Law and Public Safety, Division of Gaming Enforcement, *Report to the Casino Control Commission with Reference to the Casino License Application of Resorts International Hotel, Inc.*, 4 December 1978, p. 8.

29. Ibid., p. 9.

30. Thomas E. Dewey, "Letter to Richard C. Pistell," 10 October 1959.

31. Thomas E. Dewey, "Letter to the Purchasers of R. R. Williams Stock," 21 October 1959.

32. Pistell's fake press release is in the Dewey Papers at the University of Rochester Rare Books and Manuscripts Library.

33. New Jersey, *Report*, pp. 10–11.

34. Robert G. Barrett and J. Paul Kinloch, "Mary Carter Paint's Development of Paradise Island in The Bahamas," Report submitted to the company, 27 April 1968.

35. New Jersey Casino Control Commission, "Resorts International Transcripts: Testimony of Richard Olsen," January, 1979.

36. See Bahamas Developers Ltd., "Advertising Brochure: Queens Cove, Waterfront Wonderland of the Bahamas," prepared by Joseph Forni Associates.

37. New Jersey Casino Control Commission, "Testimony of Olsen," p. 6.

38. New Jersey, *Report*, p. 19.

39. One other company was founded, C & R Limited, to protect the interests of the Mary Carter Paint group in case the deal fell through. C & R apparently could move in and operate under the certificate of exemption if necessary. See the Nassau *Guardian, Report of the Commission . . . Casinos*, par. 230.

40. It would be compensated with regular quarterly dividends on 62.5 percent of the Realty Co. shares. Ibid., pp. 21–22.

41. New Jersey Casino Control Commission, "Resorts International Transcripts, Testimony of James Crosby," January 1979, p. 55.

42. Nassau *Guardian, Report of the Commission . . . Casinos*, par. 222, p. 21.

43. See Intelligence Division (Miami), "Memorandum to District Director of Intelligence, Jacksonville," 14 May 1965.

44. Intelligence Division (Miami), "Report to Chief Intelligence Division, Jacksonville," 14 July 1965.

45. New Jersey, *Report*, Appendix 6, 4 December 1978, p. 4.

46. Richard Oulahan and William Lambert, "The Scandal in the Bahamas," in *Life Magazine*, 3 February 1967.

47. That Cuba was most likely the initial target is supported to a degree

by C.I.A. operative Donald P. Norton, whose spy career started in 1957. Norton is part of that strange and shadowy group of operatives who planned and plotted against the Castro government, and who, more importantly, claimed Lee Harvey Oswald was among the co-conspirators. The C.I.A. sent him to Freeport in 1966, presumably on a Cuban mission to work under a C.I.A. cover provided by Groves. See William Turner, "The Garrison Commission," first published in *Ramparts*, January 1968, subsequently in Peter Dale Scott, Paul L. Hoch and Russell Steller, *The Assassinations: Dallas and Beyond* (Vintage Books, 1976), p. 288.

48. U.S. Central Intelligence Agency, "Request for Approval or Investigative Action: Subject, Wallace Groves," 30 December 1965; various reports and memoranda on File No. 473 865; and John K. Greaney, "Memorandum: Clearance Cancellation Notice," Attention Chief, Investigations & Support Division, 12 April 1972.

49. U.S. Department of State, AmConsul NASSAU, "Visit of the American Consul General to Grand Bahama," Airgram No. A–99, 3 February 1967, p. 2.

50. Hank Messick, *Syndicate Abroad*, p. 195.

51. The *New York Times*, 20 April 1967, p. 35.

52. New Jersey, *Report*, p. 94.

53. *Wall Street Journal*, 5 October 1966, p. 1.

54. *Wall Street Journal*, p. 1.

55. Messick, *Syndicate Abroad*, pp. 217–18.

56. The *New York Times*, 17 January 1967, p. 10.

57. Richard Oulahan and William Lambert, "The Scandal in The Bahamas," in *Life Magazine*, 3 February 1967.

58. Bill Davidson, "The Mafia: Shadow Of Evil On An Island In The Sun," *Saturday Evening Post*, 25 February 1967.

59. *New York Times*, 28 February 1967, p. 5.

60. The *New York Times*, p. 5.

61. Associated Press dispatch in *New York Times*, 28 February 1967, p. 5.

3

Resorts International

Resorts International was a Tradewinds' preoccupation. In particular, Sally Woodruff was determined to trace the individuals who provided the financing which allowed Mary Carter Paint to become Resorts. However, the I.R.S. turmoil which erupted over Intelligence Division operations ultimately destroyed their efforts. At around the same time, however, Resorts was in the process of expansion to Atlantic City, New Jersey. The Casino Gaming Act in the Garden State, which allowed New Jersey to withhold a gambling license from persons associated with organized crime, became the last best hope to know whether those who helped create Resorts were mobsters and their associates or not. The act stated a "license shall be denied in the event it is found the applicant or any person required to be qualified as a pre-condition to the casino license . . . is identified as a career offender or a member of a career offender cartel or an associate of a career offender cartel."[1]

The funds amassed to finance the Paradise Island ventures amounted to about $33 million. Of that sum at least 63 percent appeared to come from or through "funny-money" sources some directly related to organized crime, Castle Bank, and subsequently Robert Vesco. Mary Carter turned to several companies, individuals and brokerage firms when it was ready for the big push. Two in particular stand out when considering organized crime. The first was a Bahamian bank called Fiduciary Trust and the second, Delafield and Delafield, a well known and respected New York brokerage house.

Mary Carter borrowed $3.9 million from Fiduciary Trust which was managed by Samuel Clapp, Edward Cowett and William Sayad.[2] Clapp was an attorney from Boston who had been tax adviser to one of the world's largest mutual funds—Investors Overseas Services (I.O.S.). Working with Fiduciary Trust was equivalent to dealing with I.O.S., and I.O.S. many observers felt, was perilously close to organized crime.

I.O.S. was formed in the 1950s by the flamboyant Bernard Cornfeld and grew into the world's largest offshore mutual fund complex worth anywhere between $500 million and $2 billion. Super-salesman Cornfeld, the offspring of a Russian mother and Rumanian father, was born in Istanbul, Turkey, in 1927. Shortly after, his parents moved the family to Vienna and then to America in the worst year of the worldwide Great Depression.[3] Bernie, as everyone called him, spent the rest of his youth in Brooklyn. He graduated from Brooklyn College and for a short time played at social work and a college teaching career. Neither occupation provided what he yearned for, however, and he soon was selling mutual funds. In 1956, he convinced Jack Dreyfus, then starting his own mutual fund program, to give him the overseas selling rights. Working out of a Paris apartment, Bernie with a sales staff of eighteen (the embryonic I.O.S.), started to market the Dreyfus mutuals to American servicemen stationed at various NATO installations around France.[4]

The bearded and balding Cornfeld now with a little sales experience realized that millions of individuals all over the world would buy his funds if he could offer freedom from exchange controls and tax collectors. Bernie thought he could and moved to Switzerland to carry out his plan. There was only one hitch, Bernie was having difficulty raising money to capitalize the expansion of his sales force. The resourceful Cornfeld thought of a unique solution which became the carrot and stick of I.O.S. sales. The necessary capital could be raised from his workers themselves by selling them an equity participation based on their own sales. Putting this idea into operation became the province of the "nimble-minded" Edward Cowett eventually one of Fiduciary's bosses.

A "cum laude" graduate of Harvard Law School in 1954, Cowett was an expert on the regulation of securities sales. Cowett, like Bernie, was associated with the Dreyfus Fund when they met; his law firm was the Fund's counsel. In 1960, Cowett was kicked out of this firm for reportedly promoting "sleazy" securities. It was then that Bernie asked him to join I.O.S. and put his idea into practice. The I.O.S. Stock Option Plan was the ultimate sales device. It linked the number of shares in the firm that salesmen (called associates) could acquire (up to 20,000) to the total face amount of investment programs sold. If they sold more, they could buy more, and their investment was worth more. It was a gilt-edged whip, and still they weren't quite finished.

Building the firm on the flight capital of foreigners, often desperate to move their money out of troubled countries, usually with severe currency restrictions, and on Americans living overseas who were anxious to avoid paying the I.R.S. anything, meant that I.O.S. was a huge black market enterprise. As writer Robert Hutchinson noted, "potential clients [were] just waiting for the right kind of investment vehicle to come along and carry off their undeclared profits for safekeeping abroad."[5] But because of S.E.C. disclosure rules, American securities were not the ideal instrument for this deception. What they needed, Bernie and Cowett figured was an international investment trust; one that was unfettered by American rules and regulations.

Their principal advisor on this matter was Dr. Tibor Rosenbaum, one of organized crime's Swiss bankers. Rosenbaum worked with John Pullman in the International Credit Bank based in Geneva with a branch in The Bahamas. In the early 1960s, the mob's International Credit Bank became vitally important to Cornfeld's robust creation. It served as the laundromat for smuggled funds, mostly from South American clients of I.O.S. Bernie's sales managers provided an added service for those with at least $50,000 to move. They had the money smuggled out by special courier to I.C.B. in Geneva and then loaned back at six percent interest to the original owners. The major courier for this service was Sylvain Ferdman, a naturalized Swiss citizen who had been Cowett's Harvard roommate.[6]

Ferdman worked with Rosenbaum, Cowett, and particularly John Pullman. Unfortunatley for all the schemers, Ferdman was careless. At the Miami airport in the third week of March 1965, he inadvertently dropped a note written on International Credit Bank stationery. "This is to acknowledge," it said, "this 20th day of December 1964, the receipt of Three Hundred and Fifty Thousand ($350,000) in American bank notes for deposit to the account of Maral 2812 with the International Credit Bank Geneva."[7] The note bore the signatures of both Ferdman and Pullman. This chance event revealing the intertwining of I.O.S. and Lansky's syndicate galvanized law enforcement efforts and Ferdman eventually found himself before a federal Grand Jury in New York testifying about his role as a courier for organized crime, moving funds between America, Switzerland and The Bahamas. His most difficult moment, however, came in 1967 when *Life* magazine ran his picture identifying him as a Mafia money courier.

John Pullman's life was also made at least moderately miserable because of the Ferdman mishap. Canadian authorities bugged and wiretapped a Royal York Hotel room Pullman used when he was in Toronto. The electronic surveillance started in September 1966 and confirmed Pullman's standing in organized crime and his relationship with Lansky called "the Chief, the Little Guy," and "Dupont." Talking about "Dupont" one day, Pullman and attorney Gerson Blatt exchanged remarks about Lansky's wealth, estimated then at $300 million. Pullman said he hadn't seen a nickel of it, while Blatt asserted with awe that Lansky didn't even have an accountant. Investigators learned Pullman and his racketeer associates had recently closed a complex deal in Bolivia involving mines and other industrial enterprises. At another point, Pullman mentioned he was working with the greatest stock manipulators in the world including his partner Chesler, and a very prominent financier and art collector. Pullman proudly stated: "They're putting up a special building in Washington to house his collection."[8]

The Bolivian arrangement was one part of an elaborate organized crime network of businesses then being constructed. This particular one centered on a Liechtenstein company which branched out to encompass at least fifteen known subsidiaries. The multinational structure permitted organized crime enormous flexibility in moving and laundering funds as subsidiaries were placed in the United States, Europe, and the Caribbean. There were single companies established in Delaware, Florida, Missouri, The Bahamas, and Holland. Multiple enterprises were formed in the Cayman Islands, the Netherlands Antilles, and in Vaduz, Liechtenstein's capitol and only town. All the firms dealt in one way or another with land development. They were in construction, especially shopping centers, and condominiums, and in finance, particularly mortgages.[9]

Pullman, however, was unable to concentrate on this project because of anxiety over tax matters. He squirmed under the heat of an I.R.S. investigation which stemmed from Dick Jaffe's discovery of the Bank of World Commerce in Nassau. Afraid to travel to the United States he said: "I can do nothing in the United States; I have to have people that I can trust in the United States, because I can't even go to the United States, . . . I'm not in a position to answer questions." He was, however, in a hurry to talk to Alvin Ira Malnik because he had to file amended tax returns for 1962 through 1964, and referring to Malnik he said "I don't know what he told them [law enforcement] in New York."[10]

On 27 September 1966, the Canadian police recorded a Pullman and Malnik conversation which detailed some Pullman investments, and elements of their relationship. They were partners in many enterprises besides the Bank of World Commerce. During the talk Malnik became exasperated with Pullman and said: "No, no! What this is, is this; these are escrow accounts on deals that I was handling for you."[11] Malnik went over Pullman's complicated finances involving several firms and fairly obscure foreign banks. Some people owed Pullman money including "Fat Tony" Salerno from East Harlem and South Florida.[12] In addition to tax problems, they talked about buying a small Paris casino. Later, the police listened as Pullman discussed the Paris casino with Morris Lansburgh the owner of the plush Eden Roc Hotel on Miami Beach.[13]

Cornfeld's creation and the Lansky syndicate were very tight. However IOS did maintain some degree of independence. Bernie decided to buy his own Swiss bank (the Overseas Development Bank), although Tibor Rosenbaum thought it unnecessary, arguing in vain that Bernie could always rely on the I.C.B. This wasn't real separation; I.C.B. held a 20 percent equity interest in Bernie's bank.[14] Fiduciary Trust was one of many IOS subsidiaries and affiliates and thus automatically suspicious because of its parent's organized crime connection. In addition to that issue, in 1968, Fiduciary's management ran into legal trouble. According to the S.E.C., Clapp and Sayad had engaged in several flimflams while handling the Mary Carter Paint shares. They received mild sanctions from the S.E.C. Cowett (who died suddenly on an airplane in 1974) also tangled with the S.E.C. and in 1971 he was forbidden to work as a stock broker.

Fiduciary had two rounds with Mary Carter/Resorts. The first occurred in the summer of 1966 when the bank and Sam Clapp took $100,000 worth of the paint company's promissory notes. The following year the bank again invested for itself, and for two of its clients. The clients were the Fiduciary Growth Fund totally owned by Louis Chesler's son Alan, and the Troconis Family Trust whose principal beneficiary was the family of William Mellon Hitchcock. One other Fiduciary manifestation, Fiduciary Investment, lent Sy Alter $70,000 which he invested in Resorts.

Stockbroker William Mellon Hitchcock is an American original. He is the grandson of William Larimer Hitchcock founder of Gulf Oil, and the nephew of Andrew Mellon whose fortune in the 1920s was somewhere between one and two billion dollars. Andrew Mellon was ranked second to John D. Rockefeller in power, wealth and influence in the whole country, wrote Cleveland Amory in his chronicle of the American aristocracy.[15] But Billy Hitchcock marched to a more complicated tune than the industrial tycoons in his family. He reached for both an emotional and aesthetic experience nurtured by LSD, as well as the more traditional reverie brought on by conquering the boardrooms of Wall Street. His quest for internal enlightenment was helped by a substantial inheritance and trust fund that provided him with $15,000 per week in spending money. That money enabled him to bankroll the manufacture and distribution of LSD.[16]

Originally turned onto acid by his sister, the director of the New York branch of Timothy Leary's International Federation for Internal Freedom, Billy Hitchcock gave one of the family's estates to Leary as a center and playground for psychedelic fun and games. Leary, the nation's best known apostle of LSD, disbanded the Federation and replaced it with something called the Castalia Foundation once he was in place at the Hitchcock spread in Millbrook, New York. The Millbrook experience, according to researchers Martin Lee and Bruce Shlain, was like a fairy tale. The Hitchcock mansion was transformed into a Victorian Ashram; psychedelic art mixed with Persian carpets, dark woods, and crystal chandeliers. Several dozen acid trippers moved in and "people stayed up all night tripping and prancing around the estate. . . . Some dropped acid for ten days straight. . . . Even the children and dogs were said to have taken LSD.[17]

Although a devotee of LSD and Leary, Hitchcock retained a certain aloofness from the more frenetic acid-trippers. He stayed at Millbrook but chose to live away from the mansion in a sumptuous "cottage." From there he carried on with business keeping in close contact with investors and brokers. He spent mornings on the phone talking with Bahamian and Swiss bankers setting up meetings and fast-money deals. Those who visited him at Millbrook from the financial world were invariably and routinely turned on.

The party at Millbrook lasted until 1967 when Leary left for California. By that time the Hitchcock estate was being fought over by three different bizarre acid sects including one called the Neo-American Boohoo Church. It was also constantly watched by the New York State Police. Billy Hitchcock decided to leave and after evicting all the "freaks" left for Sausalito, a few miles north of San Francisco.[18] It was then Hitchcock decided to underwrite two amateur chemists, Nick Sand and Tim Scully, in the manufacture of LSD, STP and other hallucinogens.

They relied upon a most remarkable group known as "The Brotherhood of Eternal Love" to distribute the drugs. Incorporated in California as a tax-exempt religious entity in October 1966, the Brotherhood really was a segment of the Hell's Angels motorcycle gang. Jack-booted and adorned with various Nazi symbols, the Angels added a savage touch to the new Church whose avowed purpose was to achieve a heightened awareness of God, love, and wisdom through the teachings of prophets and wise men including Christ, Buddha, Ramakrishna, Yogananda, and Mahatma Ghandi.[19] They settled south of Los Angeles at Laguna Beach considered something of an artists' colony. Getting in touch with God and one's spiritual essence, they felt, was immeasurably aided by large doses of LSD and other drugs. Supported by guru Leary in his California incarnation, the tax-exempt zealots of the Brotherhood ran the largest illicit LSD ring in the world.[20]

The deal between The Brotherhood and the manufacturers was made at Hitchcock's Sausalito home. With the organization set, Hitchcock, mimicking his industrial forbears, proceeded to rationalize the manufacturing process. He bought property in a small northern California town and set his chemists to work with new equipment. His arrangement with Sand and Scully called for him to keep them on very modest $12,000 yearly retainers. They were turned loose in the laboratory eager to concoct the best LSD ever. Within six months they had turned out at least ten million hits of the soon-to-be-famous acid called orange sunshine.[21]

Hitchcock and Sand went to The Bahamas in the spring of 1968 in preparation for an expected economic bonanza. They stayed with Sam Clapp who had been one of Hitchcock's college pals. A secret account for the LSD chemist was established at Fiduciary Trust. The acid entrepreneurs were also in The Bahamas to scout locations for a possible offshore LSD laboratory.

The family of Mary Carter Paint investors from I.O.S and its affiliates who had connections to Billy Hitchcock was extensive. There was Seymour Lazar who described himself as a personal associate of Bernie Cornfeld and a friend of Billy Hitchcock. Lazar, called by California acid cronies "The Head," also worked with Big Lou Chesler. In 1967 Lazar bought $84,000 worth of Class A Mary Carter Paint shares in a private placement.[22] According to the S.E.C. in a later investigation, Lazar and Jim Crosby's friend and broker Richard Pistell engaged in securities violations for which they were punished in 1973. There was also Fred Alger and his two mutual fund firms—the Alger Fund and Security Equity Fund. The Alger Fund sank $2,546,000 and Security Equity another $950,000 into Mary Carter Paint. This Fund was directly related to I.O.S at this time; it was the subsidiary of an I.O.S. subsidiary with the beatific name "Fund of Funds." Alger's investments were apparently worked out in negotiations with Clapp, Hitchcock, and Jim Crosby.[23]

While Hitchcock worked his LSD wonders he was also a registered securities broker employed first by Lehman Brothers and then with the venerable brokerage house of Delafield and Delafield.[24] That financial institution played a key role in the Mary Carter Paint transformation. One of the large transactions handled by Delafield, for instance, involved several companies owned by a fabulously wealthy Greek shipping family named Goulandris. The Goulandris companies, registered in Panama, invested over $4,500,000 in the paint company. A financial scoundrel named Frank Mace handled the Goulandris investment for Delafield. The S.E.C. took action against Mace in June, 1969, because of his manipulation of Mary Cater stock and barred him for life from engaging in the business of a broker.[25] Hitchcock and Mace were not the end of the crooked line running into Delafield and out again to Mary Carter Paint. Joining them at Delafield was Sam Clapp's wife who was also barred by the S.E.C. in the summer of 1968 for more "funny business" with Mary Carter stock.

No Delafield "hotshot" has quite the deservedly bad reputation as J. Jay Frankel. Even Hitchcock's LSD syndicate pales in comparison with the activities and associates of Frankel, who committed suicide the police believe, or was murdered as his wife claims, in November 1983. Frankel fell to his death from a window in his Park Avenue apartment. Frankel had a hand in at least $12 million of the $33 million which went into Resorts. First of all, he was likely involved in one of the Mace transactions, and in two 1968 fund purchases of Mary Carter stock worth $1,050,000.[26] The funds were Republic Technology and Equity Growth, both part of the Equity Funding Corporation of America which was then constructing the most colossal business fraud ever. It reportedly had over $3.5 billion in insurance policies by the early 1970s, but it didn't. Federal and state investigators found that over $2 billion of its declared assets were bogus.[27] Part of the fraud went through Bishops Bank & Trust in The Bahamas which had a number of its own subsidiaries including one called Global Finance Corporation Ltd. It was an associate of Frankel's, Yura Arkus-Duntov, from Global who handled the investments for both Republic Technology and Equity Growth.[28]

More importantly, Frankel participated in the biggest transaction of all—the $10,500,000 deal paid to Mary Carter for the paint division itself. This was the moment when Mary Carter became a "leisure industry" company called Resorts International. The arrangement was worked out by the Delafield Capital Corporation and Frankel was its chief officer.

Joseph Jacob (he preferred to be called J. Jay, or J. J. or Jay

J.) Frankel was born on Staten Island in the summer of 1937. He graduated from a New York prep school and attended college for a few years. J. Jay was first noticed by outsiders in the latter 1950s when he was excused from mandatory military service in order to participate in the Eastern European Cultural Exchange Program under the sponsorship of the U.S. State Department.[29] He travelled in both the U.S.S.R. and Romania. This experience which convinced some that J. Jay was an occasional agent for American Intelligence led directly to his becoming a junior impresario in the foreign film industry. He made a substantial contribution to cinematic history by importing the great Soviet film about World War II entitled "Ballad of a Soldier."

Frankel formed several music and film companies in New York. In 1962, these failed and he filed for bankruptcy, a practice he would soon perfect. Frankel also lived well beyond his apparent means if his business failures and a landlord suit were reliable clues to his finances. They probably weren't, as he was reportedly renting a $1,700 per month Park Avenue duplex when he claimed no assets.

At some point in the early 1960s, Frankel teamed up with Charles "Ruby" Stein and Nicholas "Jiggs" Forlano who were major organized criminals.[30] Stein was a renowned bookmaker with an extensive criminal record for gambling and income tax violations. He and Forlano ran New York's largest mob loan-sharking operation. In 1977 Stein was shot and hacked to pieces with his head, hands and feet chopped off. Among his past associates were the infamous racketeers Joe Bonanno, Carmine Lombardozzi, Ed McGrath, and Hugh Mulligan.[31] Forlano was equally well-known in organized crime circles as a member of the Colombo crime syndicate headquartered in Brooklyn. His rise to mob fame came from his role in New York's Gallo-Profaci mob war which claimed nine dead and scores wounded. Forlano's arrest record listed narcotics, gambling and assault violations.[32] During the 1970s, he moved to Fort Lauderdale and there helped funnel mob money into local businesses. He died of a heart attack at Hialeah race track in 1977.[33]

Frankel's racketeer connections were very extensive. Besides those already noted, he was also allied with "Fat Tony" Salerno in a Bahamian corporation, SeaFerro, which manufactured cement-bottomed boats.[34] In the post Delafield years, Frankel's affiliations with the underworld persisted. In one particularly serious situation, his activities unmasked another individual, Joel Mallin, tied to the mob, Resorts International, and Castle Bank. This occurred after an organized crime homicide in New York had sparked an investigation into Automated Ticket Systems Ltd., a vending machine company with a suspiciously lucrative contract to supply New York State with lottery tickets.[35]

Despite the state's generosity, the company's president, Arthur Milgram, needed financial help in 1975 and he turned to Frankel, and attorney Joel Mallin.[36] They re-organized the firm bringing in money and new and dangerous partners. The changes were in place by September 1975. Two new companies were formed leaving Automated Ticket Systems as a shell.[37] With this new structure came new investors. Frankel and Mallin brought in Regents Associates a Connecticut Limited Partnership, and gathered $808,000 from both General and Limited Partners. The General Partners were Mallin and Frankel and they put up only $8,000. There were eleven Limited Partners who provided the rest. The largest single investment was $320,000 from a partnership called SOROVI Ventures which took its name from partners Joseph *So*lce, Richard *Ro*cco and Frank *Vi*serto, Jr. They were organized crime figures primarily working in the importation and distribution of heroin. In fact, they were arrested on 19 December 1977 and charged with selling 200 kilos of heroin worth $40 to $50 million. The following year they were sentenced to federal prison.[38]

Arthur Milgram's problems were not resolved by the actions of Frankel and Mallin. His bullet-riddled corpse was found in the parking lot outside his Queens luxury apartment on 9 December 1977. Milgram had been shot seven times in the head and chest by a .22 caliber automatic the trademark of an East Harlem organized crime group called the Purple Gang. Frank Viserto, Jr. and his SOROVI partners were charter members of this exceptionally murderous gang. The Milgram homicide was one of a series committed by gangsters using pistols bought in South Florida gun shops by Purple Gang members using phony names. Viserto probably transported the weapons from Florida to the New York/New Jersey area selecting some for distribution to other organized crime killers from the Genovese syndicate.[39] Federal law enforcement also believed that Frankel dealt with gangster Joseph Pagano a leader of the Genovese syndicate and a known loan shark, gambler and union racketeer who used the Purple Gang killers several times.[40]

Following Milgram's killing, Frankel testified before a New York State Senate investigating committee. He unequivocally denied he "had at any time any ties with the Mafia, an organization, the actual existence of which is wholly unknown to me, nor did I have any ties with any member of any such organization."[41] He also stated the same held true for Milgram and added if he had the slightest suspicion otherwise, he "would never have sought or obtained the substantial term insurance policies that I did obtain for the protection of our investors."[42] Shortly before Milgram was murdered, he had been insured through the efforts of Frankel for $1 million payable to Regents Associates.

No one was convinced by Frankel's denial of mob association; the record of his affiliation was far too strong and extensive to be believably denied. With Frankel's history so well known, attention focused on Joel Mallin and the law firm representing SOROVI in the lottery investment. SOROVI's Counsel was Wagman, Cannon & Musoff a well known Manhattan firm. According to Frankel, it was attorney Wallace Musoff who directly handled SOROVI. Musoff was a former I.R.S. Special Agent in New York; a man knowledgeable about organized crime.[43] Musoff's involvement led to a charge of conspiring with the gangsters in a tax evasion scheme in 1977. Part of the charge stated that he listed $180,000 of the Regent investment as a legal fee thus deductible on the tax returns filed by Viserto, Rocco and Solce.[44] After a jury trial, however, Musoff and the mobsters were acquitted.[45]

Joel Mallin was born in New York in 1934, and educated at Columbia University receiving his law degree in 1960. He was a very able student becoming a James Kent Scholar and member of the Board of Editors of the *Columbia Law Review*. After graduation he joined Roberts & Holland specializing in taxation. In 1972, Mallin pled guilty to a stock market scam having to do with margin requirements. He was placed on probation and fined a small sum.[16] New Jersey officials report that the following year Mallin was convicted of federal banking violations in connection with the sale of $500,000 worth of stolen securities back in 1968.[47]

Mallin and Frankel shared office space in Manhattan during the time they put together Milgram's deal. And Mallin's interests in the enterprise were at least as complete and extensive as Frankel's. Among the Limited Partners in Regents, besides SOROVI, was Petrus Associates which was reportedly Mallin's creation fronted by his legal assistant and two others from his law office.[48] The shared pursuits of Mallin and Frankel involved The Bahamas as well. While J. Jay raised money for Resorts, Mallin represented I.O.S. stalwarts Bernie Cornfeld, Ed Cowett, Sam Clapp, and the clumsy Sylvain Ferdman. In addition, he provided counsel to Fred Alger, Seymour Lazar, and Billy Hitchcock.[49] Mallin was also part of Castle Bank—a "closet" partner in one of the law firms which founded and partially owned the bank. He had an account with the bank, and solicited others to deposit in the tax haven sanctuary.

The Delafield money for the Paradise Island deal totalled over $15 million, the lion's share coming when the Frankel run subsidiary, Delafield Capital, brokered the sale of Mary Carter's paint division. There was no known profit for Delafield from this most important arrangement, however. There was no quick turn around, no buyer waiting to move in. Delafield held on to Mary Carter Paint for a few years, then sold it at a substantial loss to Twin Fair, Incorporated, which was formerly the Unexcelled Chemical Company.[50] Crosby's original companies, changed in many ways, were made whole again. Some speculated that this indicated a mysterious and insidious understanding between Crosby and Frankel. But Crosby commented his Unexcelled stock was sold in 1965, thus he had nothing to gain from this curious development. New Jersey investigators, their curiosity aroused, looked through S.E.C. records for information on Crosby's stock sale and came up empty. They reported there was no S.E.C. record of this sale.[51]

Resorts International, seeking New Jersey approval for a casino license, tried hard to distance itself from cartel associates like Frankel, downplaying as much as possible the Cornfeld (I.O.S.) connection. Crosby even denied knowing Frankel at all testifying that he had worked only with Frank Mace and Yura Arkus-Duntov over various Delafield investments. His Delafield contact for the crucial sale of the paint division, Crosby noted, was a young man named Jack Hesse.[52] But given the structure of Delafield Capital, it is hard to fathom how Crosby could have avoided Frankel.

Among the tasks Mary Carter was obliged to accomplish when it secured its Bahamian gambling license, building a bridge to connect Paradise Island and Nassau was paramount. This particular project which built a beautiful toll bridge was handled by Crosby outside the financing channels already discussed. The Paradise Island Bridge Company Ltd. was formed on 13 January 1966 by attorney Noel Roberts and then immediately transferred to Sir Stafford Sands' office. The original shareholders were Crosby (president and a director of the bridge venture), Irving George Davis (vice president, treasurer and a director of the new company), and a couple of Bahamians employed by Sands.[53] I. G. Davis joined Mary Carter as an officer in 1960. He eventually became President of Resorts International, second in authority only to Crosby.

The Bridge Company's administrative structure was changed in April 1966, with the introduction of a little more capital and stock divided into A and B shares. Holders of A shares were entitled to vote on company business whether in person or by proxy, while owners of B had no managerial rights. Two thousand A and an equal number of B shares were issued. The RoyWest Bank (an amalgam of the Royal Bank of Canada and the Westminster Bank) held a mortgage on the company in 1967. That was quickly followed by a Bridge Company debenture to RoyWest, a second mortgage to Crosby, and then a mortgage transfer to Cosmos (Bahamian) Ltd., a Swiss bank subsidiary.

The earliest company statement on file is dated 15 April 1968; it shows both the A and B list. Most of the B shares were held by Crosby, the RoyWest Banking Corporation, and C. Gerald Goldsmith from New York in a ratio between them of around 5:1:1. The controlling A shares were in the hands of the Cosmos Bank, its officers, and several of its subsidiaries. The Bridge company's major officers were Crosby, Davis, and Murphy from Resorts, and Hans Ulrich Rinderknecht from Zurich, Switzerland. Rinderknecht was president of Cosmos Bank which was a Swiss Joint Stock company established in Zurich in 1959.[54]

A few years after its creation, Cosmos was strategically placed in a controversial American land development scheme involving organized crime. In 1964, Cosmos loaned millions of Swiss francs to builder Irvin J. Kahn for his Rancho Penasquitas project near San Diego, California. The loan was concealed through the use of City National Bank of Beverly Hills as trustee for the transaction.[55] One of the conditions for the hidden loan called for Kahn to purchase a $1 million life insurance policy naming Cosmos as the beneficiary. Additionally, the agreement between Kahn and Cosmos forbade Kahn from entering into any joint venture, merger, trust, partnership, consolidation or any other business without the written consent of Cosmos.[56]

This agreement was a prerequisite for vastly larger loans from the racketeer-managed Teamsters Central States Pension Fund. With the permission of Cosmos, Kahn borrowed very heavily from the Pension Fund. It ultimately lent $150 million to the project.[57] One of Kahn's partners in this undertaking was mob attorney Morris Shenker who co-signed one note worth $37.5 million. Kahn and Shenker were associates in several resort complexes on the West Coast and partial owners of the Dunes Hotel.

Cosmos Bank and Resorts were brought together by C. Gerald Goldsmith, described by Crosby as a man around town involved in Freeport.[58] Crosby was right, Goldsmith had been around the Grand Bahama development scene for quite some time. He was among the original Port Authority and DEVCO investors, and apparently listed an affiliation with Cosmos Bank in 1959. Goldsmith played a key role in all the bridge financing.[59] Besides his relationship with Cosmos Bank, he was friendly with the leadership of the Royal Bank of Canada and acted as Crosby's representative with them.

At the same time that he was a director of the bridge company arranging the complicated financial packages, Goldsmith was Board Chairman of the Port Authority, DEVCO and several related firms. This put him in the middle of one of the largest political payoff scams in The Bahamas. Underlying the corruption were certain governmental and corporate changes centered on Freeport's unique status.

Change was inevitable when Pindling came to power, but where and how he would act was the preoccupation of many white businessmen. Pindling's initial moves were administrative. He notified the British that The Bahamas was ready for another constitutional advance, allowing more autonomy. Next he scheduled another election.[60] Having squeaked to power only through the good offices of Randol Fawkes in 1967, the government's majority was as slim as a 1960's *Vogue* model. Even this margin vanished when a P.L.P. representative died, forcing a new election. In April 1968, the P.L.P. won a decisive victory and overt white political rule was forever finished. The Constitutional changes hammered out in the fall of 1968 which became fundamental Law on 10 May 1969 placed in the elected government's hand control over police and internal security. The Bahamas was still a colony, but its colonial status was never more tenuous.

In the winter of 1968, the Port Authority notified the government of negotiations intending to amalgamate the Port Authority with Benguet Consolidated, Inc., a Philippine company organized in 1903 as primarily a mining venture. Behind this maneuver was the Allen consortium of Port Authority investors, especially Charles Allen's brother, Herbert, who held the largest single bloc of Benguet's stock.[61] Actually, more than 97 percent of Benguet was owned by non-Filipinos. The Philippine Constitution mandated, however, that Filipino companies with investments in the nation's natural resources and a majority of foreign stockholders must reorganize by 3 July 1974. The Allens therefore planned to merge Benguet with another foreign corporate entity (the Port Authority) which would later enable them to spin off assets other than its natural resources properties in the Philippines and thereby secure their long-term interests.[62]

The transfer of Port Authority shares needed governmental approval. The Benguet arrangement thereby put into motion an opportunity for Pindling to alter the terms of the Hawksbill Creek Agreement. In discussion between the government and usually Herbert Allen representing the Port Authority, Pindling proposed four changes: (1) the government should be represented on the Boards of both Benguet and the Port Authority; (2) the licensing of businesses in Freeport should be brought under government control and supervision; (3) certain administrative functions carried out by the Port Authority should be transferred to the government; and (4) customs and immigration procedures in Freeport should be brought into line with the rest of The Bahamas.

Allen replied on 12 August 1968 that Benguet would certainly agree with almost everything, with just a slight demur on point number 4, as soon as the government approved Benguet's acquisition of the Port Authority.[63] Understandably testy, the Government remarked the power transfer in Freeport would take place whether or not the Benguet transfer did. The Port Authority again agreed in general but strongly suggested the government adhere to certain procedures for change specified in the Hawksbill Creek Act. This small wrangle produced a bitter controversy.

The fight was over immigration controls with the government insisting on standardization and an active commitment on the part of the Port Authority and its licensees to try much harder to employ and train Bahamians.[64] The P.L.P. was moving to carry out its policy of integrating Freeport both politically and racially with the rest of The Bahamas. Freeport's population was 63 percent non-Bahamian.[65] The quarrel was settled in 1970, with the government inevitably winning, and with the transfer of stock between Benguet and the Port Authority.

Although the battle was over, it embittered many in Freeport who would always believe the government had acted in bad faith, disregarding the real interests of Bahamians by attacking white entrepreneurs. Wallace Groves, in particular, was angered and bewildered, unable to understand why the government had chosen to take this action, why it would "stupidly wish to destroy a city that was furnishing approximately one-fifth of their governmental revenues."[66] The assertion of P.L.P. power affected the business climate and community on Grand Bahama Island. The American Consul reported business activity in Freeport was notably down and that some expatriates were ready to leave; dreading the future under P.L.P. management.

Everyone was aware of Pindling's agenda for change announced at his party's convention in October 1970. His platform entitled "Building a Nation Through Peace, Understanding, Love," called for national independence within the next four years. Pindling asserted the nation must control its destiny by controlling development. He called for a government development corporation, central bank, banking corporation, insurance corporation, and airline. Moreover, he warned something had to be done about the casinos; ways had to be found for establishing stronger government control over them. Lastly, he mused that perhaps it was time to consider an income tax only for non-Bahamian companies operating in The Bahamas.[67] There was plenty of "advertising," as Sally Woodruff called it, in Pindling's speech setting the agenda for future private financial negotiations.

The Benguet transfer was only half the game. Philippine law required Benguet to dispose of the Port Authority and its subsidiaries such as DEVCO within a few years. As part of the Allen plan, there was a new firm called Intercontinental Diversified (I.C.D.) waiting in the wings to take over the Bahamian operations. Everything seemed to go smoothly with only a slight hitch suggesting a brief Philippine squeeze. But after payment of $329,439 to a Hong Kong Bank (possibly into a Marcos account), Benguet transferred operations to I.C.D. which was eventually spun-off to the shareholders in early 1974.[68]

The financial winners in this complicated series of moves naturally included the Allens. They enhanced and secured their Benguet holdings and received $1,300,000 in financial fees and $200,000 for dealer-manager costs in engineering the spin-off. As for the government, it dynamically affected the balance of power on Grand Bahama Island fulfilling campaign promises, and received from I.C.D. $8.7 million for its approval of the deal.[69]

Goldsmith was in the middle of these corporate and political alterations. After the spin-off, he headed Intercontinental Diversified. And one of his duties was the illegal siphoning of company funds into hidden bank accounts for political payoffs. Political reformation in The Bahamas was, as usual, far more entrepreneurial than ideological. Although the government had every imaginable legitimate reason to abrogate the Hawksbill Creek Agreement, it also had in mind the development of leverage for private economic interests. Goldsmith diverted $4,431,600 for political payoffs in The Bahamas with perhaps a little falling into his own pocket. The last point was raised after an investigation by the S.E.C. When its accounting was completed, and the millions in off-the-books political contributions discovered, there was still almost $1.4 million missing.[70] Where else could it have gone, investigators wondered, but into some secret Gold-smith account probably in Castle Bank which was the vehicle used in this payoff operation.

The diversion of funds from I.C.D. managed by Goldsmith coincides in time with allegations that a significant portion of the tolls collected from the Bridge was hidden from the normal ac-counting system. Indeed, some held that this was yet another method of illegal payment worked out for President Nixon. In this version, the money was surreptitiously deposited in Rebozo's Key Biscayne Bank for Nixon's benefit.[71]

No one was angrier and more suspicious about Resorts' bridge activities than Huntington Hartford who was still a company di-rector in Paradise Island Limited. In a suit filed in 1973, Hartford charged Resorts International with forcing him out of Paradise Island. He demanded a court order declaring the bridge to be a corporate asset belonging to Paradise Island Limited and asked for a proper accounting of the bridge's revenues and expenses.[72] Hartford was convinced Resorts was operating the bridge to the detriment of Paradise Island Limited, the only part of the complex in which he still held an interest.

Hartford's anger and his insistence on an accounting of bridge receipts were stimulated to some degree by the malice of his former associate Sy Alter who had switched sides and allegiances. After betraying Hartford, he had become an insider close to Crosby and particularly I. G. Davis. A Resorts employee noted Alter was always hanging around the Davis office reminding him of some repulsive dog. "The office used to start before breakfast," he stated, and "Sy would come to sit across from I. G. Davis's secretary, hacking, spitting, coughing, belching until the poor girl would flee to another part of the building or to the washroom to be sick."[73]

Alter held important posts at Resorts which were apparently off-the-books. There was also a claim from Tradewinds' agents that Alter really managed "the Paradise Island Bridge Company from the time it was built until recently [1974]."[74] It was Alter's connection to the bridge which convinced some investigators that Nixon was being paid off with the bridge receipts. They knew Alter was quite friendly with Rebozo, and that he had accounts at Rebozo's Key Biscayne Bank. Suspicion was immeasurably increased when they learned Alter actually hand delivered some cash deposits to Rebozo outside normal banking hours.[75]

Resorts International had a predilection for funny-money often connected to organized crime associates. It also had a preoccupation with corporate security. In 1967 Crosby convinced Robert D. Peloquin, the Department of Justice attorney who had been investigating organized crime in The Bahamas and written the embarrassing memo about Lansky, and William G. Hundley formerly Peloquin's boss as head of the Organized Crime and Racketeering Section of the Justice Department, to join the new team. With the financial backing of Resorts, Intertel Inc. (standing for International Intelligence Incorporated) was formed.

Its primary job, so it was said, was to keep mobsters away from Resorts International. Interestingly enough, however, Sally Woodruff found a company with the same name incorporated in New York in 1962, which must have been an organized crime enterprise of some type aimed at The Bahamas. Its officers were publicist Tex McCrary, and Lansky syndicate gamblers Frank Ritter and Max Courtney two of the men who ran the Monte Carlo casino. The coincidence perplexed Sally who had also discovered Peloquin's new company used the Bahamian cable/Telex and postal address of the original Intertel.[76]

The progress of Resorts' Intertel was spectacular. In addition to security for Paradise Island, its client list by 1971 included most of the Howard Hughes hotel and casino empire in Nevada. That year Intertel performed security and detective work for several Fortune 500 industrial and communication companies, as well as international financial firms. Intertel then had offices in The Bahamas, Washington, New York, Toronto, Los Angeles, and Las Vegas. Specialists from almost every important law enforcement and intelligence service were on Intertel's staff from the start. The Secret Service, Customs, Border Patrol, New York and Los Angeles Police Departments, Department of State, Royal Canadian Mounted Police, INTERPOL, F.B.I., Federal Bureau of Narcotics, C.I.A., National Security Agency, and the I.R.S. were just some of their former employers. Clearly, Intertel hired prominent security officers and former chiefs, several with exceptional political experience and contacts.

All this expertise and law enforcement sophistication seemed to count for little, however, when it came to Eddie Cellini. Brought over from Freeport to manage Mary Carter's first casino venture the Bahamian Club, Eddie had outlasted the organized crime scandal of 1966–1967. And though the prudent course for Mary Carter and then Resorts International was complete disassociation from the Cellini brothers, plus anyone else known to have a criminal past or belong to a crime syndicate, this didn't happen. Although still characterized as a worker for the Lansky syndicate Eddie Cellini was hired as Paradise Island's casino manager at the end of 1967. He was given a three-year contract eventually worth one half million dollars.

Cellini's continued presence angered the Bahamian government then particularly sensitive to overt flaunting of its recent campaign theme "racketeers out." Thus, the government decided to declare Eddie "persona non grata" when his Bahamian work permit expired in November, 1969, which gave Resorts two years to use and then replace him.[77] This was far more charitable than Great Britain had been. The year before, British authorities had banned Eddie from entering the country. And that had followed Britain's deportation of Eddie's infamous brother Dino. Great Britain plainly wanted nothing to do with Cellinis.

Peloquin and I. G. Davis fought the anti-Eddie Cellini forces first in Britain and subsequently in The Bahamas. Once Dino was finished at the London croupier school, Eddie was proposed as his substitute; that was what had triggered the British ban. The Paradise Island interests pushed the British to rescind their decision and allow him in to run the school. Peloquin believed Eddie was unfairly treated, that he was a person of excellent character.[78]

For help on this issue, Intertel hired an English legal firm, but even they felt it was clear that nothing would change the situation. This conclusion stemmed from an investigation conducted by a highly regarded British private detective—A. S. Baker of Q-Men. Baker's report which was forwarded to Peloquin found Dino was a member of a crime organization and that Eddie and Dino are very close and have been in the same business for years. "Is it conceivable in these circumstances," Baker remarked, "that only one brother is tainted?" Moreover, Eddie had worked for Meyer Lansky as the night manager of a couple of his Cuban casinos. The English detective flatly stated it was unbelievable "that Meyer

Lansky would employ anyone as a Night Manager unless he was a member of the Organization."[79] The British would not be budged and Eddie remained barred.

With London out, Resorts International found it imperative to keep Eddie in The Bahamas. A silly cat and mouse game then took place: the government would demand Cellini's ouster, and Resorts would hesitantly agree and then hide him. Later Resorts turned to obfuscation claiming Eddie was not the casino manager only a consultant "on certain collection matters." Other similar statements were made from time to tome. Eddie's employment was "sensitive" enough that Resorts tried to hide it by moving his salary off the books. Resorts International sent Eddie's 1970 payment to a law firm in South Florida which in turn disbursed the money.[80] This immoderate devotion to Eddie Cellini made Intertel appear especially ineffective.

I. G. Davis evidently believed Eddie was indispensable because of his unique ability to evaluate potential new casino projects. In the early 1970s, Resorts sent Eddie to Sint Maarten in the Dutch West Indies to evaluate a fashionable resort complex which also involved Castle Bank. While Davis was no doubt sincere in wanting Eddie's help for new gambling ventures, the real issue underlying the Cellini fight was Paradise Island's determination to keep him because of his experience in handling the casino's credit gambling operation.

The credit arrangements resulted in part from "junket" operations to Paradise Island while Eddie was the manager. Junketeers are credit gamblers with cash transactions taking place after the gamblers have left the casinos and returned to their point of origin. And unlike the tourist who casually gambles, junket participants are hard core gamblers first and foremost. Racketeer and junket operator Vincent Teresa succinctly stated the issue: "We didn't want anyone on the junkets who wasn't going to gamble. We didn't want tourists or 'sun worshippers' as we called them."[81] Junkets were the mainstay of successful casino gambling providing Resorts in its early years with about 66 percent of casino profits.[82]

Credit gambling and junkets are a major way in which organized crime skims a percentage of gambling revenues. Collection of gambling debts is often in the hands of gangsters who take their cut first before remitting the rest to the casino. Eddie Cellini was affiliated with several junket operations while he worked for Resorts International. His junket partners included old-time bookmakers and members of organized crime syndicates. Lurking behind these was Eddie's old boss, Meyer Lansky.[83]

Freeport's gambling scene was so obviously "bent" no one bothered to deny the obvious. Paradise Island, on the other hand, which emerged from the Aryan grip of Wenner-Gren and the effete one of Huntington Hartford, took great pains at all times to rhetorically distance itself from criminality. Although this was done for political and economic reasons that doesn't negate the hypocrisy. Clearly, it is a fact that Paradise Island worked with "criminal cartel" associates and "career offenders" on the financial side, and well-heeled political corrupters like Goldsmith in the bridge enterprise, and brazenly and stubbornly held onto Eddie Cellini come what may. Its repeated disclaimers of taint from organized crime were always misleading. Paradise Island was, as Peloquin so embarrassingly observed, ripe for mob infiltration, and what if anything was done to avoid that penetration has never been divulged.

The history of organized crime's first decade in The Bahamas centers as it must on the development of casino gambling. The Freeport enterprise which was so tightly bound in so many instances with the Lansky syndicate is the historical precedent. And the progression from Freeport to Paradise Island naturally follows. But, as should be clear by now, casino gambling was itself only an instance in the evolution of the underground economy, the subterranean movement of money from country to country outside the tax man's grasp.

In The Bahamas and nations like it, their role in the "underground economy" is perhaps their most distinguishing feature. It is so prominent, of course, because it is government policy to provide a haven for the world's wealth no matter who owns it or how their fortunes were made. That is the prime directive. There are, however, dozens of situations in which the general principle is abrogated, when foreign crooks are indeed handed over. Almost always, these breaches of the code and laws of silence on fiscal matters depend upon the kind of pressure foreign law enforcers can bring upon haven governments. These always involve delicate negotiations. Equally testy are the negotiations within law enforcement agencies whose responsibility include's the investigation and prosecution of the rich and crooked. In the case of American criminals using The Bahamas, the only agency which pursued the issue was the Internal Revenue Service and even it did so haltingly and grudgingly at first.

Notes

1. New Jersey Casino Control Commission, "In the Matter of the Casino License Application of Resorts International Hotel, Inc.: Statement of Exceptions," *Report*, 4 December 1978, pp. 3–4.
2. New Jersey, *Report*, p. 27.
3. Robert A. Hutchinson, *Vesco*, (Praeger, 1974), p. 54.
4. Hutchinson, *Vesco*, pp. 55–56.
5. Ibid., p. 58.
6. Nicholas Faith, *Safety in Numbers: The Mysterious World of Swiss Banking* (Viking Press, 1982), pp. 214–215; Hutchinson, *Vesco*, 66–68; and TW–5 Folder, "International Credit Bank."
7. Faith, *Safety in Numbers*, p. 223.
8. Royal Canadian Mounted Police, "Pullman Transcript No. 1" pp. 124–25.
9. TW–5 Folder, "American Realequities."
10. Royal Canadian Mounted Police, "Pullman Transcript No. 1," p. 18.
11. Hank Messick, Special Consultant to Florida Governor Claude R. Kirk, Jr., "A Report on Crime and Corruption," p. 152.
12. Ibid., p. 154.
13. Ibid., pp. 8–11.
    The wiretap established Pullman and Malnik were part of the organized crime hierarchy with ready access to "muscle." In the fall of 1966, for example, Pullman was asked for help by a friend in Florida threatened by a 270 pound "goon" about to "break all [his] bones." Frustrated because he couldn't get to the U.S. to help, Pullman told him not to worry, that he would give him "somebody to talk to, a very nice kid." He told his worried friend to see Al Malnik who could be found in a stockbroker's office on Miami Beach. The broker, incidentally, was Yiddy Bloom's son. Pullman's advice was "Talk to him; tell him you know me. He can make a telephone call and everything will be taken away." Ibid, p. 154.
14. TW–5 Folder, "IOS/VESCO/RESORTS."
15. Cleveland Amory, *Who Killed Society?*, (Harper and Brothers, 1960), p. 351.
16. Martin A. Lee and Bruce Shlain, *Acid Dreams: The CIA, LSD and the Sixties Rebellion* (Grove Press, 1985), p. 97.

17. Lee and Shlain, *Acid Dreams*, p. 99.
18. Ibid., p. 238.
19. Ibid., p. 237.
20. Ibid., p. 236.
21. Ibid., pp. 242–243.
22. Ibid., p. 31.
23. Ibid., pp. 29–31.
24. New Jersey, *Report*, pp. 28–29.
25. Ibid., p. 33.
26. Ibid., p. 38.
27. Ronald L. Soble and Robert E. Dallos, *The Impossible Dream: The Equity Funding Story: The Fraud of the Century* (New American Library, 1975), p. 1.
28. Sally Woodruff, "Folder; Bishop's Bank & Trust for Fenelon Richards, Intertel."
29. New York State Senate Select Committee on Crime, "Report on J. Jay Frankel," 1975.
30. New Jersey, *Report*, p. 40; also, New York City Police Department, "Wiretap Summaries and Excerpts from Plants #40 (1962) and #105 (1965)," 3 March 1977.
31. New York State Senate Select Committee on Crime, *Report on Organized Crime, 1970* (Albany, 1970).
32. Ibid.
33. Brian Donovan, "Mob Power Links to Lottery Vending," *Newsday*, 22 May 1977.
34. See New Jersey, *Report*, p. 40.
35. The contract provided for a higher than standard and usual commission on the sale of lottery tickets through its 350 vending machines. See Brian Donovan and Tom Demoretcky, "U.S. Jury Indicts 3 in Lottery Ticket Firm," *Newsday*, 22 December 1977, p. 2.
36. Selwyn Rabb, "Despite Hint of Mafia Tie, Lottery Let Promoter Take Vending Role," *The New York Times*, 1 March 1977, p. 3.
37. J. Jay Frankel, "Letter to Mr. Russell V. Gladieux, Administrative Director, New York State Lottery Commission," 18 February 1977.
38. New Jersey, *Report*, p. 41; Max H. Seigel, "14, Including Alleged Charter Member of Purple Gang, Charged in a Heroin Conspiracy," *The New York Times*, 20 December 1977, p. 27.
39. U.S. Department of the Treasury, Federal Bureau of Alcohol, Tobacco and Firearms, "An Analysis of the Twenty-Two Caliber Homicides in the Northern New Jersey-New York Areas, Re: Genovese—Organized Crime Family and Purple Gang," July 1979.
40. Ibid., p. 17.
41. New York State Senate Select Committee on Crime, "Statement of J. Jay Frankel," n.d., p. 2.
42. Ibid.
43. Frankel, "Letter to Russell V. Gladieux . . .," 18 February 1977, p. 3.

44. U.S. District Court, Southern District of New York, *USA v. Wallace Musoff, Frank Viserto, Jr., Joseph Solce and Richard Rocco*, Indictment No. 77 Cr. 895, 21 December 1977.
45. Arnold H. Lubasch, "Lawyer and 3 Reputed Mobsters Acquitted of Tax-Evasion Charges," *The New York Times*, 25 February 1978, p. 36.
46. *The New York Times*, 1 March 1977, p. 1.
47. New Jersey, *Report*, pp. 43–44.
48. Brian Donovan, "Lottery to End Pact With Vending Firm," *Newsday*, 6 March 1977.
49. Donovan, *Newsday*, pp. 43–44.
50. New Jersey, *Report*, p. 43.
51. Ibid.
52. New Jersey Casino Control Commission, "Resorts International Transcripts, Testimony of James Crosby," January 1979, p. 65.
53. TW–5 Folder, "Paradise Island Bridge Co., #9200/66."
54. Rand McNally International, *Bankers Director*, Final 1969 Edition, p. F456.
55. Homer Clance, "Cosmos Bank Loans Aided Kahn's Project," *San Diego Union*, 11 September 1974, p. A–15.
56. Ibid.
57. U.S. Senate, Permanent Subcommittee on Investigations, "Oversight Inquiry of the Department of Labor's Investigation of the Teamsters Central States Pension Fund," Report No. 97–177 (Government Printing Office, 1981), p. 8.
58. New Jersey Casino Control Commission, "Reports International Transcripts, Testimony of James Crosby," January 1979, p. 37.
59. Paradise Island Bridge Company, Limited, "Company Statement received by the Registrar General's Office," 15, April 1971; 15 April 1972; 15 April 1973; 15 April 1974.
60. U.K., *Report . . . Hawksbill*, Vol. 1, p. 36.
61. U.K., *Report*, p. 46.
62. Ibid.
63. Ibid., p. 47.
64. Ibid., p. 52.
65. Stanley Penn, "Benguet Grand Bahama Unit Warns of End to Island's Spectacular Economic Growth," *Wall Street Journal*, 19 December 1973.
66. AmConsul NASSAU to Department of State, "Discussion with Mr. Wallace Groves at Freeport, Grand Bahama," 27 March 1970.
67. Lynden O. Pindling, "Digest on Building a Nation Through Peace, Understanding, Love," presented at the P.L.P. Convention, October 1970.
68. Pindling, "Digest," pp. 6–7, 26.
69. Stanley Penn, 19 December 1973.
70. Board of Directors, Intercontinental Diversified Corp., "Report of

the Audit Committee," p. 31; United States District Court for the District of Columbia, *Securities and Exchange Commission v. Intercontinental Diversified Corp., C. Gerald Goldsmith*, 6 January 1978.

71. TW–24 Interview; TW–5 "Reports on Resorts/Vesco/IOS."
72. Supreme Court of the State of New York, Huntington Hartford, Plaintiff-against—Resorts International, Inc., James M. Crosby, and Bank of Commerce, defendants, Index No. 13082/2, July 1973.
73. TW–5, "Report on Seymour, a.k.a. Sy, Alter," 15 January 1974.
74. The official manager was Tom Blum whose father had been in charge of construction work at Paradise Island.
75. Rob Elder, "Figure in Probes Admits Visits to Nixon Compound," *Miami Herald*, 18 January 1974, p. 10A.
76. TW–5 Folder, "Intertel Personnel."
77. New Jersey, *Report*, p. 47.
78. Ibid., Appendix 17.
79. Ibid., Appendix 19, n.p.
80. Ibid., p. 52.
81. U.S. Senate, Permanent Subcommittee on Investigations, *Hearing: Organized Crime, Stolen Securities* (Government Printing Office, 28 July 1971), p. 790.
82. New Jersey, *Report*, p. 54.
83. Ibid., Vol. II, Appendix, p. 78; Toronto *Daily Star*, 2 December 1972, p. 1; and, William Davidson, "The Mafia: Shadow of Evil on the Island in the Sun," *Saturday Evening Post*, 26 February 1967, pp. 33–34.

4

Operation Tradewinds

Dick Jaffe, I.R.S. Special Agent from the Intelligence Division's Miami Office of the Jacksonville District, started a Bahamian intelligence gathering project in 1962. It lasted in one form or another until the mid–1970s. The Bahamian project was completely involved with Dick Jaffe's professional life. He was its inspiration and prime architect. It is literally impossible to follow the contours of the I.R.S. effort in The Bahamas outside the context of Jaffe's career. It was neither easy nor simple to move the I.R.S. to support Jaffe's investigative inspiration, as there was internal opposition almost from its inception. If not for Jaffe's doggedness, the operation would have quickly faltered. But he stubbornly persisted and it didn't, although there was a future heavy price he would pay for his initial success.

Special Agent Jaffe was born and raised in Brooklyn, New York, and moved to Miami in 1948. Tall, balding, soft-spoken and articulate he went to the University of Miami where he studied business administration, marketing, and advertising, graduating in 1950. Less than a year later, he was in the Army heading for Korea. A forward artillery observer in the 7th Infantry Division, Second Lieutenant Jaffe fought in the famous battles of Old Baldy and Pork Chop Hill in the waning months of the war. He returned home in 1953 as a First Lieutenant. Jaffe returned to school, this time earning a degree in accounting. A few years later, because of a friend's prodding, he took the I.R.S. Civil Service exam (scored the highest mark in the Southeast Region) and joined the Service as a Special Agent with a yearly salary of $4,525.

Jaffe investigated criminal violations of revenue statutes, including the wagering tax law designed to ferret out bookmakers and lottery operators. In 1957, he was assigned several cases involving small-time gamblers on the periphery of major organized crime syndicates. The following year, he spent 22 weeks in Washington at Treasury's Law Enforcement Officer Training School where he graduated first in his class. Back in Miami, he continued working on routine investigations until 1960, when he was assigned to an important organized crime case. It was this investigation which sparked Jaffe's interest in pursuing racketeers in The Bahamas.

The case dealt with the finances of Michael "Trigger Mike" Coppola who came from Fricheno, Italy (the Naples district), at the turn of the century. Before he was 25, Coppola was a rising gambler and bootlegger running with gangsters from his East Harlem neighborhood, home to scores of racketeers and gunmen. Three years later he began a long association with "Lucky" Luciano and Meyer Lansky. In years to come, Coppola would be identified as a high ranking member of the Genovese organized crime syndicate, one of New York's most powerful mobs.[1] Coppola's principal gang underling was "Fat Tony" Salerno (Frankel's partner in SeaFerro) whose own racket career advanced steadily until the mid–1980s when he was sent to prison. At the time, Salerno was reputedly the richest so-called "Cosa Nostra" leader in America. He still ran major rackets from his dingy headquarters in the ever grimmer East Harlem neighborhood, although he had an elegant Florida home much like his mentor Coppola had earlier. It was in the 1950s, that the short and stocky "Trigger Mike" moved to Miami Beach. He was known to Florida police as a "national crime syndicate" figure arrested many times for assault, robbery and homicide.

Racketeer Coppola came to the attention of the I.R.S. following a brief arrest in Las Vegas in the fall of 1958. He had been on a gambling spree and lost $165,000 at the crap tables. The local F.B.I. assumed that far exceeded his reported income and passed their information to the I.R.S. Revenue Agent Joseph A. Wanderscheid was assigned the job of auditing Coppola's returns for the prior several years. While doing his evaluation, Wanderscheid was casually told by Jaffe (who noticed the item in a local newspaper), that Coppola was being sued for divorce. Realizing the potential significance for his case should she be willing to help, Wanderscheid interviewed the estranged wife, Ann Drahman Coppola. Having been systematically abused and brutalized by Coppola for years, and after much coaxing by Wanderscheid, she became the principal witness in the investigation and subsequent prosecution.

In many ways "Trigger Mike" was none too bright, and he committed several serious gaffes during the investigation. One took place at the manager's office at the Fountainbleu Hotel. Ann Coppola had a safe deposit box there filled with money and jewels given to her by Mike. One day as Jaffe and Wanderscheid were in the office inventorying the contents of the box, "the stubby mobster tipped off by a hotel executive, burst on the scene and in a blind and foolish rage pointed to $24,000 in currency and shouted—'Dat's my money!' " When he realized what he had just said, he quickly shifted gears and claimed "It's her money, and anyway, that'll be on this year's tax."

Coppola had given Ann about $250,000 during four years of marriage while reporting an annual income of $15,000. He hid a great deal of his unreported income around his Miami Beach house. By 1960, this totalled $340,000. Most of the money came by courier from East Harlem. It was Coppola's cut from the numbers racket run by his lieutenant "Fat Tony" Salerno. Around Christmas of each year, approximately $200,000 in cash was delivered to him. Coppola was increasingly nonchalant about this money, actually leaving his 1959 bundle of $219,000 in his card club's freezer. It was delivered later by a local gangster when Coppola finally remembered leaving it.[2]

"Trigger Mike's" only chance to escape conviction for tax evasion was to get to Ann. He tried to frighten her by sending two thugs to beat her. It didn't work, however, as she was long past the point of intimidation. Coppola was indicted and Ann left for Europe on vacation. Special Agent Wallace Musoff (later to represent the Purple Gang after getting his law degree and leaving the I.R.S.) was assigned to guard her. The overseas security operation also involved the I.R.S. Office of International Operations (O.I.O.), the State Department, Treasury officers assigned to European stations, and the French, Swiss, and Italian national police. Nevertheless, her ex-husband arranged to have a mob lawyer confront her in Rome. She was offered $200,000 not to return to Florida for the trial. Ann Drahman cooly turned it down.

The defense won the first round, successfully moving for a mistrial only three days into the trial because several jurors had seen news stories detailing Coppola's organized crime background. The government scheduled his retrial for February 1962. Just prior to trial, Coppola surprised everyone by pleading guilty. He was sentenced to a year's incarceration and $40,000 in fines. The 61-year-old racketeer went to prison for the first time in 40 years. It was the end of his career, his underworld prestige destroyed by his gritty ex-wife. When he got out of prison he was closely watched by law enforcement. In 1966, he died of a kidney ailment in a Boston hospital.

Ann's life was not much better. Threatened many times and deserted by all her friends, who were primarily professional gamblers and their wives, she became deeply depressed. Following Mike's guilty plea, she moved to Europe where she committed suicide one night in a Rome hotel room. She left behind a long note calling on the law to do more against organized crime and ending with this farewell: "Mike Coppola someday, somehow, a person or God or the Law shall catch up with you, you yellow-bellied bastard. You are the lowest and biggest coward I have had the misfortune to meet."

Immediately after the Coppola case, the I.R.S. turned to The Bahamas. Material from several organized crime investigations indicated Bahamian financial activity on behalf of many racketeers. A pilot trip to The Bahamas was arranged for December 1962 with Jaffe selected to spearhead the inquiry for the I.R.S.[3] Of some significance, Jaffe had an Intelligence connection that could provide cover for any I.R.S. probing in The Bahamas. In 1959, Jaffe had resigned his Army Reserve commission for one with the Coast Guard Reserve—the Coast Guard was also then part of the Treasury Department. The Coast Guard had an active Intelligence section and Jaffe knew several of the officers. Coast Guard personnel made frequent trips to Nassau to discuss "search and rescue" operations in Bahamian waters, and they had a liaison officer in the American Consulate. The exploratory visit made in the waning days of 1962 by Jaffe and an I.R.S. agent from the O.I.O. coincided with a "covering" Coast Guard visit.

Jaffe's Coast Guard contacts introduced him to influential sources, laying the foundation for many subsequent I.R.S ventures. That achievement aside, there was conflict between Jaffe and the O.I.O. agent because of significant differences over the function of law enforcement between the two I.R.S. divisions. The O.I.O. had primary responsibility for overseas intelligence gathering, but it had little or no interest in that kind of work. O.I.O. leadership resolutely opposed overseas investigations, which meant there would be an inevitable clash with the Intelligence Division. The O.I.O. was obstructive, always attempting to stop Intelligence Division Special Agents from going abroad on the grounds that their kind of work caused diplomatic problems. These tensions existed from the project's inception.

It was in the Registrar General's office in Nassau that Jaffe first perceived what was happening in The Bahamas, what was really at stake. One of the first items he chanced upon was the company file on The Bank of World Commerce, which listed all the stockholders, officers and directors of the bank. Jaffe could hardly believe what was in the public record. He recognized many of the Bank's officers and stockholders as Las Vegas gamblers and organized crime associates, names he was familiar with from working the Coppola case and gambling collaterals (requests for investigative aid from other I.R.S. Districts).

The information was put into a report which noted that Lansky's men, John Pullman and Al Malnik, were the principal officers of this mysterious bank. Jaffe alerted the F.B.I., particularly about Malnik's activities, which were less well known than Pullman's. The report was well received by the Regional Intelligence Office in Atlanta, and I.R.S. Intelligence in Washington. However, it encountered stiff opposition from the O.I.O. section, which claimed his report was inflated, insignificant and misleading.

Subsequently, the O.I.O. stubbornly fought an Intelligence Division recommendation to establish a Bahamian operation to be run by Jaffe. One part of the recommendation called for the operation to receive an exemption from O.I.O.'s offshore jurisdiction in order to work The Bahamas without interference. O.I.O.

battled the Intelligence Division for over two years before the recommendation was finally approved. Jaffe did not patiently wait the two years it took for his operation to be institutionalized. With the approval of his superiors in the Jacksonville District he began his activities earlier. Reports he wrote from material gathered in The Bahamas were enthusiastically passed to Washington and by Troy Register, Chief of the Intelligence Division in Jacksonville to Jim Sutherland, the Regional Organized Crime Coordinator in Atlanta. It was the pressure brought by the Intelligence Division, armed with Jaffe's "extramural" reports, which finally overcame O.I.O. opposition and secured the project's endorsement. In 1965 the operation, codenamed Tradewinds, officially began.

That Tradewinds was now an official Intelligence Division project did not automatically mean it was ringed by bureaucratic restrictions. On the contrary, Tradewinds for the first few years, was principally Jaffe and his contacts, although he did have a capable partner. Later it expanded somewhat when four agents were formally added. But even then, it was still essentially Jaffe's operation; he made about three-quarters of the trips to The Bahamas by himself.

As soon as Tradewinds was approved, a special group of I.R.S. personnel, from both the Intelligence Division and O.I.O. went to Nassau to discuss procedures for the Special Agents, and to start the process of establishing cooperation and rapport with the U.S. Consul General and his staff and Bahamian police officials.[4] The group conferred with Consul General John Barnard, stating their principal interest was to develop information on American racketeers who have taken "hot money" to The Bahamas and invested it there. Barnard suggested contacting Nigel Morris, Bahamian Commissioner of Police, and Stanley Moir, his chief assistant. Others noted as important contacts were Leslie Cate, the principal police officer in Freeport, and Godfrey Higgs, who was, in Barnard's opinion, an honest and knowledgeable lawyer.

Barnard also told them that two Department of Justice attorneys, including Robert Peloquin (several years from Intertel) had recently been in The Bahamas and had spoken with Sir Stafford Sands. The Consul General agreed to give the I.R.S. a report on the Freeport racketeers, which he was preparing for Peloquin. The group visited all those noted and found them cordial and potentially helpful. They also made useful contacts with the Bahamian Comptroller of Customs and the Chief U.S. Customs Inspector at the Nassau airport. They returned to Florida satisfied with their progress.

Less than a month later, Jaffe, accompanied by I.R.S. Group Supervisor Richard B. Wallace was back in Nassau. They made the rounds talking with their new associates. Assistant Police Commissioner Stanley Moir remarked that there was a serious problem brought about by American swindlers forming Bahamian banks for the purpose of bilking American investors.[5] He had already turned over material about one of these scams called Trans World Investment Bank to the American S.E.C., and would provide the same to the I.R.S. agents. But information would have to be a two-way street. Moir told them he wanted intelligence on Ben Novack, the owner of Miami Beach's Fountainbleu hotel.

Novack was pushing for a gambling license in order to construct a new casino on Bimini, and Moir was worried. Jaffe described Novack as an associate of prominent American gangsters Lansky, Coppola, and others including Max Eder, a loanshark and suspected labor racketeer with a history of gambling, robbery, narcotics, and homicide arrests. Eder lived on Miami Beach, had a residence in New York, a business in Los Angeles, associated with numerous national organized crime figures particularly gamblers, and owned a lingerie shop in the Fountainbleu.[6] That hotel, Jaffe added, was used to collect substantial gambling debts and permitted "the well organized fleecing of wealthy players in the card room."

Moir listened, and then confided he was under pressure to permit Novack a free hand. He produced an unsolicited letter from the Miami Beach Chief of Police commenting on Novack's good character, and a telegram from J. Edgar Hoover stating Novack had no criminal record. Hoover's telegram was tucked inside the Police Chief's envelope. Jaffe later made a special trip to Nassau and gave Assistant Commissioner Moir a well documented file on Novack, which enabled him to stop any hopes Novack had of getting a license for a casino on Bimini.

From Moir, they paid visits to others cultivated earlier. Eventually, Jaffe ended up at the U.S. Consulate where he met Lieutenant Michael Miller, the Project Liaison Officer for the Navy's important Atlantic Undersea Test and Evaluation Center (A.U.T.E.C. tested submarines, underwater weapons, and sonar detection systems) on Andros Island. As a result of their conversation, Miller offered to help, and introduced Jaffe to John Davis, former Assistant Secretary of Agriculture in President Eisenhower's Administration. Miller knew him quite well and set up a meeting for the next morning. Davis was even more enthusiastic than Miller, anxious to work as an undercover operative, becoming the first official Tradewinds agent (TW-1).

A publisher of farm journals and small town newspapers in Ohio, Davis had been a politically active Republican. Also, he was familiar with important organized crime figures, such as Cleveland racketeers Morris Kleinman and Moe Dalitz, both of whom had worked with Meyer Lansky in casinos in Kentucky, Florida, and Nevada. Davis had been around The Bahamas since 1940, when he became an alien resident, although he returned to the States to serve Eisenhower. During World War II he conducted secret surveillance work, keeping quiet tabs on the Colony's Governor, the Duke of Windsor, correctly suspected of having Nazi sympathies.[7]

The I.R.S. mission urgently needed someone who could get information from the British and Canadian banks. To this Davis responded that "under the proper circumstances, . . . he was confident that he could obtain information of a *specific* nature from a bank such as Barclays." Additionally, his eagerness for the project led him to volunteer a cottage at the rear of his house for a combination residence, safe house, and photography center for the agents. Davis finally offered much more than housing. He recruited his wife, daughter, and a close friend as operatives. His wife Ruth became TW-1A; his friend, an officer at Barclays Bank, TW-3; his married daughter Sarah (Sally) Woodruff TW-5. Having enrolled his family as undercover workers for the I.R.S., Davis had only one apparent worry. He was adamant that the State Department, which he believed wholly incompetent, be uninformed of his secret work.

During Jaffe's first meeting with TW-3, he gained general and useful information about the bank's procedures. But most importantly, Jaffe was given a transcript of the major deposits and withdrawals from the Barclays' Bank of World Commerce account from July 1961 through July 1963. TW-3 furnished a similar record of John Pullman's transactions, and thus opened several windows into Meyer Lansky's syndicate financial operations. TW-3 also asked if the I.R.S. wanted details on a cash deposit of $233,700 made by a "scruffy-looking American wearing dirty clothes and carrying a nondescript satchel." The bag contained mostly hundreds and a few fiftys, which appeared new and in consecutive, serial-numbered order. Moreover, the deposit was made in the names of two New Yorkers and exchanged for a Certificate of Deposit paying lower interest than did the major New York banks. Yes, the I.R.S. was interested, and plans were made to pull the material together.

No matter how spectacular the Barclay's source was, there was no Tradewinds operative quite like Sally Woodruff. She turned out a seemingly endless supply of company records, analyses of documents, and sophisticated speculation on Bahamian affairs. Sally had intelligence, wit, and style, and all this and more would show in the course of future events.

Born in Cleveland and raised in both Cleveland and Boston, she wanted to be an artist and writer. Her early education was at the Katherine Gibbs school in Boston. Dark-haired, slightly plump, about 5 feet and 5 inches, she studied English at the Cleveland College of Western Reserve University, and art at the Cleveland Institute of Art. As an artist Sally had several minor Cleveland exhibits. She had others at the Kansas Institute of Art and the National Press Club in Washington. Combining interests, she illustrated articles and booklets. Her interest in writing was somewhat satisfied when she went to work for the Cleveland *Plain Dealer*, the most influential paper in Ohio. Sally was an editorial assistant in both the feature department and Sunday edition; she later became secretary to the chief editor.

Sally married in Cleveland, but it was a disaster for several reasons, including her husband's more catholic sexual preferences. That was disturbing enough, but Sally's bad news was just beginning. She hadn't been feeling well for some time, and finally was carefully examined. The dreadful diagnosis was cancer of the breast. She went to the acclaimed Cleveland Clinic where she was treated successfully. The tumor was removed, and there were no further signs of the disease. Beating cancer for the time being (it would ultimately return to kill her in 1982), she determined to leave Ohio and her divorce behind. She headed for her parents' Bahamian home and turned her talented hand to finance. In 1962, she participated in the establishment of the first savings and loan institution in The Bahamas. Later, she was a consultant when the original (1965) Banks & Trust Act was drafted.

Sally Davis met Ed Woodruff early in her expatriate days. He had also left a marriage gone sour, as well as a career in television and film. A New Yorker, Ed broke into television working for his uncle, the television pioneer Alan Dumont, the original producer of Jackie Gleason's show. Ed was overweight and overwrought; feeling ill and trapped in New York, he chose The Bahamas to start a new life. With no experience, he sailed from Miami to Nassau and beyond. His destination was the almost deserted island of Rum Cay, a long way south and east of Nassau. There he intended to build a home, regain his health and a sense of proportion. He stayed on Rum Cay for awhile, and then sailed back to Nassau where he met and married Sally.

Sally took to the secret work with a firm belief in the value of the mission. She knew first hand the methods of the scam artists in The Bahamas, and Tradewinds gave her a unique chance to do something about the situation. It was also a project that emotionally appealed to her because of its clandestine side. There was something about being an operative, the constant alertness, the hidden routine within the public life, the satisfaction of knowing what's really going on, that had for her its own relentless fascination.

But the first time she produced material as TW-5 occurred before Jaffe met her. About this, Jaffe wrote "we expect to eventually meet TW-5, who was temporarily off the Island during this official visit." She had forwarded material through her father concerning American George P. Davis (no relation), president of Bahamas Savings and Loan Association. Davis, Sally reported, was "siphoning funds" from the institution for his personal use. Sally knew this because she was working for Bahamas Savings and Loan, which gave her an inside track on both her boss and the chummy world of Bahamian banks and trusts.

The Davis and Woodruff families lived in Nassau, and Jaffe still needed someone who knew Freeport. He was able to enroll a successful businessman with a detailed knowledge of Freeport's commercial, industrial, political, and social affairs as TW-4. In his initial meetings with Jaffe, TW-4 shed considerable light on local politics and details on how Freeport's shadier characters were moving money and themselves back and forth to the United States, without passing through customs and immigration. They were using private planes owned by resort businesses, and charter airlines like the Flying Tigers, which flew numerous "junket" flights bringing gamblers to and from Freeport. There was no formal clearance carried out by the U.S. Immigration Service, TW-4 commented, especially when the money movers were listed as crew members on the private planes.

Tradewinds seemed securely in place no later than the summer of 1965. Vital private contacts were established, U.S. Embassy officers consulted, top Bahamian police officials informed, and productive sources engaged. Yet before it had a chance to get underway, Tradewinds had to overcome an obstacle brought about by a change in Bahamian law. Prior to November 1965, it was a civil offense in The Bahamas for someone to divulge information protected by the Bank and Company Secrecy Laws; after November, it became a criminal offense. Because of the legal modification, Jaffe and the Tradewinds Special Agents made it a point never to make a direct contact in The Bahamas for information passing. The explicit guidelines for Tradewinds developed subsequently forbade such contacts with Bahamians. Documentary information had to be transferred to an intermediary who would take it to Miami, or the Bahamian sources themselves would bring or mail the material to the I.R.S. in Miami. Sources were paid a fee for information received, and had their expenses covered when they delivered material to Miami.

The evolution of Tradewinds' guidelines during this period reflected continuing turf battles among I.R.S. Intelligence, O.I.O., and the State Department over just which service had hegemony in The Bahamas. These types of battles were also fought out within the I.R.S. itself. This inner turmoil surfaced once again as soon as the new bank secrecy law was passed in the fall of 1965.

A series of meetings took place between representatives of the Departments of State and Justice over what effect this new law would have on Tradewinds. On 28 February 1966, senior I.R.S. management officials, including the Assistant Commissioner of the Compliance Division, as well as the Director of the Intelligence Division met in Washington and decided to suspend Tradewinds pending a review of the project by the I.R.S. Chief Counsel's Office. The suspension lasted eight months. Tradewinds was finally reinstated on 10 November 1966, when the Assistant Commissioner for Compliance, authorized the Intelligence Division to resume its Bahamian contacts under the new procedures.

1967 should have been a watershed year for Jaffe, Operation Tradewinds, and the Internal Revenue Service. It was the year that American newspaper exposes had forced a Royal Commission to hold explosive hearings on casino gambling, Bahamian corruption, and the American mob. But during the time the Royal Commission labored over the casino gambling problem, the I.R.S. was caught in another skirmish over Tradewinds. It was a reprise of the preceding two years' battles. This 1967 fight was ignited by the jealously disruptive opposition to Tradewinds of the Office of International Operations. There were times when this opposition crystallized in encounters revealing the O.I.O.'s distaste for Tradewinds and apparent naivete about organized crime. This was one of those revealing times.

In the morning of 14 March 1967, just two days before the Royal Commission began its hearings in Nassau, there was a dramatic conference held in the Internal Revenue building in Washington.[8] Present at the meeting were Leon Green, Executive Assistant to the Assistant Commissioner for Compliance; William Kolar, the Director of the Intelligence Division; C. I. Fox, the Director of O.I.O., Donald Durkin, who was Fox's assistant; Edward Mould, the Assistant Chief of the Coordination Branch; Charles Knight, the National Office Coordinator; Troy Register, the Chief of the Intelligence Division for the Jacksonville District; and Special Agents Jaffe and his first Tradewinds' partner, James A. Barrett. Taking the lead in exceptionally harsh criticism of Jaffe, Barrett, and Tradewinds was O.I.O. Director Fox.

After introductory remarks by Kolar describing the purpose of

Tradewinds, Fox launched into his attack. In general, Fox stated, his office was deeply concerned with the manner in which the project was directed. He produced copies of three telegrams sent to The Bahamas Desk Officer at the Department of State from the American Consul General Turner Shelton (successor to John Barnard) in Nassau. Wrongly interpreting the telegrams, Fox claimed that Jaffe and Barrett were meddling in internal Bahamian affairs causing great concern in the State Department. What Fox meant by meddling was revealed when he specifically mentioned contacts that agents had with the well known Dupuch family in Nassau, publishers of the *Tribune*. These contacts were preliminary to a meeting with Stafford Sands.

To Fox, it was obvious the State Department disapproved of such contacts, and, moreover, he too was against them. Fox continued the critique, pointing out Jaffe had also met with Cecil Wallace-Whitfield, a member of the P.L.P. (at that time), and Minister of Works. Jaffe's meeting with Wallace-Whitfield was sufficient reason, in and of itself, Fox argued, to call for Jaffe's removal from Operation Tradewinds. Other objections raised included material Jaffe had written in his latest Tradewinds report, which detailed a conversation between Jaffe and Stanley Moir, Assistant Commissioner of Police in The Bahamas. What most upset Fox was that Jaffe, responding to a question from Moir, suggested a better way for The Bahamas to control the mushrooming casinos.

While Fox caught his breath, Special Agent Barrett stated he had every reason to believe the Dupuch family was trustworthy and was appropriate to employ as intermediaries in arranging a meeting with Sands. Barrett added that Consul General Turner Shelton was completely informed prior to the meeting with Sands as to how the meeting had been arranged. And, he stated, after the meeting Shelton was given a full account. Barrett remarked the State Department had not objected to the meeting with Sands so long as it did not involve the Consul General. Fox countered, questioning the purpose and authority for interviewing Sands. He was told it was done to inquire about Sands' financial transactions with Lou Chesler and Mike McLaney who were at the time, it was pointed out, subjects of full-scale O.C.D. (Organized Crime Drive) investigations.

Exasperated, Fox asked what in the world the Intelligence Division was doing investigating Chesler, who was a Canadian. He forcefully said the I.R.S. had no business investigating foreigners who filed no U.S. tax returns. Barrett's answer should have given Fox pause. He commented that Chesler was in fact a resident alien with a home in Brooklyn, New York. Chesler had filed a U.S. tax return in that district for the previous ten years. Lastly, Barrett stated that Chesler was currently being investigated by a special agent from the Brooklyn office. As for McLaney, he filed in the Jacksonville District, which properly made him a Miami Office target. The objections, nevertheless, continued unabated.

Fox turned to Wallace Groves and an apparent investigation of him by Jaffe and Barrett. Again Barrett responded, acknowledging contacts with Groves, but denying Groves was a target. He also indicated that Groves agreed to furnish information about Chesler and McLaney. That, however, prompted Fox to complain about I.R.S. involvement with the Department of Justice in its drive against organized crime. He added to this complaint the charge that Tradewinds' special agents seemed to be running errands for Bob Peloquin of the Justice Department, and Robert Morgenthau, the U.S. Attorney for the Southern District of New York. Jaffe and Barrett completely denied performing any services for either man.

Jaffe then explained in detail the nature of his contact with Wallace-Whitfield. It began, he recounted, when an informant suggested to Wallace-Whitfield that he should speak with Jaffe about an issue of mutual concern—organized crime's International Credit Bank. Wallace-Whitfield agreed and the informant contacted Jaffe. When Jaffe learned what the informant had done, he went to the American Consul-General, Turner Shelton, and asked him whether or not he should meet with the Minister. The Consul General told him to make the meeting but to establish that it was strictly informal and done only as a favor for a mutual friend. Jaffe and Wallace-Whitfield finally met one dark night on a bluff above Nassau's harbor. Jaffe told him what he knew about the bank and the racketeers associated with it. Wallace-Whitfield in turn asked what he could do to help. Jaffe noted it would be very useful if he could obtain a record of the deposits made by the bank to its accounts in the Bank of Nova Scotia and the Canadian Imperial Bank of Commerce.

Wallace-Whitfield then poured out his own tale of grief to Jaffe, which consisted mostly of his government's difficulties dealing with many Americans of questionable background. It seems the new Bahamian government was drastically limited in its ability to check out these individuals. As far as Wallace-Whitfield knew, their only contact was a Bahamian official's cousin, a Deputy in the Dade County Sheriff's Office. Jaffe thought it would be easier and more reliable for the Minister to consult directly with Consul General Shelton, who had access to federal law enforcement agencies and was anxious to help the government achieve stability and avoid the numerous confidence men. The contact was made, and clearly, both Wallace-Whitfield and Shelton were pleased at establishing this new avenue of consultation.

After Jaffe finished this account, the O.I.O. people resumed their carping. They didn't like Operation Tradewinds and special agents Jaffe and Barrett, and nothing was going to change their minds. They belittled the accomplishments of Tradewinds, and constantly claimed the agents' activities "could conceivably disrupt delicate arrangements made by O.I.O. in countries all over the world and result in cutting off many sources of information." Perhaps most astonishingly, Fox announced he could not possibly understand why Bahamian gambling casinos were being investigated at all. He emphatically stated they were an external matter of no possible interest to the United States, adding we should be happy American gangsters had taken to The Bahamas and were no longer our problem.

It was at this point that Troy Register, the Jacksonville District Intelligence chief (Jaffe's and Barrett's boss), spoke up. He forcefully told Fox that "it is our concern." Money from Bahamian casinos was skimmed by and for the American underworld using U.S. bank accounts. To make this point crystal clear, Register produced copies of five cancelled checks which had been drawn on the account of Bahamas Amusements at the Bank of Miami Beach in 1964 and 1965. The checks came to over $500,000 and were signed and endorsed by Chesler, Max Courtney, and Max Orovitz. Register remarked that a witness identified the checks as a portion of the "skim" from the casino receipts transmitted to Meyer Lansky. The casino, Fox was told, was at the Lucayan Beach Hotel in Freeport.

Still the meeting went on, with O.I.O. insisting that the State

Department was upset with Tradewinds. When pressed on this, Durkin (Fox's assistant) replied the concern was obvious in the tone of Consul General Shelton's messages to State. Then, in what must have been a dramatic interlude, a secret message for Fox arrived from the Department of State. He read it, paled and passed it to William Kolar, the Director of the Intelligence Division. Kolar read the message aloud. It came from Turner Shelton, the American Consul in Nassau, and stated that any criticism of agents Jaffe and Barrett by their superiors in Washington was unjustified; that he was convinced of their responsible and professional conduct; and that he was aware of all their activities in The Bahamas. On that sour note for O.I.O., the meeting was adjourned until later in the afternoon.

In the afternoon session, the key I.R.S. officer in attendance was Donald Bacon, the Assistant Commissioner for Compliance, who would ultimately decide Tradewinds' fate. Fox declined to attend the afternoon meeting, reflecting just how dispirited the O.I.O. had become. The only issue raised at this time concerned Barrett's relationship with the Dupuch family. Barrett explained how it evolved. He had a very close personal friend living in The Bahamas whom he asked for help on a confidential government project. Without being told what the project was about, the friend gave Barrett the use of an office in Nassau and offered to introduce him to Sir Etienne Dupuch, a member of the Bahamian Senate and owner of the *Tribune*. Barrett and Dupuch met, and the publisher volunteered to help by providing introductions to various Bahamians and resident expatriates. According to Barrett, Dupuch never asked, and was never told the purpose of Barrett's mission, nor did he ever receive any favors or payments for his help.[9]

Bacon closed the meeting and announced he would make his decision after further consultations with the State Department. March 14 had been a difficult day, made remarkable by the short-sightedness of the Office of International Operations, whose antipathy to organized crime investigations was perplexing if not worrisome.

Assistant Commissioner Bacon's answer came on 3 April 1967. He ruled that Tradewinds could continue with its procedures somewhat changed. It was felt by Jaffe and others in the Intelligence Division that some of these new bureaucratic procedures had the potential to "significantly and substantially reduce the effectiveness" of Tradewinds. The first of these required that all contacts with sources who had information culled from anyone working in a Bahamian bank, had to take place on American soil. This meant Jaffe could not accept information from John Davis in The Bahamas, even though Jaffe often stayed in his cottage. Moreover, it was not sufficient for Davis to send all confidential Bahamian bank material to a Miami post box. The other new wrinkle added to the routine, called for advance notice of trips to The Bahamas, including notification of "itinerary and proposed contacts."[10] Jaffe's complaints were similar to those of his Miami Group Supervisor, J. A. McRae, who wrote, if the new restrictions and limitations were not lifted, he would recommend Tradewinds be abandoned.[11] Negotiations over the restrictive procedures followed and some leeway was granted on contacts in The Bahamas, but the travel restrictions were adamantly enforced.[12]

Tradewinds limped on with a budget of $15,000 for the 1968 calendar year.[13] Although woefully underfunded, the project always produced substantial money for the government. At the end of 1971, it was estimated that Tradewinds had produced $25 million in taxes and penalties since its inception, and had initiated thirteen full-scale investigations ending in recommendations for criminal proceedings. It was an inexpensive deal for the government.[14] Moreover, some of the information gathered was of critical significance. Tradewinds reported a very disturbing sidelight of the Vietnam War in 1970. Late in the summer, agent TW-19 informed Jaffe that he had been approached by a Washington, DC lawyer representing a group with $1 million to invest in land development on Great Exuma Island. The attorney was a former Naval Captain with extensive contacts in the Far East, who worked as an assistant to the Navy Department official responsible for the annual procurement of $9 billion of services and hardware.[15] His group was composed of five U.S. Army Generals serving in Vietnam, along with some other U.S. officials stationed there. The lawyer told TW-19 that his organization controlled about $50 million, which was sitting in a Hong Kong bank waiting for the right investments. Tradewinds passed this disturbing information up the line of I.R.S. Intelligence where it made its way into the higher reaches of the State Department.[16]

Tradewinds normal routine was augmented by the turn of the decade. Collateral requests for information in The Bahamas from other I.R.S. offices, which had been routed to the sluggish and disinterested O.I.O., were now sent directly to the Jacksonville District Intelligence Division and then on to Jaffe. Several of the collaterals concerned organized crime figures and drug dealers, while others dealt with stock swindlers and scam artists. One collateral request, however, involved Howard Hughes, the grotesque and lunatic billionaire who had purchased several Las Vegas casinos in the 1960s. There were numerous signals flashed to Tradewinds by other I.R.S. offices alerting it to Hughes and his machinations, because of the connections between Vegas casinos and money laundering operations in The Bahamas. The signals increased when Hughes retained Intertel, Resorts' private security outfit.

Hiring Intertel in 1970 was one step in a process of changing the billionaire's palace guard. The battle for control of Hughes and his fortune was arranged and skillfully managed by a cadre of executives known as the "Mormon Mafia." This force was led by Bill Gay, Chester Davis, and Raymond Holliday, who headed the Hughes Tool Company, the empire's foundation. Their enemy in the struggle for mastery over Hughes was Robert Maheu, the ex-director of security, who was also in charge of the Nevada casino operations. Maheu was a former F.B.I. agent and C.I.A. operative directly involved in the Agency's plan to murder Fidel Castro. The Mormons manipulated the result of a fractious split between Maheu and the codeine-addicted Hughes.[17] It was the Mormon Mafia which hired Intertel to replace Maheu, and thereby set off major sparks in Nevada, and later The Bahamas.

The initial meeting with Intertel's Peloquin took place in Washington where Gay stated Hughes wanted Intertel to secretly conduct an audit of his Las Vegas casinos. Shortly after this first contact, Holliday and Peloquin met again in Los Angeles. This time it was explained an audit was really secondary to a plan for a complete management change in Nevada.[18] Maheu was to be ousted; moreover, Hughes was leaving Nevada. He was departing, unnerved over the Atomic Energy Commission's continuing nuclear tests in Nevada. For a man paranoid about common germs, Hughes was near apoplexy thinking about radiation.[19] One reason for his disenchantment with Maheu supposedly stemmed from Maheu's inability to convince President Nixon, the recipient of cash payoffs from Hughes totalling $200,000, which were masked by Rebozo, to stop the A.E.C. testing program.

Hughes determined to go to The Bahamas, after eliminating Mexico (Baja, California), and Puerto Rico from consideration. He was prepared to leave in August 1970, and settle on Paradise Island. Hughes' men, now including Intertel, had reserved, and then sealed off two floors in two different Paradise Island hotels for his use. Beyond this, it seems Hughes was thinking of buying the entire island. Because he was so irrational, the Bahamian adventure was almost scuttled when he learned that "Sixty-six tons of lethal nerve gas, one-ninth of the Pentagon's entire poisonous stockpile," was about to be sunk into the ocean about 150 miles from Paradise Island.[20] It was a terrible nightmare for Hughes and he immediately commanded his forces to stop it, no matter the cost. This demand was conveyed to President Nixon, already living in dread whenever contemplating Hughes for a variety of reasons, especially the sensible one that the disguised bribery would be disclosed. Indeed, the previous month a Hughes executive had slipped $50,000 in cash (the second half of the payoff) to Rebozo, who placed the money in safe-deposit box #224 in his Key Biscayne bank.[21]

Ever solicitous, therefore, the Administration wanted to know if Hughes had an alternative in mind for the gas. He did—the North Pole. Although mighty efforts were made to halt the dumping, it finally happened on August 18. The poison gas terrified Hughes, but other matters in Las Vegas scared him even more. At long last, on 25 November 1970, the nearly emaciated and unbelievably filthy billionaire left for The Bahamas. He was carried on a stretcher from his Vegas penthouse and flown to The Bahamas in one of his jets.

Waiting for Hughes at the Nassau airport was Lou Crosson, the American Consul, Mrs. Barbara Pierre of Bahamas immigration, and Jim Golden (former Vice President Nixon's chief Secret Service guard, and later head of security at the 1968 Republican National Convention) from Intertel. A Hughes aide handed eight immigration cards to Pierre. She then went on board and talked to the pilot. When it was time for Hughes to actually leave the plane, Golden requested both Crosson and Pierre to turn around and walk away from the plane keeping their backs to the scene.[22] They complied without any reported complaint, and the American Consul heard what he thought was a wheel chair moving, and then a van rumbling away.[23] Hughes was finally carried to a darkened penthouse bedroom in the Britannia Beach Hotel on Paradise Island.

His routine in The Bahamas was much the same as in Las Vegas; he neither bathed, shaved, cut his hair or nails (fingers and toes), dressed, nor left his self-imposed prison. He watched movies day and night, over and over again. Daily needs were attended by a very few trusted aides, and consisted of codeine shots, a little food and enemas. While Hughes existed within this sad-mad reverie, the political world was laying the foundation for its own St. Vitus dance; forces rotated around the fixed point of the living skeleton in cyclonic fashion.

Nixon was always in a state of high anxiety over the bribery. The President was further panicked by a Jack Anderson column in the summer of 1971, which reported that $100,000 had been "siphoned" out of the Hughes' Silver Slipper casino and given to Rebozo for the President.[24] Nixon desperately wanted to prove that Lawrence O'Brien, Chairman of the Democratic Party and former Kennedy assistant in the days of "Camelot," was also sucking at Hughes' dessicated tit. The President was determined to bury his own crime under what he believed was O'Brien's corruption. And so he pushed his little band of White House spies and burglars to get the goods on O'Brien, and they rushed pell-mell into Watergate.

Meanwhile, in the continuing battle between Intertel and the Mormon Mafia on one side, and the still-powerful Maheu on the other, events were heating up. Intertel used its influence (with whom it is unclear), to instigate an I.R.S. investigation of Maheu, which was the apparent fulfillment of the original plan to secretly audit the casinos. But bringing in the I.R.S. had far-reaching, out-of-control consequences. Starting with the casinos, I.R.S. investigators inexorably advanced to the Nixon payoffs.[25] They also uncovered a major theft within Hughes' organization.

Ralph R. Kaminiski from the Reno office was the I.R.S. Special Agent in charge of the investigation into the looting operation, which, peripherally at least, involved Nixon's brother Donald. Jaffe and members of his Tradewinds' team worked closely with Kaminski assembling proof on the Caribbean part of the scheme. The theft was planned and carried out by John H. Meier, an executive with the Hughes Tool Company, and his accomplice Anthony G. Hatsis from Salt Lake City. They were aided by three California attorneys, Charles Adams, John R. Suckling, and Robert Kahan, and two individuals from the world of offshore banking. Simple in design and complicated in execution, Meier, Hatsis, and the others conspired to sell $9 million in phony mine claims to Hughes Tool.[26] The money was moved through a series of companies, subsidiaries, and affiliates, in Nassau, Panama, the Dutch Antilles, and the Cayman Islands. Hatsis and Meier filed fraudulent tax returns showing the proceeds of the mining sales going to a Dutch firm named Maatschappij Intermovie, the conduit used by the thieves. There were many reasons why the I.R.S. was interested in Hughes, and why Jaffe and Tradewinds were busy gathering data.

But if all that had transpired wasn't sufficient stimulation for law enforcement, along came novelist Clifford Irving, and the case of the bogus biography. Irving decided to write an account of Hughes' life after accumulating news accounts of the struggle for control of Hughes Inc. He believed the reclusive billionaire was dead, or so far gone that neither he nor any of his official party would find it in their interests to contradict his story. Irving convinced McGraw-Hill that he had Hughes' cooperation and signed for a fat advance. The publisher announced the coming book on 7 December 1971, and thereby unknowingly raised Nixon's apprehension that his bribe would soon be public knowledge.[27]

In preparation for writing his fake account, novelist Irving and his wife did a little research in The Bahamas. Through a local newspaper reporter, they were put in touch with Sally and Ed Woodruff. The Irvings tried to pump them for information, without the slightest idea they were dealing with an I.R.S. undercover agent.[28] A dinner party was arranged at the Bahamian Club, now on Paradise Island on 30 April 1971. The Woodruffs thought

Irving was writing "an historical novel concerning the Bahamas." During dinner, Sally and the writer had a lengthy discussion; she realized he knew nothing about The Bahamas and seemed to care less. What he wanted instead, was information about Howard Hughes, but she had none to offer.[29]

Irving's audacious fraud finally caused Hughes himself to surface in a manner of speaking. Hughes held a telephonic press conference on 7 January 1971. Stoned on codeine, while in his blacked-out Paradise Island penthouse, he spoke on a conference line to seven reporters gathered in a Los Angeles hotel. This was the first press conference in a decade and a half. Hughes convincingly disposed of Irving—never heard of him, never saw him. That done, he returned to his macabre existence and "settled back to watch another movie, *Topaz*, shot up four more grains of codeine, they stayed up all night for a fourth and fifth screening of *Funeral in Berlin*."[30]

The press conference (along with subsequent events) was enough to expose Irving, but not sufficient to satisfy everyone that Hughes was indeed alive. Among the skeptics was Jaffe and other I.R.S. personnel who pushed for indisputable proof.[31] What they wanted was a face-to-face interview. The press picked up the story, commenting that "if Hughes refuses to meet in person with I.R.S. agents, the tax men could seize his immense financial empire until his proper tax status is determined."[32] The I.R.S., it was noted, could conceivably declare him dead and move to collect millions in estate taxes unless he shows himself. The demand to interview him was orchestrated by Jaffe among others. It was considered urgent because Hughes was about to leave The Bahamas. His next sanctuary was Nicaragua, then under the despotic control of Anastasio Somoza.

Jaffe was particularly concerned because no American official had actually seen Hughes when he arrived in 1970, and, of course, none since. Troy Register and Jaffe contacted the U.S. Ambassador to Nicaragua, Turner Shelton (former Bahamian Consul General and Tradewinds' savior during the difficult 1967 fight with the O.I.O.), and pressed him to confirm Hughes' existence. He told Jaffe and Register that although he didn't know Hughes and had never seen him, and wouldn't know him if he did see him, he nonetheless had no doubt he was alive and competent.

This confidence rested upon Shelton's acquaintance with two of the billionaire's most trusted assistants.[33]

Hughes was not pleased with Nicaragua, especially as Somoza tried to sell him very expensive portions of Somoza's many companies in plywood, pharmaceuticals, travel, and real estate. Hughes may have been crazy, but he still recognized extortion and knew it would never end. He thus decided to leave a month or so after arriving.[34] Before leaving, this time for Vancouver, Canada, he resolved to actually meet with Somoza and U.S. Ambassador Shelton in order to end the dangerous speculation that he was dead or completely comatose. Careful preparations were made: an aide trimmed his beard, hair, and nails, and as a finishing touch, Hughes consented to a shower.[35] Shelton and Somoza met him on his airplane where they had an amiable conversation. Shelton described Hughes as tall, very thin, with grey hair and a trim Van Dyke beard. He wore tattered slippers and an old robe. Shelton thought the outfit would have sold at a bargain basement for less than a dollar.[36] Hughes confided he hadn't spoken to outsiders in person for almost 24 years. The Ambassador was impressed, finding him both eccentric and fascinating—"an authentic genius," he remarked.[37]

The billionaire left Nicaragua, but returned several months later, again isolating himself in the same Managua hotel. Two days before Christmas 1972, a devastating earthquake struck Managua. That surely did it; the following night Hughes was gone forever. He was now on his way to England. His plane had to stop in the United States, however, before it could continue across the Atlantic. The executive jet with Hughes and some of his devoted Mormons flew into Fort Lauderdale, Florida. It was his last stop in America; the last chance for the I.R.S. to chat with him. The I.R.S. had a subpoena stemming from the Nevada investigations waiting for Hughes.

Not wishing to be intercepted by anyone, Hughes' agents launched a deceptive ploy requesting the "courtesies of the Port" for his entry at Miami International airport. His real destination was Fort Lauderdale. Several Customs and I.R.S. Special Agents, including Jaffe were at the Miami field. With some prior knowledge of the Mormon Mafia's deceptive practices, Jaffe had taken the precaution of calling the Federal Aviation Administration (F.A.A.).

He requested notification of all inbound flight plans to the United States from Managua. In mid-flight Hughes' jet filed a flight plan to Fort Lauderdale, not Miami. Jaffe and the agents notified by the F.A.A., raced to Fort Lauderdale where a tense confrontation took place—agents milled about demanding to get on the plane, aides refused to let them. Telephone calls to various VIPs in Washington were made. A compromise was reached. One Customs agent was allowed on the plane to briefly speak with a perturbed Hughes. At the same time, an I.R.S. Special Agent, William C. Ryan, was permitted to peek at Hughes from outside the plane through the open door, helped by the illumination cast by a flashlight flickered on for a moment by the Customs Agent.

This brief encounter was characterized as a law enforcement triumph by a high I.R.S. official, who wrote that the special agents proved resourceful, tactful, discreet, more than equal to the task, and ultimately successful in accomplishment of their mission.[38] Tradewinds' involvement in the Hughes' matters ended on this enigmatic "high note"; this passing glance at a loony billionaire, covered by a blanket, wearing a pulled-down fedora, crunched in the claustrophobic gloom of a Lear Jet.

Notes

1. Material on Coppola's criminal activities and background is derived from U.S. Department of Justice, Federal Bureau of Investigation, "The Fur Dress Case," Report #60–1501 (7 November 1939); New York State Crime Commission, "Confidential Digest of Information on Certain Arrest Records," (1952) in New York State Crime Commission papers in Butler Library, Columbia University; U.S. Department of Justice, Federal Bureau of Investigation, "Interrogation of Joseph Valachi," File #NY92–1459 (1962); State of Florida TriCounty Intelligence Unit of Broward, Dade and Palm Beach Counties, *Known Offenders*, April, 1959; and Hank Messick, *Syndicate Wife: The Story of Ann Drahman Coppola* (MacMillan, 1968).
2. The account of investigative details is from a summary prepared by Richard Jaffe entitled "NAT 5 JAX, AN OCD CASE HISTORY."
3. The following material on the origins of Operation Tradewinds is from author's interviews with Richard Jaffe, Miami, Florida, 1984, 1986, 1987, and 1988.
4. Richard B. Wallace, "Re: Official Visit to Nassau, B.W.I.," 4 and 5 March 1965.

5. Intelligence Division (Miami), "Report," 1–2 April 1965.

6. The material on Eder comes from Florida, *Known Offenders*, p. 37.

7. Peter Allen, *The Windsor Secret: New Revelations of the Nazi Connection* (Stein and Day, 1984).

8. The following reconstruction is drawn from Intelligence Division, "Memo of Conference, 14 March 1967," 24 March 1967; Department of State, AMCONSUL Nassau to Secstate Wash DC Priority, Secret Nassau 433, "REF: Nassau's 408," 10 March 1967; and D. W. Bacon, Assistant Commissioner (Compliance) to William J. Bookholt, Regional Commissioner, Southeast Region, "Operation TRADEWINDS," 3 April 1967.

9. Years later and under totally different circumstances Dupuch and his paper would find themselves under savage attack by the Pindling government. They would be accused of working with American drug agents to undermine Bahamian stability. The truth of the matter was quite different. By then, drug corruption had reached to the very highest office in The Bahamas, and the *Tribune* was being punished for its splendid work reporting on this menace. See Chapter Ten for more of this story.

10. Intelligence Division (Miami) to District Director, "Operation TRADEWINDS," 11 April 1967.

11. Intelligence Division (Miami) to District Director of Internal Revenue, "OPERATION TRADEWINDS," 11 April 1967.

12. I.R.S. Regional Commissioner, Southeast Region, to All Assistant Regional Commissioners, All Directors, Southeast Region, "Memorandum: Advance Approval of Foreign Travel," 29 February 1968.

13. D. W. Bacon, Assistant Commissioner (Compliance) to William J. Bookholt, Regional Commissioner, Southeast Region, "Confidential Expenditures, Jacksonville District, Southeast Region, OPERATION 'TRADE WINDS,' " 9 September 1968.

14. Intelligence Division (Miami) to Chief, Intelligence Division, Jacksonville, "Operation Tradewinds Work Plan—FY 1972," 13 August 1971.

15. Director, Intelligence Division, Washington, D.C. to Regional Commissioner, Southeast Region, "OPERATION 'TRADE WINDS,' " 27 October 1970.

16. Turner B. Shelton letter to Honorable Edwin W. Martin, American Consul General, American Consulate General, Hong Kong, 28 August 1970.

17. Michael Drosnin, *Citizen Hughes* (Holt, Rinehart and Winston, 1985), pp. 392–393, et passim.

18. Drosnin, *Citizen Hughes*, p. 392.

19. Ibid., p. 347.

20. Ibid., p. 379.

21. Ibid., p. 385.

22. Donald E. van Koughnet Papers, "Memorandum of Telephone Call

between Richard E. Jaffe and H. Clay Black, American Consul, Nassau," 18 February 1972.

23. Van Koughnet Papers, "Memorandum of Telephone Call between Jaffe and Lou Crosson, former American Consul Nassau," 18 February 1972.

24. Ibid.

25. David Wise, *The American Police State: The Government Against the People* (Vintage, 1978), pp. 339–342.

26. Ralph R. Kaminski, Special Agent, Reno, Nevada to District Director of IRS, "Memorandum: Subject: Hatsis and Meier," 18 April 1972.

27. Drosnin, *Citizen Hughes*, p. 421.

28. New York State Supreme Court, County of New York, "Rosemont Enterprises, Incorporated, against McGraw-Hill Book Company, . . . Clifford Irving . . . ," *Affidavit of Sarah Jane Woodruff*, Exhibit Index No. 800/72.

29. Ibid.

30. Drosnin, p. 424.

31. James Savage, "Will IRS Solve Riddle of Hughes?" *Miami Herald*, 18 February 1972.

32. Ibid.

33. Van Koughnet Papers, "Memorandum of Conversation between Dick Jaffe and Ambassador Turner B. Shelton," 18 February 1972.

34. Drosnin, p. 432; and "Somoza Eyes Airline Deal With Hughes," New York *Daily News*, 21 February 1972.

35. Drosnin, pp. 432–33.

36. Van Koughnet Papers, "Memorandum of Interviews with Ambassador Turner B. Shelton and Special Agent Thomas A. Lopez," 10, 11 and 12 April 1972.

37. Ibid.

38. John J. Olszewski, IRS Intelligence Division, "Memorandum: Howard R. Hughes," 5 January 1973.

5

Vesco

Robert Lee Vesco was probably the most audacious crook ever to land in The Bahamas, and his effect was extraordinary. He intended the country to provide him sanctuary, if need be, from American justice. To make sure of his welcome, he spent millions buying influence and loyalty from the very top of Bahamian life on down the ranks. He transformed as much of the government and population as he could into criminal accomplices. Corruption was nothing new to Bahamian life, but with Vesco the scale dramatically changed. He and Progressive Liberal Party members were in so many conspiracies they appeared permanent criminal partners—a new Bahamian criminal cartel. Vesco supported his subversion of government and people with millions in stolen money.

He engaged in one of the boldest financial crimes of the era, targeting Bernie Cornfeld's mutual fund in all its permutations. The Fund was constructed by Cornfeld on the backs and dreams of any army of salesman literally tramping the world, helping the financially nervous from several tottering nations. The 1960s was the decade of the big push; to the thousands of metaphysically inclined brokers nothing could contain the inevitable growth of Investors Overseas Services (I.O.S.). They deluded themselves and many others believing I.O.S. was an expression of a stock market that could only rise.

One had to believe in the upward market spiral, which guaranteed I.O.S.'s success, or face an empty future. A loss of confidence and nerve would endanger the entire I.O.S. edifice. That is one reason why I.O.S. executives sounded so insipid. They were fanatic sellers and nervous believers in "confidence" itself as a product. They were "positive thinkers," smiling hucksters speaking the distinctive "jive" of boiler-room stock operators the world over. With I.O.S., though, it was difficult to separate the suckers from the wiseguys.

When the big stock push ended at the turn of the decade, I.O.S. was in immediate trouble, even though it had more than $2.1 billion in assets under management at the end of 1969.[1] Its dilemma was caused by a collapse in the value of its common stock. I.O.S. had gone public in September 1969, selling eleven million shares at $10 each. The price rapidly rose to a high of $19 and then went into a wrenching decline. Within three months or so, I.O.S. shares could be had for $3 if anyone wanted them. Moreover, only about half the money raised in the public offering went into the I.O.S. treasury, the rest belonged to I.O.S. "insiders." When the value of I.O.S. paper crashed, their paper fortunes vanished and they viewed the I.O.S. ruling triumvirate, Cornfeld, Ed Cowett, and Alan Cantor, with increasing animosity. I.O.S. quickly had to find major outside financing.[2]

None of these problems was missed by the larger world of financial crime. The word was out that Bernie had trouble and the scam artists, some racketeer-connected, began to gather. The first was Denver oilman John M. King whose own company was in its death throes. King wanted I.O.S.'s still substantial assets to salvage his firm. He teamed up with the irrepressible J. Jay Frankel, Vice Chairman of Delafield Capital Corporation, still flush from helping arrange the Resorts International deal.[3] Frankel, King, and I.O.S. management worked out a $40 million debt financing package secured by I.O.S. shares, which amounted to 77 percent of the company. The plan was put into motion and special deposit accounts were opened at the Bank of New York. In May, 1970, $8 million was transferred from Delafield to King.[4] But the plan failed. King's own financial problems were too severe, within months his company was bankrupt.[5] The King interlude was a bad dream for I.O.S. people, and in their frustration they turned to the greatest thief of all.

Vesco was born in Detroit on 4 December 1936. His father was a first generation American of Italian heritage who worked the line at Chrysler most of his life. His mother, Barbara Sasek, migrated from Yugoslavia. The family lived in an Italian, Jewish, and Black neighborhood.[6] Vesco went to high school where he was drawn to mathematics. He didn't stay long, however; he was far too restless and, more importantly, soon had a wife and child to support. Early in 1953, he dropped out of Detroit's Denby High after marrying sixteen-year old Patricia Melzer, who hailed from Bad Axe, Michigan. Before the year was over they had a son, and Vesco had a job reading blueprints in training as a draftsman with the Packard Car company.[7]

From Packard he went to another Detroit company as a junior engineer. About a year later, Vesco moved from this post to the Reynolds Metals Company working in sales. For the next eighteen months he stayed put. But he was already absorbed, so he retrospectively stated, in plotting how to become the president of his own company. He had fashioned a master plan for self advancement.[8] The ensuing step came when he joined the Olin Mathieson Chemical Corporation in 1957. At first he was unhappily stuck in the Detroit regional office, but was presently promoted and transferred to the New York headquarters.

Vesco ached for business success and soothed this pain with movement and experimentation. Although he stayed with Olin longer than any other firm, he left before he was 24, angry when he wasn't promoted to an executive position.[9] From then on he was an entrepreneur; his own boss in charge of his future. He became a manufacturer's representative, humping his way around New Jersey, working out of his car buying and selling things, looking for the right score. It came in the form of Eagle Aluminum Products, which was his first important independent business connection. He worked out an arrangement with Eagle that let him use some of their idle equipment for his new company, Aluminum Services Incorporated. Borrowing furniture and a secretary, Aluminum Services made and sold storm windows, aluminum awnings, etc., splitting the few profits with Eagle.

It was not part of his plan to build corporate success through product development and strategic marketing. A business was a means to a different end. He wanted to acquire companies in order to acquire more companies; success, growth, and acquisition were synonyms. Even at the beginning, with his aluminum

company, when small-time companies couldn't pay for their aluminum siding, Vesco accepted their stock instead of cash and
took the loss. He wanted the stock because he wanted ownership.
When he became an equity owner for the first time, it excited
him.[10] He experienced an inner ecstasy through the joy of acquisition.

Vesco still had much to learn, and, fortunately, he found his
first significant mentor in Malcolm Evans McAlpin. A suave,
tweedy, Princeton graduate and stockbroker with a seat on the
New York Exchange, McAlpin was almost thirty years older than
Vesco. His impressive experience and style enabled him to teach
Vesco how to behave around bankers and others with cash at
hand. It was a hasty course in entrepreneurial etiquette.[11]

Vesco was ready for his next business step. He secured control
of a small valve manufacturing plant, Captive Seal, entirely on
credit. He then placed Captive Seal's few assets and greater lia-
bilities into the brand new International Controls Corporation
(I.C.C.), which he had formed only the previous month. This
marked the true start of Vesco's ascent to the top of the financial
crime heap. I.C.C., not as it was, but as it would become, was
the vehicle he prepared for dominance.

To accomplish this, he took over and merged I.C.C. with a
nearly broke Florida company named Cryogenics Incorporated,
which was a public corporation. Cryogenics provided an opportunity to transform I.C.C. into a public corporation, while avoid-
ing S.E.C. filing requirements and other burdensome rules and
regulations for the issuance of securities. The "sci-fi" sounding
firm was his back door into the market.[12] When the merger took
place, I.C.C. became a Florida corporation and went on an acquisition binge. By the end of 1967, I.C.C. owned Fairfield Aviation, I.C.C. Manufacturing (formerly Lowden Machine), The
Special Corporation, Silber Products, and the Moeller Tool Corporation.[13] The next year brought more of the same, although
the quality of the firms acquired dramatically improved. Also in
1968, Vesco sold 220,000 shares of I.C.C. common stock and
realized more than $6 million. Finally, during that busy year,
Vesco began the process of purchasing a manufacturing company,
Electronic Specialty. He raised $50 million in cash through bank
loans, and then more money by selling various debentures, hold-

ing another public offering, and finally a private placement. By 1969 Electronic Specialty was a wholly-owned subsidiary of I.C.C. It was one of its most important acquisitions at this stage, providing all of I.C.C.'s profits in 1969.[14]

Beginning with McAlpin, Vesco found a wide variety of talented and helpful people, many of whom became part of his permanent crew of "sharpsters." One was Wilbert J. Snipes, a banker from New Jersey. With only an eighth grade education, Snipes started his banking career in North Carolina as a guard, and then a clerk. After military service in World War II, he returned to banking as the head credit clerk at Chase Manhattan. He left Chase to start the credit department at American National, a New Jersey bank which had gone through several name changes. When Vesco met him, late in 1965, Snipes was the bank's vice president and senior loan officer. Six months later, Snipes joined the board of I.C.C., with the authorization, he stated, of the bank. Upon Snipes' approval, American National then loaned Vesco money, which he used to buy stock in the bank's holding company. It was a typically cozy arrangement, and American National was exceptionally helpful in Vesco's rise to financial power.[15]

Snipes and the bank arranged loans and widened Vesco's world of contacts. He was introduced to Gilbert Straub, a politically influential money-man.[16] Straub and others like him were valuable because of their experience in politics and offshore finances. Before formally joining Vesco's expanding conglomerate in 1968, Straub had already shepherded at least one minor Bahamian company called Bank Securities, which subsequently disappeared.[17] But his major offshore work came with an outfit called Capital Growth Fund, originally managed by New Providence Securities out of Nassau. Its boss was a legendary "flim-flam" artist, Clovis William McAlpin from Texas (no relation to Vesco's Ivy League friend from Princeton). McAlpin managed to drain money from hundreds, perhaps thousands, of victims, while searching for a resting place for Capital Growth. He dropped in everywhere the "funny-money" game was played in Europe, the Caribbean, and Latin America.

Through the efforts of Snipes and Straub, Vesco was brought

into the murky world of New Jersey and national politics. One early contact was Harry L. Sears, who was the New Jersey State Senate majority leader until he retired from politics in 1971. Vesco met him in 1969 when Sears was running for the Republican gubernatorial nomination. Sears needed campaign money and Vesco was happy to contribute. Between Vesco's donations and American National's loans, Sears was well cared for.[18] Vesco ingratiated himself with Sears because he craved political influence and wanted Sears to join his growing I.C.C. empire as its counsel. The New Jersey politician failed to secure the nomination and accepted Vesco's offer at the end of 1971. This was a fateful move with important Watergate consequences, as it was Sears who later asked his friend Attorney General John Mitchell to rescue Vesco from several difficulties. Knowledge of these actions would later emerge and feed into the generalized Watergate scandal.

Vesco's Republican associates were Nixon loyalists. Howard F. Cerny, who was a lawyer, although better known as a private detective, and expert on wiretaps and electronic bugs, is an important example. Cerny's value for sensitive clients was partly his reassuring discretion; when contracts were prepared, the drafts were destroyed; when bills were paid, records of time charges and disbursements were thrown out; and when calls came in or meetings held, no notes were taken or memoranda retained.[19] The security-minded Cerny claimed to represent Donald and Edward Nixon, the President's two brothers.[20] Cerny joined Vesco's camp and helped bring in Donald Nixon, Jr., the President's nephew.[21]

Called Don-Don, he entered Vesco's world in the summer of 1971, apparently as a favor to his worried father, and was placed under Gil Straub's tutelage. By then, Vesco had grabbed much of Cornfeld's I.O.S., including the Swiss facilities, and the idea of depositing Junior in Switzerland was appealing. The young Nixon was not ambitious. Following military training at the Great Lakes Naval Center in Illinois (far from Vietnam), he took to the California hills spending time in what was believed to be a hippie commune. This distressed the Nixon family and they called upon Anthony Ulasewicz, a former New York City detective then serving on the White House Special Investigations Unit, to bring Don-Don out of the hills. The blunt talking detective, later to gain notoriety from his Watergate testimony, brought him to the Western White House for a sit-down with presidential aide John Ehrlichman, who had a reputation for frankness. Ehrlichman told him of the Vesco offer, urged him to take it, cautioned him to behave, and warned him to tell people he was working for Straub and not Vesco.[22] Discretion was not part of Don-Don's temperament, and he told anyone interested that he was a Vesco man.

At the decade's end, Vesco had the nucleus of an organization ready to play in the rough and tumble of politics and financial crime. He had the backing of his New Jersey banker and many political friends. And since 1968, he had formed a critically important alliance with a Bahamian bank run by Allan C. Butler in Nassau. Born in Cambridge, Massachusetts, in 1926, Butler attended Harvard and then Johns Hopkins, training for a career in international banking. In 1958 he got a job with the First National Bank of Boston. A short while later, he was in The Bahamas anxious to have his own bank.

In Nassau, Butler married Shirley Oakes, the second daughter of the very wealthy Sir Harry Oakes. Sir Harry had discovered Canada's largest gold deposits and was the richest baronet in the British Empire. He headed for The Bahamas at the tail end of the 1930s when his Canadian taxes reached about $3 million a year.[23] An early developer of The Bahamas, Oakes was mysteriously murdered in his beautiful Nassau home in 1943. The Oakes children, Shirley and two others, inherited money and extensive land holdings on New Providence Island, including most of the center of old Nassau. It was Shirley's inheritance that provided the capital her husband needed to form Butlers Bank in the early 1960s. The bank was the centerpiece in a growing Butler conglomerate of local businesses under the corporate name, General Bahamian Companies.[24]

Butlers Bank was used by Vesco for many parts of his I.O.S. looting scheme. It ended up as the foundation for Vesco's own banking institutions, held together by a creation called International Bancorp Limited (Bahamas). This company, which was topped off by the Bahamas Commonwealth Bank (Vesco's temporary financial flagship), gathered much of I.O.S.'s banking structure into the Vesco system. Butlers Bank was then cleaned out by Bahamas Commonweath, which itself suffered a similar fate from another Vesco company after its money, credit, and usefulness were gone.

When the King-Frankel deal fell apart in the summer of 1970, certain I.O.S. people were already negotiating with Vesco. The I.O.S. panic stemmed from a cash-flow problem, not from either structural or legal issues. Indeed, I.O.S. was in far trimmer shape than Vesco's corporation. But Vesco had so skillfully handled I.C.C.'s precarious debt financing that the real condition of near penury wouldn't surface for a year or two.[26] In the meantime, Vesco greedily viewed I.O.S. as an imperative acquisition, the next great extension of his empire.

That summer there were hurried meetings of baroque proportions, usually within the Swiss and French compounds of I.O.S. In venerable European settings, a score of American plunderers finally set in motion the Vesco takeover.[27] Vesco's chief lieutenant in Geneva was Milton F. Meissner, holder of a PhD and former Rhodes scholar, who had met Vesco years earlier at Olin Mathieson.[28] The I.O.S. and I.C.C. negotiations were stormy, and at one point Vesco's offer of help was rejected. Some I.O.S. representatives still believed they could secure cash from establishment sources. This illusion didn't last long, and they rushed back to Vesco who promised I.O.S. both enough cash to get through the crisis, and, equally important, its continuing independence.[29] This was not supposed to be a conventional buyout and takeover.

In order to consummate the agreement, Vesco had to convince I.O.S. he commanded the necessary funds to manage and overcome their liquidity problem, which approached the $15 to $20 million mark. To demonstrate his worth he called on Butlers Bank and American National. Telegrams from both institutions stated that I.C.C., or one of its subsidiaries, had $5 million on deposit and thereby certified Vesco's financial credentials.[30] Of course neither message was accurate: I.C.C. did not have $5 million in American National, and the $5 million at Butlers was really a "back to back deposit" against a bank loan to I.C.C. It was fluff and smoke, but convincing enough, particularly when Vesco falsely intimated that the Bank of America and Prudential Insurance quietly stood behind his offer.[31] Later, Vesco denied he suggested

Prudential backed him stating "Prudential thought that I.O.S. was a bunch of schmucks and would not touch it with a ten foot pole."[32]

Part of the dynamics of the action came from I.C.C.'s internal affairs. There were those from Vesco's company skeptical of its ability to lend anybody anything. But Vesco so completely controlled the Board that important questions about I.C.C.'s capabilities and the deal were never asked.[33] Permission to aid I.O.S. was presumed by Vesco who provided less information to the I.C.C. Board than Colonel North and Admiral Poindexter gave to Congress about their Iran-Contra scam.

Flaunting I.C.C.'s approval, and bamboozling I.O.S. with telegrams of phony net worth were convincing. On 3 September 1970, the agreement was signed. It called for a newly-formed Bahamian subsidiary of I.C.C. to lend I.O.S. $5 million in cash, and provide it a line of credit for the same amount. Additionally, Vesco's firm agreed to consider a second line of credit for $5 million should it be necessary. The cash was supposed to stabilize I.O.S., enabling it to reduce its debt by selling off certain valuable assets. The agreement also held that Cornfeld and Ed Cowett could have nothing to do with the business. Vesco required an iron-clad guarantee that Cornfeld was really out: "Absolute assurance must be given that Mr. Cornfeld, his affiliates or associates will not be represented on the Board of Directors nor involved in any way with the management of I.O.S. during the life of the proposed agreement," was the language employed.[34] Even with this, though, Cornfeld's separation from I.O.S. was not over. He threatened a tough proxy fight causing Vesco to momentarily back off. Vesco's dislike of Cornfeld could not match in vituperation Bernie's contempt for him. Cornfeld characterized his former I.O.S. associates now working with Vesco as traitors, dolts, idiots, and imbeciles.

With the I.C.C. loan came its right to sit on the I.O.S. Board and Executive Committee. In addition, a new and powerful Finance Committee that could stop any independent I.O.S. financial action was created. This committee, chaired by Vesco, was at the center of the takeover, providing Vesco all the leverage he needed. He had the power to control I.O.S. through what were called "the negative covenants of the Loan Agreement": nothing of any significance could be done without his approval, which meant, Vesco said, he had the "right to put I.O.S. into default."[35]

One of his first moves was to hit Butlers Bank for cash. On Vesco's promise to deposit I.O.S. money as soon as possible, Allan Butler lent him $4 million so he could buy out another group of "interim" I.O.S. investors. Around this time, Vesco suggested the I.C.C. Board should select a new leader, because he had little time to supervise its daily affairs, consumed as he was with the details of the I.O.S. acquisition and restructuring.[36] Vesco's maneuvers to dominate I.O.S. came rapidly. Using the Finance Committee's power, he caused a row which eliminated the line of credit provisions, and also saved him from repaying Butler the $4 million. In the following months, he artfully drained more I.O.S. money into, and quickly out of Butlers.

Next he went after Cornfeld's I.O.S. stock, which represented about sixteen percent of all the preferred shares. To buy him out, and give the appearance I.C.C. had nothing to do with the purchase (he hinted this time that the Union Bank of Switzerland was actually behind the plan), Vesco used a Panamanian shell company named Linkink. After establishing its seeming independence from I.C.C., and consummating the purchase, Linkink was acquired by a Canadian subsidiary of I.C.C. Vesco's intermediary in this was again Butlers Bank. The operation was intended to involve the usual "flim-flam": Vesco would take a little more I.O.S. money, deposit it in Butlers, and then borrow it back to buy a little more of I.O.S, in this case, Cornfeld's shares. His intention had to be slightly modified because Butler and Vesco had just about driven the bank into the ground; it tottered on the edge of bankruptcy.[37] The Vesco pattern of lying to everyone continued unabated. However, he wasn't able to keep the I.C.C. Board completely in the dark. There came a time, for example, when it learned and accepted the fact that an I.C.C. Canadian subsidiary named American Interland (later renamed Hemispheres Financial Services) had acquired Linkink. The Board knew that the "arms length deal" established to avoid certain I.C.C. agreements with lenders, and mandatory S.E.C. disclosure requirements, was an inside and crooked one.[38]

The criminal "wheeling and dealing" couldn't last forever, it was bound to be noticed and scrutinized by some agency or other.

Therefore, it shouldn't have been a surprise when the S.E.C., on 25 March 1971, notified the I.C.C. Board that it was looking into the deal and wanted company documents.[39] Nothing that had happened to Vesco up till then would match the consequences of this S.E.C. action. It didn't appear very threatening at first, but it wouldn't go away. The probe expanded and every attempt made to stop it was unsuccessful. The investigation didn't peak until late in 1973, however, and in the meantime, Vesco plundered ahead.[40]

The pace of looting increased, millions of dollars were wired around the world; the business of I.C.C. was now almost entirely the total acquisition and obliteration of I.O.S.[41] Along with the flight of money went the fantasies it had sustained. Knowledgeable former I.O.S. "wheeler-dealers" realized they had been taken and were angrier and more uncomfortable with each passing day.

The complex maneuvers carried out in this frenetic atmosphere guaranteed considerable stress and strain. Vesco's tussle with Swiss legal authorities was one result. In the early summer of 1971, he moved to gobble up about 60,000 shares of I.O.S. preferred owned by David Tucker, the former I.O.S. sales director. Tucker had placed the certificates in I.O.S.'s Overseas Development Bank (Geneva) in order to collateralize a small loan of around $35,000. Vesco had become one of the bank's directors by virtue of his position with I.O.S., and he demanded the shares be turned over to him based on the incorrect premise the loan had defaulted. He used a heavy hand, physically browbeating bank officers into opening the safe and handing him the securities.[42] A few weeks later, Tucker lodged a criminal complaint on the theft of his shares. An investigation started, and in November, Vesco and two of his accomplices, Meissner and Ulrich Stickler, were called to testify. They did and were promptly thrown into a Swiss lockup charged with "disloyal conduct."[43] Word of their predicament flew to Vesco headquarters in New Jersey activating the channels of political influence. Harry Sears contacted Attorney General Mitchell, who asked the U.S. Embassy in Berne to help out. It complied, and the following day Vesco and the others were released on bail.[44] This Swiss affair, which infuriated Vesco, was quickly resolved. The complaining Tucker, after experiencing various unpleasantries, was finally given over $78,000. He then withdrew his complaint. This gave the Geneva Attorney General's office the opportunity to suspend the charges and refund the bail money.[45]

This was the kind of situation Vesco's political allies were able to handle with some ease. It was far less complicated than undermining the S.E.C.'s investigation. Nevertheless, the Swiss affair bore an unexpected price when Watergate investigators surveying the Vesco misalliances found Mitchell's fingerprints, so to speak, all over the evidence. It provided another link in the chain of shabby service to bribers that preoccupied the Attorney General.

Around this time Vesco took on another associate who became second only to the boss in villainy. This was Norman LeBlanc, a French Canadian and 1958 graduate of McGill University in Montreal. LeBlanc was an accountant employed in the Paris office of Coopers & Lybrand, one of the world's largest accounting firms, when he met Vesco. Coopers & Lybrand was involved in I.O.S. affairs and moved LeBlanc to Geneva in 1970 to work with the Cornfeld group on various deals. In the summer of 1971, LeBlanc was on I.O.S.'s payroll. Not long after, he had become Vesco's primary confederate.[46] The giant accounting firm had no cause to complain, for it too went to work for Vesco handling part of I.C.C.'s books. It did such a snappy job that a special counsel hired by I.C.C. after the Vesco theft concluded "that Coopers & Lybrand aided and abetted" the crooks "permitting the illegal conduct to continue unchecked."[47]

LeBlanc's accounting talents were enhanced by his links to Canadian racketeers, some involved in the international drug trade. This would later become known when Sam Peroff, an informant shared by the Bureau of Narcotics and Dangerous Drugs (B.N.D.D.) and the Customs Service, stumbled onto LeBlanc's, and more significantly, Vesco's Canadian heroin connection. The B.N.D.D. and the narcotic enforcement portion of the Customs Service were both reorganized during the midst of this affair and placed into the new Drug Enforcement Agency (D.E.A.), a part of the Justice Department. Peroff told his story to the Senate Permanent Subcommittee on Investigation. His chilling account was itself the subject of an intense investigation because of charges of D.E.A. corruption.[48]

Basically, Peroff, who had perfected many of his criminal tech-

niques and connections in The Bahamas, was working an organized crime heroin case involving major Canadian smugglers,
when it turned into a Vesco-LeBlanc affair. Vesco was supposed
to provide $300,000 to buy 100 kilos of heroin in Europe.[49] Peroff
reported this to his government control and suddenly everything
changed. Once Vesco's name surfaced, Peroff was in jeopardy.
He believed government agents were in league with Vesco and
the Canadians, and attempted to have him murdered. Thoroughly
frightened and underestandably suspicious of law enforcement,
he searched for help. In the fall of 1973 he turned to the Senate
committee for support and protection.[50]

Vesco and LeBlanc had a particularly close relationship with
federal drug enforcers. In 1972, cooperative drug agents from
California, Robert P. Saunders, a member of B.N.D.D.'s electronic surveillance team in Los Angeles, and Sergio Borquez, his
supervisor, flew to Vesco's New Jersey home and headquarters
to search for electronic bugs. Their mission was arranged and
paid for by Thomas Richardson, a Los Angeles stockbroker working for Vesco in 1969. He had become part of Vesco's "inner
circle" late in 1970, and sat as I.C.C.'s president and chief operating officer while Vesco was Chairman of the Board.[51] Richardson's contact in the Los Angeles B.N.D.D. office was John
L. Kelly, the Assistant Regional Director. With Kelly's approval
and Richardson's money, the two agents headed east one week-
end in June checking for any "government planted" electronic
listening devices.[52] Once other agents became aware of the Borquez and Saunders trip, they concluded Vesco and high level
narcotics officials were likely partners in large-scale smuggling
operations.[53]

With LeBlanc in the second spot, the Vesco team was ready
to finish off I.O.S. The Bahamas was central for this stage and
Vesco had to finish crafting Bahamian political alliances. Prime
Minister Pindling was critical, and Vesco had no difficulties given
their already established mutuality of interests. In the winter of
1969, Pindling, his former law partner Kendall Nottage, and Vesco
formed a new Bahamian bank called Columbus Trust. Four years
later, when Watergate investigators were pursuing Vesco connections, his shares were "transferred" to a young man named
Donald B. Aberle who became the bank's president.

Columbus Trust was initially used by Vesco for part two of his plot, which was the sinking of the I.C.C. ship as soon as all the I.O.S. assets had been removed. I.C.C. was Vesco's great filter through which the hundreds of millions sucked from Cornfeld's creation passed—it was a clearing house for I.C.C. money, which then was picked clean.[54] The bank was later revitalized with millions of cocaine dollars as The Bahamas became a transshipment center for tons of Colombian cocaine around 1975.

There was more than Colombus Trust and Butler's Bank in Vesco's Bahamian operations. He created an interrelated series of Bahamian companies designed to momentarily park and then move money around, and others that had an influence on the daily life of Bahamians. Amidst the "shelf" and "shell" firms were Central Garage Ltd., Michael Maura's Tourist Service, and the Cole-Thompson Pharmacies. These companies were run and staffed by native Bahamians making Vesco a local benefactor. Vesco also created his own banking empire in The Bahamas built around the Bahamas Commonwealth Bank, which he claimed was founded to provide capital for low cost housing mortgages. He realized the value of this role and often referred to his concern for the people. In an interview in 1973, he spoke of using Bahamas Commonwealth Bank to provide capital for low cost housing and mortgages. Bahamas Commonwealth was not, Vesco stated, another brass-plate transit bank: "It was established as a Bahamian bank to prosper with the growth of the Bahamas while at the same time helping local Bahamians."[55] Most of these future bootstrap plans remained totally ephemeral.

Bahamas Commonwealth was a bank with serious political purposes. It was used to buy influence with as much of the government as possible, making a specialty of financing projects for Progressive Liberal Party (P.L.P.) bigwigs. The bank loaned money to Pindling associate Garrett Finlayson so he could control the catering facilities at the airports in Nassau and Freeport. Another major loan went to a P.L.P. supporter to purchase a restaurant, and almost $1 million was given to P.L.P. Chairman, Andrew Maynard, for two bottling companies. Approximately $14 million was "donated" by Vesco to the party through the simple device of phony loans to Bahamas World Airways.[56] And so it went, until approximately $30 million was spread over Pindling's friends, associates and party machinery. On the social side of the ledger, this spending had a considerable "trickle down" effect. It was a hefty investment in Bahamian businesses, helping to bring more locals under his sway, and tying their economic futures to Vesco's ventures.

All this was critical for Vesco and the Prime Minister, who was preparing The Bahamas for independence. In anticipation of that event, Pindling had called for elections in September 1972, which would serve as a referendum on the independence question. Vesco was a major contributor to the P.L.P. campaign chest, giving $200,000 in cash outright and upfront, and millions under the table.[57] Vesco expanded corruption on vertical and horizontal planes, laying the groundwork for the country's leap into the cocaine business.

Vesco was a supreme juggler with an ever increasing number of companies, politicians, mobsters, twirling in the air. While perfecting his Bahamian alliances, stealing everything not bolted down, he was also constantly trying to block the S.E.C. probe. It had tentatively started in January 1971 and was officially ordered three months later. Vesco tried bribery, intimidation, and legal "falderol" to check the Commission, but nothing worked. Barely two months after the inquiry opened, he had Sears write Attorney General Mitchell for help. This was the connection that expertly handled the Swiss problem, and Vesco couldn't quite grasp its difficulties with the S.E.C. Sears initially asked Mitchell to lean on S.E.C. Chairman William Casey, later President Reagen's C.I.A. chief.[58] Subsequently, Casey met several times with one of Vesco's lawyers, but was unwilling to do more than listen.[59] Casey and Vesco were not strangers to one another. In fact, they had a business connection, which Casey preferred to keep quiet, involving a firm called Multiponics. It had been founded in 1968 to perfect hydroponic farming, soilless agriculture. Casey was the largest investor, legal counsel, and corporate secretary; Vesco one of the largest investors. Multiponics, which owned around 40,000 acres, principally in Louisiana, went bankrupt like so many companies touched by Vesco. An inquiry into its failure indicated some shoddy practices on Casey's part.[60]

Maintaining and energizing the political arrangements in The

Bahamas and Washington, trying to handle the S.E.C., pushing the awesomely complex I.O.S. and I.C.C. strategy forward, working a drug deal here and there, did not tire Vesco out. He was so addicted to action, that his next desire was perhaps the most natural of all. He wanted his own casino.

On 27 January 1972, he announced at an I.C.C. meeting in New Jersey that he planned to buy Resorts International. His interest in acquiring Paradise Island was stirred by stockbroker Richard Pistell, the early booster of Crosby-Miller, then Mary Carter Paint, and finally Resorts International. A close friend of Crosby's, Pistell had been one of the money movers finding investors for the original Mary Carter and Resorts amalgamation. He had a large block of Resorts stock stemming in part from shares in its predecessors.[61] Vesco also must have had a healthy share of Resorts through his grab of I.O.S., which was a major Resort investor, primarily through the "hinky" Fiduciary Trust. In the 1967 private sales of Resorts stock, I.O.S. subsidiaries purchased more than half of those sold.[62]

Pistell, the ultimate insider, was Resorts' major negotiator in the Vesco deal, and clearly someone working both sides of the street. Prior to entering the talks, Pistell had picked up $4 million from I.O.S. funds, under Vesco's personal control, for two projects. And while he worked for Resorts, he also represented Gil Straub and other Vesco people in a reputed $10 to $12 million deal for a Moroccan resort. Additionally, Pistell introduced Vesco to Costa Rica and its president, Jose Figueres, and then brokered an unsecured loan for more than $2 million from one of Vesco's I.O.S. companies, to one partially owned by the Costa Rican president.[63] Pistell was almost as intimate with Vesco as he was with Jim Crosby of Resorts International.

In the early 1970s, Resorts, which was fearful of Bahamian independence, and thus insecure over keeping its casino license, looked for a buyer. Pistell introduced Vesco to Crosby and the bargaining began. The talks went on for some time, partly because Vesco wasn't the only suitor. When Vesco expressed serious interest in purchasing Resorts, Howard Hughes was still around in his darkened chamber on the ninth floor of the Britannia Beach Hotel.[64] There was still the possibility, however remote, that the goofy billionaire might buy the whole place.

Vesco's move on Resorts was carefully watched by Tradewinds operatives. They were especially intrigued because there was an organized crime angle to the negotiations. Vesco thoughtfully included the Cellini brothers (Dino and Eddie) in his Paradise Island calculations. To get them interested, he had already paid a $50,000 "finder's fee" to gambler Jimmy Neal for an introduction to Dino. They met in Rome at the Fiumicino airport in July, 1972.[65] In reports back to Jaffe, Sally described Neal as a Lansky operative specializing in junkets and slot machines for several Bahamian casinos.[66] She added that Neal was close to the Cellinis, and then noted that sometime after Eddie finally left The Bahamas, he had gone to Colombia to run a small but unprofitable casino. Sally wondered if this casino covered other illicit activities like cocaine trafficking. She also established that Jimmie Neal visited Colombia so often, he appeared to her a commuter between Miami, Paradise Island, and Eddie's Colombian casino.[67] Sally suspected the Cellinis, and therefore Lansky, might be a hidden force behind Vesco.[68]

Much of Sally's speculation about Neal's relationships with professional criminals was confirmed by New Jersey's Casino Control Commission in its 1978 investigation of Resorts. Neal, whose real name was Loia, had been an illegal bookmaker and subsequently a major junket operator to Paradise Island, personally approved by Resorts executive, H. Steven Norton.[69] Moreover, he was associated with the Cellinis and Canadian racketeer Albert Volpe, one of three brothers among Canada's organized crime elite. Albert's specialty was stock promotions and financial crime, while his older brother, Paul, commanded a loose confederation of professional criminals operating in extortion, the construction industry, loan-sharking, gambling, illegal diamond deals, and land frauds. From late in 1969 until 1978, their prime operating areas were Toronto and Ottawa in Canada, and Atlantic City and New York in the United States.[70]

Neal's affiliation with Vesco lasted beyond his Resorts period well into his Costa Rican interlude. Neal and other racketeers worked with him in the munitions business. One of their arrangements in 1974, involved Marti Figueres (the son of Costa Rica's president), Mitch Werbell III, and Gordon Ingram, two well-known American arms merchants. The delivery of weapons to

Central America was handled by Neal's brother-in-law, Dominic Salerno, formerly a cashier at the Paradise Island casino (as was Neal's brother).[71] These transactions took place while Neal and Eddie Cellini continued their association with Paradise Island through a junket company known as Tourist Entertainment Enterprises.[72]

The selling of Resorts International was a major topic of conversation in The Bahamas during the summer and fall of 1973. In November, a two-tiered deal for Paradise Island was struck. Gulf Stream (Bahamas) Limited, a Vesco subsidiary with Gil Straub as president, was to buy the casino and toll bridge—the only significant Paradise Island moneymakers—for about $25 million. Half of Gulf Stream would go to the Bahamian government to guarantee a peaceful future. The rest of Paradise Island, the hotels, restaurants, golf course, some undeveloped land, and other bits and pieces, which produced nothing but a "negative cash flow" and seemed to Sally run down, tattered, and so much untended junk, was to be sold to another Vesco firm.[73] But just as the bargain was concluded, it suddenly failed.[74] The S.E.C. filed a civil fraud complaint against Vesco in the Federal District Court in Manhattan that month, and Resorts could not afford to openly deal with him.[75]

Interestingly, when the deal fell apart, the casino company claimed it had been fortunate to fail. Crosby said there had been a change in atmosphere and attitude toward investors on the part of the Bahamian government, and Resorts now was confident of the future. While the Bahamian operation looked a good deal healthier because of a change in the government's attitude, still the company's earnings for the coming year depended on how well Resorts' "Marine World theme park," located close to San Francisco, did. Certainly Crosby hoped it would enable Resorts to shake off the doldrums experienced by the company's lack of real estate sales in The Bahamas. They sold hardly anything at all.

Vesco was quite distressed over his failures to buy Paradise Island and stop the S.E.C. Neither Vesco's past political cronies nor his new Caribbean friends, particularly in Costa Rica, were able to muster enough support to stop the action, although they tried. Only the past July, Costa Rica's President wrote a strong letter to President Nixon urging help for his friend and business associate unfairly bothered by the S.E.C. President Figueres said:

> Vesco has been visiting Costa Rica with a view to helping us establish some new instruments of finance and economic development. . . . I am impressed by his ideas, . . . He may provide the ingredient that has been lacking in our plans to create in the middle of the Western Hemisphere, a show piece of democratic development. . . . Vesco has had difficulties with the Securities and Exchange Commission, . . . John Mitchell, your former Attorney General, is familiar with the matter. I am concerned that any adverse publicity emanating from the S.E.C. against Mr. Vesco might jeopardize the development of my country. . . . This matter is of importance to our two countries.[76]

Figueres mentioned that Vesco had recently introduced him to Nixon's brother, Edward, who was invited to visit "our country." However pleased Nixon was to hear from Figueres in the summer of 1972, it wasn't long before Vesco and many others were causing him a dreadful headache. The Vesco and S.E.C. matter, his $250,000 cash contribution to Nixon's 1972 campaign, his relationships with the president's family, all became part of the Watergate hydra.

A year later, amid the crumbling ruins of his presidency, Nixon watched as Vesco, John Mitchell, and Maurice Stans, former Commerce Secretary and head of CREEP's finance section, were indicted on criminal charges. Government prosecutors argued that Vesco's $250,000 contribution was a bribe given to get Mitchell and Stans to "pull the plug" on the S.E.C. investigation. But the prosecutors were unable to produce Vesco for the trial, and without his testimony winning the case was quite impossible. At the end of April, 1974, Mitchell and Stans were found not guilty of obstruction of justice, perjury and conspiracy.[77]

This was not the exoneration some claimed it to be. The government's case had been critically weakened by Vesco's absence, and he wasn't there because U.S. authorities suspiciously failed in their attempt to extradite him from The Bahamas. Vesco's extradition was formally requested on 9 June 1973. The final decision was made in December. Led by the U.S. Attorney from Manhattan, the Americans tried to pry Vesco loose from The Bahamas on the wrong charge. Bahamian records state the extradition application was refused "for the reason that the offense or offenses of 'wire fraud' with which Robert Vesco was charged in the United States had no counterpart in Bahamian law,"[78] There never was the slightest chance Vesco would be extradited on the grounds presented and U.S. authorities knew that. Moreover, no "fresh application for extradition on the basis of a charge which was a criminal offense both under the laws of the United States and The Bahamas" was made.[79]

No one seriously questioned the conclusion that Vesco's extradition was a farce. Daniel Oduber, Figueres replacement as Costa Rica's president, confirmed it in an extraordinary public letter to Robert Vesco on 6 May 1974:

> I want to tell you [Oduber said to Vesco] that friendly governments have kept me informed on possible legal actions against you and your firms, *but at no time has your expulsion from the country been requested*, . . . Now that a new government is beginning in which no one—I repeat, no one—among its members can be accused of being a shareholder in firms in which you are also one, the situation is different and the country will be able to see more objectively the problems caused by your arrival in Costa Rica. As I told you before, friendly governments have kept me informed about the controversies concerning companies that you temporarily headed, and others which you still head. There are two areas in which those controversies are situated. In the criminal area they may result in a request for extradition. *It was attempted once, but in such a way that it seemed aimed at the extradition failing, just as it did*.[80]

President Oduber warned Vesco to obey the law, to stop flouting Costa Rican customs requirements, importing unknown and unexamined, "merchandise," and to leave his government alone or get out.[81]

The United States clearly did not want him back, although he reportedly has returned every once in a while to visit in New Jersey and Florida.[82] How often he illegally entered the United States is relatively unimportant compared to his continuing impact on crime and politics, whether from The Bahamas, Costa Rica, Panama, or now Cuba.[83] Vesco moved munitions, drugs, and money around the world, and made a major try at corrupting the Carter Administration. One part of his intricate tactics employed during the Carter years included a Libyan gambit. Vesco worked out a three-way deal for the release of planes paid for by Qaddafi, but embargoed by the Department of State, when Libya was sanctioned as a terrorist state. The arrangement called for Vesco, and supposedly certain members of the Carter Administration to split $15 million paid by the Libyans, who would finally get their planes. Vesco's Libyan partner, he said, was Major Abdul Salaam Jalloud who was Qaddafi's Deputy, the number three man in the government. Following meetings in The Bahamas between several of the principals in the plot, two planes were released. Later when these schemes became part of a Senate scrutiny, some of those involved claimed the planes were released because Libya "agreed to provide in writing assurances that the aircraft involved in the sale would not be used for military purposes." On such thin reeds were major foreign policy decisions made, or retrospectively made to stand upon.[84]

Even though Vesco currently lives in Cuba under the protection of the Cuban Intelligence Service, his real home still seems to be The Bahamas. Nowhere else was he more fully appreciated. Indeed, when Vesco was finally placed on The Bahamas' Stop List (the foreign press was vigorously investigating the drug trade at the time), a local group came forward and petitioned the government to allow him to stay. The National Progressive Committee (N.P.C.) led by William "Life" Curtis and Samuel Miller, both close friends of Pindling, wrote: "We of the NPC feel that the only humanitarian and civilized thing to do is to grant Mr. Vesco some status in this Commonwealth." The reason was his vast contributions "made to the Bahamian people both individually, severally, and jointly and . . . to the Commonwealth of the Bahamas as a whole." Finally though, the spokesmen for the ephemeral National Progressive Committee argued he must be allowed to stay because he was a man who "loves" The Bahamas.[85]

Vesco had won the admiration of many ordinary Bahamians. However, neither "Life" Curtis nor Sam "Daddy-O" Miller of the National Progressive Committee were just plain folks. They were, or shortly became, two of the new drug entrepreneurs springing forth from the Bahamian population. A few years after the plea for Vesco, Curtis was wanted by American authorities on drug charges, which he dismissed as a "harmless hoax," a spoof he pulled on the D.E.A. He never meant smugglers could really use a particular island airstrip for cocaine importation if he was given an $80,000 payoff. Miller, on the other hand, was caught in the United States and, joke or not, was convicted in this same case.[86] The effusive statement about Vesco made by the National Progressive Committee was simply crass bunk. Yet, there is no denying it was the truest expression of the consequence of Vesco's generosity with other people's money.

Vesco was one of a kind. His action, along with the watches on the Lansky crowd, Resorts, and Howard Hughes, was enough to keep Operation Tradewinds working full tilt. But soon there was much more, as Jaffe chanced upon Castle Bank in the midst of all this.

Notes

1. U.S. District Court, Southern District of New York, *Securities and Exchange Commission, v. Robert L. Vesco, et al., Report of Investigation by Special Counsel*, 72 Civ. 5001 (CES), 23 November 1977, p. 235.
2. Ibid., p. 236.
3. Delafield Capital Corporation, *John M. King—I.O.S. Ltd. $40,000,000 Financing Agreement Confidential Memorandum*, May 1970.
4. J. Jay Frankel, Vice Chairman, Delafield Capital Corporation to Harry S. Oliver, Jr., The Bank of New York, "Letter of Instructions," 13 May 1970. On Dundee and Castle see Ron Wilson, Special Agent IRS, to Richard E. Jaffe, Special Agent Miami Group 902, "John King—DBA: Dundee International Corporation, 6 May 1976.
5. U.S. District Court, *Sec v. Vesco*, p. 237.
6. Robert A. Hutchinson, *Vesco* (Praeger, 1974), p. 10.
7. Hutchinson, *Vesco*, p. 11.
8. Ibid., p. 13.
9. Ibid., p. 14.
10. Ibid., p. 15.
11. Ibid., pp. 16–17.
12. Ibid., pp. 18–19.
13. U.S. District Court, *SEC v. Vesco*, p. 117.
14. Ibid., pp. 117–118.
15. Ibid., pp. 80–81.
16. Ibid., p. 52. The introduction took place sometime in the early to mid–1960s; in the beginning, Straub and Vesco had some small business interests in The Bahamas. Straub was probably already at

work there, but his deals were unsuccessful and nondescript. One was a land development project on Eleuthera Island which collapsed when Straub's property title was challenged. Hutchinson, p. 48.

17. Ibid.
18. U.S. District Court, *SEC v. Vesco*, pp. 83–84.
19. Ibid., p. 61.
20. Hutchinson, p. 48.
21. U.S. District Court, *SEC v. Vesco*, p. 53.
22. Hutchinson, 210–211.
23. James Leasor, *Who Killed Sir Harry Oakes?* (Houghton Mifflin, 1983), p. 7.
24. Sally Woodruff, "Report on Allan C. Butler," for INTERTEL assigned 28 March 1972.

    Eventually this company was bought by a Canadian firm in which Lou Chesler and his son were the major stockholders. The Butlers worked with Chesler and many others mentioned earlier including Inge Mosvold of Mercantile Bank and Trust. Mosvold and the Butlers had a project to develop low-cost housing mortgages for The Bahamas. This was an idea whose populist value attracted Vesco's attention and he later proposed but never implemented it.
25. U.S. District Court, *SEC v. Vesco*, p A–38.
26. Hutchinson, p. 5.
27. Ibid., pp. 4–7.
28. U.S. District Court, *SEC v. Vesco*, p. 56.
29. Ibid., p. 240.
30. Ibid., pp. 248–249.
31. ibid., pp. 249–250.
32. Ibid., p. 252.
33. Ibid., p. 262.
34. Ibid., p. 241.
35. Ibid., pp. 264–265.
36. Ibid., pp. 274–275.
37. To complete the transaction Vesco was forced to "seed" Butler's funds. He did it with a friendly $6.2 million deposit to a Butler account from the Arthur Lipper Corporation which expected, in return, either to handle half of I.O.S.'s future U.S. brokerage business or a $1 million a year consulting fee for five years. Ibid., p. 304. U.S. District Court, *SEC v. Vesco*, p. 304.

    Lipper soon learned Vesco wasn't going to live up to the bargain and withdrew his money from Butlers. Vesco countered the Lipper withdrawal with I.C.C. funds drawn from, among others, Electronic Specialty, one of the few viable Vesco companies.
38. Ibid., p. 325.
39. Ibid., pp. 318–319.
40. In the months following the Cornfeld stock purchase there was a brush-fire of protest from a group of ousted I.O.S. officers. Vesco

beat it out by using the power he held as Finance Committee Chairman. He also floated stories picked up by an eager press indicating I.O.S. was near collapse and I.C.C. was considering further help. It was the old stick and carrot routine again in which the press always plays a crucial role. Reporters presented other views and interpretations, but they couldn't possibly counter the impact of the bogus ones strategically placed by Vesco. For example, Vesco's line was disputed by a former I.O.S. executive who challenged the doom and gloom statements and bitterly noted "except for very short periods of time, I.O.S. actually had not required any outside financing, and that the loan from I.C.C. had been more of a burden than a benefit to I.O.S." Ibid., p. 331. This was absolutely correct, duly reported in the financial papers, and entirely beside the point. The dream factor of I.O.S. had been captured and was now being inexorably dismantled.

41. Ibid., p. 331.
42. Ibid., pp. 347–353.
43. Ibid., p. 355.
44. Ibid., p. 355.
45. Ibid., p. 357.
46. Ibid., p. 44.
47. Ibid., p. 775.
48. See U.S. Senate, Permanent Subcommittee on Investigations, *Staff Study of the Frank Peroff Case* (Government Printing Office, 1975).
49. Ibid., p. 209.
50. Meanwhile the newly formed D.E.A. tried to steal a march on the Senate committee by conducting an in-house investigation which concluded, not surprisingly, Peroff was wrong. The D.E.A. found there was no evidence to substantiate the charge narcotics and customs agents "attempted to discontinue an ongoing narcotics investigation when Robert Vesco's name was mentioned; that agents threatened and intimidated him; that someone, presumably the agents, burglarized his apartment in an effort to recover tape recordings mentioning Vesco's name. Ibid., pp. 2–3.

   The D.E.A. conclusions were challenged by the Senate committee which determined, after a careful examination, the heroin investigation failed because of the conduct of the drug agents and officials, not Peroff. Moreover, Peroff was correct in stating that Federal officials did not pursue the Vesco–LeBlanc connection: ". . . some Federal officials and agents conducted themselves in a highly unprofessional manner once the names of Vesco and Le Blanc came into the picture." Ibid., p. 197.
51. U.S. Senate, Permanent Subcommittee on Investigations, *Hearings: The Robert Vesco Investigation*, 22 July, 17 September, and 7 October 1974, p. 43; and U.S. District Court, *SEC v. Vesco*, p. 71.
52. Senate, *Vesco Investigation*, pp. 44–45.

53. Author's interviews with former Federal Bureau of Narcotics and I.R.S. Intelligence Division Special Agent John Daley, February 1984 and June 1986.
54. U.S. District Court, *SEC v. Vesco*, p. A29.
55. Oswald T. Brown, "Robert Vesco Breaks His Silence," *International Bahama Life*, June 1973, p. 14.
56. See Collin Higgins, "Vesco made 'large donations' to PLP," Nassau *Tribune*, 1984.
57. Hutchinson, p. 247.
58. Ibid., p. 368.
59. U.S. Senate, Committee on Banking, Housing and Urban Affairs, *Hearing: Nominations of William J. Casey and Ralph D. DeNunzio*, 12 December 1973, pp. 15–18.
60. Ronald Brownstein and Nina Easton, *Reagan's Ruling Class: Portraits of the President's Top One Hundred Officials* (Pantheon Books, 1983), pp. 619–620.
61. Sally Woodruff, "Documents from Resorts International including Schedules I–VII, Schedule V *Resorts International, Inc. and Predecessor Companies, Shares Issued on Conversion of Series A and B Subordinate Debentures*.
62. Ibid., "Schedule II."
63. Stanley Penn, "Some of Cash Vesco Allegedly Diverted Financed Ventures Promoted by Pistell," *Wall Street Journal*, 5 December 1972.
64. U.S. District Court, *SEC v. Vesco*, pp. 534 537–38.
65. Hutchinson, p. 272.
66. Sally Woodruff, "Report on Casino Operations in The Bahamas," 31 May 1977.
67. Ibid.
68. Sally Woodruff, "Report on F. Marvin and Betty Marion," 13 December 1972; and "Report on UNION PROPERTIES LTD., BUTLER–GRESHAM SECURITIES LTD., GRESHAM SECURITIES NASSAU LIMITED," 12 August 1974.
69. New Jersey, *Report*, pp. 57–59.
70. James Dubro, *Mob Rule: Inside the Canadian Mafia* (Totem Books, 1986), pp. 77, 85–86.
71. U.S. Senate, *Vesco Investigation*, pp. 110–112, 155.
72. New Jersey, *Report*, p. 59.
73. Hutchinson, pp. 289–81.
74. Ibid., p. 281.
75. "Resorts International Suggests Failure to Sell Casino Was Good Luck," *Wall Street Journal*, December 1972.
76. Hutchinson, p. 369.
77. U.S. Senate, Permanent Subcommittee on Investigations, *Staff Study of the Frank Peroff Case*, (Government Printing Office, March 1975), pp. 1–2.

78. Bahamas Commission of Inquiry Appointed to Inquire into the Illegal Use of The Bahamas for the Transshipment of Dangerous Drugs Destined for the United States of America, p. 70.
79. Ibid.
80. Senate, *Vesco Investigation*, pp. 113–114.
81. Ibid.
82. Author's Interview with William Metz, Attorney for Milton Meissner, July 1986; interview with Detective in the Intelligence Division of the Washington Police Department, May, 1986.
83. Bahamas Commission of Inquiry, p. 70; and Arthur Herzog, "Stalking Robert Vesco," *Fortune*, 24 November 1986.
84. See U.S. Senate, Committee on the Judiciary, *The Undercover Investigation of Robert L. Vesco's Alleged Attempts to Reverse a State Department Ban Preventing the Export of Planes to Libya*, Government Printing Office, September 1982, pp. 6–7.
85. "Group backs Vesco's bid to remain in Bahamas," Nassau *Guardian*, 18 April 1981.
86. *Miami Herald*, Special Report, by Carl Hiaasen and Jim McGee, "A Nation For Sale: Corruption in the Bahamas," 1985, p. 5.

6

Castle Bank

It was spring 1972 when Jaffe received a collateral request for aid and information from I.R.S. Intelligence in San Francisco. The subject was Allan George Palmer (also known as Allan Houseman), who was absorbed in the manufacture of LSD and the distribution of it and marijuana in the San Francisco area. Active since 1968, Palmer was a major producer of LSD, mescaline, and THC (another powerful hallucinogenic drug), and a "grass" dealer. The I.R.S. still had its Narcotics Traffickers Program; Alexander was still a year away from becoming the Commissioner. This program utilized a Target Selection Committee to choose individuals for investigation, and it had zeroed in on the green-eyed, blond, and mustachioed Palmer.[1] As part of the government's drive, Palmer and three others were arrested in Marin County, California, on 17 October 1971. Federal drug agents watched the conspirators unload around 900 pounds of "pot" from a private plane at the Oakland airport.[2] Indicted, Palmer skipped out on his trial, after which a "No Bail" bench warrant was issued for his capture.

Jaffe was brought into the Palmer affair because several checks the drug merchant received in May 1970, were drawn by a Bahamian bank on an account it maintained in the American National Bank and Trust Company of Chicago. (The Bahamian bank was identified as the Castle Trust Company, Inc. The name was changed in 1972 to Castle Bank and Trust Company Ltd.; other slight name changes followed. In common parlance it is called Castle Bank.) The checks worth $22,500 were found in the course of the drug investigation. San Francisco agents requested I.R.S. Intelligence in Chicago and Miami to pursue the money. The Chicago agents located the Castle account at American National and the signature card on file. There were nine names: A. Alipranti; A. R. Bickerton; L. A. Freeman; E. J. Foster; M. S. Gilmour; A. J. T. Gooding; H. M. Wolstencroft; Paul L. E. Helliwell; and Burton W. Kanter.

The first individual from the signature card list interviewed by the I.R.S. was Chicago attorney Burton Wallace Kanter. A special agent talked with Kanter on 16 March 1972, and the lawyer admitted he had introduced the Castle Trust Company, Ltd., to the American National Bank for the purposes of opening a checking account.[3] Asked about others on the signature card, Kanter indicated Gooding was Castle's president and a personal friend, and that Miami attorney Paul Helliwell was Castle's legal counsel. Kanter explained that he was only an Illinois tax consultant for Castle. He added it was unlikely the private bank would provide the I.R.S. with any information on Palmer. He didn't think he could possibly persuade it to cooperate.[4]

Kanter was lying. He and Paul Helliwell were the bank's master builders. They were its principal owners, its primary managers. Castle Bank was their scam, although not their only one. Additionally, both men, but especially Kanter, had direct ties to organized crime. Helliwell's outside interests tended to fall more often within the parameters of the C.I.A.

Burt Kanter was born in Jersey City, New Jersey, in the summer of 1930. Illinois, however, was to be his bailiwick. He was educated at the University of Chicago, receiving an undergraduate degree in 1951, and an LLB the following year. He became a teaching associate for a couple of years at the University of Indiana Law School. Kanter next clerked for two years for Judge Morton P. Fisher of the U.S. Tax Court.[5] Kanter had been a superior student with the potential to be an exceptional lawyer specializing in tax issues. In time, he was admitted to practice before the U.S. District Court, the Court of Appeals, the Court of Claims, the Tax Court, and the Supreme Court.[6]

Kanter joined the David Altman firm on South La Salle Street in Chicago as an associate in 1958. The firm concentrated on federal taxation, estate planning, wills, and trusts. It was headed by Altman, who had worked for the I.R.S. in the Chief Counsel's Office, and later its Office of Division Counsel from 1938 through 1943.[7] Another associate, Gerald W. Brooks, had more extensive I.R.S. experience. Brooks was at one time the Assistant District Counsel, then Assistant Regional Counsel for the Service in charge of appellate matters.[8] In 1963, Kanter and Milton A. Levenfeld, another graduate of the University of Chicago Law School, became partners in the Altman firm.[9] The next year, Kanter and Levenfeld broke from Altman and started their own firm, which became a powerhouse with exceptionally strong I.R.S. connections.

When Kanter was contacted in 1972 by the special agent for discussion about Castle, the firm had grown in both size and prestige. The senior partners were Kanter, Levenfeld, Charles A. Lippitz, and Roger S. Baskes. According to Martindale and Hubbell's directory of attorneys, there were fifteen lawyers working at Levenfeld, Kanter, Baskes and Lippitz in 1972, including Elliot G. Steinberg, who was titled a resident member of the firm practicing in San Francisco.[10] Not listed was Kanter's partner Joel Mallin in midtown Manhattan.[11]

In the period when Resorts was created, Kanter (like Mallin) was very active in The Bahamas shaping up Castle Bank. He was also energetically at work in California on one of the largest resort projects in the Golden State. Kanter and Richard K. Janger, a young attorney from his firm, were the registered agents for the La Costa Land Company.[12] An Illinois corporation created in 1968, its purpose was to aid in developing Rancho La Costa, a resort and country club complex north of San Diego first planned in 1963.[13] The La Costa undertaking also involved racketeer Moe Dalitz, a principal in the Desert Inn, and, as mentioned previously, a member of the Cleveland syndicate. Working closely with Dalitz and other Rancho La Costa investors were fraudster Allard Roen, also from the Desert Inn, and like Dalitz an investor in Meyer Lansky's enterprises, and Clifford Jones, Nevada's former Lieutenant Governor. Jones' organized crime connections were impeccable; he had been an original Bank of World Commerce partner.[14] In order to move the project along, provisions were made to bring in one of Lou Chesler's top real estate salesmen at the proper time.[15]

The La Costa Land Company received funding from a foreign investment group headquartered in The Netherlands and from the Teamsters Central States Pension Fund. Teamster money for La Costa eventually came to about $50 million.[16] The arrangement was strikingly reminiscent of the 1964 "Rancho Penasquitas/Cosmos Bank/Teamsters Pension Fund settlement. The Department of Labor perceived this in 1975 after formally studying the Pension Fund's organic relationship to organized crime, using data collected during fifteen years of investigations.[17]

They found that Pension Fund loans traditionally went to risky resort ventures involving organized crime. In the 1950s, these developments were around Miami Beach. The action then moved to Southern California and Las Vegas. Two of the latter loans mentioned in this context were the ones to La Costa and Penasquitas. In 1976 the Fund was worth around $1.4 billion. Of that sum, $902 million was in real estate and collateral loans. An examination of a portion of the Fund's real estate portfolio—82 loans worth $518 million—revealed $425 million went to seven entities controlled by three men with organized crime connections. They were Allan Robert Glick, Morris Shenker, and Alvin Malnik.[18]

Kanter's access to the Pension Fund likely came from Allen Dorfman, a friend and business associate. Murdered in 1985 to prevent him from talking about mob investments, Dorfman was an important Fund official and racketeer. He was considered by government investigators the primary mover of Pension Fund loans, particularly after Jimmy Hoffa went to prison.[19] Dorfman was in the same league as Glick, Shenker, and Malnik.

In early 1972, I.R.S. knowledge about Castle Bank was minimal. There was the Palmer connection, the American National Bank account, the names on the signature card, and the little that Kanter told. Special agents rapidly learned more. After the Kanter talk, the Chicago agent pulled American National's bank statements specifying the Castle account. The 1969 and 1970 figures showed Castle maintained a sizeable commercial account; deposits were as large as one million, and several were in the $200,000 to $500,000 range. The account's size aroused I.R.S. interest beyond the issue of Palmer's funds. "We are," wrote the Intelligence Division Supervisor from San Francisco, "concerned about the source of funds being deposited by Castle Trust Company with the American National Bank in Chicago."[20] Soon, it was determined that Castle had accounts at two other Chicago banks, Continental Illinois National and First National. There was also evidence that requests from Castle to Chicago ordering cashier's checks were disbursed to associates of organized crime.[21]

A $70,000 cashiers check, for example, was issued to Yale Cohen, a convicted felon and known gambler from Cleveland and Newport, Kentucky. Cohen received Castle Bank money while he was the manager of the Stardust Casino in Las Vegas, and an associate of Chicago mobster Anthony Spilotro, who was shot to death in 1986. Further probing turned up other Windy City mob connections in the Stardust. The pit boss was a Chicago gambler close to Chicago crime czar Sam "Momo" Giancana, and Jimmy "The Weasel" Fratianno, one of his henchmen (famous now as an informant). In addition, there were numerous money transfers between Castle and a Chicago investment firm indicating money laundering on behalf of Tony Accardo, yet another Chicago crime boss.

The spotlight on the Stardust Casino also illuminated Cleveland racketeer Morris Kleinman. It had been Kleinman, along with his partners Moe Dalitz, Sam Tucker, and Lou Rothkopf, who formed Cleveland's primary organized crime syndicate during Prohibition. After repeal, this Cleveland mob joined with Lansky and his confederates controlling numerous rackets and businesses. This expanded group was so criminally creative that they formed the core of the most sophisticated national crime syndicate in America. The Kleinman material found in the Castle Bank probe revealed his partnership in a company called Karat, Inc., which operated the Sardust Casino until it was sold in 1969. More importantly, it was detected that Kleinman's attorneys were Kanter and Helliwell.[22]

At this time, the I.R.S. also discovered just who brought drug dealer Palmer into Castle Bank. The evidence was developed by Norman Casper, a new Tradewinds operative. The Palmer connection was made by Roger S. Baskes, a senior partner in the Kanter firm. On 11 May 1970, he wrote to Castle opening Palmer's account. The instruction from Baskes also notified the Bahamian office that a Castle depositor called Seven Seas Brokerage had agreed to lend Palmer's account (number 4084) an additional $10,000 without interest.[23]

Casper's original source of information was F. (Francis) Eugene

Poe, the president of two small South Florida banks at Perrine and Cutler Ridge, which were affiliated through a holding company, and often called the Bank of Perrine-Cutler Ridge. Paul Helliwell was the actual boss of both banks. In addition to Poe's stateside banking, he was also a Castle Bank director. He was in his mid–40s when Casper made his pitch telling Poe he was investigating narcotics. The suspect was Palmer, and Casper asked the banker for assistance. Poe had known Casper for almost twenty years, and believed the line that he was working undercover for the federal narcotics bureau. Poe was glad to oblige.[24]

With Casper's help, Jaffe determined that Castle, with its own bank accounts in Chicago, South Florida, and New York, was an underground conduit for untaxed money. Through Gene Poe, it was learned that drug merchant Palmer had personally brought some of his money south to the Perrine-Cutler Ridge Bank for deposit in a Castle account. Most importantly, Jaffe discovered that Palmer's money never actually left the United States. The cash stayed in the Castle account at Perrine-Cutler Ridge. Jaffe thus suspected Castle merely provided bookkeeping services, crediting and debiting accounts in which the funds remained in the States. He wrote, "when the depositor requires them again, a debiting entry is made in Nassau with a check or cash paid out by the Miami bank charged only to the CASTLE TRUST account thereby providing the anonymity of the transaction."[25] That Castle was actually operated in the United States was a potentially significant conclusion. It meant that Castle was not really a foreign bank, and myriad criminal charges might follow for the owners as well as depositors.

The question of Castle's true situs was clearly recognized by the Castle people as soon as the I.R.S. served a summons on the Chicago bank for its Castle records. The response in Nassau was interesting and immediate. Castle's resident managers applied to the Bahamian government for a name change, and more significantly, a general banking license that would at least legitimize transactions for outsiders. This was clearly and patently illegal under their existing Bahamian license, and the applied-for-charges would help mask that it was a foreign corporation working on American soil.[26] Castle secured the name change (from Castle Trust to Castle Bank & Trust Ltd.), but not the desired unrestricted banking license. Their operating license had been issued on 12 May 1971 and had the following restrictions: "a) it [Castle] carries on no banking business with the public; and b) it only carries on banking business for its shareholders and persons, firms or corporations affiliated with or controlled by its shareholders."[27] Castle's owners knew that restriction B might prove extremely troublesome if ever their depositors became known. It was a ticking bomb leading to the explosive conclusion that Castle was a foreign entity run by Americans in the United States.

Castle Bank had two poles of ownership and management: one was in Chicago with Kanter and his firm; the other in Miami, where the main force was the stout, chain-smoking, asthmatic, Paul Lionel Edward Helliwell, the Chairman of the Perrine-Cutler Ridge Banks and, so Kanter said, counsel to Castle Bank.

Helliwell was born in Brooklyn, New York, in 1914, and like Jaffe moved south. He attended the University of Florida as an undergraduate and then law school, graduating with an LLB in 1939. During his last two years in law school, Helliwell joined the Reserve Officer Training Corps (R.O.T.C.) and was appointed a Second Lieutenant upon graduation. He was called to active service on 26 August 1941.

Helliwell's vocation was Military Intelligence and he served in the Army's G–2 Intelligence group in the Middle East, later transferring to the Office of Strategic Services (O.S.S.) as Chief of Intelligence in China, commanding 350 Army and Navy personnel and thousands of Asians.[28] In the O.S.S., founded and directed by William J. Donovan (also correctly credited with being the "progenitor" of the Central Intelligence Agency[29]), Helliwell earned several high decorations.[30] China and Southeast Asia were his prime areas, and there he was involved in matters of great importance. It was Helliwell and members of his O.S.S. group who had contact with Ho Chi Minh during the latter days of the war.[31] Ho Chi Minh and Helliwell had three meetings between January and the end of March 1945. Ho asked for arms and ammunition to fight the Japanese; Helliwell refused unless Ho gave categorical assurances the weapons would not be used against the mutually despised French. They deadlocked over the issue, and nothing much was done. The only weapons given Ho by the

O.S.S. in China, were six revolvers personally handed over by Helliwell after Ho's guerrillas rescued American flyers shot down in Indochina.

When the O.S.S. disbanded at the end of the war, Helliwell became Chief of the Far East Division of the Strategic Services Unit of the War Department until the spring of 1946. This was an interim intelligence unit bridging the gap between the O.S.S. and the C.I.A., which was created in 1947.[32] After Helliwell was mustered out of the military, he joined a small Miami law firm, Bouvier, Helliwell & Clark, specializing in real property, insurance, tax, trade regulation, and similar matters.[33] General corporate law kept the firm moderately busy. The rest of Helliwell's time was taken by the C.I.A. In the beginning, his C.I.A. activities centered on Asian problems, brought to mind by the famous and controversial Major General Claire L. Chennault, known as an "acerbic warrior, at odds with his superiors for decades."[34]

Chennault was one of the first exponents of the Southeast Asian domino theory of Communist expansion. The doctrine went like this: Mao's victory in China would result in massive Communist support for Ho Chi Minh in Indochina, causing the French to fall; then, like tipping dominoes, the regimes in Thailand, Burma, Malaya, and perhaps India would topple to the Communists. Finally, the Pacific from the Bering Sea to Bali would feel the inexorable pressure of Communist imperialism, unleashed and unchecked.[35] Chennault had a plan to stop this catastrophe of his own imagination. Through the skillful use of air power, supplying war material to the indigenous anticommunist Chinese, coupled with the employment of American military advisers for training and planning, Chinese communism could be contained, thus saving Southeast Asia. The necessary logistical support would be furnished by certain civilian airlines, such as the Civil Air Transport (C.A.T.) owned by Chennault and a partner.

There were few takers in Washington for Chennault's plan, even though he had the lobbying help of attorney Thomas G. "Tommy the Cork" Corcoran, an early FDR brain-truster, zealously committed to New Deal policies until he found how lucrative the other side was. Corcoran was then known for sleazy influence peddling, questionable lobbying tactics, and backdoor deals.[36] Chennault was stymied until his friend Paul Helliwell intervened.

It was Helliwell who broke the impasse by suggesting to Frank Wisner, an important C.I.A. official, that he use C.A.T. for Southeast Asian operations. The powerful and well-placed Wisner was in charge of the Office of Policy Coordination, a covert action organization somewhat tenuously tied to the C.I.A. in 1948–1949 but entirely within it a few years later.[37] Wisner agreed, and requested Helliwell to figure out a clandestine way to subsidize the airline, which was at that moment in desperate financial trouble.[38]

In the autumn of 1949, a formal agreement was reached and signed by Corcoran for his airline and a C.I.A. representative from the Office of Finance.[39] Helliwell helped construct the C.I.A.'s commercial cover organization for the airline and its Southeast Asian covert missions. This was the Sea Supply Corporation set up in Florida with its main office in Bangkok, Thailand.[40] In 1952, Helliwell's law firm became general counsel for Sea Supply. That same year Helliwell was made the general counsel for the Royal Consulate of Thailand.[41] Naturally, the C.I.A. controlled the Consulate. Under the stewardship of C.I.A. functionaries such as Helliwell, Sea Supply did far more than cover the C.A.T. operations. It also channeled assistance to the Thai Chief of Police who was implicated in the region's extensive opium trade. With Sea Supply's help, the Chief built a police force of 42,835 men which rivalled, most likely surpassed, the Thai army in organization, pay, and efficiency.[42]

Helliwell also worked C.I.A. operations in the Caribbean area as early as 1953–1954. In those days the target was Guatemala and its government, led by President Jacobo Arbenz, which was overthrown by the Agency. Helliwell worked closely with the main architects of the Guatemalan coup, which included Wisner and Corcoran, now on the United Fruit payroll as a lobbyist. It was the C.A.T. team joined by other spies like E. Howard Hunt (later of Watergate infamy), which carried out this action, far more in the economic interests of the United Fruit Company, than the national security interests of the United States.[43]

Helliwell was not yet finished with the C.I.A. In 1961, a C.I.A. army of Cuban emigres disastrously invaded Cuba at the Bay of Pigs, one of the island's least hospitable spots. The operation was an unmitigated failure and an international scandal. Helliwell's role in this affair was that of paymaster. The Bay of Pigs brought together several of the C.I.A. men who had triumphed in Guatemala and formulated much of the Thai campaign. Their common root was the O.S.S. and China under Helliwell's command.

In addition to his espionage activities during the 1950s, Helliwell became a well known political lawyer. He was among the key organizers for the Republican Party at a time when it was little more than a curiosity in Florida. Helliwell was instrumental in carrying the state for Eisenhower in 1952, thereby contributing to the rise of the national Republican Party in the former solidly Democratic South. Around Florida, Helliwell was called Mr. Republican.[44] The making of Florida's Republican Party also brought Helliwell into close contact with Bebe Rebozo. They became companions and attentive associates from then on.[45]

In 1954, Mary Jane Melrose was hired as an associate. This argumented the Helliwell firm's political bent. The Pennsylvania born (1919) Melrose, a 1953 University of Miami law school graduate, was a Young Republican National Committeewoman when hired and remained one for several years.[46] By 1956, she was a partner and the firm was named Helliwell, DeWolf, Melrose & Sanderson.[47] Melrose rendered an important service in the firm's Bahamian associations. She took a leave of absence in 1969, moving to Freeport where she worked directly for DEVCO.[44] From that point through 1976, Melrose was alongside Gerald Goldsmith during the crucial period of political change modifying Freeport's unique status. She served as the vice president, secretary, and director of the Port Authority and Freeport Commercial. After the struggle between Pindling and the Freeporters, Melrose was vice president, general counsel and, director of Intercontinental Diversified.[49] She worked very closely with Goldsmith in arranging the payoffs to the Prime Minister with money diverted from Intercontinental Diversified through Castle Bank.

While Norm Casper worked Poe and his other sources, and the Special Agents roamed through Chicago accounts, Jaffe had Sally Woodruff busily mining Bahamian records. Her task was to plot Castle's history, to outline its permutations, and figure out its connections. This was Sally's specialty in the same manner as espionage and subversion was Helliwell's.

Jaffe asked Sally to focus her research and analytical talents on the mystery bank. Shortly after, Sally learned Castle was formed in Freeport on 8 October 1964. Its officers were nominee shareholders from a Bahamian attorney's office.[50] The 1965 annual return showed some consequential personnel changes, and one item of abundant interest. Sally discovered a Castle connection to the Mercantile Bank and Trust; it owned one of the five shares of Castle stock. The Mercantile Bank, which boasted of being the first locally-owned bank in Freeport, was Castle's parent company. Sally naturally wondered why a bank would form another bank. Wouldn't they be rivals, she pondered in a communication to Jaffe. Perhaps Castle was really a subsidiary of Mercantile, but then she asked why would they call it Castle instead of the Mercantile Merchant Bank or something similar? On the other hand, what if they formed Castle for a particular client? Possibly, she thought, but why not run the operation as other banks do through their trust department?

The Freeport bank was itself probably formed from the Cayship Investment Company of Panama and several other companies owned by billionaire D. K. Ludwig. However, the paper trail indicated Mercantile was founded by Inge Gordon Mosvold, an extremely wealthy Norwegian shipbuilder. Sally concluded, as did others, that Mosvold was partly fronting for the even richer Ludwig in the Mercantile companies.

The bank originally was the Mercantile Bank of the Americas Limited, registered on 11 January 1962. It became the Mercantile Bank and Trust in November of that year. The officers and directors were several nominees from the attorney's office, the Norwegian shipping magnate Mosvold, and Keith Gonsalves, one of the original settlers in Freeport who appears in many of the early companies. In 1964, the shareholders were three firms—Cayship Investment Company Incorporated, in Panama; Security (Bahamas) Limited; Cia. De Navegacion Mandinga S.A., a Panamanian company with a Nassau address; and two office nominees.

Company records in 1965 produced Sally's critical lead on Castle's origins. They showed Paul Helliwell had become a Mercantile director.[51] That made the Castle puzzle part of a Helliwell offshore banking complex, which hooked into various wealthy and secretive types like Ludwig. Sally was unaware at this time that

Kanter and Helliwell had known each other since the late 1950s; that they had met while working on a deal between a Kanter client and Mosvold, represented by Helliwell.[52] Apparently they got along well. A few years later, Kanter even opened an account for his mother at Helliwell's Bank of Perrine.[53] It is also certain, as Roger Baskes later emphasized, that from its founding in 1964, the Levenfeld & Kanter firm worked closely with Helliwell's firm.[54] Moreover, it was Burt Kanter, more so than Helliwell, who was instrumental in Castle's formation. Years after the fact, Kanter revealingly commented "It was originally organized per instructions for the organization from a client of mine in conjunction with the organization of several companies." When Kanter made these remarks he was no longer able to remember the name of the local lawyer who did the actual incorporating. And citing the lawyer and client privilege, he would not divulge his client's identity.[55] Speculation held that it was racketeer Morris Kleinman.

For Sally, innocent of the Kanter and Helliwell relationships, and certainly of Kanter's client and his role in the founding of Castle Bank, her first keys to the riddle were Helliwell and Mercantile. The 1965 Mercantile officers, she reported, were Mosvold, Helliwell, Gonsalves, Karl Glastad from New York, and several others from Freeport. The Mercantile company file showed relatively little action over the next few years. However, in 1970, two new officers appeared: Gene Poe was one; the other was Peter A. Tomkins, a Cayman Islands banker. The annual return, as well as the appearance of Tomkins, reflected the opening of a Mercantile branch in the Cayman Islands.

While searching and arranging material on Mercantile, Sally discovered another Helliwell bank. This was the Bank of the Caribbean Limited registered in The Bahamas on 10 December 1963. Sally spent time running down leads on this bank hoping information from one Helliwell project would shed light on the others.

This particular bank was even more mysterious than most, and ultimately Sally thought it probably was involved in Intelligence matters. It was also in some ways a mirror image of Castle. The Bank of the Caribbean, registered by Mosvold and other Mercantile people in 1963, with Helliwell somewhere in the background, was picked up two years later by a client of Helliwell's law firm. This was an insurance conglomerate with suspected ties to the C.I.A. in Southeast Asia. In 1968 the bank changed name and hands. Its new name was Underwriters Bank Limited and its directors were people associated with Castle Bank, including Helliwell and Anthony James Tullis Gooding (called Jim or Tullis by Kanter and Helliwell), May Gilmour, and Ernest J. Foster.[56] Gooding was a British subject with many years residence in Argentina as well as The Bahamas. He had his own business, Gooding & Company, which was interwoven with Castle and several other related firms, and he was the primary manager for Underwriters Bank. Gooding was also on the Castle signature list found in Chicago; he was subsequently identified by Kanter as Castle's president.[57]

Meanwhile, Sally's Castle research indicated Castle was not activated until 1967 when new officers and shareholders came on board. The increasingly busy Jim Gooding became president, and Ernest J. Foster, a chartered accountant formerly with Touche, Ross & Company, became Castle's new vice president (and soon a director of Underwriters Bank). Gooding and Foster were joined at Castle by A. Alipranti and G. Bebas, two Greek executives supposedly resident in Athens, who were both listed as Castle directors. Alipranti was also reported as the bank's secretory. The four new officers each owned a share of Castle stock. The required fifth share was held by a Panamanian firm named Fomentos. Castle was clearly preparing for business and moved from a "shelf" in Mercantile's Freeport office to its own quarters in the lovely Norfolk House in downtown Nassau.[58]

From 1967 on, those who owned Castle Bank were engaged in an ongoing fraud, a major criminal conspiracy. The managers of Castle Bank had first of all deceived the Bahamian government by creating two wholly fictitious shareholders and bank officers; namely Alipranti and Bebas, likely conjured up by Helliwell and Kanter. Bebas was totally imaginary according to a close Helliwell associate, Colonel Demetrius Stampados. Friends since the O.S.S., Stampados later worked in the Mercantile companies and Helliwell's law office. Stampados recently remarked that Alipranti may have been a Greek marathon runner before the turn of the century, and, if so, was dead for decades prior to Castle's founding.[59] Every time a legal document, such as a Deed of Settlement, was signed with the names Bebas and Alipranti, the fraud compounded itself. The same was true when the two Greeks were listed as Castle officers, directors, or shareholders as in the 1970 company registration forms.

Once Castle primed itself for commerce, major developments followed. In 1968, the shares owned by the Panamanian company jumped to over 35,000 and the following year Gene Poe and Columbus (Chris) O'Donnell became Castle officers. Sally wrote to Jaffe that Castle must have been pleased to land O'Donnell who was Huntington Hartford's nephew, and probably had some rich contacts for the bank. O'Donnell's mother was thought to have retained "every penny" of her inheritance and was considered by the Castle conspirators a "great heiress," unlike her strange, spendthrift brother Hartford.[60]

When O'Donnell joined Castle he was contemporaneously employed by the Deltec International banking firm headquartered in Nassau, a firm listed on the New York Stock Exchange, which was formerly "the principal investment banking firm that organized financing for Brazil and Argentina."[61] Around this same period, O'Donnell also went to work for Resorts International as a special assistant to Jim Crosby. O'Donnell was not quite finished with his many pursuits. In 1972 it was reported that he formed a trust company along with Robert Vesco.[62] A very busy man by all accounts, whose employment record and family connections touched many of the key players and institutions in Bahamian affairs, O'Donnell's first Resorts International assignment was the creation of a private bank called Vortac. This bank was formed to lend money to South American entrepreneurs, similar, in that respect, to Deltec International. But according to I. G. Davis of Resorts, Vortac never really developed because the advantageous interest rate structure, upon which its lending ability rested, collapsed soon after the bank was formed.[63]

Castle Bank had a markedly nervous propensity for change. "I think I could safely say," remarked Sally, "that I've never seen such a restless company. I don't think they ever went a full year without a change of directors."[64] Her insight was confirmed on 27 November 1970 when the "ghostly" Alipranti resigned as a diretor. The Castle board added two Nassau residents as officers. H. M. Wolstencroft became the trust officer, and lawyer Lawrence A. Freeman a vice president. The following year the "spirit" Alipranti quit as secretary and was again replaced by Freeman.

Sally's information, combined with the documentary material from Chicago, San Francisco, and Miami, plus Casper's contributions, gave the I.R.S. a large cache of Castle documentation. Late in the summer of 1972, the I.R.S. summarized what it had: twenty-one identified Castle directors, officers, and shareholders; over half a dozen Castle commercial accounts in American banks; several organized crime associations and four narcotics targets; many prominent U.S. citizens involved in stock transfers to Castle, which then acted as their trustee; and six American brokerage and investment companies, which paid Castle dividend income. The I.R.S. intended to start a grand jury investigation in the very near future.[65]

Before that happened, Gene Poe gave the I.R.S. its single greatest investigative opportunity. He paved the way for Casper to actually get inside Castle Bank in Nassau. It was quite casual. One day at the Bank of Perrine, Poe introduced Casper to Samuel B. Pierson, the relatively young, somewhat unkempt, slightly walleyed, tall, and heavy-set president of Castle Bank. (Pierson's presidency, which sort of flip-flopped with Gooding's, only lasted a short time—part of that nervous restlessness Sally commented on.) Poe told the president of Casper's good anti-narcotics work. Sam then wrote a note on the back of his business card to Castle officer Mike Wolstencroft. The message said—"Mike, give this man any thing he wants." Casper was inside Castle by October 1972.

During this autumn visit to Nassau, Casper learned of important Castle changes then being discussed. There had been an internal squabble over closing down the bank in The Bahamas and moving the operation to the Cayman Islands. This was the period when many investors and businesses prepared to leave The Bahamas in the wake of Pindling's smashing 1972 electoral victory, and in anticipation of independence from Great Britain. No matter how reassuring Pindling may have appeared after his 1970 speech calling for national independence, which was known locally as the "bend or break" announcement, a great deal of commercial uneasiness remained. The financial future of The Bahamas looked bleak for some, and hazardous for others.

Castle in the Bahamas, was not closed, despite Sam Pierson's push for the radical Cayman solution. Instead, a half-way remedy was accepted at a meeting held in Florida. This meeting was dominated by Helliwell, with either Kanter or an attorney from his firm in attendance. The Nassau facility would remain, but a new Castle Bank in the Cayman Islands must be prepared to take over at a moment's notice. Moreover, all Castle records were to be duplicated and copies sent to Grand Cayman for safe-keeping. The Castle conspirators were so security conscious at this time, they also placed copies of account records in the vault at the Canadian Imperial bank.[66] Pierson was to leave Nassau and operate Castle from an office in the Bank of Perrine, although, ever mindful of an I.R.S. summons, no records would be kept in Miami. The Pierson move was probably predicated on the desire to avoid any hassles over Bahamian work permits.

Another personnel decision made at this time in response to the changing Bahamian conditions concerned Gene Poe. He was dropped from the Castle board in order to open a slot for a Bahamian, as the government was insisting on more local participation. Poe was retained as a consultant. Wolstencroft related that these alterations were implemented in case business was disrupted by the government. Castle feared the possibility of sudden and abrupt Bahamian nationalization, the final reason why complete business records had to be maintained in Grand Cayman.[67]

On this October trip, Casper's infiltration paid dividends. He was given a look at the Castle office, which included their small IBM data processing facility. They were only learning the system, he was told, and they certainly knew nothing about "system security." Casper was asked if he could recommend something in that line. He coolly responded yes, in an off-handed, slightly bored way. Among the items Casper saw was an IBM printout several inches thick with lots of corporate and individual names. Left alone for a moment, Casper casually thumbed through it.

While doing so, he was genuinely shocked to read the name Richard Nixon on the Castle printout. Later, under trying conditions, Casper would state that he had no idea whether the Richard Nixon entry he saw was actually for President Nixon, or whether someone had put the name there as a joke.[68] At the time, however, Casper believed he had stumbled onto one of the most important investigative leads on political corruption in the history of the United States.[69]

Beside the Nixon name, Casper also noticed others, such as Moe Dalitz, familiar to him as a racketeer. When he excitedly reported his findings to Jaffe, he was asked if he could possibly obtain more names? Casper wanted to know if Jaffe would like the printout. Of course, Jaffe replied. From that moment on Casper sought a solution, a way to produce either the list or the information.

The method came about through his friendly relationship with Wolstencroft. Since they first met, Wolstencroft confided to Casper an interest in extra-marital female companionship.[70] He often travelled and asked Casper to get him dates in Miami.[71] Casper demurred just a bit and then agreed to help. Wolstencroft and other Castle people frequently commuted from Nassau to Chicago to straighten out the bank's confused books with the Kanter firm's help. The confusion in accounts between Nassau and Chicago was partially caused by the new computer system which befuddled many.[72] They also mistrusted the Bahamian government's postal service. Castle, therefore, had instituted a policy of hand-carrying important documents to Miami and Chicago, rather than using the mail.[73]

The opportunity to get the account list came in the winter of 1972–1973. Wolstencroft planned another Chicago trip, and asked Casper to arrange a date for him in Miami. Such arrangements were routine by then. Casper suggested he see Sybil Kennedy, a woman he had introduced to Wolstencroft a few months earlier. Wolstencroft thought it a fine suggestion and called her. The Castle officer had not the slightest idea she was a former police-woman who was now a free-lance operative aiding Casper. It was known to Casper that Wolstencroft would be carrying the account list and other important Castle documents in his locked leather briefcase when he arrived in Miami on 15 January 1973. The papers included, he believed, a complaint intended for Kanter's consideration, stating that Pierson and Helliwell were misman-aging Castle.

Casper shaped a plan. He instructed Kennedy to bring Wol-stencroft from the airport to her apartment. On the way, she was to recommend dinner at the Sandbar restaurant on Key Biscayne—a place over at least an hour's distance. Casper was confident Wolstencroft would leave the briefcase in the apartment. He notified Jaffe in a memorandum on 9 January that Wolstencroft would be in Miami on the fifteenth, adding that there was an excellent chance the material could be obtained. The scenario did leave dangling a potential legal problem. Casper discussed this dilemma with Kennedy. He didn't wish to commit a burglary to get the briefcase. Her response was what he expected, direct and helpful: "Here is the key to my apartment. If I am out to dinner, anything in the apartment is yours."[74]

Two days before the anticipated event, Casper spoke to Jaffe and presented him the plan in detail. He said he would enter the apartment with the key and take the briefcase out. At that point Jaffe told him to stop; he could't and would't authorize this plan without first checking with his superiors and getting their permission. Later that day, Jaffe told him to proceed; the plan was approved.[75] On the night of the fifteenth, the operation went off without a hitch. Casper grabbed the briefcase and took it to another location where a locksmith made a key to open it and then to where Jaffe was waiting. It was then opened and the account list photographed and microfilmed.[76]

The documents were wondrously revealing—the master list of accounts had the names and numbers of over 300 individual and company clients, and other material found within the briefcase had the identification and location of around 39 U.S. brokerage accounts for Castle.[77] Jaffe and those involved in this operation were well pleased. They had turned an offshore bank inside out.

In the rush of success, Casper and Kennedy worked out a scheme to pluck the Castle rolodex out from under the easily distracted eyes of Wolstencroft. This was needed to further identify many of the names on the Castle account list. Kennedy flew to Nassau and ripped it off. Casper than presented it to Jaffe who hadn't any notion this last maneuver was in the works. Nevertheless, he was pleased to have it.[78]

From the moment the film was developed, Jaffe and the I.R.S. Intelligence Division were busy figuring out what they had and how to proceed. This was to be an enormous project and coordination was imperative. The first difficult problem was the identification of the accounts, many of which were in names like

Pythagoras, Helwan, Emanon, Topaz, and Inversiones Mixtas. Once that was accomplished, they would have to assign investigations and cases to the appropriate I.R.S. districts. There was a mountain of satisfying work ahead.

Getting inside Castle Bank was the Intelligence Division's alpha and omega. For the first time ever, it possessed the inner workings of a functioning tax haven. It didn't matter that Castle was just a modest size operation in comparison with others in The Bahamas and elsewhere (with total accounts valued at approximately $250 million). What was important was knowing how these havens functioned; identifying the creators, managers, and depositors; uncovering exactly how mob money was converted into legitimate investments and repatriated; and gaining a better idea of the scope of the problem. Castle's records could do that plus give some measure of the vitality of the "underground economy." Shaking Castle's tree, it was also believed, would send shivers up and down the spines of the "underground economy's" many patrons. Moreover, it was time, I.R.S. intelligence thought, for the "wheeler-dealers" to face prosecution. This was potentially among the most fruitful enforcement coups in I.R.S. memory.

That was the cheeful news. The bad news was slower coming. Those seeking to protect Castle perceived a weakness in the operation. All the evidence from the "briefcase caper" they would argue later, was tainted; it was inadmissable in court, deriving as it did from inexcusable conduct on the part of the Intelligence Division. That argument would be enunciated time and again by Commissioner Alexander as he used Casper's "caper" in this battle with the Intelligence Division. Over the next few years, every detail of the Castle Bank affair would be scrutinized by a widening audience, some sympathetic to Jaffe's coup, others quite the opposite. But before that happened, the investigation rolled on, oblivious to the coming furor.

Notes

1. Paul H. Wall, Group Supervisor, Intelligence Division, San Francisco District to District Director, IRS, Attn: Chief, Intelligence Division, Jacksonville, Florida, *Memorandum Subject: Allan G. Palmer 94–22–179–4–7 (NTP)*, 22 May 1972.

2. *San Francisco Examiner*, "Half Ton of 'Pot' Jails Four," 18 October 1971, p. 3.
3. Paul Wall, *Memorandum*.
4. Ibid.
5. Martindale and Hubbell, *Law Directory*, 1958; p. 1189.
6. Cayman Conferences Limited, Cayman Islands Tax Seminar 1974, "Biographies of Speakers—Burton W. Kanter, et al."
7. Martindale and Hubbell, 1958.
8. Ibid.
9. Ibid., 1963; p. 1753.
10. Ibid., 1971; pp. 254B–255B.
11. Chairperson, Judicial Council of California, Judicial Council Co-ordination Proceedings No. 1040, San Francisco Superior Court No. 764340, Santa Barbara Superior Court No. 121771, "Musical Group Investment Cases, Proceedings Re: Deposition of Burton Kanter," 10 December 1981, p. 756.
12. On Janger see Martindale and Hubbell, 1969; p. 223B.
13. Phil Manuel, *"Chronology: Possible Infusion of Foreign Funds into Rancho La Costa."*
14. Ibid.
15. Ibid.
16. U.S. Senate, Permanent Subcommittee on Investigations, *Oversight Inquiry of the Department of Labor's Investigation of the Teamsters Central States Pension Fund*, Report No. 97–177, (Government Printing Office, 1981), p. 8.
17. Ibid., pp. 7–8.
18. Ibid., p. 33.
19. Ibid., pp. 8–9.
20. Ibid.
21. Intelligence Division (Miami) to District Director of Internal Revenue, Attn: Chief, Intelligence Division Jacksonville District, "Memorandum: Joint Compliance Program, Quarterly Narrative Report," 7 July 1972.
22. Norman J. Mueller, "Summary Report, Castle Trust Company, Nassau, Bahamas," 5 September 1972, p. 4. Also see Musical Group Investment Cases, "Deposition of Burton W. Kanter," Vol. VI, 10 December 1981, p. 888.
23. Intelligence Division (Miami) to Chief Intelligence Division, San Francisco District, "Collateral Reply," 27 June 1972.
24. Musical Group Investment Cases, "Deposition Summary of Normal L. Casper."
25. Ibid., p. 2.
26. Intelligence Division (Miami) to District Director of Internal Revenue, Chief Intelligence Division, Jacksonville District, "Joint Compliance Program, Quarterly Narrative Report," 7 July 1972.
27. Sally Wooddruf, TW-5, "Report on Castle," 23 June 1972.
28. U.S. War Department, M.I.D., "HELLIWELL, Paul L. E." 26

September 1946, in William J. Donovan papers, U. S. Army Military Institute, Carlisle, PA.

29. Anthony Cave Brown, *The Last Hero: Wild Bill Donovan* (Times Books, 1982).
30. U.S. War Department, "HELLIWELL," 26 September 1946. They included the Oak Leaf Cluster to the Legion of Merit, the Asiatic Campaign Medal with two bronze stars, and similar awards for outstanding Intelligence work in Egypt.
31. Paul L. E. Helliwell to Bernard B. Fall, Department of Modern Languages, Cornell University, "Letter," 14 October 1954, in Donovan papers Box 9A.
32. William R. Corson, *The Armies of Ignorance: The Rise of the American Intelligence Empire* (Dial Press, 1977), pp. 221–290.
33. Martindale and Hubbell, 1949; p. 453.
34. William L. Leary, *Perilous Missions: Civil Air Transport and CIA Covert Operations in Asia* (University of Alabama Press, 1984), p. 3.
35. Ibid., pp. 67–68.
36. Bob Woodward and Scott Armstrong, *The Brethren: Inside the Supreme Court* (Avon Books, 1981), p. 88.
37. Leary, pp. 70–71.
38. Ibid., p. 72.
39. Ibid., p. 82.
40. Ibid., p. 129; and Martindale and Hubbell, 1952; p. 661.
41. Ibid.
42. Noam Chomsky and Edward S. Herman, *The Washington Connection and Third World Fascism* (South End Press, 1979), pp. 220–222.
43. Stephen Schlesinger and Stephen Kinzer, *Bitter Fruit: The Untold Story of the American Coup in Guatemala* (Anchor Books, 1983), p. 119.
44. Author's interview with attorney Donald E. Van Koughnet, Naples, Florida, May, 1985.
45. Van Koughnet interview.
46. Martindale & Hubbell, 1954; p. 797.
47. Ibid., 1956; p. 920.
48. Ibid., 1969; pp. 2391B–2392B.
49. Board of Directors of Intercontinental Diversified, "Report of the Audit Committee," 15 November 1979, pp. iii–v.
50. In registering a Bahamian company there must be a minimum of five company shares held by five entities, usually nominees from the local attorney's office doing the incorporting. These shares are not typically reflective of a bank or company's real owners, although they can provide important leads, which is what happened with Castle.
51. The records were slightly ambiguous and it was not clear whether Helliwell was with Mercantile at the start or joined after a year or two, although the former seems probable.

52. Musical Group Investment Cases, "Deposition of Burton W. Kanter," Vol. VI, 10 December 1981, pp. 756–758.
53. Ibid., p. 774.
54. Musical Group Investment Cases, "Deposition of Roger S. Baskes," Vol. 1, p. 108.
55. Musical Group Investment Cases, "Deposition of Burton W. Kanter," p. 130.
56. The 3 January 1969 annual report showed the following company personnel and ownership:
American International Underwriters—9,995 shares;
Paul L. E. Helliwell—1 share;
A. J. T. Gooding—1 share;
May S. Gilmour—1 share;
Ernest J. Foster—1 share;
Ron E. Strange (a chartered accountant)—1 share.

57. There were several reasons why Sally suspected Underwriters Bank was a CIA proprietary: its ownership by the American International Underwriters Overseas company (renamed in 1970 the American International Reinsurance Company and headquartered in the off-shore insurance capital of Bermuda with subsidiaries in Australia, Argentina, Belgium, Brazil, Colombia, West Germany, Guatemala, South Africa, Thailand and Venezuela), believed to have had a hand in Intelligence work in Southeast Asia; its management by Helliwell with his known spy background; and finally its shift to Gooding who Sally believed worked for American, and possibly British Intelligence from time to time. See Sally Woodruff, "Documents on #6289 Underwriters Bank Limited," n.d. The scenario didn't seem far fetched, and it was the kind of enigma she found almost irresistible.
58. Sally Woodruff to Dick Jaffe, "Report on Castle Trust," June 1971.
59. Author's interview with D. G. Stampados, Orlando, Florida, 17 July 1986.
60. Musical Group Investment Cases, "Deposition of Roger S. Baskes," Vol. II, 20 October 1981, p. 167.
61. Ibid., "Deposition of Burton W. Kanter," p. 798. Some of the information on O'Donnell came from my interview with him in the summer of 1987 at his office in Resorts International, Atlantic City.
62. Musical Group Investment Cases, "Testimony of Samuel Pierson," 5 April 1983, p. 118.
63. New Jersey Department of Law and Public Safety, Division of Gaming Enforcement, "Testimony of I. G. Davis," 1979, p. 81; Author's Interview with Colombus O'Donnell, July 1987.
    Vortac was unknown, even to Tradewinds, until one of the agents accidently stumbled upon it. While visiting another bank in an office

building, an operative noticed an empty office across the hall with three telephones and a telex—Vortac Bank. Securing the telephone number and telex listing, and asking Bahamian authorities to identify them was no help. The authorities could not find the telephone or telex listing in their records, and thought the telex "may be operating illegally." TW-5 to Jaffe, "Resorts," 19 September 1973.

64. Sally Woodruff, "File: Castle Bank–Gooding–Mercantile."
65. Norman J. Mueller, "Summary Report, Castle Trust Company," 5 September 1972.
66. Musical Group Investment Cases, "Deposition Summary of Norman L. Casper," p. 4.
67. TW-24, "Memo to File," 13 October 1972.
68. U.S. House of Representatives, Subcommittee of the Committee on Government Operations, *Oversight Hearings into the Operations of the IRS: Operation Tradewinds, Project Haven, and Narcotics Traffickers Tax Program*, 94th Congress, first session, 6 October, 4 and 11 November 1975 (Government Printing Office, 1976), pp. 157–158.
69. Ibid., p. 179.
70. The compact Scot, born in 1932, educated at Trinity College, Glenalmond, Scotland, and years later at Sir George Williams University in Montreal, Canada, where he earned a Bachelor of Commerce degree with a major in General Administration, was married and had a ten-year old daughter at the time of his request to Casper. See Herbert Michael Wolstencroft, "CURRICULUM VITAE," in author's possession.
71. House of Representatives, p. 159; and TW-24, "Memo to File . . .," 13 October 1972, p. 3, attached to Jaffe "STATUS REPORT: Castle Trust, et al.," 30 October 1972; and, "Affidavit of H. M. Wolstencroft" taken by the IRS in the Commonwealth of The Bahamas, 13 January 1976.
72. House of Representatives, p. 160.
73. Musical Group Investment Cases, "Deposition Summary of Norman L. Casper," p. 5.
74. House of Representatives, p. 177.
75. Ibid., p. 178.
76. Musical Group Investment Cases, "Deposition Summary of Norman L. Casper," p. 7.
77. Intelligence Division (Miami) to Chief, Intelligence Division, Jacksonville District, "Castle Trust, et al., and Operation DECODE, Briefing Summary," 29 March 1973.
78. Musical Group Investment Cases, "Deposition Summary of Norman L. Casper," pp. 7–8.

7

Inside Castle

The evidence collected by the I.R.S. was more than sufficient to initiate a new special project separate from Operation Tradewinds. At first it was called DECODE, an acronym for Detection and Exposure of Concealed Overseas Deposits for Evasion. But shortly after it began in June, 1973, the use of acronyms was discouraged. DECODE became Project Haven, descriptive and straightforward.[1] The Project Haven field managers were Jaffe and David L. Ellison from the Intelligence Division, and Gerald Z. Applebaum from Audit. They gathered the Castle Bank material in order to shape the many-linked investigations and eventual prosecutions. The Service was confident cases could be made against Castle for failing to file as a foreign corporation conducting business within the United States, and against many of the depositors for tax evasion, or at minimum not reporting their foreign bank interests. Castle's American owners and directors were targets for conspiracy offenses.[2]

They also kept a close watch on Castle personnel, especially the lonesome Wolstencroft. He was tailed in Miami, New Orleans, Chicago, and San Francisco. Sometimes the surveillances were very extensive. The precedent for Haven surveillances was set in anticipation of Wolstencroft's mid-January trip to Miami and then Chicago. The I.R.S. arranged to follow him in Chicago, assigning 27 special agents to monitor his every action.[3] They tailed him on 16 January, the day after his briefcase was snatched, to Kanter's South La Salle Street office.[4] Keeping Wolstencroft in sight eventually paid off. In 1976 the Castle officer was charged with participation in a swindle based on phony silver options, refining contracts, loan advancements, and equipment options.[5] Castle was integral to the scheme. It was the offshore depository for investors' funds, most of which were apparently kept by the conspirators. After his indictment, Wolstencroft stayed out of the United States and a warrant for his arrest was issued by the federal court in Dallas.[6] He never returned.

As far as the Haven investigation was concerned, Wolstencroft was only a subordinate, a means to an end. His job, the I.R.S. knew, was to try and keep some order in the bank's relatively untidy affairs. The computer system had brought chaos. Wolstencroft plaintively wrote to Helliwell one day that "We are currently trying to devise a system of numbering which will eliminate all the inherent problems of different locations, different types of account and even different currencies."[7] He was a $36,000-a-year file clerk and messenger. The prime players were the lawyers behind the Castle conspiracy and the other major depositors who were clients of the Kanter and Helliwell firms.

Castle was not an organized crime bank in the way the Bank of World Commerce had been. That bank was formed by racketeers as part of a complex casino laundering scheme, though it may have had other purposes as well. Castle was a tax haven first and foremost, formed by lawyers who had mob connections, and used from time to time to launder illicit funds generated by some, like Palmer, and others, like Hitchcock. Its real job covered the panoply of white-collar crime hiding otherwise legitimate profits, aiding in financial frauds, evading taxes, and investing in various projects for its clientele, most of whom were not from the ranks of organized crime.

To understand Castle's business requires more than the 1972 master list of accounts foolishly carried by Wolstencroft, and purloined by Casper. It provided a cast (Kanter, Helliwell, Roger Baskes, Milton Levenfeld, Mary Jane Melrose, Morris Kleinman, Moe Dalitz, Billy Hitchock, Joel Mallin, etc), but it lacked any particular information concerning the accounts themselves. The master list is mute about the nature of Castle's investments as trustee for its depositors, the partnerships, and the quantity and flow of money. Fortunately, the account list can be supplemented by what were thought to be securely hidden Castle files left in the Cayman Islands by Helliwell and Kanter.

The two partners decided they had to cover their trail after publicity from Project Haven erupted in the mid-1970s. Files were reviewed in The Bahamas and many were sent to Castle Cayman, including documents from Helliwell's trust (numbered 705095), which were received in Grand Cayman on 2 March 1976. Other Bahamian documents were destroyed. In August 1976, Kanter, aided by Wolstencroft, spent about three weeks shredding bank files in Castle's Bahamian office. Helping them was Dorothy Ann Strachan, who was employed by Castle from 1973 through September 1976 as a receptionist, telex operator, and file clerk in what she called "the filing and shredding room."[8] She participated in the file destruction under the explicit direction of Kanter and Wolstencroft. To make doubly sure the files could never be reconstructed, the shredded material was bagged and burned.[9]

The Cayman end of the cover-up was handled differently. Helliwell contacted Castle Cayman's resident director, Tony (Anthony R.) Field, and told him that Kanter would be down in a few days to go through the expanded "Cayman Trust files."[10] Kanter flew down and instructed Field to put all the files in a conference room for review. When the review was completed, he told Field to destroy some documents, to put others back in the office files, and to hold another batch in special security. Instructions dealing with these documents followed by telephone from Helliwell. Field was told to buy a "very secure, fire-proof safe or filing cabinet" for the selected files, put them in and lock it. Then he was to place the cabinet with one local attorney, Ian Paget-Brown, and the key with another. This arrangement was to last for several years.

The cabinet, filled with selected documents, ultimately was taken from the Cayman Islands by Florida attorney Donald E. Van Koughnet, who represented several Castle employees including Tony Field. Told about the special material in the early 1980s, Van Koughnet made up his mind to secure the cabinet. With permission from his client Tony Field (the legal owner of the file cabinet), he persuaded the Cayman attorney holding the cabinet to relinquish it. The 800 pound cabinet was driven to the Cayman airport and flown to Miami. Once secure in Florida, the lock was drilled out.[11] Documentary material on investments and partnerships, money transfers, and bank policy was at last available. There was now indisputable proof of the closeness between Kanter and Helliwell and how they directed Castle Bank affairs. What made this so convincing, of course, was that the documents had been pre-selected by the conspirators themselves.

Castle catered to the financial needs of racketeer Morris Kleinman. On 21 September 1970, Settlor Hans Bossard from Zug, Switzerland, and attorney Paul Helliwell established the Gizella (Kleinman) Family Trust with $10,000 at Castle. It was assigned account number 706076.[12] Within days, Castle Vice President Larry Freeman sent off a revealing letter to the Bahamas Controller of Exchange, noting that the Kleinman trust "will participate in certain business activities in affiliation with either or both Compania de Fomentos Internacionales S.A. or Mr. A. Alipranti."[13]

While this was occurring, both Helliwell and Kanter were already avidly at work with another Kleinman trust account (T–1157) held by Mercantile Bank. A number of their deals involved Florida real estate. Kleinman's trust had bought in 1969 a 50 percent interest in 344 acres located in South Dade County called the "Doral Property" or SR–27 (State Road 27).[14] The other half was split equally between one of Kanter's Castle accounts (T–5075) and one of Helliwell's (T–5095).[15] The nominee or Trustee for the property was Ralph C. Datillio, a member of the Helliwell law firm in Miami.

Mercantile Bank was in some confusion over the Kleinman account, which was characterized as quite an involved Trust, and advised Kanter and Helliwell of certain problems. The response to these problems wasn't seen as adequate, and Mercantile complained to a Bahamian law firm about Kleinman's trust, stating the bank wanted to straighten it out, but Kanter resisted.[16] The problems stemmed from a complicated series of deals between Mercantile and Castle involving Kleinman, Helliwell, Kanter, Roger Baskes, several other Trusts (M. K. Revocable, Everglades 1 through 5), and the Doral property. At some point in this process, Wolstencroft sent Kanter copies of correspondence and documentation dealing with Kleinman's Castle account.[17] It was finally put right at the end of January 1972, when Mercantile received a Castle Bank Certificate of Deposit worth $135,000. This money came to Castle from a firm named Sheridan Ventures headed by Kleinman's nephew.[18]

For awhile the Doral real estate caused no more problems. The trustee for the property during this less contentious period was Helliwell's Administrative Assistant, Maria Theresa Cueto. Mortgage payments were sent to Helliwell from Castle. The checks, around $44,000 a quarter, were made out to M. T. Cueto, Trustee. Castle, under the direction of Helliwell, drew the mortgage money from Morris Kleinman's account. Negotiations to sell the real estate started in 1972, and the contract was finally settled in February, 1974.[19] The property was bought by Maule Industries, controlled by Maurice Ferre, the Mayor of Miami. There were several Ferre-owned Maule companies, including one in Freeport in which Lansky's associate, Max Orovitz, had an interest.[20]

The Doral sale caused another group of problems to surface as correspondence between Wolstencroft and Cueto make clear. Over a year and a half after the sale, Wolstencroft pointed out to her that Castle was still missing money from the deal. He noted the bank received $2,173,786 which made the bank short by $40,988. "We are anxious to finalize this matter," he said tactfully.[21] He was tactful because Morris Kleinman was the beneficiary of most of the money from the Doral sale.

Alert to Kleinman's interests, Castle shifted his money around for his benefit. As part of this Doral deal, for instance, Castle deposited $1,000,000 with the First National City Bank in Nassau. The million earned $83,694 in interest, which First National was authorized to transfer to the Irving Trust Co. in New York. There the interest was deposited into Castle's account number (4161590).[22] Later, it was wired out of New York and laid to rest, at least temporarily, in Kleinman's Castle account.

Kleinman, Helliwell, and Kanter had numerous real estate investments in common. Helliwell and Kleinman each owned half of a 20 acre tract in South Dade County, which ended up in the path of a proposed new superhighway. The State of Florida took almost seven acres of the property for around $57,000. The money kept flowing in. Kleinman added a $200,000 certificate of deposit to his Mercantile account (T–1157), and received $22,500 in interest for a matured CD at Castle. By the end of April 1972, his Mercantile account had a balance of $430,545.[23]

An unexpected complication occurred around this time, causing Castle employees a great deal of worry. In 1972, Mercantile Bank went into a financial tailspin, making it imperative to move certain accounts out of Mercantile and into Castle before they were wiped out. Apparently, Kleinman's Mercantile account was among those saved by transfer to Castle. This was probably accomplished at the vigorous urging of Kanter. On this matter, Castle president Sam Pierson had an intriguing tale to tell. He stated "Mercantile was on the verge of going broke at that point, and Kanter had clients, trust clients in Mercantile, . . . we had to support that bank so that it didn't go broke because those clients had certificates of deposit with Mercantile."[24] When the rescue effort was completed Castle took over the troubled Mercantile accounts— "in other words, if they had a CD, Mercantile CDs, they were exchanged for Castle CDs on a one-for-one, par basis."[25] Kanter's urgent advocacy was explained to Pierson by Paul Helliwell: "'If you don't do it, Kanter will end up face down in the Chicago River. We have to do it.'"[26]

Mercantile's downfall began as early as 1969, when the bank made several substantial demand loans to the numbered Trusts of its own American investors and officials. The loans were used to purchase securities, on a very large margin, which was traded on the American Stock Exchange. The securities were then fraudulently used as collateral for the loans. This scam fell apart when the stock market drastically declined and the value of the securities plummeted. Mercantile wanted, needed, the loans repaid. The trusts couldn't cover the losses, especially because various guarantors refused to honor their guarantees.[27]

Faced with catastrophic problems, Mercantile's contemporary leadership—Inge Gordon Mosvold, Paul Helliwell, and his former O.S.S. associate Demetrius Stampados apparently conspired to "disguise and conceal the existence of the defaulted loans in order to defraud depositors and creditors of the Bank as well as Bahamian Government banking authorities."[28] They filed phony reports and set up shell corporations, one in Panama and two in The Bahamas, to shuffle the disastrous loans around, attempting to create the impression they were soundly collateralized.

The conspiracy took on a new dimension when officers from the International Bank, a bank holding company headquartered in Washington DC, decided to acquire 66 percent of the capital stock of Mercantile in The Bahamas and its subsidiary in the Cayman Islands. International's officers knew the actual state of Mercantile's financial health—during negotiations they were told the bank recently had very serious losses and much of the loan portfolio was tenuously secured by real property that was not, unfortunately, readily marketable.[29] Unperturbed, they went ahead with the purchase, which closed at the end of March 1973. A couple of months later, they knew the scam's every jot and tittle. Still they didn't complain. On the contrary, they proceeded to lustily join in.

What remained of the bank was drained dry through more fraudulent loans, totalling at least $17,000,313 made to seven companies controlled by the conspirators. These firms were primarily engaged in Florida land deals in the Orlando area.[30] Castle naturally played an important role in the bilking of Mercantile. The primary corporate villain in this round robin of fraud was a company known as Dacca S.A., which sat snugly as Castle savings account 504110. In the summer of 1977, over 90 percent of Mercantile's claimed assets were actually uncollectible liabilities.[31] Too much even for The Bahamas. That August, the government revoked Mercantile's banking and trust license; the game was over at last.[32]

Whatever the motivation to save Kleinman's funds may truly have been (and it's difficult to believe concern with life and limb wasn't primary), he lost nothing in the Mercantile disaster, remaining solvent with a great deal of money safely housed in Castle. Perhaps to insure nothing similar happened in the future, large amounts of Kleinman's resources were transferred from Castle in Nassau to Castle Cayman. In the spring of 1976 his Castle Cayman balance sheet recorded total assets of $3,540,418.[33]

Kleinman was a very important Castle depositor (and perhaps a hidden owner), but by no means the wealthiest. The most affluent were members of the fabulously rich Pritzker family from Chicago, clients of the Kanter firm.[34] In approximately forty years, this family rose from relative obscurity to incredible affluence.

The Pritzkers' best-known company is the Hyatt Corporation, which features the famous hotel chain. Kanter, one of their attorneys, served on the Hyatt Board of Directors. By 1980, just three of their many holding companies reportedly generated revenues exceeding $3 billion annually.[35] The Pritzkers embodied that old maxim of the rich, which holds that if you can count your money you're not that wealthy. In the mid–1970s, it was reported the family's holdings were far too numerous for any member of the family to remember them at any given moment.[36]

Like many others with so much money, a little digging into their background produced troubling questions. It was discovered that the source of some Pritzker money came from the racket-ridden Teamsters Pension Fund. One deal in particular stood out. This was their purchase of a Nevada hotel and casino owned by the Pension fund, in which the Pritzkers were assisted by a $30 million Pension Fund loan. The loan, in turn, was secured by another Pritzker casino venture—the Four Queens Hotel and Casino in Vegas.[37] The Pritzker's had several casino interests, at least one of which also involved another Castle depositor—Hugh Hefner of *Playboy*. Hefner's ill-fated New Jersey casino venture, the Playboy Hotel and Casino, was partly owned (46 percent) by the Pritzkers.[38]

Investigators probing the Pritzker empire were intrigued by its connection to the Pension Fund. This was especially so when it was learned that both Jimmy Hoffa and Allen Dorfman personally worked on Pritzker loans. The major Pritzker link to the Teamsters was crafted by Stanford Clinton, "a former associate of the Pritzker's law firm, a man who represented some of Chicago's leading hoodlums and, after becoming general counsel of the Teamsters pension fund, assisted the Pritzkers in obtaining pension fund loans."[39] The Clinton family, like the Pritzkers, was in Castle Bank; they had Settlement Account (705062).

Sally determined the Pritzkers had been in The Bahamas since the autumn of 1964. That was when their Transnational Trust Company Limited, was formed by attorneys from McKinney, Bancroft and Hughes. Transnational was held by Mercantile Bank in a trust account (1740), which Tax Court records for 1970 showed earned over $50,000 in interest from one investment. Much more significantly, capital gains totalling over $28 million were placed into the account from the liquidation of a firm established to hold Pritzker's hotel interests.[40] When Mercantile's fortunes dipped, the Pritzker trust was transferred to Castle and placed in an account numbered 108055. On the first of March 1972, Transnational changed its name to Anjado Limited.[41]

As far as Castle Bank was concerned, the Pritzkers were the wealthiest clients, while Kleinman was certainly one of the most dangerous. There were many other clients and indeed partners. Castle's action encompassed major real estate projects, film and recording ventures, and a variety of other undertakings. One particular resort enterprise, above all others, captured the Castle crowd and brought them together with Resorts International, and fleetingly with J. Jay Frankel.

At just about the northern end of what English and American cartographers call the Leeward Islands (and conversely, Dutch geographers style Windward), rimming the Caribbean Sea, due east of Puerto Rico and the Virgin Islands, lies a curious anomaly from the colonial past. It is a tiny island, only 37 square miles, politically and culturally divided in two. The northern part is a French colony, the southern a Dutch one. The division came in 1648, a creation of the Peace of Westphalia, which finally ended Europe's agony known as the Thirty Years War. St. Martin, the French possession, is unmistakably Gallic with an ambience reminiscent of the small towns on the French Riviera prior to the 1960s. Dutch Sint Maarten, on the other hand, has given itself wholeheartedly to American tourist culture.[42]

In 1969, Frankel arrived on the French side; one year later Resorts was working the Dutch part. Frankel, who had just finished the Mary Carter Paint and Resorts International arrangement, was described then by *Fortune* magazine as the head of Delafield & Delafield's venture-capital section.[43] Frankel was brought to St. Martin to rescue a resort project tottering on the brink of financial disaster. Called La Belle Creole, it was "the ruin of an obsessed man's dream."[44]

Although Frankel had successfully raised a good deal of the capital necessary for the emergence of Resorts, most other Frankel projects had dismal histories of bankruptcies. Overall, he did not seem to be an ideal choice for corporate deliverance. Still, he was invited in by La Belle Creole's owner upon the advice of a loan officer at a New York bank.[45] His penchant for expensive failure became obvious once again. With his attention diverted time and again to other issues, it took a while before he finally realized La Belle Creole precariously floated on a bog of uncertainties, costing money with no certain return. Frankel was somewhat unfocused because he was also working with Denver oilman John King, who was then rashly trying to buy I.O.S., Bernie Cornfeld's sickly mutual fund goliath.[46] Always a "wheeler-dealer," Frankel, and probably Joel Mallin, introduced John King to Castle Bank. A Castle account was established for a King company known as Dundee International.[47]

Frankel's St. Martin adventure was a grand mistake; he had stepped into the muck only to learn too late that even title to the land was unclear. The St. Martin adventure ended nastily, and the project, barely shuffling along, was shut down.[48] The stillborn resort was abandoned for about fifteen years until the Hilton hotel chain came along and finished the job.[49] But Frankel was never one to sit idly by, pondering his mistakes and misfortunes. He was soon working on his cement boat venture with "Fat Tony" Salerno.

While Frankel has his problems on the French side of the island, both Resorts and Castle people had the opposite experience on the Dutch half. There, all attention was fixed on the development of a resort complex along the beautiful beach facing south southwest, called Mullet Pond Bay. The Mullet Bay Beach Hotel and Casino opened in December 1970.

Interest in the area started as far back as the late 1950s when Henry Ford II considered building a home somewhere in the Caribbean. He sent one of his company executives, Herbert Merser, as an advance scout. Merser contacted Eric Lawaetz, a resident of the Virgin Islands and one of the largest landowners in the Caribbean, for advice.[50] The two men flew around the Caribbean viewing various choice parcels of real estate. At one point they cruised over the Mullet Bay section of Sint Maarten. Pointing out its exceptional location and natural beauty, Lawaetz thought it a grand site for a hotel. The Ford executive readily agreed, excited at the prospect. His enthusiasm was communicated to his boss and they and Lawaetz turned to resort development.[51]

A company called Island Gem Enterprises was formed and registered in the Netherlands Antilles to act as developer. Early on, Merser brought in the Levenfeld, Kanter firm both to act as tax counsel and help plan the development.[52] Joining Burt Kanter in legal work for the venture was his younger brother, Carl I. Kanter, a lawyer with the prestigious New York firm of Stroock, Stroock and Lavan.[53] Carl Kanter prepared the prospectus for Island Gem's successful fund raising and remained associated with it through at least 1981.[54]

Henry Ford and his beautiful, vivacious wife Christina, Herbert Merser, and several other Ford executives, such as Lee A. Iacocca, bought Island Gem stock. They weren't all Island Gem "insiders," however. Those truly on the inside paid far less than the average for Island Gem stock and had Castle Bank act as their trustee. The stock usually sold for $10,000 a share, which is what Iacocca and almost everyone else paid.[55] Christina Ford, however, bought her 100 shares for $1,500 each. Herbert Merser, Burt Kanter, and his close friend Chris O'Donnell purchased theirs for $625 a share. So did Edward J. Gerrits, the head of a large construction company which actually built the resort. Eric Lawaetz had an even better deal. Castle handled the Sint Maarten money for Kanter, Lawaetz, O'Donnell, Merser, and Gerrits.[56]

Island Gem was crossed by various partnerships such as Mullet Pond Development Venture Limited and Largesse Development Venture. In the spring of 1970, shortly after the Mercantile Bank scam began, ten percent of Lawaetz's holdings in these partnerships and his stock in Island Gem was used as collateral for a deal with Mercantile. Perhaps it played a role in momentarily shoring up some of those diastrous investments mentioned before, because a couple of months later Mercantile returned it to Castle as Trustee for Lawaetz.[57] Two years after this, Castle divided and turned over one part of the Lawaetz option package to trust 705164, and the rest to another called Topaz Trust through Helwan S.A., a Panamanian firm probably set up to provide that last impenetrable layer of paper to guarantee the Topaz beneficiary anonymity.[58]

Topaz and many other Castle accounts were routinely involved in complicated (because hidden) property deals. For instance, Topaz and another mysterious settlement called Emanon ("no name" spelled backwards) shared in a large Florida real estate package in Ft. Pierce. They were joined in this venture by two individuals with Castle accounts, who were probably using money siphoned out of a very sizable Toyota fraud and tax scam which ran through Castle. Topaz and Emanon were also partners in another Florida land deal with record and film producer Saul Zaentz, best known for *One Flew Over the Cuckoo's Nest* and *Amadeus*. Zaentz had two trusts in Castle, one of which owned stock in Island Gem. Unlike the other Castle owners, however, Zaentz apparently paid the standard $10,000 per share for his slice of the Sint Maarten pie.

Working on a large development project such as Island Gem provided a springboard for Kanter's creative talents. In time he gathered 6.2 percent of Island Gem's stock into sundry trusts and became a director of the company. He also took care of his brother, who shared in Burt's percentage of Island Gem through what was foggily described as "in an indirect ownership through a limited partnership."[59]

The original Mullet Bay undertaking developed a luxury hotel and casino. It was the latter that brought Resorts International and casino manager Eddie Cellini together with Island Gem. The two companies signed a joint venture agreement in October 1970 calling for the Paradise Island company to operate the casino.[60] Concerning the Sint Maarten casino, Sally believed the actual management contract was made between Intertel, Resort's private security subsidiary, and Island Gem. If indeed so, this suggests a reason for Robert Peloquin's curiously vigorous defense of Eddie Cellini remarked on earlier.

Clearly, there was a working relationship between Eddie and Resorts and Intertel, and the officers and directors of Island Gem. It lasted for some time. Almost a decade later, Resorts of the World, a quite special Cellini company, metamorphosed into the St. Maarten Gaming Corporation and leased the casino at the Mullett Bay Beach Hotel from Island Gem. Involved in this 1981 arrangement, was Carl Kanter acting for Stroock, Stroock and Lavan, and Cellini's man from Resorts of the World, Rosario Spadaro.[61]

Resorts of the World probably started business on Sint Maarten in 1967, when Eddie was still managing the Bahamian Club for

Mary Carter Paint, well before the opening of Paradise Island.[62] It was a subsidiary operation of the well-known Concord Hotel located at Kiamesha Lake in New York's Catskill Mountains. In 1976, Cellini and Rosario Spadaro from Sicily, with many years experience in casino and resort development and management in Sicily, Nigeria, and Sint Maarten bought out the Concord people.

The original owners of the Concord and Resorts of the World were almost as deeply enmeshed in organized crime as Cellini himself. They had mob ties dating from the mid–1950s. Congressional testimony in 1959 established a relationship between the Concord and corrupt Teamster officials, particularly one who was the administrator of a large New York local's welfare fund.[63] Even more telling, in 1955 the Concord had hired a labor relations firm headed by Carlo Gambino, one of America's most notorious gangsters.[64] It is probable that the Concord's ties to organized crime increased during the 1960s and 1970s as the Sint Maarten deal developed. The Organized Crime Control Bureau of the New York City Police Department determined that Matthew "Matty the Horse" Ianiello, a major power in organized crime (who was recently convicted on racketeering charges) had considerable interests in the Concord's Caribbean operation, including casino management, junkets, and debt collection using various "leg breakers" to persuade credit players to pay their debts.[65]

Castle Bank and Resorts International had met prior to, and outside the beautiful byway of Sint Maarten. Certain individuals representative of the two groups had earlier operated together in The Bahamas. Burt Kanter, for one, stated he labored to find a reputable outside hotelier to manage the Paradise Island hotel, in order to satisfy a Bahamian government concern.[66] There was reasonable doubt that a paint company, even one in partnership with Huntington Hartford, had the necessary expertise to handle a resort hotel. The Bahamians were right, and the original Paradise Island Hotel was managed by Laurence A. Tisch's Loews Corporation.

But it was in the commonality of political payoffs that Resorts and Castle most obviously shared interests and personalities in The Bahamas. Gerald Goldsmith, who embodied the diverse interests of Freeport and Paradise Island, used Castle Bank for hidden payments to Prime Minister Pindling, and probably other members of his administration. He, and his partner Mary Jane Melrose, did it by looting funds from Intercontinental Diversified. Goldsmith and Melrose secured the money by having Intercontinental Diversifed pay for fictitious consulting and legal services. The phony invoices were obtained from seven offshore corporations by Goldsmith, Melrose, and Helliwell, who put the money into Castle accounts called Zodiac and Atlantic. The funds were then disbursed in two streams. Some flowed to the Bank of Perrine where it was converted to cash, picked up, and flown back to The Bahamas and paid out. The other stream was like a desert wash; what entered this one, at least $400,000, just vanished.[67]

The payoffs from Goldsmith through Castle to Bahamian politicians represented a sign of the times; the inevitable shift of political power that had gone to the Progressive Liberal Party. This theme was positively echoed when Resorts International was discovered doing much the same thing (with bag men other than Goldsmith) during the same period of time. At its annual shareholder meeting in 1976, when the subject was raised and Chairman Crosby refused to comment, a vocal shareholder, in suport of company payoffs to politicians, announced that's how business gets done in The Bahamas.[68] The Goldsmith and Castle story surfaced in May, 1976, the Resorts one in September.

If Castle had a theme besides creative tax evasion and diverting money for political payoffs, it was the magic of real estate. Whether Island Gem and its derivatives, the Doral property, the Topaz Trust and Saul Zaentz, Castle promoted real estate for every sort of investor, for many reasons. From Orlando, Jacksonville, South Miami, Ft. Pierce, the Dutch Antilles, to dozens of other places worldwide, Castle trust money floated in and out of myriad property ventures. Castle's emphasis on land was based on something much more than typical investment potential, more than the sum of its many property deals. At the heart of Castle stood a huge real estate scam—a fraud that by itself was enough to take an offshore bank from the shelf and put it to work. The name of the scam was International Computerized Land Research (I.C.L.R.).

Sally was convinced the relationship between I.C.L.R. and Castle was absolutely fundamental, almost as significant as its connection to Mercantile Bank. She believed that figuring out I.C.L.R. would reveal some as yet undiscovered essence of Castle. She established that I.C.L.R. was formed in the autumn of 1968 by A. J. T. Gooding, acting as a nominee, and lodged in his Nassau office. This was fairly standard practice. The office of Gooding and Co. was also used by Castle Bank when it first came off the shelf in 1967. I.C.L.R.'s cable address was PALOMAR, which was later adopted by Castle as its address, and subsequently became the name of Castle's Panamanian branch. Sally's research turned up some of I.C.L.R.'s shareholders. There were Gooding, Kanter, William J. Friedman, and two people unfamiliar to her— James McGowan and James Farrara. The minimal yearly company fees for I.C.L.R. were handled by Gooding and Co. until 1970, then by CAMACO (a Castle Bank management company) for three years. Castle itself paid for the next two years, and from then on I.C.L.R.'s fees were paid by the Canadian Imperial Bank of Commerce. The listed personnel in this land company were by now familiar: Gooding, Ernest Foster, and Wolstencroft were directors and officers.

In the I.C.L.R. company file, Sally came across an intriguing letter dated 27 June 1972. It was on I.C.L.R. company stationery and at the bottom listed three important foreign banks: the Bayerische Vereinsbank in Munich, West Germany; the Creditanstalt Bankverein in Vienna; and the Schweizerische Kreditanstalt (the Swiss Credit Bank) in Zug, Switzerland, close by Zurich. She wondered if this meant a substantial European marketing scheme. Her instincts, as usual, were on target. I.C.L.R. had opened a sales office in Munich in 1968, and began selling overvalued California desert land to investors in Germany, Switzerland, and Italy. Land in California's Antelope Valley was criminally misrepresented by I.C.L.R. and sold to well over 2,000 unwitting Europeans.

The Castle master list of accounts indicated two primary I.C.L.R. accounts, two others for McGowan, and the same for Farrara. There were perhaps two dozen others linked to this enterprise. Farrara was a fairly sleazy operator with a criminal record stretching back to 1926, when he was fined for running a whore house. He spent some time in prison in the 1930s and 1940s for violations of the Mann Act, having to do with transporting women across state lines for immoral purposes. In Los Angeles, he endured a series of arrests for bookmaking but no convictions.[69] McGowan (called Mac) was not as criminally colorful as his partner, having only a single conviction in New York for violations of the housing code in 1955, and an arrest in Los Angeles for assault with a deadly weapon. The charge was dropped.[70]

Mac and Farrara apparently started their real estate adventure in 1964, under the company name Far-Mac, buying up chunks of high desert land northeast of Los Angeles. Their company changed in 1968 and 1969, spawning not only I.C.L.R. but three other firms. Two of them were incorporated in the Netherlands Antilles, Inversiones Mixtas and Gorgias; and one in California called Trebor Land Consultants.[71] The primary firm among these three was Inversiones Mixtas, which had two Castle accounts and was used, at times, as a general Castle repository of funds. Inversiones Mixtas was an important conduit for many of Castle's "funny-money" deals.

In the summer of 1969, the Castle and I.C.L.R. scam began in earnest. Inversiones Mixtas purchased certain assets from Far-Mac Investments on 28 February 1969.[72] Mixtas, in turn, made Castle the Trusee for the following people whose ownership interests of I.C.L.R. are represented.

Castle Account Number	Name	Percentage of Ownership
T–5063	J. McGowan	25.5
T–5064	J. Farrara	25.5
T–6070	Levenfeld Family	1.5
T–6072	Baskes Family	1.5
T–6075	Burton W. Kanter	20.25
T–6089	W. J. Friedman	23.25
T–6096	M. J. Melrose	2.5

A few years later there were minor changes in ownership, with some I.C.L.R. money going into a disguised account called Claudette Investments.[73] The Kanter firm made most of the policy decisions concerning I.C.L.R., such as authorizing the Castle comptroller A. R. Bickerton to distribute the monthly cash statements of the partners to accountant Jerry Weiss in Chicago.[74] In the spring of 1971, Kanter indicated how he wanted Castle to structure its reporting on I.C.L.R. accounts and investments.[75]

At one point, due entirely to frustration, Kanter revealed his own role in the origins of I.C.L.R. and its direction. He was quite irritated about the matter of overdrafts in the McGowan and Farrara accounts, and he wrote Mac reminding him of their original understanding. Friedman "and I," he said, "would in essence put up a maximum of $150,000. This was to be put up by way of loan to a venture in which you would have 51% and we would have 49%. That loan was to be fully repaid from sales of the venture. Obviously this did not transpire."[76] Kanter was upset because the loan was overdue, and I.C.L.R. financing was costing both Kanter and Friedman more and more. The way out, he told Mac, was to borrow money from Mercantile Bank through the "conduit," Inversiones Mixtas. That would hopefully resolve all their current financial woes.[77] It is doubtful whether this aided Mercantile's financial problems.

The use of Inversiones Mixtas as a Castle conduit by the bank's principal partners is clear from other correspondence as well. On instructions from Levenfeld, Kanter, Baskes and Lippitz, Castle's assistant secretary, May S. Gilmour, signed various Inversiones Mixtas documents as its attorney of record.[78] Among these papers was the Far-Mac agreement commented on above. The ghostly Alipranti also signed for Mixtas on occasion, usually when it involved some Helliwell deal.[79] In fact, Helliwell as well as Kanter had directions for Wolstencroft concerning I.C.L.R. Helliwell's attention, however, seems to have been confined primarily to discrepancies of I.C.L.R. money in Mary Jane Melrose's trust account (706096). Reviewing monthly I.C.L.R. statements, Helliwell wrote that the inconsistencies drove him back to the statements and they put him "in a state of hopeless confusion" dangerously close to "insanity."

Wolstencroft was requested to recalculate account 706096 with proper explanations of debits and credits.[80] Helliwell was answered by Castle's comptroller Alan Bickerton who explained, "as you are aware, the ICLR receipts from European sales are placed into the appropriate Castle account to be disbursed to the partners' trust monthly." Lately, Bickerton added, instructions on payouts and accounting had been received from I.C.L.R.'s accountant, Jerry Weiss, a close confidante of Kanter's, and the implementation of their suggestions caused a few glitches.[81] Bickerton concluded that now everything should proceed smoothly.

The law finally caught up with McGowan and Farrara, who

died before anything legally significant took place. That left Mac, who was eventually convicted on 19 counts of conspiracy and mail fraud.[82] There are literally hundreds of civil claims from Europe and the United States that are still grinding their way along through one system of justice or another. Nothing happened to the Castle conspirators besides Farrara and McGowan; Kanter skated by claiming, falsely but effectively, the attorney-client privilege whenever questioned by anyone about I.C.L.R.[83] As long as his partnership interest was unknown he was able to fend off the curious.

There is one last illustration of Kanter's management of Castle found in the special Cayman files. Beckwith Carbon was a research and development firm looking for ways to build and market products manufactured from Vitreous Carbon. There were potential biomedical applications including its use in orthopedic, dental, and cardiac-arterial implantations. It also had industrial potential as a substitute for materials such as graphite and molybendum, and as a crucible for low oxygen crystal growth, which is vitally important in the semiconductor industry. Like many research and development firms, Beckwith didn't make money in its early years. In April 1972, Beckwith requested its debenture holders, unfortunately for the second time, to waive their rights to interest payments until the company turned the corner.[84]

The Castle investors in Beckwith were the bank itself and its inner core of principals—Kanter, Levenfeld, Baskes, Friedman, Melrose, Helliwell, and E. P. Barry (the last remaining mystery man from Castle Bank). Kanter and the bank had the largest investments in Beckwith, and even they weren't all that large (in 1971 Kanter had $10,000 and Castle $19,000).[85] While the amounts involved were relatively minuscule, events affecting Beckwith revealed the unmistakable control of Castle management. On 26 April 1972, Wolstencroft signed the "Waiver of Debenture Agreement Provisions" for Castle. When Kanter received his copy of the agreement, he shot off a telex to Wolstencroft telling him he must withdraw the waiver. Kanter instructed him to send a letter to Beckwith Carbon immediately, explaining the waiver was signed inadvertently "without prior approval of our general counsel." He also informed Wolstencroft that he had already sent Beckwith a wire stating Castle's withdrawal. To clear the situation, Wolstencroft was instructed to wire Beckwith's president "confirming that you requested me to wire him withdrawing consent."[86] Wolstencroft complied, sending an urgent telegram to Beckwith containing the false statement.[87] Kanter always understood the importance of maintaining the fiction of Castle's administration.

Kanter and Helliwell were indisputably Castle's owners, managers, and administrators. They were aided in these tasks by members of their respective law firms and individuals like Gene Poe, from controlled institutions such as the Bank of Perrine, which was of paramount significance in the conspiracy. The conspiracy was so complete that Helliwell, Kanter, Melrose, and a few others held the vast majority of Perrine-Cutler Ridge shares through corporations named HMT and Florida Shares.[88]

The fact of Castle's ownership is beyond question. In addition to the proofs from the special Cayman files, there are the official filings of ownership made in Nassau. Jim Gooding was the Managing Director of Castle Trust on 14 July 1970. As required under Bahamian law, Gooding wrote to the Superintendent of Banks in the Ministry of Finance and stated:

For your private and confidential information, subject to possible minor amendments. I ratify that the following persons or corporate entity will ultimately own the issued share capital of this company, however restructured, whether the shares be registered openly, concealed behind a nominee or held by a non-resident Bahamian settlement:

Fomentos	$33\frac{1}{3}\%$
Paul L. E. Helliwell *Attorney at Law*	$16\frac{2}{3}\%$
Burton W. Kanter *Attorney at Law*	$16\frac{2}{3}\%$
A. J. T. Gooding (local)	*12%*
E. F. Poe *President of the Bank of Perrine*	*8%*
E. J. Foster (local)	$6\frac{1}{3}\%$
Columbus O'Donnell *Deltec Banking Corp. Ltd. (local)*	*3%*
Staff and Others	*4%*

Fomentos was another Castle conduit similar to Inversiones Mixtas set up by the conspirators. Additionally, it was rumored to represent racketeer Kleinman's main Castle interest, used by him in 1964 to capitalize the new bank with $600,000, and thus made him, Kanter, and Helliwell, the largest shareholders by far.

One year later, when Castle filed its annual Statement with Bahamian authorities, it was noted that Gooding (and his wife) owned 72,000 shares, Ernie Foster another 38,000, A. Alipranti and George Bebas merely two, Fomentos 199,998, while five trusts numbered 001 through 005 held the remaining 290,000. That same year, again according to Bahamian law, Castle informed Mr. L. S. Evans of the Bahamas Monetary Authority that the beneficiaries of those five trusts were Helliwell, Kanter, Poe, Melrose, and O'Donnell.[89] Helliwell and Kanter had 100,000 shares each; Poe 48,000; Melrose 24,000; and O'Donnell 18,000.

In addition to Bahamian records, Castle directors and others associated with the bank used the Republic of Panama's quite liberal company laws (with its provisions for anonymity) on several occasions, including registering Castle Trust Company Limited, S.A. on 27 February 1969. This was like an insurance policy, supplying another layer of secrecy. However, on 11 May 1972, Castle filed a Certificate of Election in the Republic of Panama, and named Pierson, Poe, Helliwell, Kanter, and Melrose as the bank's directors ("quienes constituyen toda la Junta Directive de la Compania"). This Panamanian game resurrected Alipranti; Wolstencroft certified the spiritual Greek's reelection as Castle's secretary.[90] Castle (Panama) changed its name to Compania Fiduciaria Palomar (I.C.L.R.'s cable address) in 1977, after damaging publicity about the Bahamian operation had emerged from the general tumult associated with Project Haven.

If the I.R.S. had had timely access to the Cayman files and the Panama documents, the conspirators would have been in extreme jeopardy. But those files weren't found and retrieved until long after Project Haven had come and gone. On the other hand, the Bahamian Monetary Authority records signed by Gooding, ratifying Castle's ownership, were pried loose while Haven still existed. These records were never utilized to their potential. When this latter evidence was at hand, Project Haven was directed by the Justice Department, which was overly cautious (to put it charitably) about utilizing any evidence from The Bahamas not directly certified by the government. That put prosecutors in an impossible situation because of both Bahamian law and Bahamian corruption. Pindling was after all, paid off, through Castle Bank.

The Castle conspirators mounted a complicated counterattack, putting Jaffe, Norm Casper, and several others from the I.R.S. Intelligence Division on the defensive as often as possible. In the early stages of the counterattack, there was a good deal of posturing in the hope of prying loose information and planting "disinformation." In February 1974, Gene Poe called Casper and invited him for an important chat over lunch. Poe had several items he wanted to confide. The major one was that he and Helliwell thought Joel Mallin was a crook; that Kanter still associated with him; and they could hardly stand Kanter anymore. Poe said that the Helliwell people were doing everything they could to disassociate themselves from Kanter and his group. But it was hard; he had to understand. Poe offered Casper the complete cooperation of the Helliwell side in pursuit of drug dealers in Castle. He stated categorically and in good faith that Helliwell wanted nothing to do with money from narcotics or organized crime.

Then came the warning. Poe confided Kanter was exerting a lot of pressure in an attempt to identify the man who had been snooping around Castle, talking to Wolstencroft. No question his cover was safe with him, said the banker, but Kanter already "knows you live on Key Biscayne." Be very careful, Poe suggested. There was one last twist in this talk. Dramatically, and certainly enigmatically, Poe said, "When I signed up for 20 years, the agreement was that I could not talk for a number of years after my contract is terminated." Surely this was also true for Casper, he quickly added. Now that the secret was out, there was an offer of elderly comradeship. While the proper time comes, "if we are both still alive, I would like to sit down and compare bedtime stories." But raising the specter of the C.I.A. did not impress Casper.[91] He understood the chat was designed to give him conflicting and tantalizing messages as part of the information and disinformation process.

But it wasn't all simple play acting. Because Poe was concerned

with his own safety, like all informers he gave some solid news.
The most important was that Project Haven had sprung a large
leak, which meant Kanter was receiving vital information. That
worrisome detail was discussed by Jaffe and the other Project
Haven manager David Ellison on 13 March 1974.[92]

The leak wasn't their only problem. It was also becoming clear
the briefcase incident was developing into a major issue. Almost
a year to the day after the Casper coup, William Hyatt from the
Tax Division of the Justice Department came to Miami to discuss
the manner in which the Castle documents were obtained.[93] In a
couple of weeks, Joseph Salus, an attorney from the Chief Counsel's Office commented that he was writing a memo to protect
Jaffe, although it was unclear from what. A draft of the unwanted
memo was sent to the Director of the Intelligence Division for
comment. It was, as Jaffe and Ellison described it, written in an
extremely negative, highly critical manner of Project Haven. Even
after Salus rewrote parts, it still retained its critical, accusatory
tone. The issue was the briefcase "caper," and what the Chief
Counsel's Office felt was a lack of prior consultation.[94] The pressure built just a little bit more.

A week later, the Haven people met with the assistant commissioner for Compliance, and his deputy. The assistant commissioner had urgently requested the talk after receiving an inquiry about Haven from an undisclosed source in the Department
of Justice. All this disturbed Jaffe and Ellison, who put together
a report on the Castle investigation including a section on Casper
and Wolstencroft. They reminded the director of Intelligence that
prior approval had been granted, and that detailed notification
through the Intelligence Division had been provided to Justice.[95]

These developments were very perplexing for the Haven managers. The operation was over a year old, and a great deal of
time and manpower had been devoted to the investigation since
getting the list. The manner of its acquisition was never hidden.
No one had violated any known internal Service procedures. They
wondered what was going on. For the time being a diffuse anxiety
settled in. There was no resolution because there was nothing
well defined. They went about their business; so did Kanter and
Helliwell.

The two attorneys were themselves perturbed over the Haven

investigation, and they did know much more about it than Jaffe and Ellison ever imagined—there was a hemorrhage of information, not a leak. In August 1974, Kanter and Helliwell had a strategy session in which Poe, and perhaps another (racketeer Kleinman's nephew, Al Morrison) attended. Kanter read from a secret report containing details about Haven. Part of this exercise was to alert Helliwell about what to say and what to avoid in an upcoming interview with Agent Ellison. As Kanter put it, "I also have to very carefully delineate what it is that you should or should not know." He was very distressed, anxious that there be no errors and "no accidents of disclosure."[96]

For a long time Kanter read from the report that identified Jaffe, Ellison, and the fact of a Castle account list getting into the possession of the I.R.S., but not exactly when or how, and about DECODE and a Haven-related operation called the Bahamas Project. The report contained a precis about the Howard Hughes investigation and named the I.R.S. agent in charge. They knew about the Wolstencroft surveillance in San Francisco, although they were apparently still unaware of his connection to the purloined list. Kanter commented, "how they ended up figuring out to tail Michael or anything else, I don't know, but it was definitely a cover on Michael." Poe who was sitting attentively through all this, offered no guess or information about Wolstencroft and Casper. Other agents and supervisors who were part of Haven were also named. Kanter concluded, noting the project was definitely a fishing expedition spurred on by the malign and ambitious Ellison, and by that "rough character" Jaffe.

What to do was discursively discussed. Kanter reported that the project goes on even though "we keep poking around trying to put on pressure." He asked Helliwell to check out whether there was any State Department involvement in this investigation. If so, he added while Helliwell murmured, that would be very helpful. Helliwell piped up and forcefully stated, that if we can get rid of stocks and bonds as an issue, "if we eliminate that, we eliminate, you know, rackets, Mafias, and all this damn foolishness."

They both talked a great deal about playing tough from now on. Helliwell remarked he was about ready to close the investigators out of the Perrine bank and go to court. Kanter chimed in, "Now, we've made the same threat, and we're making it more and more affirmatively. . . . we've indicated that not only will we shut everything down—by everything you have no idea the scope of audits all over the country that will be shut down, but, we may bring separate lawsuits and we have been exploring the theories of injunction; theories of restraint, restraining orders, and other suits that we could bring in certain districts that are sympathetic to taxpayers and taxpayers' representatives as distinguished from this one."

They also mentioned rather mysteriously and cryptically, "the political matter, the overseas political matter"; and whether those people "will go to bat and say yes we did it." Their particular anxieties were showing. For Helliwell it was primarily the stocks, bonds, and checks cashed at Perrine, while for Kanter it was making sure Helliwell didn't divulge any of their secretly leaked government information, and keeping the investigators away from American National in Chicago. They were both concerned with Gooding who was in the Cayman Islands, either delivering or checking on Castle documents sent there. Helliwell had put the pressure on him "to get the hell down there, and see what was going on because Tony [Field] is going to be gone five and a half weeks." As usual, Gooding was a bit confused, and now they weren't sure all the right documents had gone to the right places. The conspirators were nervous, but still confident not shaken. They had plenty of political muscle left, and they clearly intended to use it.

There was a lull between the early warning signs of problems over Haven's evidence and the full blast of controversy. Thus, in the summer of 1974, the Project was driving confidently forward. More and more documents were found and new leads appeared. An attempt by the Kanter firm to avoid an I.R.S. subpoena of its Castle records was denied in federal court, and Jaffe was sure the investigative net was closing in on both Kanter and Helliwell. The Haven team experienced the thrill of new powers: "We have expanded the scope of the HAVEN Project to include all aspects of worldwide international tax fraud," wrote Applebaum and Ellison, two of Haven's managers.[97]

They weren't being immodest; Haven had subsumed many of the functions of two important I.R.S. task forces working on worldwide issues: the North Atlantic Region Task Force—International Finance, which was established to investigate tax fraud and Swiss banks; and the North Atlantic Region Securities Task Force. Haven team members were I.R.S. pioneers operating in what Jaffe described as a virgin, highly specialized area of law enforcement.[98] Their work was also organizationally innovative. They provided guidance, documents, and coordination for those I.R.S. Districts (Chicago, San Francisco, Reno, New York, etc.), which had the majority of Castle cases. It was their most assured period; they felt at the center of an I.R.S. reformation.

Notes

1. Nine other acronyms had been considered before settling on DE-CODE. They were: 1) CODEDUST—Concealment of Overseas Deposits to Evade Domestic U.S. Taxes; 2) COASTLID—Concealment of Overseas Accounts and Securities Transactions by Lawyers Illegal Diversions; 3) DATABUST—Domestic Account Transactions by Attorneys Bypassing U.S. Taxes; 4) DATAFIB—Domestic Account Transactions by Attorneys Foreign Illegal Bank; 5) COST—Concealment of Overseas Securities Transactions; 6) FEECOST—Foreign Entity Evasion by Concealment of Overseas Security Transactions; 7) FATCAT—Foreign Account Transactions by Conspiracy of Attorneys and Taxpayers; 8) FAST—Foreign Accounts and Securities Transactions; and 9) FASTCAT—Foreign Accounts and Securities Transactions by Conspiracy of Attorneys and Taxpayers.
2. Intelligence Division (Miami), "Project MINT," 29 January 1973.
3. Project MINT, "Memorandum of Surveillance: In re: H. M. Wolstencroft," pp. 16–19 January 1973.
4. The surveillance entry reads: "At 12:45 PM subject arrived at *10 South La Salle Street* carrying the brown briefcase and went to the offices located on the 8th floor. The elevator doors all open on this floor in the reception area of the law firm of Levenfeld, Kanter, Baskes & Lippitz," Project Mint, p. 1.
5. U.S. District Court, for the Northern District of Texas at Dallas, *United States of America v. C.W. Deaton, et al.*, Criminal Number CR 3–76–132, 5 May 1976 p. 2.
6. U.S. District Court for the Northern District of Texas, *United States of America v. H. M. Wolstencroft, Warrant of Arrest*," Magistrate's Docket No. 3–76; Case No. 58M, 28 April 1976.
7. H. M. Wolstencroft to Paul Helliwell, 21 November 1972.
8. California Superior Court in and for the City and County of San

Francisco, Musical Group Investment Cases, "Testimony of Dorothy Ann Strachan," 16 March 1983; Reporter's Partial Transcript of Proceedings, p. 9.

9. Ibid., p. 12; also Commonwealth of The Bahamas, "Affidavit of Ann Strachan," January 1979.

10. Author's interview with Donald E. Van Koughnet, Naples, Florida, 30 May 1986.

11. Ibid.

12. Deed of Settlement, "Hans Bossard Settlor to Castle Trust Company Limited Trustee," Nassau, 21 September 1970.

13. Lawrence A. Freeman to The Controller of Exchange, Exchange Control, Nassau, Bahamas, "Re: Settlement 706076," 1 October 1970.

14. Paul Helliwell to Mr. R. G. Winfield, Vice President Mercantile Bank & Trust, Freeport, Grand Bahama, "File: 10.911–2," 18 June 1970.

15. Helliwell to Winfield, "File: 10.911–2, 10.911–4," 4 June 1970.

16. Mercantile Bank to Paul H. Bethel of McKinney, Bancroft & Hughes, "Re: Settlement T–1157 and Conveyance Raleigh Investment Company Ltd. to Yourselves," 24 March 1971.

17. H. M. Wolstencroft, Vice President, to Mr. Burton W. Kanter, Levenfeld, Kanter, Baskes & Lippitz, Suite 838, S. 10 La Salle Street, Chicago, "Re: 706076," 2 November 1971.

18. Paul Helliwell to William A. Kledzik, Vice President Mercantile Bank & Trust, "File: 10.911–2," 31 January 1972.

19. Paul Helliwell to H. M. Wolstencroft, "File: 10.506," 21 March 1972.

20. Sally Woodruff to Richard E. Jaffe, "File Folder, Maule (Bahamas) 7156; Maule (Overseas) 15926." Within a very short time of the Doral purchase, Maule Industries was in financial trouble finally ending up bankrupt. See "Maule in Court Over Foreclosure," *Miami Herald*, 10 December 1978. Part of the problem emerged from a dispute between the Florida side of the Ferre family, and the Puerto Rican branch which included, Luis A. Ferre, the former Governor of the island. See Carolyn Jay Wright, "Ferre Families Dispute Validity of 3.5 Million Shares in Maule," *Miami Herald*, 26 April 1975; and Andy Taylor, "Life After Wealth," *Tropic*, 28 October 1978, pp. 9–14.

21. H. M. Wolstencroft, Deputy Managing Director, Castle Bank & Trust (Bahamas) Limited to Mrs. M. T. Cueto, Trustee, Miami, Florida, 30 October 1975.

22. J. S. Whylly, Assistant Trust Officer to First National City Bank, Nassau, Bahamas, Attn: Sidney Outten *Euro Currency Dept*, 18 February 1975.

23. Mercantile Bank, "Statement Account No. 3553 (M), T–1157," 30 April 1972.

24. California Superior Court in and for the City and County of San

Francisco, Musical Group Investment Cases, Coordination Proceedings Special Title (Rule 1550 (b)), "Transcript of Proceedings, Testimony of Samuel B. Pierson," 5 April 1983, p. 109.

25. Ibid., p. 111.
26. Ibid., p. 113.
27. United States District Court for the District of Columbia, *Dennis Cross and David Hamilton, Plaintiffs, v. Price Waterhouse & Co., et. al.,* Civil No. 80–0410, 12 February 1980, p. 7.
28. Ibid., pp. 7–8.
29. Ibid., p. 12.
30. Ibid., p. 22.
31. United States District Court for the District of Columbia, *Canadian Imperial Bank of Commerce, Trust Company (Bahamas) Limited as Successor Trustee . . . , Plaintiff, v. Carl Rupert, Managing Partner Price Waterhouse & Co., et al., Civil Action No. 80–0002, Complaint for Damages,* 2 January 1980, p. 6.
32. U.S. District Court, *Dennis Cross . . .* p. 29.
33. Castle Bank & Trust (Cayman) Limited, Trustee, "*Interim Report: Settlement 805532,* 31 March 1976.
34. See Musical Group Investment Cases, "Deposition of Burton W. Kanter," et passim.
35. Knut Royce, "The Operators: Chicago's Pritzker Family and Kansas City's Hyatt Regency," *Kansas City Times,* 8 March 1982, p. 1.
36. Ibid.
37. Ibid.
38. Ronald Koziol, "Four Won't Testify in New Jersey Playboy Hearings," *Chicago Tribune,* 9 March 1982.
39. Ibid.
40. Royce, 10 March 1982.
41. TW-5, "File: Transnational Trust Company Limited #7311."
42. Margaret Zellers, *Fielding's Caribbean 1984* (Morrow, 1984), pp. 579–580.
43. Allan T. Demaree, "When the Money Ran Out at a Grand Resort," *Fortune,* May 1972, p. 248.
44. Ibid., p. 171.
45. Ibid., p. 246.
46. Delafield Capital Corporation an affiliate of Delafield & Delafield, "John M. King—I.O.S. LTD., $40,000,000 Financing Agreement, Confidential Memorandum," May 1970.
47. Ron Wilson, I.R.S. Special Agent, "John King DBA: DUNDEE INTERNATIONAL CORPORATION," 6 May 1976.
48. Ibid., p. 250.
49. "The Art of Travel: The Caribbean Islands," *Harper's* May 1986, p. T–14.
50. Musical Group Investment Cases, "Deposition of Roger Baskes," Vol. 1, p. 33.
51. Ibid.

52. Ibid.
53. Martindale and Hubbell, 1963; p. 4398.
54. Securities and Exchange Commission, "Lease Between Island Gem Enterprises Ltd. N.V. and St. Maarten Gaming Corporation, N.V.," 21 December 1981.
55. Island Gem Enterprises Ltd. N.V., "Common Stock Purchasers."
56. However, one of the Cayman files brought to Miami by Van Koughnet contains a letter from Wolstencroft to Baskes about Lawaetz's account with a notation hinting the Topaz Trust was also his. At the same time, Sally discovered Topaz's listed officers were apparently four women from New York—Elsa Strokirk, Sandra Lobraico, Donna Scott, and Sandra Hockins. Sally Woodruff to Richard E. Jaffe, "File Folder: Topaz Trust Ltd., # 14359/68." Whether they were linked to Lawaetz was unknown.
57. See Optioner: Castle Trust Company Limited, not individually but solely as Trustee of Settlement T–5003 *OPTION* to Optionee: Mercantile Bank and Trust Company Limited; and Assignor: Mercantile Bank and Trust Company Limited *ASSIGNMENT* to Assignee: Castle Trust Company Limited.
58. See Assignor: Castle Bank & Trust *Assignment* to Assigness: Helwan S.A. as Trustee of the Topaz Settlement, Castle Bank & Trust as Trustee of Settlement 705164, 21 September 1972.
59. Resort and Urban Timeshares, Inc., "Prospectus," 20 August 1981, p. 31.
60. "Resorts International Signs to Run St. Maarten Casino," *Wall Street Journal*, 27 October 1970, p. 14.
61. "Lease Between Island Gem Enterprises Ltd. N.V. and St. Maarten Gaming Corporation, N.V." 21 December 1981.
62. Securities & Exchange Commission, "Resorts of the World, N.V. Form 10–K," 16 March 1978, p. 7.
63. "Teamster Aides Linked to Drugs," *New York Times*, 2 July 1959, p. 14.
64. Waterfront Commission of New York Harbor, "Summary of Information," 25 November 1964.
65. New York City Police Department, Commanding Officer, Intelligence Section, Organized Crime Control Bureau to Chief, Organized Crime Control, "Subject: Organized Crime in Mid-Town Area—Matthew Ianiello," 23 October 1975.
66. Musical Group Investment Cases, "Deposition of Burt Kanter," et passim.
67. See the ICD Audit Report, pp. 17, 32–35.
68. Jane Scholz, "Resorts Firm Refuses to Detail Bahamas Payments," *Miami Herald*, 9 September 1976.
69. German police report on Farrara and McGowan based on F.B.I. Investigations, translated by Donal Murray, a private investigator retained by the San Francisco law firm of Brobeck Phleger & Har-

rison, which represents scores of European victims of the I.C.L.R. fraud, 24 November 1982.

70. Ibid.
71. Al Delugach, "Deal in Desert Just a Mirage?" *Los Angeles Times*, 25 April 1976.
72. M. S. Gilmore for Inversiones Mixtas, N.V. to Castle Trust Company, Limited, 3 June 1969.
73. Graff, Weiss & Company, Certified Public Accountants, Chicago, "I.C.L.R. Schedule of "4062" Account Transactions, Section: Distribution to Partners, October 1972; November 1972; December 1972; January 1973.
74. Calvin Eisenberg to A. R. Bickerton, 28 December 1971.
75. Burt Kanter to M. S. Gilmour, M. Wolstencroft, "RE: ICLR," 22 April 1971.
76. Burton W. Kanter to James McGowan, 22 March 1971.
77. Ibid.
78. Calvin Eisenberg to Miss May S. Gilmour, 13 June 1969; M. S. Gilmour to Calvin Eisenberg, 17 June 1969.
79. A. Alipranti "Trustee," Inversiones Mixtas, N.V., *Declaration of Trust* with Castle Trust Company Limited as Trustee under Settlement T–5095, 14 April 1969.
80. Paul Helliwell to H. M. Wolstencroft, "File: 10.506–3," 12 February 1973.
81. Alan R. Bickerton to Paul L. E. Helliwell, 16 February 1973.
82. U.S. Department of Justice, Criminal Division, "Criminal Division and United States Attorneys Monthly Report of Significance Criminal Cases and Matters," September 1983, p. 24.
83. Delugach, 25 April 1976.
84. Sanford E. Glick, President Beckwith Carbon Corporation, "To the Debenture holders of Beckwith Carbon Corporation," 26 April 1972.
85. Burton W. Kanter to Mr. Michael Wolstencroft, RE: Beckwith Carbon, 21 April 1971.
86. Burton W. Kanter, TAXLAW CGO, PALOMAR NS137, to Michael Wolstencroft, RECEIVED 25 May 1972.
87. Bahamas Telecommunications Corporation, Telegram, J. S. Whyllym, sender, to Beckwith Carbon Corporation," 23 May 1972.
88. Paul L. E. Helliwell, President Florida Shares, Inc., "Dear Stockholder," 21 August 1973; HMT Corporation, "*Consolidation of Shares by Accounts*," undated; Paul L. E. Helliwell, President and Chairman of the Board of Directors, HMT Corporation, "To The Shareholders of Bank of Perrine, Bank of Cutler Ridge, Florida Shares, Inc.," 19 March 1973.
89. M. S. Gilmour, Assistant Secretary, Castle Trust Company Limited to Mr. L. S. Evans, Bahamas Monetary Authority, 29 September 1971.
90. Republica De Panama, Provincia De Panama, Notaria Segundo Del

Circuito, COPIA Escritura No. 2928 DE 11 DE Mavo DE 1972, Por La Cual sa protocoliza un Certificado de Eleccion de la socciadad anonima denominada CASTLE TRUST COMPANY LIMITED; S.A.

91. TW-24, "Memorandum to File, Castle Bank & Trust Co.," 14 February 1974.
92. Haven Project Managers to Director, Intelligence Division CP:1, "Project Haven," 13 March 1974, pp. 7–8.
93. Ibid., p. 6.
94. Ibid.
95. Ibid., p. 3.
96. Recorded and transcribed telephone conversation among Kanter, Helliwell, and Gene Poe, August 1974; turned over to the I.R.S. by an employee of the Bank of Perrine. This conversation was preserved on Dictabelts by Helliwell.
97. Project Managers (Audit and Intelligence) to Program Managers (Audit and Intelligence), Memorandum—SUBJECT: Project HAVEN Status Report—Quarter ending 12/31/73."
98. Field Project Managers to Assistant Regional Commissioners, North Atlantic Region, "Project HAVEN Current Status and Future Plans," 11 November 1974.

8

Crisis in the Internal Revenue Service

The perception of an I.R.S. reformation didn't last long. The trend for the Intelligence Division was completely opposite. Indeed, there quickly emerged an unprecedented internal I.R.S. war. On one side stood a new commissioner and his staff, on the other the renowned Intelligence Division. Skirmishing began when Donald C. Alexander was appointed I.R.S. commissioner in April 1973 by a beleaguered President Richard Nixon. Under Alexander's stewardship, the I.R.S. underwent a long, complicated, and bitter struggle over what and who the Internal Revenue should investigate and recommend for prosecution.

The vendetta took place during Watergate, a huge public distraction that eased the Commissioner's task in dismantling the I.R.S. Intelligence Division. First, Watergate monopolized the news so that hardly anyone commented on Nixon's appointment of Alexander. In the very month that Alexander was officially selected, public attention was focused on several remarkable Watergate developments. One of the convicted burglers, former C.I.A. agent William McCord, certain he was betrayed, was immunized from further prosecution and began to testify before the Grand Jury. McCord knew a great deal about hitherto secret White House projects, and this was an exceedingly grave turn for the President. Also that month, L. Patrick Gray, Nixon's nominee to head the F.B.I., resigned as its acting direction. Gray wisely cut and ran one day after *The New York Times* reported he had destroyed vital documents taken from John Dean's safe, and thus had contributed to the cover-up, the obstruction of justice.

The April bombshells continued. Attorney General Richard Kleindienst removed himself from the Justice Department's Watergate investigation, because of potential conflicts-of-interest. He turned it over to Assistant Attorney General Henry Petersen. And on the last day of that crucial month Nixon announced with deep regret the resignations of his closest aides, the Teutonic chiefs of staff, H. R. Haldeman and John Ehrlichman. The President also declared that day he had fired his former counsel John Dean.

Little wonder Alexander's nomination passed practically unnoticed. Even for those few who had the time to take heed, Alexander's background seemed sound enough for his new position. He was born in Pine Bluff, Arkansas, in 1921. He had married Margaret Louise Savage from Tennessee, and their union produced two sons who followed their father's educational footsteps to Yale and Harvard. Alexander's schooling had been notable. He earned his B.A. from Yale in 1942 (with honors) and an L.L.B. from Harvard (magna cum laude) in 1948. In between Yale and Harvard, Alexander served in the Army with the 14th Armored and 45th Infantry Divisions. He was awarded Silver and Bronze Stars. Alexander's specialty was taxation and he was a busy member of what is called the "Tax Bar." He wrote a number of articles published in the *Tax Law Review*, the *Tax Counselor's Quarterly*, and *The Tax Lawyer*. His last publication prior to his designation as commissioner, entitled "Tax Shelers" appeared in *The Ohio Bar*. An Ohio lawyer, he was a partner in the Cincinnati firm of Dinsmore, Shohl, Coates and Deupree when picked by the Nixon Administration for the top job.

Alexander was not a Washington greenhorn when selected. The Nixon forces had tapped him to serve on an Advisory Group to the commissioner of Internal Revenue in 1969, then kept him around as a Treasury Department Consultant from 1970 through 1972. His nomination was approved on 15 May 1973 by the Senate Committee on Finance. He had not prepared a statement and only a few dull questions were asked.[1]

Alexander's glide through the process was a consequence of the acute preoccupation with Watergate. In the absence of Congressional inquiry, there was no illumination of his tax philosophy and what plans, if any, he had for the I.R.S. under his direction. Moreover, no one asked how he came to be nominated, or what relationships he had with members of the Nixon administration. He was qualified to be Commissioner, but so were others. Who chose Alexander and why were crucial questions not asked; not least because the Internal Revenue Service, it developed, was part of President Nixon's illegal domestic spying apparatus. Even more critical was the fact that several of Nixon's closest cronies were targeted for investigation by the Internal Revenue Service's Intelligence Division.

It is well established now that Nixon used the Executive Branch to discover and punish enemies. He did not construe only ideological opponents as his enemies. Once he used executive institutions for illegal purposes, more and more enemies were created, among those, who in the course of their work, discovered and pointed out administration illegalities. There could be no end to the plotting and concealment, and therefore to the increase in the ranks of opponents. It was the hallmark of the Nixon administration to frame issues in a combative rhetoric, which separated the world into adversaries on the one side, and Nixon loyalists on the other. There never was much of a middle ground with Nixon.

Notorious for harboring grudges, Nixon's drive to get even, and to use the I.R.S. to that end, began with his 1968 victory. Upon taking office in 1969, Nixon, through H. R. Haldeman and Presidential assistant Tom Charles Huston, pressured the Service to go after political opponents—"to make them pay." In the summer of 1969, when Huston called Roger V. Barth, then a special assistant to I.R.S. Commissioner Randolph W. Thrower, and asked what the I.R.S. was going to do about "ideological organizations," there was no question of non-cooperation.[2] Barth, who operated both as a special assistant to Thrower and as deputy chief counsel of the I.R.S., had come to the Service after working "as an advance man for Julie and Tricia Nixon in the 1968 campaign."[3] His response to Huston was immediate—the I.R.S. would set up a secret new group to monitor and harass the President's ideological foes.

Within two weeks of Huston's conversation with Barth, the I.R.S. created the "Activist Organizations Committee," which was soon renamed the more innocuous, "Special Service Group and finally in the winter of 1972 the "Special Service Staff (S.S.S.)." This highly secret, relatively unstructured group, located in a "soundproof basement," operated out of the I.R.S.'s Compliance Division for two and a half years before it was discovered. It was exposed in January 1972 when a former F.B.I. agent "blew the whistle." It was then brought out of the basement, moved to a secure office on the 6th floor in the I.R.S. building, and placed in the Collection Division.

This move (acknowledged in the Internal Revenue Manual) revealed its existence, but not its real work. And nothing came of this news until the Watergate pot was set boiling. The S.S.S. worked hard. In four years it had a file system containing material on 8,585 individuals and almost three thousand organizations, all presumed enemies of the President and his controversial policies. Most of the data, almost all of it useless for tax-gathering purposes, came from the F.B.I. and the Internal Security Division of the Department of Justice.[4]

The S.S.S. was part of Nixon's domestic espionage operation that was relocated and centralized in the White House. John Dean characterized the domestic intelligence operation as a project "to restructure the Government's intelligence-gathering capacities vis-a-vis demonstrators and domestic radicals."[5] The tactics included the wiretapping of groups and individuals suspected of radical activity, the monitoring of their mail, and the burglaries of their apartments, homes and offices. These actions were part of the infamous "Huston plan," named after the zealous presidential assistant who conjured it up upon presidential instruction, following his success with Barth in establishing the secret I.R.S. unit.

Donald C. Alexander was cut from a mold similar to the President's. He was quick to anger, bursting with bravado, and felt surrounded by enemies whom he once dubbed "faceless liars."[6] Former colleagues, when asked about Alexander, first recollect his "ego," his stubbornness, and his intolerance of conflicting opinions.[7] Perhaps it was his personality, as much as anything else, which made him Roger Barth's candidate for commissioner. For it was Barth, the head of the S.S.S., who selected Alexander for the top post in the I.R.S.. Barth, who was Erhlichman's mole in the I.R.S., pushed Alexander's candidacy through.[8]

What set this in motion was Nixon's anger in the summer and

fall of 1972 with what he believed was I.R.S. footdragging on his enemies' list, enlarged after the arrest of the Watergate burglars. Since the initial understanding between the White House and Barth, there had been a change of commissioners. Thrower was replaced by Johnnie M. Walters who, despite Barth's best efforts, was very reluctant to play along with the White House. His interests were in moving aggressively against both organized and corporate criminals, not political dissidents. During Walters' term, George Shultz was secretary of the treasury.

The Watergate burglars were indicated on 15 September, and that prompted President Nixon to hold a strategy session with Haldeman and Dean. They discussed numerous issues including the role of the F.B.I. in the investigation, ways of muzzling a Congressional inquiry into campaign irregularities, and the means to "screw" the *Washington Post* and its attorney Edward Bennett Williams.[9] At one point Dean mentioned there were bitter feelings among former members of the Committee to Reelect the President (CREEP), and that there might be "some finger pointing—false accusations." Nixon lashed out and the following exhange took place:

NIXON—We are all in it together. This is a war. We take a few shots and it will be over. We will give them a few shots and it will be over. Don't worry. I wouldn't want to be on the other side right now. Would you?

DEAN—Along that line, one of the things I've tried to do, I have begun to keep notes on a lot of people who are emerging as less than our friends because this will be over some day and we shouldn't forget the way some of them have treated us.

NIXON—I want the most comprehensive notes on all those who tried to do us in. They didn't have to do it. If we had had a very close election and they were playing the other side I would understand this. No—they were doing this quite deliberately and they are asking for it and they are going to get it. We have not used the power in this first four years as you know. We have never used it. We have not used the Bureau and we have not used the Justice Department but things are going to change now. And they are either going to do it right or go.

DEAN—What an exciting prospect.[10]

Although the last part of Nixon's statement about his holding back during the first term was clearly disingenuous, the tone, style, and substance of this meeting perfectly represented how much the Oval Office resembled a command post for outright political warefare.

Before that meeting ended, the plotters got around to the Internal Revenue Service. Dean complained he wasn't getting sufficient cooperation from the I.R.S. in nailing a McGovern supporter. Nixon shot back in anger, stating the I.R.S. would be much more cooperative after he fired Commissioner Walters. He would be gone as soon as the election was over. He followed that outburst with one aimed at Shultz, just in case the Secretary tried to interfere with Nixon's plans for the post-election I.R.S.: "I don't want George Shultz to ever raise the question, because it would put me in the position of having to throw him out of office. . . . He didn't get to be secretary of the treasury because he has nice blue eyes. It was a goddam favor to him to get the job."[11]

Donald Alexander wanted one of the important posts at Treasury ever since Nixon had become president, but his chances were not very promising during Nixon's first term. Alexander's name surfaced when the I.R.S. chief counsel's spot opened, and then quickly submerged when the idea was nixed by Ohio Senator Robert Taft, Jr.[12] Grandson of the rotund President, son of U.S. Senator Robert A. Taft, known as Mr. Republican, and the leader of the conservative wing of the Republican Party for years, Taft Jr. disliked Alexander, which was enough to end the matter, due to Senatorial courtesy. Taft's reason was quite straightforward. Alexander had worked for the Taft law firm (Taft, Stettinius and Hollister) headquartered in Cincinnati, and had left it to join the rival firm of Dinsmore, Shohl, Coates and Deupree.[13] It is commonly believed that Taft must have mellowed by Nixon's second term or Alexander would not have been selected commissioner.[14]

Even in the absence of objections from Taft, Alexander was far from a popular selection. He was no one's first choice. He had no White House sponsor. White House "bully boy" Charles Colson had another candidate in mind, according to John Ehrlichman, but when he failed to secure support, Colson did not pursue it. With the Watergate issues looming larger and larger, the White House had far more on its mind than who would replace Walters. In the end, the selection of commissioner was simply left in the hands of Roger Barth. There was no process in this affair at all—no nominations, committees, discussion, recommendations, and so forth. Barth just knew his man. In fact, it was the head of the S.S.S. who had earlier worked to get Alexander a post on the I.R.S. Advisory Group. Barth supported Alexander because he was convinced Alexander understood and agreed with the president's policies concerning the Service.

Time has a way of radically changing issues, and during this period in American political life time itself seemed to have radically accelerated—yesterday's secret became the next day's headline, and the following day's taboo. Almost at the very moment Alexander accepted his new position, Barth had passed his pinnacle and was tumbling down. In the spring of 1973, the news about the administration's spying and criminality, about the political use of the I.R.S., was pouring out from seemingly endless sources. Testimony before the Senate's Watergate Committee finally sealed its fate.

The Special Services staff was one of the first domestic spying groups to go, and, ironically enough, it was Commissioner Alexander who rather carefully and circumspectly announced its demise on 9 August 1973. He said that it had been established primarily because of congressional findings and pressure, and, since 1972, the S.S.S. only investigated tax rebels.[15] It was a deft job of revisionism later contradicted when the Joint Committee on Internal Revenue Taxation revealed that the White House had sent another enemies list of 575 persons to the S.S.S. in September 1972.[16] This was Dean's contribution following Nixon's tirade.

Nixon's range of I.R.S. interests, evident during that September meeting, had irrevocably shifted by the beginning of Alexander's term. The aggressive "make the enemies pay" attitude was tempered, replaced by increasingly counterproductive efforts to save himself from the Watergate swamp. The carefully-crafted White-House-directed espionage efforts had become a millstone around his neck. Every detail about them jeopardized Nixon's future in two related ways. They proved long-standing past abuses of power, such as the burglary of Dr. Fielding's office (Fielding was Daniel Ellsberg's psychiatrist), and as more information about previous crimes emerged, it fueled the contemporary cover-up, forming the basis for a charge of obstructing justice. Using the

"Plumbers' to burgle and harass political enemies was one thing, paying them off to keep silent after they were caught was another.

The Watergate scandal was not limited to illegal espionage organizations and their crimes, it leached into all aspects of Nixon's campaign. Despite the president's attempts to contain the damage, the scandal inexorably led to other crimes, including the bribery of public officials, extortion by public officials, and the evasion of taxes, to name the more elemental issues. Every time a campaign contribution was given that was used for something other than legitimate election expenses, it was someone's income, and someone had to report it as such. Sometimes, those who received illegal contributions, like Nixon's most intimate friend "Bebe" Rebozo, fretfully claimed the money was never spent and then returned it or a reasonable facsimile. Part of this more standard corruption was connected to espionage matters. Campaign officials used every device they had to raise and divert funds necessary for those operations and later their cover-up. Campaign law violations were legion. While espionage decisions were made in the White House, CREEP was the money machine. The known Nixon receipts for the 1972 campaign totalled over $37 million; another $1.6 million was borrowed. This phenomenal figure was compiled by the Government Accounting Office, and didn't list contributions under $100 or those made before 7 April 1972.

The point was this: gobs of money were collected by Nixon agents who put the squeeze on corporate friends and others in order to finance the total campaign, which included spying. And those who gave, did so because they too had things they wanted, sometimes specific and immediate favors, at other times merely a claim on the future. The Teamsters were an example of a contributor with an immediate need. Although their total contributions are not known (Jimmy Hoffa claimed the G.A.O. missed about 80 percent of it), the money was given with the clear understanding it was to pay for Hoffa's release from prison. The Teamster package consisted of one thousand dollars from each of the union's business agents, and undisclosed amounts supposedly contributed by Las Vegas mobsters, who had borrowed from the Teamster Pension Funds. After the money was delivered, the president did commute Hoffa's sentence, but added a special clause to the commutation decree which barred Hoffa from union office until 1980. A bitter Hoffa believed he had been double-crossed by Nixon at the urging of Charles Colson and the incumbent Teamster president Frank Fitzsimmons.[17] Former I.R.S. Intelligence Director John Olszewski, who spent years investigating the Teamsters, inclines to Hoffa's opinion.[18]

There were many more instances of influence peddling and bribery involving corporate giants like American Airlines, Gulf Oil, and Goodyear Tire and Rubber. In the United States, corporations have been barred from direct or indirect campaign contributions for federal offices under the Corrupt Practice's Act, originally passed early in the twentieth century and refined many times since.[19]

Gulf's case is the most interesting. The bulk of Gulf's illegal contributions came through a subsidiary known as Bahamas Exploration (Bahamas Ex.) located in Nassau. For years Gulf executives carried out surreptitious transfers of funds from Gulf to Bahamas Ex., which then disbursed the money. It was a massive exercise in bribery and, of course, extortion. In thirteen years over $9.5 million found its way into campaign coffers or the pockets of important politicians. Americans from both parties and every level of government, from the Pennsylvania Turnpike Authority to the White House, received in total about $4.5 million. The remainder primarily went to Italians, Koreans, and Bolivians.[20] Nixon's 1972 campaign cost Gulf $100,000. In this particular instance, it appears Gulf was shaken down by Nixon's campaign chiefs—extortion rather than bribery.

There were so many parts to the phenomenon known as Watergate, and so many levels of criminality. "Follow the money," Deep Throat told Bob Woodward, and he, as well as others, did. That simple maxim partially unearthed the shadow government of espionage and corruption, and exposed, as nothing before or since, the character of a sitting president and his inner circle of friends and associates.

Donald Alexander, however, was never brushed by the political spying issues because of the timing of his appointment. It is thus not known whether he was prepared to go as far as Nixon, Dean, and Barth might have wanted. But clearly Alexander was selected by Barth because of his opinions about the proper role and function of the I.R.S. And in this regard nothing was quite as significant as Alexander's dislike of the Intelligence Division. He believed there was no real place for it in the Service; it went against his grain; it upset his vision. He had the kind of "laissez-faire" view naturally in tune with many of those caught in the web of Watergate criminality, as well as others involved in more traditional organized crime. Financial privacy was as much his intellectual cornerstone as theirs.

Take Rebozo, for instance. His primary problem during Alexander's term had to do with accepting the illegal campaign contribution of $100,000 in cash from Howard Hughes. The money came in two installments, the first in 1969 and the second in 1970. They were really bribes to insure Nixon's approval for Hughes' purchase of Air West, and to smooth Hughes' path past the Anti-Trust Division of the Department of Justice so he could acquire a sixth hotel-casino in Las Vegas.[21] The Hughes money was never reported, and that left Rebozo subject to a tax evasion charge. To wriggle out of it, Rebozo argued the money stayed in his bank, never used, never touched, and squirreled away and forgotten. This artless explanation could hardly deter the I.R.S. Intelligence Division from continuing its probe, which included not only Rebozo and the $100,000, but also the activities of the president's brother, (F.) Donald Nixon.

The Intelligence Division had discovered a Hughes executive named John Meier who swindled millions from his boss. Working closely with Meier in a number of other highly questionable schemes was Don Nixon. The president's anxiety over his brother's clumsy intrigues and the Hughes bribe fueled his anger with his brother, and no doubt the Intelligence Division, which must have seemed dedicated to his destruction.

During the heyday of Watergate, it looked like the Intelligence Division was everywhere pushing criminal investigations into one touchy area after another. The Rebozo probe was broadcast by ABC News in the summer of 1973. A day later, Spiro Agnew was informed he was the target of a criminal tax investigation. In the midst of this unprecedented development, several corporate confessions about illegal contributions were made.

When Commissioner Alexander bloodied the Intelligence Division, it inevitably provided relief for many under examination.

Philosophically speaking, he was a financial crook's delight, as a glance at his original intentions makes plain. Few policies better served members of that community than Alexander's ones dealing with foreign tax havens and offshore investigations. Alexander's significant position on offshore questions was clear before he officially took office. As commissioner-designate in early 1973, he tipped his hand by proposing a small, but most important change in the tax return format itself. Alexander lobbied hard for the elimination from the tax form of the question that asked taxpayers whether or not they had a foreign bank account. This "Foreign Bank Account Question" had been placed on tax forms only a few years earlier to encourage compliance by taxpayers considering the illegal use of secret foreign bank accounts.[22] Falsely answering left an individual guilty at least of perjury.

Alexander was opposed in this move by the director of the Intelligence Division, but persistence paid off. The commissioner finally succeeded in removing the question for the 1975 tax year, after someone had altered the Intelligence Division's written opinion. After a change in the Intelligence Division's leadership, Alexander asked for its input on the question. A memorandum written by Charles McCalmont, the National Office program manager, and *initialed* by Alexander's new head of Intelligence, recommended retention of the question. The memo was then sent on its bureaucratic way. But it disappeared and in its place a different document appeared. This one was *signed* by the head of Intelligence and it agreed with Alexander's policy. When McCalmont asked what happened, he was told never to mention the issue again.[23]

Alexander didn't like the foreign bank account reporting requirement, and he most certainly didn't approve of Intelligence Division investigations into financial crimes utilizing foreign banks in places like The Bahamas, the Cayman Islands, and the Netherlands Antilles. These investigations often involved proactive undercover work aimed at "potential" or "suspected" tax evaders and therefore, Alexander maintained, were wholly inappropriate to the reactive, civil tax enforcement Service he wanted.

He also opposed in principle and fact the Intelligence Division's targeting of organized crime syndicates and narcotics smugglers.[24] Alexander was especially at odds with the two-year-old Narcotics

Traffickers Tax Program (N.T.P.) which used a special Target Selection Committee to choose appropriate individuals for investigation, even though he did recognize the effectiveness of the Service's "war" on drug merchants.[25] Effectiveness didn't matter for someone as conservatively-minded as he was. It was much the same when it came to organized crime investigations. He wanted the I.R.S. out of the Federal Strike Forces, no matter what the need was. Since 1970, there had been an ongoing Senate investigation into massive worldwide swindles carried out by organized crime using offshore banks in foreign tax havens to negotiate stolen or counterfeit securities. The Senate Permanent Subcommittee on Investigations urged law enforcement coordination at the same time Alexander was planning I.R.S. disengagement.[26]

In attacking the Intelligence Division, Alexander successfully but wrongly portrayed the Division as out of control, involved in projects and operations that smacked of political spying, run by special agents devoted to illegal and unfair practices in their zeal to catch crooks. There were few, if any, who realized just how ironic this was, as Roger Barth's man accused the Division of spying. In this offensive against the Intelligence Division, there was a blurring of issues and the timing of events in order to take the fullest advantage of the Watergate theme. Normal and practical investigative procedures, which used informants and conducted covert surveillances, were labelled by the commissioner as the hallmark of political policing.

Determined to either tame or terminate the Intelligence Division prior to his leaving office, Alexander and his staff turned every found procedural mistake (large or small, meaningful or irrelevant) into a "post hoc" justification for his claim and policy. At times, this called for them to testify falsely under oath about their motivation and actions. In the drive against the Intelligence Division, it was the assault on Project Haven and Jaffe which assumed the greatest significance. There were, nonetheless, important antecedents.

In the months before the concentration on Haven, Alexander halted the work of an Intelligence Division unit known as the Intelligence Gathering and Retrieval System (I.G.R.S.), which had been accused (ironically in retrospect) of suspicious contact with members of Nixon's White House staff.[27] The press picked up on the I.G.R.S. in February 1975, reporting that the Internal Revenue Service was investigating a special Miami unit that gathered information concerning the personal habits and activities of prominent citizens believed to be anti-Nixon.[28]

A few days later the Service denied these allegations, but added it was still investigating. It also announced that Commissioner Alexander's Deputy, William E. Williams, would closely monitor the Miami inquiry. Indeed, it was later learned that Williams had already started an informal probe of intelligence gathering practices that past December. This was followed in a month by an announcement that all Intelligence Division activities were to cease except those connected with active tax cases.[29] And then Alexander and Williams were handed an Intelligence Division nightmare, an operation that seemed to confirm all suspicions of illegality and ineptitude.

"Justice Dept. Is Linked to Sex Spying," announced the startling headline on 16 March 1975. But it was I.R.S. Intelligence, not the Justice Department, which ran "Operation Leprechaun," a poorly managed affair that grew out of a serious professional probe. Since the early 1970s, there had been a coordinated investigation involving the Miami Strike Force, I.R.S. Intelligence, the Dade County Public Safety Department, and the Miami Police Department into the association of public officials with organized crime figures in Dade County.[30] Under surveillance were several members of Meyer Lansky's Miami Beach syndicate who regularly met with a circuit court judge and other public officials. The thrust of the investigation was aimed at Richard Gerstein, a state Attorney, who was characterized by the chief of the Miami Strike Force as unquestionably "a knowing handmaiden of organized crime in Dade County."[31]

Leprechaun was run by Special Agent John T. Harrison. He worked closely with a veteran informant named Elsa Gutierrez, who was previously employed on a casual basis by the Secret Service, Drug Enforcement Administration, and Organized Crime Strike Force. According to Gutierrez, her job was to "get dirt on" about 30 Dade County public officials, including three federal judges and Gerstein. Gutierrez implied she was supposed to have sex with at least one of the targets, but refused and quit instead.[32]

Some of the targets were amused by the attention. "My sex habits are not a taxable item," said Alfonso Sepe, a Dade County circuit judge. Sepe added a wry note stating "if anything, I think I'm depreciating and should get a tax writeoff."[33] Others, naturally enough, were not quite so entertained.

Leprechaun was a perfect foil for slashing away at the Intelligence Division. With its charming name and strange characters, it became a symbol of the Intelligence Division running wild, gone "dotty." And though it had absolutely nothing to do with Project Haven, it did have a major impact on its future.[34] Leprechaun formed part of the indispensable backdrop for those committed to stopping it. Could the Intelligence Division be trusted? Leprechaun was the answer and the excuse they needed.

Project Haven was suspended just before it could disseminate Castle Bank file material to the appropriate I.R.S. regions. A meeting in New York was arranged for 19 and 20 August 1975, to provide regional audit and intelligence personnel with the files.[35] The assistant commissioner for Compliance, concurred with the schedule, but went on record noting that possible adverse publicity might still be generated concerning how the Castle Bank master list of accounts and certain other records were acquired.[36] The hedge should have been a tipoff. Within a week or so, Compliance had changed its mind and the meeting was cancelled. The turnabout was peculiarly done, and would provide questions for years of inquiry.

Jaffe's own difficulties started during the first week of August with the shock of having his rights read to him by I.R.S. inspectors sent to conduct an official interrogation. This was an exceedingly serious inquiry, he was told. The matter had already been referred to the Department of Justice for investigation and perhaps prosecution. Jaffe gave them various relevant memoranda and related that his superior, Troy Register, chief of the Intelligence Division, Jacksonville District, had been informed of Casper's plan in advance and approved. After the operation the appropriate I.R.S. and Department of Justice officials were notified and supplied with the pertinent details.[37]

Guilford Troy Register, Jr. supported most of Jaffe's recollection when he testified several years later during one of the few

Haven cases. Register remembered he took the copied briefcase documents to Atlanta, and presented the material both to the regional commissioner of Internal Revenue for the Southeast Region, and the assistant regional commissioner for Intelligence, the head of Intelligence for all the Southeast. From Atlanta, Register transported the documents to Washington and turned them over to the Director of Intelligence, John Olszewski.

Register and Jaffe disagreed over the question of prior knowledge of the briefcase incident. The former district intelligence chief remembered a telephone conversation with Jaffe asking for permission to receive and photograph documents brought by an informant. But he recalled only a brief talk during which no mention was made of how the informant gathered, or intended to gather the material. In any case, he authorized the receipt and reproduction of the documents. Even when he did learn the details, Register didn't pause for a moment in moving the project forward.[38]

Jaffe ultimately contacted Jack B. Solerwitz, a lawyer employed by the Federal Criminal Investigators Association, retaining him as counsel after the interrogation by the inspectors.[39] Solerwitz had recently represented other special agents from the Intelligence Division who were in deep conflict with Alexander. The primary issue for them was Alexander's policy directive on informants, which constitutes one of the most sensitive factors in professional law enforcement. Sometime during the first half of May 1975, special agents were ordered to identify their informants or suffer disciplinary proceedings. Among the many objectionable features of this policy, reasoned the critics, was the fundamental one that it put informants at extreme risk. A civil action on behalf of six special agents in New York was filed in the federal court by Solerwitz. The plaintiffs claimed the policy would wreck their work against organized crime, drug traffickers, corrupt public officials, and make informing exceptionally risky and therefore unlikely.[40]

In the early autumn, both Jaffe and Casper joined the New York litigation. Jaffe's claims were consistent with those of the special agents. Casper's, on the other hand, were derived from statements made by Alexander at a press conference held late in September. During the conference, the commissioner all but revealed Casper's identity. He referred to the briefcase incident in sufficient detail that Castle Bank partisans were easily able to identify Casper as an I.R.S. operative. Casper was angry and worried, particularly when he thought of returning to The Bahamas.[41] He also retained Solerwitz as counsel.

It was impossible to keep this dispute out of the press; a brawl of this magnitude within the I.R.S. was a major story. During the last week of September, stories about the row monopolized the headlines. Certain details about Tradewinds, Jaffe's current predicament, and Alexander's request for a congressional investigation of the project were now public knowledge. As expected, the Intelligence Division's dislike and mistrust of Alexander was one major theme. Sources were quoted saying Alexander's qualifications were grossly inadequate for the post.[42]

The press began asking embarrassing questions of Commissioner Alexander. One report stated there were allegations that Alexander conspired to undermine a Customs Service prosecution of one of his former clients, the Proctor and Gamble company. There were other charges of improper behavior on Alexander's part, which finally forced Treasury Secretary William E. Simon to publicly state he had complete confidence in Alexander.[43] After that rhetorical back-slap was reported, the bad news flowed once again. Bob Woodward of the *Washington Post* noted that Alexander's action had "jeopardized one of the largest potential criminal and civil court tax recovery operations in the history of the I.R.S."[44]

The material in the American press jarred Bahamian sensibilities in several ways. One particular story in the *Miami Herald* produced a corresponding answer from The Bahamas. The Miami account reported that Jaffe had confidential informants in The Bahamas who were in top political and financial circles in Freeport and Nassau.[45] The following day the Bahamian government announced it had known of Tradewinds since 1972, considered it an attempt by the I.R.S. to breach the country's bank secrecy laws, and had sacked an immigration officer for aiding the operation.[46] Secretary of State Henry Kissinger instructed the ambassador in Nassau, if questioned by Bahamian officials, to respond that the Service was conducting an internal investigation of Tradewinds.[47] By the end of September, tempers in The Bahamas were frayed over the revelation of Tradewinds. At one point, Prime Minister Pindling threatened to punch out the few teeth of Clarence Lightbourn, an independent representative in the House of Assembly who had the temerity to call for an investigation of foreigners using The Bahamas for illegal purposes. Pindling shouted that Lightbourn himself might be involved with an I.R.S. informant. Joining Pindling in attacking Lightbourn was the deputy prime minister, who threw a book at the beleaguered representative.[48]

Bahamian stories about Operation Tradewinds raised the anxiety level of every resident TW agent. For Sally it was an especially difficult time. There were pressing financial problems mixed with the dangerous possibility of exposure. She unquestionably felt the strain.[49] During the following year, her position did not materially improve. The bottom was probably reached in August 1976, when a Justice Department prosecutor, Bernard S. Bailor, accompanied by James Lane from the Intelligence Division, both of whom were unknown to her, came to Nassau for a talk. Sally was staggered to learn Bailor's mission included disclosing her identity to the Bahamian Government.[50] He wanted her permission for what seemed perfect madness; she strenuously resisted.

She wrote to Jaffe: "Boy! was I mad when I saw that they wanted us [Sally and her husband Ed] to sign a legal document that could/would be filed in public record in Dade County! Mon Dieu! Dios Mio! Obviously no one gave us a thought on that one. Then they got real cute and tried to pressure us." Sally had decided it was time to turn the tables. "I pretended to get very angry at him, saying what did he mean calling me on an open line at a time like this and discussing this matter. He must know that everyone listens in on calls here. What did he mean by putting me in jeopardy."[51]

Protecting her identity as an agent was becoming an ever more pressing problem for Sally. A few weeks after the Bailor incident, two members of the CBS show *60 Minutes* arrived literally on her doorstep, asking about Operation Tradewinds. They had at least two confidential I.R.S. memos with details about the operation and job descriptions of TW-1, TW-1A, and TW-5. She was irate, knowing it could be even more unpleasant for her if identified on television. After putting the CBS people off, Sally considered who might have sent the reporters to her and why. Where did they get secret I.R.S. memos? Sally thought this indicated probable collusion between Castle Bank, the Justice Department, and I.R.S. management. "Was the idea," she wrote, "to destroy what is left of the TW operation?"

It was not an irrational question to ask in the summer of 1976. By then, Sally knew Tradewinds was just about finished, and that Project Haven was in desperate shape. However, she was able to maintain her cover, which was critically important for her future in The Bahamas. She was secure despite the national publicity when *60 Minutes* aired its Bahamian investigation on 21 November 1976. That night, Mike Wallace reported that "Norman Casper was hired by the Intelligence Division of I.R.S. to try to finger U.S. tax evaders in the Bahamas and that is where Castle Bank came under scrutiny."[52] Wallace interviewed both Casper and Sybil Kennedy about Wolstencroft and the briefcase. He also questioned Burt Kanter about tax evasion and Castle Bank. When asked who owned the bank, Kanter responded, his eyes dancing evasively, "I don't know . . . I really don't know." Paul Helliwell was equally in the dark when questioned about who directed Castle. He confusingly phrased his answer this way: "much of the direction of their operation did not come from me."[53]

The show covered most of the important issues, including Pindling's relationship to Castle. Standing in front of the Prime Minister's home, Wallace said it cost $450,000, part of which was borrowed from Castle Bank.[54] The Pindling connection was the segue to a section dealing with Commissioner Alexander. Wallace announced that "Last year Norm Casper's work and the secret IRS investigation were revealed and temporarily roadblocked by the then new head of the I.R.S., himself, Donald Alexander."[55] The show then cut to an interview with Alexander.

The I.R.S. fight shifted to the congressional arena when a Subcommittee of the Committee on Government Operations, chaired by Representative Benjamin S. Rosenthal of New York began an inquiry. Hearings opened on the morning of 6 October 1975 at the Rayburn House Office Building. Members of the Subcommittee included Elliott H. Levitas from Georgia and Father Robert F. Drinan from Massachusetts. Appearing as a witness the first day was Commissioner Alexander. He was accompanied by some from his administration involved in the Haven battle, including Deputy Commissioner Williams, and the Acting Assistant Commissioner for Compliance Edwin Trainor.[56]

Alexander quickly got down to it. He would not stand for uncontrolled law enforcement, for aberrations like Operation Leprechaun, he informed the Subcommittee.[57] The commissioner was worried about illegally obtained evidence, believing I.R.S. policy on civil cases should match the scrupulousness brought about by the exclusionary rule in criminal matters. Chairman Rosenthal, to the contrary, thought this affair was primarily about the problem of Americans fraudulently bringing money into The Bahamas, deceiving the United States Government, which was attempting to discover the crimes and collect the taxes. With that history in mind, Rosenthal noted different undercover methods were used to gather the information, and that these methods generally stayed within the law, but sometimes veered a bit to the right or left. The response to his statement was surprising. Deputy Commissioner Williams said the Service wasn't sure about the evidence issue yet; it was still under investigation. With some exasperation, the witnesses were asked how long it took to get the facts about Casper's "caper."

Although not mentioned, the Alexander administration already had the facts, and at least one legal opinion on the briefcase incident, which stated, in effect, the material was usable. Bank secrecy in The Bahamas was not law in the United States. Jaffe had committed no crime.[58] The examination of the briefcase caper was carried out by the Justice Department's Criminal Tax Division in 1975. The primary questions asked were whether the action constituted an illegal search under the Fourth Amendment and an invasion of Wolstencroft's privacy. It was reckoned that the controlling statute which protects the civil rights of both Americans and aliens as to warrantless searches by federal agents, is predicated on the action being malicious and without reasonable cause. As far as the briefcase was concerned, the report held, there was plenty of reasonable cause and the search was not malicious. On the most important points, the general conclusions were "no federal criminal statute has been violated through participation in the securing in this country of the records protected by Bahamian law," and the "Bahamian Banks and Trust Companies Regulations Acts of 1965 has not been violated in the course of the briefcase incident, regardless of any question of extra-territorial effect of the Act."[59]

What the congressional subcommittee was most interested in determining was exactly when Project Haven was suspended, who did it, and why. Alexander was asked, for instance, about press allegations that he had personal reasons both for exposing Operation Tradewinds and closing down Project Haven. The commissioner denied that was so, adding he "did not shut it [Haven] down."[60] Alexander later strongly reiterated this point, which became a theme of the hearing. He could not have served private interests in this affair because he didn't shut Haven down. Ed Trainor made the decision and neither the commissioner nor the deputy commissioner were involved at all. They were only briefed after the fact.[61] He tried to make the Subcommittee understand the Service faced a dilemma. It desired effective, not irresponsible, tax law enforcement. For his commitment to honest and aboveboard enforcement, he said dramatically, "I have been berated by a group of faceless liars."[62]

Some members of the Panel found Alexander's testimony difficult to accept. Congressman Levitas pursued the critical issue of timing, establishing for the record that high officials in both the Justice Department and Internal Revenue Service had known the facts about the briefcase since very early in 1974. Not only that, the congressman remarked, but just this past July the question of whether Project Haven should proceed was discussed by officials of the I.R.S., specifically in the Compliance Division, and it was given a green light. Levitas carefully enumerated the troubling sequential issues in the commissioner's account. Then Father Drinan asked, "What brought everything to a screeching halt?" Deputy Commissioner Williams took a stab at an explanation. It was Operation Leprechaun that made them examine all intelligence work in the state of Florida.[63]

But making Leprechaun the cause could not end the issue. The chronology of Alexander's increasing anger with the Intelligence Division could not support this explanation. First of all, Deputy Inspector Williams halted Intelligence Division activities on 22

January 1975, with nary a thought about Leprechaun or Project Haven. His immediate concern is unclear, but he soon focused on the Intelligence Gathering and Retrieval System. About two weeks later, an official investigation into I.G.R.S. started, which was handled by the I.R.S. Inspection Service, staffed from the Internal Security and Internal Audit Divisions. The inquiry thus followed the deputy inspector's first actions concerning the Intelligence Division.[64] Second, it was in the midst of this investigation that adverse publicity about Operation Leprechaun surfaced. On 14 March, Inspection included Leprechaun in its probe. Inspection's *Report* on both I.G.R.S. and Leprechaun was completed on 23 June 1975. Neither Jaffe, nor Operation Tradewinds nor Project Haven were mentioned in the 28 page single-spaced document.[65] Once again Leprechaun's disturbing reputation lent a certain plausibility to the claim that all I.R.S. criminal investigations using undercover techniques and informants were necessarily suspect. But it did not lead to Jaffe and his projects. Indeed, if it had, Compliance surely should have been in trouble. It approved the Haven dissemination meeting in July **after** Inspection's *Report* was received.

Much of what Alexander and his staff had to say at the congressional hearing was soon shown to be either false or foolish, in any case. At the end of 1975, press reports rebutted much of Alexander's testimony. They went right to the commissioner's repeated statement that he did not suspend Project Haven. Reporters discovered Alexander was at a meeting and did participate in the decision despite what he and his staff told the Rosenthal Committee. I.R.S. internal documents directly contradicted the commissioner's testimony. Although Trainor did authorize the Project's suspension, his action followed a meeting with the commissioner in his own office at precisely 1:30 in the afternoon on 14 August. One hour later, Trainor telephoned New York I.R.S. officials and told them Haven was to be placed on hold.[66] Trainor finally remembered, the *Chicago Sun Times* reported, that the action was taken after speaking with Alexander. Nevertheless, he still claimed he had made his decision the day before and it was accomplished without benefit of the commissioner's input.

An I.R.S. spokesman tried to explain the damaging account. Alexander "had no advance knowledge of the decision—that is clear. . . . He had advance knowledge of the suspension."[67] The act of suspending Project Haven was now broken down into tiny, willful, independent steps. Alexander and Trainor talked about doing it, but only after Trainor had determined to do it. It wasn't a very clever explanation, but it was the best one fashionable from such slight material.

Alexander broke the back of the Intelligence Division, and understandably some of the victims were rankled. In 1975, for instance, while the Rosenthal Subcommittee worked on the difficult issues, the Federal Criminal Investigators Association (F.C.I.A.) sent to the secretary of the treasury a resolution on the havoc caused by Alexander to the Intelligence Division. Included in the resolution, passed at the society's Detroit Convention in October, was mention of the Strike Force and Narcotic Traffickers Programs disruption, the routine harassment and humiliation of district directors and managers causing them to further restrict the activities of special agents, and the jeopardizing of informants. The F.C.I.A. proposed that the secretary of the treasury transfer the criminal investigative functions of the Intelligence Division out of the I.R.S., and place them under the wing of the assistant secretary of the Treasury for Enforcement, Operations and Tariff Affairs.[68] The F.C.I.A. had several thousand members and it is hard to imagine a better gauge of broadly held anger and outrage. Almost a year later, certain high ranking Intelligence Division officials from the Southeast Region requested congressional intervention, claiming an ongoing process of harassment and forced retirement.[69]

Getting rid of Jaffe was policy for several years, but it proved a difficult task. Unlike his Intelligence Division colleagues who retired or backed off under pressure, Jaffe not only stayed in the service, but remained on Project Haven, much to the discomfort of high I.R.S. officials. The Project itself was moved in late November 1975 from I.R.S. control to the Department of Justice, and placed under the administration of Senior Oversight Attorney Bernard S. Bailor, yet to visit Sally in The Bahamas. Under the direction of the Justice Department, I.R.S. representation was also changed. No longer a National Office Program headquartered in New York, Project Haven responsibilities were, in a sense, reassigned to the Jacksonville District's Miami Field Office.

By then, I.R.S. directors and managers in that district reflected the profound changes which had taken place under Alexander's stewardship.

From the moment Haven went to Justice, the Jacksonville managers pressured Bailor to release Jaffe from the Project. Although this wasn't accomplished until the spring of 1977, they were able to marginalize him much earlier. Careful and systematic steps were taken to detach him from the more sensitive Project areas and the decision making process. This was obvious by the summer of 1976, when important planning sessions were held dealing with Castle Bank and Jaffe was not in attendance.[70]

In addition, I.R.S. management prolonged the internal investigation into the briefcase incident, which finally ended as Jaffe always predicted. The Inspection Service judged there had been no basis for the charge he had illegally obtained foreign bank documents. Jaffe received an official "clearance letter" from Charles O. DeWitt, district director, Jacksonville, in mid-December 1976. The Jacksonville director regretted any inconvenience the investigation may have caused; the matter was officially closed.[71] But there was still the Justice Department to contend with. The I.R.S. had referred the Jaffe case to Justice for possible prosecution in the summer of 1975. In time, the Department of Justice made exactly the same determination as the I.R.S. A Federal Grand Jury which heard the evidence declined to indict, which greatly pleased the U.S. attorney who was sure Jaffe was the subject of a vendetta.[72]

Despite these findings, I.R.S. leadership still insisted Jaffe had to go. Finally a way was found which corresponded in time with the first major Castle Bank depositor case. Charged in this important action was Jack Payner from Cleveland, who failed to report his Castle Bank account, which held $442,000. Ironically, Payner's indictment was based in part on his failure to honestly answer the foreign bank account question, which so bothered Alexander he successfully fought to have it removed from the form. Because the government's evidence was linked to Wolstencroft's briefcase documents, Jaffe was an important witness. A pattern of new harassment emerged at this time, designed to take the marginal Jaffe and banish him forever from Project Haven.

A series of niggling charges were filed as I.R.S. leadership prepared to suspend Jaffe. Bernard Bailor complained to the I.R.S. Inspection Service that Jaffe's testimony at the Payner trial conflicted with earlier sworn statements made to the Inspection Service. A special inquiry was therefore begun to consider the charge on 25 March. The investigation lasted until almost the end of May. At its conclusion, Jaffe's testimony was deemed consistent.[73] However, Jaffe's problems weren't over with. He was also charged with disclosing Project Haven information to a private attorney. It took almost a year before DeWitt was once again pleased to inform him that allegation, too, was groundless.[74]

The final decision to remove Jaffe was made early in April 1977, and a plan put into motion. Support from the Justice Department for removing Jaffe was very important, and I.R.S. officials worked diligently to secure it. The forces against Jaffe were lined up no later than 22 April.[75] They were awaiting the most propitious moment. The Payner case provided it.

On a motion to suppress the evidence, Federal Judge John M. Manos, in the Cleveland District Court, levelled a staggering judgement on Jaffe and his actions. Judge Manos, on 28 April 1977, found Jaffe's testimony on certain points "unconvincing," and the "search procedure" outrageous, "shocking the court's conscience." He decided Casper's "caper" was "inconsistent with American standards of justice," and that Jaffe's and Casper's conduct was illegal. Manos thus held the government's evidence was the fruit of an illegal seizure of Wolstencroft's briefcase, and had to be suppressed.[76] The very next day, "in light of the Payner decision" he was told, Jaffe was off Project Haven.[77] The die had already been cast, but the absolutely withering opinion made the job infinitely easier. Jaffe was not surprised by his suspension, although he suspected and came to know that the Payner case covered, rather than initiated the action.

Several influential columnists and reporters commented on the case. Jack Anderson, for one, defended Jaffe and lambasted I.R.S. officials. Anderson said the Internal Revenue Service jeopardized an over $500 million investigation of rich taxpayers by removing its premier agent from the case. He added, this could only be good news for mobsters. The columnist pointed out the Manos decision was contrary to the findings of a federal Grand Jury, and an 18–month investigation conducted by the I.R.S.[78]

Jaffe had his own response to the development which he put into letter form:

ONE AGENT'S OPINION

With its customary shortsightedness and predictable propensity to over react, the IRS has taken an action that it will soon have cause to regret.

Despite more than a year's scrutiny by 23 grand jurors and several dozen inspectors which found me innocent of any improper conduct, let alone "gross illegal activity," the Service is offering me up as a sacrificial scapegoat to the opinions of one federal judge. By doing this you are announcing to the world that you agree with the judge's opinion that I and the IRS are guilty of "gross illegal acts." This action thereby falls in precisely the same category as our former commissioner's "gutter affair" comment about Leprechaun.

I would also remind you that I am still going to be called upon to appear as a witness in future cases. Your suspension of me from HAVEN will have the effect of discrediting my future testimony to the detriment of government cases. In addition, your action is going to have an adverse effect on the morale of all special agents in the Intelligence Division--not just those assigned to the project. I may not be a seer who can peer into the future, but allow me to predict what I believe is going to happen.

1)   *There is going to be a severe backlash against this judge's opinion because it is grossly unsupported by the evidence adduced in his court.*

2)   *His suppression of the evidence in this case will be appealed.*

3)   *His ruling will be reversed in words almost as strong as those used in his opinion.*

4)   *He will then find the defendant guilty as charged.*

5)   *The IRS will end up with egg on its face.*

For all of these reasons, and especially for the good of the Service, I urge you to reconsider your suspension. For my own good, I'm not entirely convinced that you might not be doing me an immense favor. Most of you here have my respect and friendship. The IRS doesn't pay you enough for days like today. Please see that Mr. DeWitt gets a copy of this statement.

Richard E. Jaffe
Special Agent
May 2, 1977

Jaffe retired from the Internal Revenue Service in January 1979. About a year later, the Payner case reached the Supreme Court. It was argued in February, 1980, and decided in June.[79]

The Manos opinion was rejected by a vote of six to three. Chief Justice Burger wrote "Payner—whose guilt is not in doubt—cannot take advantage of the Government's violation of the constitutional rights of Wolstencroft, for he is not a party to this case."[80] In this vastly imperfect world, the fruits of Casper's "caper" were ultimately determined adequate.

There is yet another and perhaps final twist to the legal proceedings which casts a new light on the Payner decision. Recently, it has been alleged that Judge Manos enjoyed a long working relationship with organized crime. Nine years after his denunciation of Jaffe and Casper, stories about the judge's supposed secret life appeared in the press. Allen Friedman, a convicted racketeer, and the talkative uncle of the late Teamster President, Jackie Presser, told federal officials that Manos took part in union shakedown schemes in the 1950s with organized crime. Friedman claimed that Manos cooperated with the Cleveland mob both before and after he became a judge.[81] The bond between the Cleveland racketeers, Kleinman and Dalitz, and Castle's owners was intricate and abiding. These disclosures certainly raise the troubling question whether the Castle conspirators had reached the federal judiciary.

The termination of Tradewinds and the battle over Haven shut the only window American law enforcement had into American criminals using The Bahamas. This was apparent as early as the October 1975 Congressional hearings when Alexander was asked questions about issues beyond Project Haven. Of particular concern was the commissioner's policy for dealing with the apprehension of tax evaders using offshore havens. In an attempt to summarize the testimony on recommended procedures for dealing with countries such as The Bahamas, Representative Anthony Moffett of Connecticut noted a counter-productive logic. He argued if a country such as The Bahamas passes bank secrecy legislation, and if the I.R.S. will not use any information on tax fraud that violates a foreign law (Alexander's position), wasn't this, therefore, a policy declaring that offshore tax evasion in countries with strict bank secrecy laws was safe from the Service? There was no satisfactory answer to Moffett's analysis. The best the commissioner could offer was the need to pursue tax fraud issues through proper diplomatic channels.

Then the commissioner was questioned about the degree of past cooperation on tax and banking matters by the Bahamian government. There was an awkward and embarrassing exchange. Neither Alexander nor his staff at the hearing had a clue concerning past Bahamian and U.S. cooperation in tax matters that came through diplomatic channels. The only historical examples of cooperation they could have cited were those forged by Jaffe with the Bahamian police, and expressed through the years in Operation Tradewinds.

MR. ROSENTHAL—Has the Bahamian Government been cooperative with our Government in the enforcement of the laws of the United States: Does anybody have an opinion?

MR. ALEXANDER—Does anybody from I.R.S. back there have any thoughts on this? Mr. DeWitt [District Director from Jacksonville]? Do you have any thoughts on this?

MR. DEWITT—I cannot speak to the period we are covering.

MR. ALEXANDER—I am sorry we cannot help you, Mr. Chairman, but we look forward to another session in which we may be able to give you some help.[82]

Alexander's homilies were grist for the press's mill. Columnist Mary McGrory (herself distinguished by making President Nixon's "enemies list") devastatingly summed up Alexander's Congressional appearance and style—a small man with a large, jutting jaw; reminiscent of a small town minister with an unruly flock; prone to sermons on his Constitutional devotion; vague to the extreme about details, relying instead on ill-prepared assistants; and finally so petulant that at one point he threw down "the little gold pencil he always carries with him to indicate his indignation."[83]

By the end of the decade drug smugglers, organized crime syndicates, and tax evaders, shielded from American law enforcement scrutiny and in cahoots with corrupt Bahamian government officials, had turned The Bahamas into a racketeer's paradise. A fair share of the responsibility for this had to be placed at Alexander's door. This was done, in fact, by David R. MacDonald who had been the assistant secretary for Enforcement, Operations and Tariff Affairs at the Treasury Department in 1974.[84] He supervised the law enforcement activities of several Treasury Department branches such as Customs, the Bureau of Alcohol, Tobacco and Firearm, and the Secret Service.

Testifying before Congress in 1980, MacDonald maintained that the adoption of Alexander's policy forced the Service to engage in reverse discrimination by concentrating on the returns of wage earners instead of hard-core criminals. Smugglers and other professional criminals, he told a congressional audience, learn to isolate themselves from the proscribed goods and services they sell and thereby avoid prosecution. But they cannot and would not separate themselves from the money, which was precisely why they went into the business of crime. He concluded that the I.R.S. was indispensable in any earnest effort against the international drug traffic, and it had to abandon the lenient, discriminating, and foolish policies of the past.

There was no legitimate reason for dropping the narcotics program and ending cooperative work aimed at organized crime. The attack on the Intelligence Division didn't advance civil liberties even by happenstance. It merely took advantage of the national uproar to supply an "after the fact" justification for a policy that made the world safer for international organized crime and its helpers in law and banking. There never was any necessity to end Operation Tradewinds, nor to treat Haven in the manner that was done. Whatever procedural mistakes were made could have been fairly treated far short of the draconian measures used.

Meanwhile, the Justice Department's Project Haven ambled on. There were several trials, although none that went to the central question of Castle Bank ownership. Nevertheless, there were prosecutions, someone had to tumble for all the rampant criminality exposed. But it wouldn't be either Paul Helliwell or Gene Poe both of whom died in 1976—Poe of heart disease in February, Helliwell of emphysema on Christmas day.

Notes

1. U.S. Senate, Committee on Finance, *Hearings on Nominations of Helmust Sonnenfeldt, Donald C. Alexander, and Edward C. Schmults* (Government Printing Office, 1973), pp. 1–4.
2. U.S. Senate, Committee on the Judiciary, Subcommittee on Con-

stitutional Rights, *Political Intelligence in the Internal Revenue Service: The Special Service Staff* (Government Printing Office, December 1974), p. 9.

3. Frank J. Donner, *The Age of Surveillance: The Aims and Methods of America's Political Intelligence System* (Vintage Books, 1981), p. 332.
4. Ibid., p. 336.
5. William A. Dobrovir, Joseph D. Gephardt, Samuel J. Buffone, Andra N. Oakes, *The Offenses of Richard M. Nixon: A Guide for the People of the United States of America* (published jointly by the Public Issues Press, Quadrangle, The New York Times Book Co., 1974), p. 25.
6. U.S. House of Representatives, Subcommittee of the Committee on Government Operations, *Oversight Hearings into the Operations of the IRS: Operation Tradewinds, Project Haven, and Narcotics Traffickers Tax Program* (Government Printing Office, 1976), p. 32.
7. Author's Interviews with John S. Nolan, former Deputy Assistant Secretary (Tax Legislation), Department of the Treasury, 22 August 1988; Charls E. Walker, former Under Secretary of the Treasury, August 1988; Edwin S. Cohen, former Assistant Secretary (Tax Policy), August 1988; and John Olszewski, former Director Intelligence Division, August 1988.
8. Author's interview with John Ehrlichman, August 1988.
9. *The White House Transcripts: Submission of Recorded Presidential Conversations to the Committee on the Judiciary of the House of Representatives by President Richard Nixon* (Bantom Books, 1974), p. 57. Bob Woodward and Carl Bernstein, *The Final Days* (Avon, 1977), pp. 83–4.
10. *White House Transcripts*, p. 63.
11. Woodward and Bernstein, p. 84.
12. Author's Interview with John S. Nolan, former Deputy Assistant Secretary (Tax Legislation), Department of the Treasury, 22 August 1988; Author's Interview with Charls E. Walker, former Under Secretary of the Treasury, August 1988.
13. Author's Interview with Edwin S. Cohen, former Assistant Secretary (Tax Policy), August 1988.
14. Edwin Cohen was especially certain that Taft had to have mellowed. Others I spoke to agreed, with the exception of John Ehrlichman, who said Taft's opinion didn't matter.
15. Evan Drossman and Edward W. Knappman, *Watergate and the White House, July–December 1973* Volume 2 (Facts on File), "Finance Controversies," p. 29.
16. Ibid., p. 124.
17. Ibid., p. 117.
18. Author's interview with John Olszewski, August 1988.

19. John J. McCloy, Nathan W. Pearson, Beverly Matthews, *The Great Oil Spill: The Inside Report* (Chelsea House, 1976), p. 3. This is a reprint of Gulf's own limited investigation into bribery and political chicanery. When McCloy finished this report, he was praised by top Gulf management for holding the line, containing the damage.
20. Ibid., p. 4.
21. Dobrovir, et al., pp. 86–87.
22. See the U.S. House of Representative, Committee on Government Operations, *Internal Revenue Service and Treasury Department Enforcement of the Foreign Bank Account Reporting Requirement of the Bank Secrecy Act: Second Report* (Government Printing Office, 1977).
23. Richard E. Jaffe, "Memorandum, Re: The Foreign Bank Account Question," in Jaffe's Diary.
24. *U.S. News & World Report*, 27 February 1976.
25. U.S. Department of Treasury, Internal Revenue Service, *Annual Report* (Government Printing Office, 1973), p. 30.
26. Consider U.S. Senate, Permanent Subcommittee on Investigations of the Committee on Government Operations, *Hearings: ORGANIZED CRIME, Securities: Thefts and Frauds* (Second Series), 93rd Congress, First Session, Part 1, 29 June, and 13 July 1973; and Permanent Subcommittee on Investigations, *Hearings: ORGANIZED CRIME, Stolen Securities*, 92nd Congress, First Session, Part 1–8, 9, 10, and 16 June 1971, and Part 3–20, 21, 22, 27, and 28, June 1971 (Government Printing Office, 1971).
27. Arnold Markowitz, "IRS: We Halted All Intelligence Except on Crime," *Miami Herald*, 29 January 1975.
28. Andy Rosenblatt, "IRS Spy-for-Nixon Report Spurs Quiz," *Miami Herald*, 2 February 1975.
29. Arnold Markowitz, "IRS Finds No Misuse of Data," *Miami Herald*, 5 February 1975.
30. Dougald D. McMillen, Chief Miami Strike Force to William S. Lynch, Chief Organized Crime and Racketeering Section, "Memorandum: Sensitive Case Report," 23 May 1974, p. 1.
31. Dougald D. McMillen, Chief Miami Strike Force to William S. Lynch, Chief OC&R Section, "Memorandum: Organized Crime—Corruption Investigation Dade County, Florida," 9 September 1974, p. 3.
32. Mike Baxter, "Sex Spy Reveals Identity: 'IRS Agent Threatened Me,' " *Miami Herald*, 16 March 1975; and William R. Amlong and Gene Miller, "Woman: IRS Probed Dade Sex Lives," *Miami Herald*, 15 March 1975.
33. Ron Sachs and Steve Strasser, "Anger and Humor Greet IRS Report," *Miami Herald*, 16 March 1975.
34. A conclusion reached by former Department of Justice Attorney William D. Hyatt who worked Project Haven through the Leprechaun period. Author's interview 7 July 1987.

35. Regional Commissioner, North-Atlantic Region to All Regional Commissioners . . . "Memorandum: Project HAVEN," 22 July 1975.
36. S. (Sing) B. Wolfe, Assistant Commissioner (Compliance) to Regional Commissioner, North-Atlantic Region, "Memorandum: Project HAVEN," 16 July 1975.
37. Richard E. Jaffe, "Diary entry," 7 August 1975.
38. See United States District Court, Southern District of Florida, Magistrate Division, *USA v. James M. Moran, et al.*, Case No. 78–189–Cr–ALH, "Testimony of Guilford Troy Register, Jr.," 12 February 1981, pp. 51–53.
39. Richard E. Jaffe to Mr. Jack Solerwitz, "Letter," 26 August 1975.
40. U.S. District Court, Eastern District of New York, *Frank J. Scodari, et al., Plaintiffs v. Donald C. Alexander, Commissioner of the Internal Revenue Service and William E. Simon, Secretary of the Treasury, Defendants*, Civil Action No. 75C813.
41. See U.S. District Court, Civil Action No. 75C813, *Affidavit in Support of Motion for Leave to File Amended Complaint* by Jack B. Solerwitz, 23 October 1975; and Fred Tuccillo, "IRS Chief Undergoing a Tough Audit," *Newsday*, 29 September 1975.
42. Charles Osolin, "Feud Between IRS Director and Federal Law Enforcers," Cox Newspapers, Washington Bureau, 27 September 1975.
43. James Savage and Phil Gailey, "IRS Chief Faces Inquiry in Probe of Bank Accounts," *Miami Herald*, 27 September 1975.
44. Bob Woodward, "IRS Shelves Inquiry Into Tax Havens," *Washington Post*, 27 September 1975.
45. See Savage and Gailey, 23 September 1975.
46. See Nicki Kelly, "Immigration man sacked over IRS link, Nassau *Tribune*, 24 September 1975.
47. SECSTATE WASHDC to AMEMBASSY NASSAU PRIORITY, "SUBJECT: IRS PROBE IN BAHAMAS," September 1975.
48. American Embassy Bahamas to SECSTATE WASHDC, AmEmbassy London, "SUBJ: IRS Probe into Bahamas," Confidential Nassau 1628, 25 September 1975.
49. Sally Woodruff to Richard Jaffe, "Letter," 4 April 1975.
50. James J. Lane, Group Manager, Intelligence Division, "Memorandum of Meeting," U.S. Embassy, Nassau, Bahamas, 3 August 1976.
51. Sally Woodruff to Commander R. Jaffe, U.S. Coast Guard, "Letter," 20 August 1976.

The day after meeting with Sally, U.S. Ambassador Seymour Weiss, according to a memorandum written by Lane, also urged Bailor not to do it. He supposedly convinced him it was somewhat premature, and the Bahamians might get the wrong idea. Bailor denies attempting to reveal Sally's identity, but the evidence is conclusive. Just what U.S. officials told the Bahamian government is unclear, although it is worth noting when Ambassador Weiss retired in December 1976, he left claiming total cooperation from Bahamian authorities for U.S. tax investigations and, less ludicrously but more ominously, he had "expressly explained what had happened" to the Bahamian government. Nassau *Guardian*, "Probe of Tax Evaders Gets 'First Class' Co-Operation," 8 December 1976.

52. Colombia Broadcasting System, Transcript of *60 Minutes* Program "The Castle Bank Caper," 21 November 1976, p. 2.
53. Ibid., p. 6.
54. Ibid., p. 6.
55. Ibid.
56. U.S. House, *Oversight Hearings*, p. 2.
57. Ibid., pp. 20–21.
58. David E. Gaston, Director, Criminal Tax Division, to Meade Whitaker, Chief Counsel, "Internal Revenue Service MEMORANDUM: *Draft Tradewinds Report dated July 3, 1975*," 24 July 1975, p. 2.
59. Ibid, p. 3.
60. U.S. House, *Oversight Hearings*, p. 30.
61. Ibid., p. 53.
62. U.S. House, *Oversight Hearings*, p. 32.
63. Ibid., p. 63.
64. IRS, *Inspection*, p. 1.
65. There is a final surprising word on Leprechaun. In the late spring of 1977, Robert W. Rust, U.S. Attorney from the Southern District of Florida, concluded almost all the "goofier" examples of I.R.S. bad behavior in this now legendary operation were fabrications. They had been either manufactured or distorted by the *Miami News* and Elsa Gutierrez for their benefit. Much ado about virtually nothing was his conclusion. Robert W. Rust, United States Attorney, to the Honorable Griffin B. Bell, Attorney General, and Honorable Jerome Kurtz, Commissioner Internal Revenue Service, "Re: OPERATION HAVEN, OPERATION TRADEWINDS," 17 June 1977.

   This was the same judgement reached earlier by a detective from a small Broward County police department who knew Special Agent Harrison, worked with the Miami Strike Force, and wrote President Gerald Ford. The detective informed the president that Alexander was out to destroy investigations of organized crime and corruption. He implored the President to remove the commissioner, described as an "incompetent bumbling nincompoop." See Detective Lieutenant Pierre Pelletier, Intelligence, Oakland Park Police Department to Mr. Gerald R. Ford, President of the United States, "Re: John Thomas Harrison and Operation Leprechaun," 24 April 1975.
66. U.S. House, *Oversight Hearings*, pp. 1269–1270.
67. Ibid., pp. 1268–1269.
68. Fred C. Denham, National President FCIA to Hon. William Simon, Secretary of the Treasury, "FCIA *Resolution*," 20 October 1975.

69. The petitioners were Ed Vitkus, Assistant Regional Commissioner of the Intelligence Division, Atlanta; A. J. O'Donnell, Jr., Regional Commissioner of the Southeast Region, Atlanta; and Troy Register, Intelligence chief in Jacksonville. See E. J. Vitkus, Assistant Regional Commissioner (Intelligence), Southeast Region to the Honorable Charles A. Vanik, Chairman, Subcommittee on Oversight, Committee on Ways and Means, U.S. House of Representatives, "Letter," 8 March 1976, and A. J. O'Donnell, Jr., to the Honorable Charles A. Vanik, Chairman, Subcommittee on Oversight, Committee on Ways and Means, U.S. House of Representatives, "Letter," 4 March 1976.

70. James J. Lane, Group Manager, Jacksonville District, "*Memorandum of Meeting*" 30 and 31 August, and 1 September 1976.

71. Charles O. DeWitt, District Director, Jacksonville, to Richard E. Jaffe, Special Agent, Intelligence Division, 20 December 1976.

72. See Rust, "Re: Operation HAVEN."

73. Jeffrey J. Motyka, Report of Investigation, 13 June 1977.

74. Charles O. DeWitt, District Director, to Richard E. Jaffe, Special Agent, 28 March 1978.

75. Anthony V. Langone, ARC (Intelligence Southeast Region), "*Memorandum to the File*," 3 May 1977.

76. U.S. District Court for the Northern District of Ohio, Eastern Division, *USA v. Jack Payner*, Case No. CR76–305, Judge John M. Manos, *Memorandum of Opinion Motion to Suppress*, 28 April 1977.

77. James J. Lane, Acting Branch Chief, Miami, Florida, to Group 902, Miami, "Memorandum: Project HAVEN," 29 April 1977.

78. Jack Anderson, "IRS Pulls the Rug Out From Top Miami Sleuth," 14 May 1977.

79. U.S. Supreme Court Reports, *United States v. Jack Payner* 65 L.Ed.2d. (1980), pp. 468–487.

80. Ibid., p. 478.

81. Ken Myers, "Judge Involved in Shakedowns? Recusal Documents Revealed," *The National Law Journal*, 30 March 1987; and Ken Myers, "U.S. Documents Tie Ex-Presser Judge to Union Shakedown Scheme in '50s," *Akron Beacon Journal*, 3 February 1987.

82. U.S. House, *Oversight Hearings*, p. 86.

83. Mary McGrory, "The IRS Answers An Audit," *Chicago Tribune*, 10 October 1975.

84. See U.S. Senate, Permanent Subcommittee on Investigations, "Statement of David R. MacDonald," *Report: Illegal Narcotics Profits*, 4 August 1980.

9

Castle Under Justice

Serious knowledge about the working of the "underground economy" in The Bahamas was safely out of the law's reach. Certainly no new cases would be made by American law enforcement, as there was no agency with either the motivation or expertise to carry out such a mission. Moreover, it was plain that The Bahamas was not about to impair one of its primary attractions. Nevertheless, the desiderata of Haven had to be handled, and there was the vague possibility something could still develop from the cases now under the direction of the Justice Department. Great care had to be exercised, first and foremost, by the Castle conspirators to contain the damage. Controlling the outcome of Haven cases was also in the interest of those in politics and finance who so ardently believed in the necessity, if not the innocence, of offshore banking. There were major forces at work trying to put out the last flickering flame of Project Haven. It may also be the case that dogged stupidity made its own significant contribution to cooling off the Haven embers. When it was over, Project Haven was most notable for the many missed opportunities for important prosecutions of the wealthy and well-placed. Under the new regime in the Justice Department, Haven's few and rather meager victories couldn't begin to compare with its failures.

Lack of accomplishment was always attributed to the ineradicable stain of Casper's "caper." Later, that explanation was supplemented with a new one. It was announced in 1980 that Haven cases didn't move ahead because of national security issues. Reporter Jim Drinkhall of the *Wall Street Journal* discovered that

C.I.A. pressure, not just legal problems stemming from tainted evidence, had induced the Justice Department to back off its investigation. Castle Bank, he reported, was used by the Agency to funnel money for secret operations against Cuba and other countries.[1] The connection was Helliwell and perhaps others from his firm.

Within a day, certain ludicrous elements appeared in follow-up stories done by anxious reporters. None was more absurd than the suggestion that Castle Bank probably laundered C.I.A. money earmarked for the Bay of Pigs invasion.[2] It was an often told yarn, though a little checking would have revealed the long time lag between the Cuban debacle in April 1961, and Castle's creation in 1964. The C.I.A. angle was blown out of proportion because it seemed plausible, explained years of prosecutorial foot drag-ging, and was confirmed to a degree by Project Haven manager Bailor. He stated the C.I.A.'s General Counsel asked him to keep away from particular accounts.[3] The best reporters, like Drinkhall, never claimed Castle Bank was a C.I.A. proprietary, only that certain accounts were used for clandestine operations, as Bailor said. It wasn't national security interests that really thwarted Project Haven, no matter how enticing the story seemed.

The greatest handicap criminal justice faced in prosecuting Cas-tle Bank conspirators emerged from a series of decisions made by the Justice Department within the difficult and demanding political environment enveloping Castle. In particular, case se-lection and development, plus the manner Justice handled the Helliwell and Kanter firms, revealed serious weaknesses in this final stage of Project Haven. This is evident when considering how a second Castle Bank master list of accounts was treated.

Shortly after Justice took over Haven, more than fifteen months before the Payner decision and Jaffe's suspension, Bailor and his boss, Cono Namorato, the chief of the Justice Department's Crim-inal Tax Division, were given a second list of depositors. It came from the Bank of Perrine. An important bank officer, who had always wished to cooperate with the investigation since its earliest stages under the I.R.S., turned the list over in February 1976. Promised immunity from prosecution, he continued to aid the investigators, providing other Castle material. As for the inventory of depositors, it was understood that Namorato would lock it away, not to be used unless absolutely necessary.[4] It never was, despite what others thought were pressing needs.

Even when the Justice Department's Project Haven team held a most important three-day conference, hashing out the strategy and tactics to follow in their work, the new list was left in Namorato's safe.[5] The conference was attended by Bailor, two other Justice Department attorneys (Dora Saharuni and Ross Mac-Beth), Dave Stetler from the I.R.S. Chief Counsel's Office, and the I.R.S. Jacksonville contingent led by District Director DeWitt. The principal discussion was the choice of tactics needed to proceed against Castle's owners and depositors. It was decided the owners should be charged with conspiracy (under Title 18, Section 371).

The Haven group, according to the minutes of the conference, was determined to prove Castle Bank was an American controlled foreign corporation set up to assist in tax evasion. There was no question of the nature and extent of the Castle conspiracy.[6] A four-step procedure was worked out to nail down the crucial ownership issue: (1) the Bahamian government would be requested to turn over ownership documents given to the Monetary Authority by Sam Pierson; (2) an analysis would be conducted of all correspondence between Castle and its American management subsidiary (CABATCO) and the Kanter and Helliwell firms; (3) a public records search would be initiated in The Bahamas and Panama for documents on the formation and stock ownership of Castle; and (4) interviews of all current and former Castle employees would be carried out.

The group decided to identify depositors and their types of accounts *solely* from the briefcase list. The Perrine directory was not to be consulted, although there seems no sensible reason why the "tainted" list was selected instead—the damaging history of the briefcase was known to all. It was this decision that ultimately allowed the defense counsel in the Payner case to raise the issue of illegal evidence. While using the neglected Perrine documents might still have resulted in a challenge on the admissability of the evidence (under a rather tortured interpretation of the doctrine known as the "fruit of the poisoned tree"), it may have been turned back by government prosecutors.

The key question is whether the government's interest in Perrine and its Castle documents preceded the purloined account list, and that answer is yes. Perrine was identified as a Castle correspondent bank during the initial investigation of drug dealer Allan Palmer. Palmer's activities led the I.R.S. to the Bank of Perrine in 1972. Jaffe sent Casper into Perrine because he already knew it was close to Castle Bank. It is apparent that a stronger case could have been made utilizing the Perrine material. Instead, Bailor inexplicably assumed it was similarly "tainted" and left it in storage.[7] Under the circumstances, one wonders why it was acquired in exchange for a grant of immunity. This same question occurred to Congressman Rosenthal. In a letter to Treasury Secretary G. William Miller, on 17 January 1980, Rosenthal noted that a second "non-tainted" list (as he put it) was available and inquired why it wasn't employed. No satisfactory answer was ever received.

The handling of the Perrine list is one puzzle. The effort to undermine Sally's cover is another. That event took place just weeks before this important Project Haven strategy conference, which affirmed the necessity of doing what Sally did best—thoroughly searching Bahamian public records for anything and everything on Castle Bank. Her research expertise was unparalleled. Moreover, the insistence on divulging her identity to the Bahamians came after Bailor knew that Pindling had a financial connection to Castle. Additionally, no one from the Department of Justice searched Bahamian records, despite the reasonableness of Point 3 in the agreed upon procedure worked out at the summer conference. Some desultory requests were made to the Bahamian government for bank records, but they were routinely denied.

What Sally could have done for Justice Department investigators is obvious. Consider her reporting (reflexively to Jaffe as Tradewinds was over) on Castle's Bahamian demise. Castle officially closed in Nassau, on 13 April 1977. The Bahamian government had revoked its license because of adverse publicity from the American investigation, which had the ability, it was stated, to undermine confidence in Bahamian bank integrity. In its announcement, the government reassuringly noted that Castle Panama, described as the parent company, promised a "full indemnity against any losses or contingencies which may result from operations in The Bahamas."[8] A few days later, Jim Gooding declared Castle had voluntarily surrendered its license in March. He did not mention either Panama or indemnifying losses.[9]

As usual, Sally knew better. In mid-November 1976, she wrote to Jaffe that Castle had been unofficially and secretly closed by Bahamian banking authorities. Everyone was keeping silent about it, she reasoned, because Castle was busy trying to negotiate reinstatement. Until a government announcement in the "Official Gazette," the closing was not quite absolute; an opportunity was left for Castle's owners to use their best persuasive talents. The bank was held in limbo and operated under the control and direction of the Central Bank.[10] The span from the fall of 1976 to the spring of 1977 also allowed time for the Castle conspirators to clear out incriminating records and lots of money. This was done while the bank was under Bahamian control, a fitting answer to those quaint notions of waiting for, and counting on Bahamian help to authenticate evidence, provide documents, etc.

The bicentennial year was full of surprises and odd occurrences when it came to the management of Haven by the Justice Department. Its actions established precedents concerning evidence and the use of operatives, which were important in each Haven case. In the following year another strange decision, this time concerning the Helliwell firm, further handicapped criminal justice. Helliwell's firm was caught in flagrant and probably criminal improprieties, but they were routinely overlooked by the Justice Department, much to the disbelief and dismay of outside observers. These particular activities began when Castle Cayman's manager, Tony Field, was subpoenaed on 12 January 1976, as he waited in the Miami airport to board a plane for the Cayman Islands.[11] He accepted service and several weeks later returned to Florida to confront the Miami Grand Jury.

In the interim, the Castle conspirators worked out a response designed to forestall the government. First, Helliwell wrote a long, reportedly impassioned, letter to the Governor General of the Cayman Islands urging resistance to this Grand Jury assault on bank secrecy. Next, he assigned a member of his firm, Jose E. Martinez, as Field's counsel with instructions to keep him silent.[12] Castle's owners were determined Field wouldn't testify.[13] Martinez moved to quash the subpoena, arguing it couldn't be enforced because of the "Comity Rule of International Law." That principle supposedly gave Field the right not to testify about Cayman banking matters, as such testimony violated Cayman law, thus unfairly exposing him to prosecution back home.[14] Any statements about Castle Bank contravened the Cayman's rigid bank secrecy law and could not be provided.[15] And, indeed, there was a letter from the Cayman Inspector of Banks and Trust Companies dated 16 January 1976, which warned Field about violating Cayman secrecy laws.

While Martinez's motion wended its way through the legal system, Field returned to Miami and appeared before the Grand Jury. Upon the advice of counsel, he refused to answer questions, citing the U.S. Fifth Amendment and the Cayman Island contravention. He was granted immunity from prosecution to satisfy the Fifth Amendment claim and ordered to proceed. He still declined to testify asserting the Cayman legal dilemma. A hearing on this matter was held in March, at which time an affidavit of a Cayman attorney, Haydn M. Rutter, was submitted to the court, which declared that should Field testify he would likely be charged on return to Grand Cayman. Rutter was a well-known and respected Cayman lawyer, a partner in the firm which represented Castle Cayman locally.[16]

The U.S. District Court did not dispute Field's contention holding, "the record should show that this court finds that there is, in fact, a reasonable probability that Mr. Field is going to be exposed to some criminal charges and some criminal punishment for violating the Cayman Bank Secrecy Act."[17] However, he still had to testify, and when he refused, the court found him in civil contempt.[18] Martinez appealed the decision but to no avail. Late in the spring the U.S. Fifth Circuit Court of Appeal flatly turned it down, concluding regretfully that Field had to talk.

By the time this drama played out, the term of the Grand Jury had expired and Field was momentarily safe, no longer in contempt of court. That moment quickly passed and he was told to return to Miami. He must testify before a new Grand Jury. Field was also informed that prosecutors were determined to indict him if his attitude didn't change. Along with this dismaying information came Helliwell's vivid suggestion to stay out of the United States. Field did as advised.[19] Meantime, the appeals process continued until it reached the Supreme Court, which declined to review the case.[20] Field had run out of all U.S. options. To make matters worse, he was indicted for his very minor part in a large tax evasion scheme involving Roger Baskes, a partner in the Kanter firm, and an accountant named George Schallman.[21] Always relying on legal advice from the Helliwell firm, Field remained abroad. He did not respond to the October 1976 indictment.

Field's legal representative knowingly presented erroneous material and withheld vital evidence from the courts beginning as early as March 1976. This material, if presented to the judiciary, would have saved Field from the various legal problems he subsequently faced. Between the original Field hearing and the first appeal of the decision, the Cayman government had notified "Messrs Helliwell, Melrose & de Wolf" that should Field be compelled to testify in the United States "he would not be subject to prosecution therefor in the Cayman Islands."[22] Field's attorney knew the true situation in the Caymans by the end of March. But this crucial information was hidden from the court and Field. Desperate to keep him outside the American judicial system, the Helliwell attorney maintained the false position through the Appellate and Supreme Court appeals.

Sometime in 1976, attorney Don Van Koughnet, the man who brought Castle's Cayman documents to Miami, informed the Department of Justice of the Cayman Island decision.[23] Van Koughnet's information was slowly but finally confirmed in February 1977. This confirmation of the Cayman's legal position moved through diplomatic channels—from the Cayman government, to the British Foreign Office, to the U.S. State Department, which finally notified the Department of Justice. It was in the form of a note from Britain to the U.S.:

> The Government of the Cayman Islands has informed us that Mr. Field was initially advised by the Inspector of Banks and Trust Companies that he and Castle Bank & Trust (Cayman) Ltd. would be prosecuted if Mr. Field in the United States contravened section 10 of the Cayman Islands Banks and Trust Companies Regulation Law, 1966. *However, subsequently and prior to the Court of Appeals hear-*

ing, Mr. Fields's lawyers were informed in writing that Mr. Field would not be prosecuted in the Cayman Islands if he were compelled by process under the laws of the United States to disclose in the United States information which would be in violation of section 10 of the law. *This latter decision is the operative one* (my emphases).[24]

Although not yet Field's attorney of record, Van Koughnet, helped by Jaffe, set out to free Field from the contempt citation, have him testify about Castle Bank, and motivate the Justice Department to prosecute Field's American counsel. "I concluded," Van Koughnet wrote, "on the basis of the official records, that the Helliwell firm's representation of Tony was the most blatant, cynical, and deliberate misrepresentation of a client to come to my attention in nearly 40 years of practice."[25] Van Koughnet's request for action against Martinez went to Bailor and met, reportedly, firm resistance. Bailor told him that he had queried Solicitor General Robert Bork about the matter, and was advised it was too late to do anything. Neither Van Koughnet nor Jaffe were convinced. They found out later that Bork knew nothing about this matter and, therefore, could not have given that opinion.[26]

This conflict produced nothing substantive over the false pleadings in the Field case, but it did further poison relations between Bailor and Jaffe. Bailor was so upset he instituted an investigation of Jaffe, charging he disclosed the "internal litigating posture of the Department of Justice" to Van Koughnet. The charge, as it concerned Jaffe, was untrue, although a member of Bailor's own Haven staff did make such a disclosure. But whatever damage Jaffe suffered from this issue, it is, nonetheless, incidental to the larger question of why nothing was done about the Helliwell firm's misrepresentation.

Herschel Clesner, Chief Counsel of the Rosenthal Subcommittee was also drawn to the Field issue. He was angered and tried to enlist the aid of Alexander's successor, I.R.S. Commissioner Jerome Kurtz. Concerning the Field case, Clesner told the commissioner, the Cayman government wished to cooperate, but Field's attorney knowingly lied to the court. He added that the Department of Justice attorneys knew the pleading was false. Clesner requested Commissioner Kurtz to marshall his power and help correct the problems.[27] It was a futile petition. Commissioner

Kurtz likely never read Clesner's epistle. At least he has no current recollection of it, or of conducting any inquiry on the matter while commissioner. He thinks probably, or possibly, an aide read it and perhaps considered it outside the commissioner's domain. Questioned about it recently, it rang no louder bell.[28]

Don Van Koughnet was determined to stay on top of the Field-Martinez-Justice Department issue. He remained irate for a long time, and several years later was able to get a small measure of satisfaction. In 1980 he read in the Miami *Herald* that Jose Martinez was considered a front-runner for the post of U.S. attorney for Florida's Southern District. Shocked, he informed Florida's Senator Lawton M. Chiles that the former Helliwell partner must not be nominated and filled him in on the history of the Field case.[29]

There is another sidelight over the issue of compelled United States testimony and prosecution in Caribbean tax havens. The Castle owners were hard pressed to maintain the Cayman fiction, and were willing to go to exceptional lengths to do so. Thus, imagine their chagrin when they solicited Bahamian legal opinion on basically the same question, and found themselves as naked before American law as Field. The distinguished Bahamian attorney Lenox M. Paton advised that, if a current or former Bahamian bank employee divulged information in Florida, he would not be liable to criminal prosecution in The Bahamas. In particular, Paton argued that Bahamian bank secrecy provisions simply could not apply to someone resident in Florida, and compelled to testify there, concerning information acquired while a Castle Bank officer in 1970 and 1971.[30] This opinion was, of course, never mentioned. The conspirators hoped the issued would remain dead, which it has.

The Helliwell firm escaped this affair unscathed. Tony Field still faced a significant criminal indictment and the likelihood of more to come. He was also out of a job in 1977 when Castle Cayman closed down. But he was promised a substantial severance allowance (he asked for $100,000, though only given $58,000) to keep him in line. The money was doled out in quarterly installments over two years to guarantee continuing good behavior.[31] When the Cayman scene ended, Field moved to England. From there, he tried to negotiate with the Justice Department to resolve his legal problems. It wasn't going to be either swift or easy.[32]

Years passed before Field reached an agreement with the Justice Department. By then, he was living in Canada and needed to resolve his American difficulties, or lose his job which required travel to the United States. He was finally questioned in Toronto in March, 1980.[33] Having waited four years for this, Justice Department attorneys were annoyed and disappointed by the result. Field was as closemouthed as one could be under the circumstances. He had few definite things to say beyond the safe statement that Helliwell (dead four years at that time) seemed to him the boss of Castle. Asked many questions, he remembered little. The Justice Department, rightfully angry, believed he was deliberately vague.[34] It was, the attorneys thought, not worth the very long wait.

A couple of years later, Field's memory radically improved. Project Haven had been over for a long time, and that probably stimulated his recollection. He was deposed as part of a private suit against Kanter and others involved in managing and "loosing" millions earned by the Creedance Clearwater Revival musical group. In the spring of 1982, Field was a much sharper witness than ever before. He recalled that Wolstencroft, Pierson, and the Cayman lawyer Haydn Rutter told him that Kanter and Helliwell owned the bank. Furthermore, he was informed by them that 60 percent of Castle Cayman's trust business came from Kanter, partners in his firm, and associates such as Joel Mallin. Field also recollected Kanter selecting certain Cayman files for destruction in 1976, and Helliwell instructing him to hide particular documents (including trusts from the Mercantile Bank period) in new cabinets. These were the ones brought to the United States by Van Koughnet. Field testified that Kanter transferred some trusts to the Canadian Imperial Bank and the Commerce Trust Company. One other recipient of Castle trusts was the Lyon Corporation in Grand Cayman. Finally, Field stated that Wolstencroft told him about shredding documents in Nassau; and that Alipranti was, in effect, really Helliwell.[35]

When he was done, Tony Field confirmed many of the facts and suspicions about the celebrated bank. His testimony was strikingly similar to information Sam Pierson passed to prosecutors

early in 1976, which was never used. At that time, Pierson commented that Helliwell was one of Castle's owners, and that its
original capital of about $600,000 came from Morris Kleinman.
Castle's former president admitted Alipranti was in his estimation
a hoax, and that Helliwell had schemed to circumvent compliance
with the government's subpoena. The Bank of Perrine, he said,
was part of the conspiracy. Pierson described how he once carried
a brown paper bag with about $87,000 in cash from Gene Poe to
Helliwell.[36] A half dozen years before Field's enlightening testimony, Pierson had already done the job.

Kanter easily suffered the Justice Department's Haven years,
emerging virtually unscathed. It was clear to some participants,
though, that someone from the Kanter firm had to fall. Roger
Baskes was the candidate selected, according to Chris O'Donnell,
the former Castle director and minority shareholder.[37] O'Donnell's opinion is shared by at least two of the Justice Department
attorneys who worked on Project Haven and had a hand in prosecuting Baskes.[38]

Baskes, Field, and George C. Schallman, an accountant, were
indicted in Florida for their part in an elaborate scheme to fraudulently shelter millions in long-term capital gains realized by Melvin Garb and Harold Stern in 1973. Garb, Stern, and another
partner made fortunes with McDonald franchises. They bought
their first one in 1957 and ended with over 32 of them. They sold
their franchises back to McDonald's in the fall of 1973, and realized approximately $7 million each in McDonald's stock. Schall-
man brought the hamburger millionaires together with the Kanter
firm, which devised a Castle Bank plan to illegally shelter part
of their money.[39] The I.R.S. Chief Counsel's office recommended
to the Florida Grand Jury that Garb and Stern not be prosecuted,
as it was evident they had relied upon counsel's advice, and had
fully cooperated in the investigation.[40]

Roger Baskes was charged with offenses in three separate cases.
That evidently was enough for him. He came in, bargained a bit,
and then gracefully took the fall.[41] He was sentenced to a few
years in the country club federal prison at Eglin Air Force base
in Fort Walton Beach, Florida. Sometime following his release,
he successfully petitioned the Illinois Bar for the reinstatement
of his license.[42]

The question of Baskes' handling by the Justice Department has various interpretations. One prosecutor feels he was treated far too gently, not at all pressured by the government to talk. He suggests Baskes should have been immunized, brought before the Grand Jury, and questioned about Castle's ownership. He believes the government let Baskes play his sacrificial part too easily. Thus Kanter's associate did not have much of an inducement to save himself by divulging what he knew. Accordingly, to see Baskes' prosecution as an example of the Justice Department energetically moving to punish the Castle criminals, is to miss the point. It was, he contends, the least that could be done under the circumstances. The Haven prosecutors were not up to the mark, he adds. They were in the main unsophisticated, neither knowledgeable nor highly competent in criminal prosecutions. Their skill was more political; they maneuvered well in Washington, but had little of the toughness found in the federal prosecutors' offices in Chicago, New York, and Los Angeles. He includes himself in this unflattering description, even though he made the Baskes case. In retrospect, this critic feels he knew little about the complex criminal and political environment within which Castle thrived.[43]

Another Haven prosecutor views the Baskes case quite differently. In his estimation, the Justice Department did adequately pressure Baskes; he was indicted three times, and faced certain prison time if he didn't cooperate. This Justice Department defender argues that this was the best way to get Baskes to open up; an unusually tough move by the government that came about after a great deal of discussion. But it just didn't work. Baskes wouldn't talk.[44]

The most relentless case worked against anyone connected to Castle Bank centered on James M. Moran of Pompano Beach, Florida. One of the premier car dealers in the country, Moran's professional career began in 1939 with a gas station in Chicago. Over the course of two decades, he built his auto businesses to mammoth proportions. His unflagging salesmanship, zest, and creativity brought money and fame—he made the cover of *Time* on 24 March 1961.[45] Later, not everything went so well. His health deteriorated badly, and in the mid–1960s Moran twice developed cancer, enduring radical chest and arm surgery. Cured for the time being, he packed up and headed to Florida. Although ill from time to time, he still looked quite good—tall, slim, and tanned—and his flair for business was unshaken. He soon was the largest and most successful Toyota distributor in the nation, boss of the hugely profitable Southeast Toyota Distributors located in Pompano Beach.[46]

Moran came to I.R.S. attention during the early stages of Project Haven (October 1973). Important evidence indicated "kickbacks" were made to secure Toyota dealerships with the money laundered through accounts at Castle.[47] As the Toyota investigation proceeded, it was apparent that Moran and others involved in his business (Jack Weiss, Donald A. Mitchell, Eugene J. Rudnik and Edward L. Johnson) had substantial Castle accounts and were engaged in massive tax evasion and fraud. The timing and extent of their involvement in this conspiracy differed. Mitchell's was shortlived; he resigned from Southeast Toyota in 1971 following a manslaughter conviction in a drunk driving accident.[48] Rudnik and Johnson joined Southeast Toyota shortly after Mitchell's departure in 1971.[49] Gene Rudnik's formal employment at Southeast Toyota was long, predated by a close friendship and business association with Moran in Chicago.

An attorney admitted to the Illinois Bar in 1943, Rudnik started doing legal work for Moran in 1962. He continued to represent certain Moran interests in Illinois after the Florida move. At Moran's urging, Rudnik came south to work for Southeast Toyota. He was described in various company ads and brochures as a vice-president and general counsel.[50] At Moran's trial there was an intense debate over whether Rudnik actually was Moran's attorney in Florida. The defense argued he was, and that his testimony should be barred on the grounds of attorney and client privilege. They lost the battle, even though Rudnik was the in-house counsel. Southeast Toyota used the Helliwell firm as outside counsel. A Helliwell partner, Raymond H. Mathisen, handled most of the legal work for Southeast.[51]

The tax evasion scheme at Southeast Toyota relied on the creative use of several phony companies, including an insurance firm and a freight broker. Expensive premiums ($25 for every Toyota vehicle sold) were paid to Cayman Assurance for so-called franchise insurance. The money ended up in secret Castle accounts held for Moran and his partners. Over 90 percent of the payments went to a Bahamian joint venture called Gemini, owned by two Castle trusts originally established for Moran and Mitchell. Additionally, the premiums were deducted from corporate tax returns: $1.2 million in 1971 and 1972, a little less the next year, a bit more in 1974.[52] The remaining ten percent or so was absorbed into the secret accounts of the master planners of the scheme, Kanter and Helliwell.

Corporate money was also poured into a Castle account for Dai Ichi Navigation (originally titled Vitacron Incorporated), supposedly to pay fees for freight forwarding. Dai Ichi was as counterfeit as Cayman Assurance, and almost 94 percent of Dai Ichi payments flowed into Castle accounts for Moran, Rudnik, and Johnson.[53] The remaining cash followed the course set for the Cayman Assurance scam.

There was no doubt about the tax evasion, but Moran had a defense and an offer. Formally uneducated (his schooling stopped at the fifth grade), he depended almost entirely upon the advice of his attorneys Rudnik and Mathisen, and accountants. Moran claimed he had been subverted to criminality by the "erroneous opinion of counsel." His victimization went further, it was argued. The money in his Castle family trusts, created on the advice and initiation of Kanter, Baskes, Helliwell, Don Mitchell, and Gene Rudnik, had disappeared.[54] To back these assertions, David M. McConnell, one of Moran's original attorneys, collected significant details on the Castle conspiracy. McConnell's material indicated the Kanter people primarily worked the Dai Ichi part of the scheme, while Helliwell's were more-or-less in charge of the fraudulent Cayman Assurance.[55] Moran, his lawyer maintained, must be viewed as a victim of subversion and theft by a pack of sophisticated organized criminals skilled in international financial crimes.

Along with the declaration of innocence, went an offer of complete cooperation with the authorities to help uncover the much greater overall Castle conspiracy. In return, McConnell wanted Moran immunized from prosecution. A deal, variously interpreted, was struck. The government would consider evidence secured by Moran and his counsel, which, if significant, would earn him a grant of immunity. Meanwhile the criminal justice process went on. Moran was indicted in June 1978 along with his associate Jack Weiss and Baskes, whose case was severed from the other defendants and moved to Chicago.

Moran and McConnell worked diligently gathering incontrovertible evidence for the government. Even before Moran's actual indictment, he and McConnell received and turned over to the Justice Department Bahamian documents including a "copy of statement as of 7-14-76 for Castle Bank & Trust (Bahamas) listing various data including names of shareholders," a file on Cayman Assurance Company and Helliwell, a copy of the Bahamian Register with the names, addresses, and occupations of directors and managers of Castle, invoices of Dai Ichi Navigation, and other documents linking Baskes and Rudnik to the crimes.[56] Much more evidence was forthcoming, McConnell wrote in his request for Moran's immunity, which would "supply the necessary evidence to connect [Kanter] to a provable conspiracy in a trail."[57]

The Justice Department didn't find the evidence persuasive, and Moran was charged. McConnell stepped up his investigative work, always sure the immunity deal would follow. On 29 November 1978, he presented two additional items on Castle's ownership. These were copies of Bahamian documents confirming Kanter's ownership of Castle in 1970. Additionally, the government was given affidavits from several witnesses who swore some Castle records had been shredded, while others had been hauled away in 91 boxes to parts unknown by command of Kanter and others.[58]

Still the Department of Justice attorneys assigned to the Moran case remained unimpressed. McConnell argued that production of these documents, and the earlier ones, meant that Moran had fulfilled his side of the bargain with the government—he had to be given immunity. Federal attorneys disagreed, holding the material was either useless as evidence, or stale, already known. It came down to a hearing before Federal Judge Henry Gonzales in Fort Lauderdale, who ruled in favor of the government. There would be no immunity for Moran.[59]

The dynamics of this little-known hearing must be kept in mind. First, it took place because Moran's lawyer was, in effect, suing the Justice Department attorneys for breach of contract. The judge listened to McConnell present his case, but as Ron Cimino from the Justice Department rose to argue the government's position, he was told it wasn't necessary. The judge had already decided on the basis of McConnell's testimony that the "specific performance" (breach of contract) charge had no merit.[60] Because of the secrecy surrounding much of the Moran case, it isn't certain on what basis the judge evaluated the evidence offered. The question of McConnell's documents is mysterious, no matter how it's viewed, particularly as the evidence was sealed by the court.[61]

Although he was increasingly suspicious of the government's actions, McConnell stayed in the fight, determined to show that the documents could lead to Kanter's prosecution and the unravelling of the conspiracy. At the same time, he kept searching for still better evidence and was successful. In fact, in 1978, the Justice Department attorneys working the case, George Kelley and Dora Saharuni, agreed to submit his proffered evidence to M. Carr Ferguson, the assistant attorney general.[62] And on 6 June 1978, according to McConnell's notes, Ferguson called him at the University Club in Washington and stated the Bahamian evidence gathered so far was "impressive and more than they had done [Department of Justice] in 8 years." He urged him to continue his efforts and to stay in touch.[63] That wasn't the support he wanted, but McConnell felt the door was still slightly ajar, and he continued his impressive efforts.

The final meeting on this issue came early in 1979. McConnell once again presented to Kelley the crucial affidavits of former Castle employees, which confirmed the shredding of Castle documents and the authenticity of the ownership letters on file with the Bahamian government. This time the affidavits were "duly notarized" and "duly authenticated and certified" by American Consuls James F. Hughes, III, and Anthony M. Santiano.[64] There they sat, conspicuous with the red seal and ribbon of the American Embassy attached. According to McConnell, Justice Department attorney Kelley finally "agreed with our arguments that the documents were admissible," and that Moran's immunity was under reconsideration.[65]

Toward the end of February, Kelley reportedly called with the good news that the Justice Department judged the affidavits admissible. Three days later, a more relaxed McConnell wrote to

Kelley pointing out that with his documents and other material given to the prosecutors at Washington's Dupont Plaza Hotel, the government must indict Kanter. Having done his part, he waited for the government's offer of immunity.[66] But it never came, and Kanter was untouched, much to the disappointment and complete mystification of McConnell. Moran then officially replaced him with Edward Bennett Williams' firm, which had already been involved in the case and had displayed no propensity whatever to pursue Kanter.

The case against Moran moved slowly along as motion after motion was made, considered, and finally defeated. One of the most telling government witnesses was Moran's old friend and attorney Gene Rudnik, who testified under a grant of immunity. Afraid of prison, Rudnik came in to deal. Moran fought to bar Rudnik's testimony, but it was allowed after U.S. Magistrate Herbert S. Shapiro reviewed it in the waning days of 1983.[67] At long last, Moran gave in. He pleaded guilty, received a suspended sentence, the maximum fine, and some community penance. Of all the Castle Bank clients, Moran paid the heaviest price, although his sentence was physically gentle. He spent a fortune on legal fees for numerous attorneys (not including McConnell), who seem to have done him little good. An even larger fortune had been lost, disappearing into the elusive Castle banks flitting between Nassau, Grand Cayman, Panama, and who knows where else. Lastly, Moran had to pay the government a rather huge sum. Moran got it from both the government, and his former comrades in crime. Once he was caught, the Justice Department must have believed he was absolutely the top conspirator they could get, for they rejected time and again his documents and deal. The Castle conspirators must have been pleased that Moran was the prime target; their joy enhanced by looting much of his Castle money. It is hard to tell what or who embittered Moran the most.

The Moran prosecution was the culmination of Project Haven. It was the most the Justice Department managed after years of hard work, internecine warfare, very complicated power struggles, legal battles over important principles, high drama, lots of money, major crimes, and possible stupefying corruption. The criminal justice result had to be disheartening and disillusioning, although not surprising. Under the most benign interpretation, criminal justice imposed crippling handicaps upon Haven prosecutions from the beginning.

The Justice Department, like the Alexander I.R.S., boxed itself into a hopeless corner when it came to Castle Bank. Nothing much could be done about the big conspiracy, because evidence always depended upon Bahamian cooperation, which was either not forthcoming (not entirely unforeseen, given that the government, both literally and figuratively, had mortgaged itself to Castle), or, in McConnell's case, rejected for some other reason. In the main, the Justice Department accepted the foolish precepts offered at the 1975 Rosenthal hearing by the I.R.S. leadership. No one could get the Castle owners without convincing Bahamian officials it was right, proper, and in their interest to turn over the necessary incriminating documents. Otherwise sensible individuals insisted that Bahamian cooperation was the indispensable element in closing the net around Kanter. At the same time, they knew perfectly well that The Bahamas was absolutely corrupt. Built into these preposterous propositions was the stubborn assumption that none of the evidence the government already possessed was good enough to do the job.

The confusing history of Castle evidence goes something like this: (1) there was tainted evidence (the briefcase documents), which could not be used, but then was; (2) there was allegedly untainted evidence (the Perrine list), which was locked away, never even tested; and (3) there was McConnell's evidence that could not be readily authenticated, and then was, and then wasn't used.

To make the case against the Castle conspirators required a more creative intelligence than was displayed. Prosecutors could never land the Castle owners so long as they held such contradictory notions. The relevance of the ownership issue was rhetorically noted, and then pushed aside.

That sorry performance is still more than can be said for the Internal Revenue Service under Alexander and Kurtz, his successor. Commissioner Kurtz never even understood why anyone cared about Castle Bank, why it mattered whether Kanter owned it or not.[68] Kurtz, like so many others in federal law enforcement, missed several consequential Castle issues, including the elementary one that its owners were supposedly targeted for prosecution for monumental frauds, etc. The big picture always eluded them.

Naturally, then, few comprehended the subtler issues which might have taken them into the larger ones. Important aspects of the case, such as Castle's license, which for Sally was the crux of the matter and the proper starting point for the development of enforcement strategy, were never grasped. Sally alerted Jaffe and Herschel Clesner that Castle was only permitted to carry on banking business for its shareholders, and those persons, firms, or corporations affiliated with, or controlled by the shareholders.[69] Therefore, the depositors weren't there by chance; they were intimately and organically connected to Castle's owners. Castle had been established to service the owners and their clients. It could do nothing else in The Bahamas, which is why the Castle people were so anxious to change their license when they got wind of the investigation. When Kanter admitted he had clients in the bank, as he did on several occasions, this was to Sally an admission of ownership. That is why a major effort to genuinely pressure depositors identified from the Perrine list was necessary. Had dozens of wealthy Castle trust holders been brought before a Project Haven Grand Jury, immunized, and forced to choose between contempt of court and testifying, they would have quickly seen the light.[70]

The Castle conspirators got away with the many enumerated crimes, and also with millions in some depositors' money. Jim Moran is only one example of those cheated by Castle. There were others, more authentically hoodwinked into putting their money in Castle, who then had to face its flight to parts unknown. One of the little known ports of call for Castle surfaced only in the spring of 1983, when a Moran attorney, Steadman Stahl (soon to be in jail for participating in narcotics violations), spotted a tiny notice in the *Miami Herald*. It announced that Castle Trust in Guernsey, the Channel Islands, a British tax haven close to the coast of France, was open for business. None of the concerned parties alerted by the notice—Pierson, Casper, Jaffe, Van Koughnet—could be absolutely certain it was **the** Castle Bank, but it seemed probable. Don Van Koughnet remembered that, several months earlier, an officer from a British merchant bank prominent in Guernsey had come to the Cayman Islands looking for Castle's special filing cabinet. The former caretaker told him he had no such cabinet. He did not mention that Van Koughnet had whisked it to Miami only two months previously.[71] When the Caribbean ship was finally abandoned, the skippers assuredly went with their pockets full.

Criminal justice was such an astounding failure in so many instances concerning Castle Bank, it seems tedious to point out it never bothered with the disappearance of depositor money. Perhaps that was just as well, given its other flops. But losing millions once thought safely tucked away, was enough to ignite some bitter and tenacious battles, which have shed the final light on the Castle saga. Fittingly, this last act took place outside the criminal justice system in the sphere of private litigation.

When it came to money, Jim Moran was really nobody's fool. That he was snookered by crooked lawyers is thus somewhat hard to accept, although there is no doubt that once he was down, the sharks feasted. He was formally uneducated, but shrewd concerning finances, not the kind of man typically befuddled by sharp practices. The same cannot be said for the Creedence Clearwater Revival (C.C.R.).

Brothers John and Tom Fogerty, along with friends Stuart Cook and Douglas Clifford formed a rock and roll group in 1959. Like so many others, they rehearsed, jammed, and rehearsed some more. Unlike most others, though, they began to produce a distinctive sound. They played for practically nothing around the San Francisco Bay area while they matured, perfecting a distinctive style. In 1964, they signed a recording contract with Fantasy Records in Berkeley. Not much happened for the group during the first few years under Fantasy; but then everything changed. In 1967 Saul Zaentz bought Fantasy and negotiated a new contract for the group, with the promise of a royalty increase if they ever had a hit.[72] Their fortune was around the corner. The Creedance Clearwater Revival clobbered the charts in 1968 with "Suzy Q," an album which sold over 5 million copies.[73] Very soon after, they were snared in Castle's sticky, complicated web.

It started when John Fogerty, the group's lead singer and major talent, asked Zaentz for the royalty increase. Zaentz countered, offering instead to sell the band a small interest in Fantasy. They weren't interested, so Zaentz tried another idea to give them more money, without tinkering with the royalty rate. He suggested a tax plan which would yield the group more money after taxes.[74] The first tax plan was one worked up by an attorney named Harry Margolis, but the group turned it down. And then Zaentz brought Creedence Clearwater and Burt Kanter together.

The Kanter plan was complicated, having both domestic and foreign components. The domestic segment shifted the bulk of C.C.R.'s income into and through new corporate entities such as Gort Functions, Son of Gort, and 40 domestic trusts. The trusts were created in order to place as much of C.C.R.'s income as possible into the hands of lower tax bracket family members.[75] When the various shifts were almost completed, the C.C.R. members along with their manager, Bruce Young, and accountant, Edward J. Arnold, owned 30 percent of Gort Functions, while the 40 trusts held the rest. A little more maneuvering and the final domestic part was complete. The band members and the trusts, in partnership, owned a Delaware corporation, which handled C.C.R.'s concert promotion, and sublicensed C.C.R. product distribution rights and royalty collections from the band's first two albums.[76]

The foreign portion of Kanter's plan relied on four overseas trusts that owned an offshore licensing entity (a Bahamian company first called King David Distributors, then more aptly Shalom Ltd., and finally Shire) created to defer U.S. taxation and, thus, substantially reduce any foreign taxes on income generated by the worldwide sales of C.C.R. records and related products.[77] King David owned everything, including C.C.R.'s obligation to perform in Europe. This particular agreement was for twelve years. King David was to pay each C.C.R. member $75,000 the first year and $50,000 per year for the remainder of the contract. To guarantee King David's performance, the troubled Mercantile bank was used.

The plan went on with King David-Shalom-Shire buying a Netherlands Antilles shelf company named Pythagorus (in certain documents and more correctly Pythagoras in others). Pythagoras, then, bought a Dutch firm Enschedesche Industrie Maatschappij. Enschedesche's role was to purchase yet a third Dutch Antilles company, this one called Erasmus. This third firm was the end of one complex line along which millions earned by C.C.R. ran, the money stopping only momentarily at various companies to pay certain fees, etc. The point, of course, was to secure better and better tax advantages. There was much more to come. A more or less parallel structure of companies was set up for that part of John Fogerty's income as a composer, songwriter, and arranger, separate and distinct from his C.C.R. work. Mercantile also guaranteed his arrangement.[78] By 1970, most of the band's money was resting in Castle trusts helpfully established by the evanescent George Bebas himself.

Creedence Clearwater was joined in offshore bliss by Zaentz. Working with the Kanter firm, Zaentz and Kanter formed a Bahamian trust structure for Fantasy Records, which had at its pinnacle a Bahamian company named Argosy-Venture. Fantasy's payments to C.C.R. were replaced by Argosy-Venture paying Shire Ltd. Everything that could go offshore did.[79]

The depositing of C.C.R. money into Castle Bank began in early 1970 and continued for seven years, much to the displeasure of John Fogerty.[80] After just a few months, the parties began to quarrel. Probably the first contentious issue was Kanter's bill sent to C.C.R.'s accountant Ed Arnold. The total fee was $300,000. This covered "out-of-pocket costs, foreign attorneys costs, acquisition and corporation costs, initial trustee set-up-fee costs, and similar items to date." In and among these and other billings, yet outside the total, was a category Kanter labelled additional billings, which were compensations payable to the Helliwell firm and to Joel Mallin.[81] A few years later, Arnold would characterize Kanter's charges as wrong and excessive. They were, he felt, part of a strategy of cheap stunts.[82]

In the first week of September 1970, C.C.R.'s attorney notified Jim Gooding at Castle to cease making unauthorized withdrawals from the group's accounts. Barrie Engel, an attorney, angrily questioned certain payments taken from the trusts, including $100,000 that went to something called Equity Financial and Management.[83] It wasn't long before everything about C.C.R. went sour, not the least of which was how their money was being managed by Castle. C.C.R. itself fell apart in the early 1970s after selling approximately $100 million worth of records in three years.[84]

The split was a result of John Fogerty's desire to solo and the internal tensions that produced.[85]

Over the years, the Creedence Clearwater Revival repatriated much of their Castle money by borrowing it from companies they actually owned, or thought they controlled, under Kanter's plan. Nevertheless, when Castle went bust it took over $4 million of the group's and John Fogerty's money. Before that happened, John Fogerty desperately tried to extricate himself from Castle and the Kanter grasp. He wanted out as early as 1972, but was advised on numerous occasions that leaving would be foolish and financially harmful.[86]

John Fogerty became particularly angry with Saul Zaentz because he held him responsible for bringing the group into the Kanter scheme. He was also incensed as Argosy-Venture continued to pay large sums of his money to Castle Bank despite his heated protests. Around the mid–1970s, John's earliest suspicions about Castle and those associated with it were accelerated by the national publicity over Castle and Project Haven. Fogerty's worst fears seemed to be confirmed by the national press, and he determined to get his money out of what he rightly perceived as a Bahamian abyss.

But it was too late; millions had either vanished or were in preparation for imminent departure. All Castle's assets, the rock group was informed by telegram on 14 February 1977, were frozen. The following day a letter of explanation from Jim Gooding arrived stating that Castle's Board of Directors had stopped withdrawals because of Paul Helliwell's untimely death.[87] Helliwell's demise, however, had actually occurred around seven weeks earlier. Gooding's letter was, of course, a stall. Castle's leadership had no intention of allowing Fogerty and the others to retrieve what rested in Castle.

John Fogerty's exasperation and distress were severe in those difficult days. So much unwanted turmoil, including the loss of rights to every song he wrote while with Creedence Clearwater, prompted him to retreat from the tumultuous entertainment scene into premature retirement. Fogerty was so enraged, it was reported, he wouldn't even sing his old songs in the shower.[88] His personal grief and exasperation were certainly increased by the I.R.S., which hit him for back taxes. When the I.R.S. audit was finished late in 1979, Fogerty and his wife Martha, paid over $1.5 million for tax deficiencies from 1970 through 1978.[89] As far as the Fogertys and the rest of Creedence Clearwater were concerned, the Kanter tax plan and its implementation were something akin to getting the plague and having it treated by Typhoid Mary.

The group sued almost everyone that had anything to do with their financial woes; that included Kanter, several members of his firm, the band's accountant, and their primary attorney, Herman Cook, who was band member Stu Cook's father. This last case was terribly tragic; the litigation drove the family apart, only to be reconciled when the elder Cook was literally on his deathbed. The burden was enormous, and for the Cook's, especially agonizing.[90]

In 1978, John and Martha Fogerty charged Kanter, his firm, several named partners and associates, Castle Bank (Nassau), Castle Trust (Panama), and C.C.R.'s former lawyers and accountants with the following: professional malpractice, breach of contract, violation of corporate securities law of 1968, violation of voluntary and constructive trust, breach of fiduciary duty, fraud, negligent misrepresentation, constructive fraud, and so on.[91] Eventually, lawsuits brought by other group members were coordinated with the Fogerty's, and were titled the Musical Group Investment Cases. When the dust cleared everyone but Arnold, the accountant, settled. Ironically enough, it was Arnold's attorney who worked out the settlements. The insurance company paying the attorney's tab turned down the settlement and told him to take it to trial. The attorney did as instructed, although he was certain they should have accepted the settlement. He was right; Arnold was pulverized with a judgement against him on 9 May 1983 for more than $5.5 million.[92] Those, like Kanter, who settled were gone. Kanter paid $1.5 million for his part in the fleecing of the Creedence Clearwater Revival.

Arnold took the most significant financial and professional beating, although Saul Zaentz may catch him. An extraordinarily talented producer of superb music and remarkable films, Zaentz became the target of an I.R.S. probe into the financial reporting of his first academy award film, *One Flew Over the Cuckoo's Nest*. The investigation started quietly around the time the Creedence civil case was ending. The I.R.S. claimed, as late as the winter of 1987, that more than $38 million in profits was moved offshore and not reported as income. The money did return, it was alleged, in the form of phony loans to Zaentz and to about twenty of his investors.[93] Kanter was questioned and again stated, as he always did, that he neither owned nor ran Castle Bank, which was an integral part of the Zaentz offshore package. Additionally, Kanter noted that he hadn't the slightest idea who did own and run the bank, and he was as mystified as everyone else when asked what happened to it.[94]

John Fogerty emerged from his retreat no doubt wiser in the ways of money, and with a desire for some artistic revenge. In 1984, he wrote, produced, and performed on a hugely successful album called *Centerfield*, which had a song descriptive of his past difficulties. It is a bitter tune with a chorus warning, "Vanz Kant Danz/ But he'll steal your money/ Watch him or he'll rob you blind." Other characters, besides the barely disguised Saul Zaentz from the Castle Bank past, include "the little pig" who is silent and quick/ Just like Oliver Twist."[95]

Whether Oliver Twist-like or not, Burton Kanter found a protective shield behind which to hide from any serious damage, either to his career or his fortune. Perhaps it was inevitable once Jaffe's eagerness and Casper's too zealous detective work cast a cloud in many minds over any Castle evidence. Given that straw to grasp, Kanter was fully capable of constructing a larger and larger impediment. Prosecuting Kanter seemed at first glance to involve the dilemma of prosecuting crooks with unconstitutionally obtained evidence. He hid in the redoubt constructed from the concerns of civil libertarians with whom he had nothing else in common. No one wanted to condone actions which had been reviled by a Federal Judge, and many who thought about Castle Bank never looked beyond the initial Payner decision.

That decision surely took some of the heart from Project Haven, even from those convinced it was erroneous, extreme, and possibly corruptly motivated. Mix that with youthful and inexperienced prosecutors handling some of the key Haven cases, and it seems a combination that was programmed to fail. But those factors still do not encompass the entire affair. The second list, the enigma of Sally, the frustrations of McConnell, the Field case, etc., are part of a troubling record in which it is also incontrovertible that Kanter received secret government information on his case. The leak, that originated in either the Justice Department or the I.R.S., was never found or plugged. Kanter's access to secret information probably continued through the entire Project Haven period. It wasn't the quality of information he received that provided his salvation; it is the fact he got it from important government officials. He was very well connected.

And what of the anxious eyes watching this endless episode from across the Florida Straits? Could the "funny-money" boys in Nassau and Freeport (not to mention the Cayman Islands, Netherlands Antilles, and Panama) miss the message of Kanter's success? Were they not encouraged when Tradewinds crashed and Haven floundered? This sad affair, which opened a window into the vast "underground economy," ultimately reassured the interconnected crowd of financial crooks, corrupt politicians, and organized criminals.

There is a perfect articulation of this conclusion. It came from a California-based tax attorney, like Kanter, under investigation by the I.R.S. for master minding an elaborate offshore tax scam for scores for wealthy clients. He boldly explained the way it was:

> *There is nothing more corrupting to our society than a system of taxation. I have no words strong enough to condemn the society in which we are living in terms of taxation. . . .*
>
> *He (the taxpayer) puts money in a Bahama central trust. Why in the Bahamas? There is no income tax or estate tax in the Bahamas. Why in a trust? A trust is like a corporation, a separate legal entity. This separate entity is a non-resident alien, and a non-resident alien can sell an asset in the United States with no tax. How delightful! Now, if that non-resident alien ties in with a distributing company in the Netherlands Antilles, which can earn interest in the United States without a tax under any circumstances, he has put together a perfect set-up. He takes losses and deductions in the United States and he takes gains and profits abroad, under a tax treaty.*
>
> *Do you think any Congress we have is going to change the laws that allow this? Let's not kid ourselves. With those savings, the rich of this country can afford to buy the entire Senate, if necessary. (My emphasis.)*[96]

Notes

1. Jim Drinkhall, "IRS vs. CIA," *Wall Street Journal*, 18 April 1980, p. 1.
2. "CIA May Have Ended Nassau Bank Probe," *Miami Herald*, 19 April 1980.
3. Author's Interview with Bernie Bailor, 6 July 1987.
4. David McDonald to Bernard Bailor, Esq., Criminal Section, Tax Division, Department of Justice, 24 February 1976.
5. Author's interview with Van Koughnet, Naples, Florida, 22 July 1987.
6. Jim Lane, "Memorandum of Meeting," 11–13 August 1976.
7. Author's interview with Bailor.
8. Edwin Lightbourn, "Castle Bank Closes as Licence Revoked," Nassau *Guardian*, 29 April 1977.
9. "Castle Bank Explains," Nassau *Tribune*, 3 May 1977.
10. Sally Woodruff to Richard E. Jaffe, "Letter," 12 November 1976.
11. Field was a timid, quiet man born in 1941 and educated almost everywhere—Lagos, Nigeria; Devon, England; The Lodge School in Barbados, British West Indies; England for "O" levels and a diploma in business administration; and finally Canada for some accounting courses at Montreal's McGill University, and work. See Anthony R. Field, *Resumé*, 1977 in author's possession.

    He was a British subject, with citizenship in Barbados and residency in Canada, when he joined Castle Bank. Sam Pierson hired Field as the resident manager for its Cayman Island operation at the beginning of 1973. Two years later, with internal concern over the I.R.S. investigation running very high, he was promoted to managing director.
12. Richard E. Jaffe, "Diary entry," 4 March 1977.

    Born in Santo Domingo, Dominican Republic, the same year as Field, the young Martinez had already gathered substantial experience as an Assistant and then Special Assistant U.S. Attorney in Florida, Puerto Rico, and Georgia, and with the military before he went with Helliwell. One of his specialties with the government was drug abuse and law enforcement. See Martindale and Hubbell 1983, 7770B. He was hired by Helliwell, Melrose, and DeWolf no later than 1972. Ibid., 1972, p. 2914B.
13. Anthony R. Field to The Honourable Henry Forde, Attorney General and Minister of External Affairs, BARBADOS, West Indies, 27 May 1980.
14. U.S. District Court for the Southern District of Florida, *USA v. John Doe, Memorandum of Law in Support of Motion to Quash Subpoena and/or for Protective Order* No. Grand Jury 76–1, 19 January 1976.

15. Ibid.
16. Haydn M. Rutter to Donald E. Van Koughnet, Esq., *"Re: Anthony R. Field,"* 29 August 1978.
17. U.S. Court of Appeals for the Fifth Circuit, *IN RE: Grand Jury Proceedings, United States of America v. Anthony R. Field,* No. 76–1739, 13 May 1976, p. 5.
18. Ibid.
19. Field to Forde, 27 May 1980, p. 2.
20. Supreme Court of the United States, October Term, 1976, *Anthony R. Field, Petitioner v. United States of America* "On Petition for a Writ of Certiorari to the United States Court of Appeals for the Fifth Circuit, Brief for the United States in Opposition," No. 76–122.
21. *U.S. District Court, Southern District of Florida, USA v. Roger S. Baskes, George C. Schallman, and Anthony Randolph Field, IN-DICTMENT,* October 1976.
22. The Governor, Grand Cayman, Cayman Islands, to Messrs. Helliwell, Melrose and de Wolf, "Letter," 29 March 1976.
23. Author's Interview with Van Koughnet, 23 July 1987.
24. Van Koughnet, "Recorded Conversation of TF USDJ, February 24, 1977, "Exhibit A."
25. Donald E. Van Koughnet, *"Memorandum* Re: Watergate revisited: Conduct of counsel to Castle Bank and Trust (Cayman) Ltd. in representation of Anthony R. Field in connection with a Grand Jury subpoena for appearance by Field before Grand Jury 76–1, USDC, SD, Florida," 26 August 1977.
26. Donald E. Van Koughnet to Richard E. Jaffe, "Letter," 15 February 1978; Richard E. Jaffe, "Diary entries," 23 January 1978, 24 January 1978; Donald E. Van Koughnet to Herschel F. Clesner, General Counsel, Commerce, Consumer and Monetary Affairs Subcommittee of the Committee on Government Operations, "Re: *United States v. Enstam* et al., No. 3–77–198M–n.d., Texas," 15 February 1978, p. 2.
27. Herschel F. Clesner, Chief Counsel, Subcommittee of the Committee on Government Operations, to Hon. Jerome Kurtz, Commissioner, Internal Revenue Service, "Letter," 4 January 1978.
28. Author's Interview with Jerome Kurtz, 17 July 1987.
29. See Donald E. Van Koughnet to Honourable Lawton M. Chiles, *"re: Disqualification of José Martinez, Esq. of the Helliwell firm, Miami, Florida to receive consideration for nomination as U.S. Attorney for the Southern District of Florida,"* 7 April 1980. Talk of the Martinez nomination quietly faded away.
30. Lenox M. Paton to Lawrence A. Freeman, Esq., Miami, Florida, "File: 5486," 11 March 1976.
31. Donald E. Van Koughnet to Honourable Frank Field, The Valley,

Anguilla, British Leeward Islands, "Re: Anthony R. Field," 9 August 1978, p. 4.

32. He first retained the firm of Berk and Wagner from Fort Lauderdale who tried to contact Bernie Bailor to cut a deal. "This is to supplement my letter of April 25, 1977, regarding Anthony R. Field," wrote attorney Bruce E. Wagner who was somewhat miffed for the moment, having difficulty tracking Bailor down. See Bruce E. Wagner to Mr. Bernard Bailor, Trial Attorney, United States Department of Justice, "Re: Anthony R. Field," 26 May 1977. The issue was a grant of immunity in exchange for Tony's testimony at the Baskes trial. Wagner notified Bailor his client was ready to cooperate, although as it turned out, this was not quite accurate. Field was more deeply concerned about his safety and future employment in banking, should he testify, than he let on to his attorney.

Bailor said he wanted information for the Baskes case, everything on a Castle insurance company known as Cayman Assurance, which was at the heart of several major Castle designed and managed tax evasion schemes, and on those who owned Castle Bank. Bruce E. Wagner to Mr. Anthony R. Field, "Letter," 6 June 1977, p. 2. The deal fell through when Tony decided to steer clear of the United States after being advised to do so by members of the Helliwell firm who visited him in England. Attorney Wagner, angry with Field, bowed out of the case and was replaced by Van Koughnet. Donald E. Van Koughnet to Richard E. Jaffe, "Re: Anthony R. Field," 28 November 1977.

The Department of Justice reopened communications with Field and Van Koughnet in March 1978. Donald E. Van Koughnet to Richard E. Jaffe, "Letter," 27 February 1978. In July of that year two Justice Department attorneys travelled to England to interview Tony. The results were unsatisfactory.

33. "*AGREEMENT*," signed by Stanley F. Krysa, Chief, Criminal Section Tax Division, Ross MacBeth, Trial Attorney Tax Division, Anthony Randolph Field, Derek T. Hogg, LLB, and Donald E. Van Koughnet, 17 September 1980; and "Deposition of ANTHONY FIELD, taken on Thursday, March 27th, 1980, at the offices of the American Consulate, Toronto, Ontario."

34. Anthony R. Field to The Honourable Henry Forde, Attorney General and Minister of External Affairs, Barbados, 27 May 1980, p. 3.

35. Musical Group Investment Cases, "Deposition of Anthony Randolph Field," 1 April 1982, pp. 63, 70–75, 86–88, 108, and 117.

36. Paul V. Hawkins, Special Agent, "Memorandum Re: Castle Bank & Trust Company—Its ownership," 9 July 1976.

37. Author's interview with O'Donnell, June 1987; See U.S. District Court, Northern District of Illinois, Eastern Division, *USA v. Roger*

S. Baskes, Burton W. Kanter, Alan H. Hammerman, and Samuel Zell, No. 76 CR 585 (Indictment originally brought in Nevada on 4 March 1976 and subsequently transferred to the above court); and Author's Interview with Bailor.

38. Author's Interviews with David Stetler, U.S. Attorney's Office, Chicago, 8 July 1987, and George Kelley, Department of Justice Tax Division, 16 July 1987.

39. U.S. District Court, Southern District of Florida, *USA v. Roger S. Baskes, George C. Schallman and Anthony Randolph Field*, n.d.; and David E. Gaston, Director Criminal Tax Division IRS to the Honorable Myron C. Baum, Acting Assistant Attorney General, Tax Division, Department of Justice, "In Re: Melvin Garb, Harold R. Stern, George C. Schallman, Robert S. Baskes," 15 December 1976.

40. Gaston to Baum, p. 45.

41. Author's Interview with George Kelley.

42. Author's interview with Dave Stetler.

43. Ibid.

44. Author's Interview with George Kelley.

45. Nancy Iran Phillips, "Jim Moran—just mention his name in Chicago . . ." *Automotive News*, 3 April 1978.

46. David M. McConnell, Counsel for James M. Moran to The Honorable Attorney General Thru George Kelley, Trial Attorney, Tax Division, "Amended Proffer," 3 June 1978, p. 17.

47. Daniel H. Foley, Group Manager Intelligence Division and C. Paul, Jr., Acting Assistant Chief Intelligence Division, "Minutes of Meeting Regarding Toyota Cases and Project Haven," 15 February 1974; and David L. Ellison, "STATUS REPORT—SHOJI HATTORI/ TOYOTA CASES," 11 November 1974.

48. Castle Trust Company Ltd., *Closing Book*, T–6073 and T–6074 Transactions, *Reference Lisa and Gemini*, July 1971.

    Mitchell and/or his wife Lois retained an interest in certain Castle accounts somewhat beyond his resignation. Lois Mitchell's account, numbered in Nassau 70604, and later moved to Castle Cayman, contained assets of about $2 million in 1975. Among those assets was a $58,000 investment in a Costa Rican corporation intriguingly known as Alajeula Castle. See "Schedule of Assets Specified in Clause 1 of That Deed of Transfer and Assignment Dated 12th Day of June, 1975 between Castle Bank & Trust (Cayman) Ltd. and Cayman National Bank and Trust Co. Ltd. of the Weisbrod Settlement," Settlement 806074, . . . "4. Castle hereby warrants that the sole beneficiary of the Settlement as at the date hereof is LOIS MITCHELL of Fort Lauderdale, Florida, United States of America."

49. U.S. District Court, Southern District of Florida, *USA v. James M. Moran, Statement of Facts*, No. 78–189–Cr–JE, 3 April 1984, p. 6.

50. U.S. District Court, Southern District of Florida, *USA v. James Moran & Jack Weiss*, *Report and Recommendations*, Case No.: 78–189–CR–JE, 28 December 1983, pp. 2–3.
51. Ibid., pp. 8–9.
52. Ibid.
53. Ibid., p. 8.
54. David M. McConnell, "Amended Proffer," p. 4.
55. Ibid., et passim.
56. Ibid., "List of Exhibits."
57. Ibid., p. 6.
58. David M. McConnell to George Kelley, DOJ Tax Division, "RE: *James Moran*," 29 November 1978.
59. Author's Interview with George Kelley.
60. Author's interview with Dora (Saharuni) Welsh, 7 August 1987.
61. Graham Button in, "Jim Moran, Master Salesman," *Forbes Magazine*, 10 October 1989, reviews the Moran case and finds that Moran's attorney and the government wanted the record sealed. Button seems to believe Moran was poorly served by Attorney Steadman Stahl, Jr., who might have been secretly cooperating with Moran's enemies.
62. David M. McConnell, Memorandum for the Record, Conference in the Office of the Attorney General Tax Division, Criminal Section—Re: James M. Moran, 18 April 1978.
63. David M. McConnell, "Conference Notes—Washington, D.C.," 6 June 1978.
64. James F. Hughes, III, American Consul, "Declaration," 10 January 1979; Anthony M. Santiano, American Consul, "Declaration," 4 January 1979; and David M. McConnell, "Contemporaneous Memorandum of Conference," 11 January 1979.
65. McConnell, 11 January 1979.
66. David M. McConnell to George Kelley, Special Assistant to the Attorney General, Criminal Section, Tax Division, "Re: James Moran Case," 25 February 1979.
67. U.S. District Court, *Report and Recommendations*, p. 35.
68. Author's Interview with Jerome Kurtz, 17 July 1987.
69. Sally Woodruff to Herschel Clesner, Subcommittee of the Committee on Government Operations, "The Implications of Trade Winds & Haven: An Analysis and Workpaper," 17 December 1976.
70. So might Chris O'Donnell had he been truly pressured by an aggressive prosecutor. O'Donnell was called before a Miami Grand Jury for a few breezy hours in 1979, and asked some questions about the bank and his position as a director. He admitted the latter, but stated the directors never held a meeting and he received no compensation. As for the rest, he did and knew nothing. Nevertheless, he was a minority shareholder of Castle stock (3 percent) and had one known and identified account (705068). Today, he has no rec-

ollection of either, and wonders if someone else didn't purchase the stock and establish the O'Donnell account without ever telling him. Author's Interview with Chris O'Donnell, July 1987.

71. Don Van Koughnet to Special Agent Robert C. Grant, Criminal Investigation Division, Internal Revenue Service: "*Re*: 'Reincarnation' of *Castle Bank*! 3 June 1983.

72. California Court of Appeal, First Appellate District, Division Five, *Douglas Clifford et al., v. Edward J. Arnold et al.*, S.F. Super. Ct. Nos. 764340, 778142, 28 March 1986, pp. 1–2.

73. Consolidated Musical Cases, Re: Fogerty v. Kanter, Deposition Summary of James (Jake) Roher, 24 May 1982, p. 2.

74. Ibid., p. 3.

75. Peat, Marwick, Mitchell & Co. to Scott T. Pratt, Esq., Keesal, Young & Logan, "Analysis, Subject: *Fogerty v. Hardin, Cook, et al.*" 15 August 1982, pp. 2–3.

76. Ibid, p. 6.

77. Ibid, p. 7.

78. Ibid., pp. 10–13.

79. State of California, Court of Appeal, First Appellate District, *Douglas Clifford, et al., v. Edward J. Arnold, et al.*, Appellants' Opening Brief, 1st Civil No. A023627, p. 12.

80. Ibid., p. 4.

81. Burton Kanter to Edward J. Arnold, "*Memorandum*—Fees," 7 May 1970.

82. Edward J. Arnold to Mr. Barrie Engel of Hardin, Cook, Loper, Engel & Bergez, "RE: *April 16, 1973 letter—Burton Kanter*," 23 April 1973.

83. Barrie Engel to Mr. A. J. T. Gooding, Castle Trust Company Limited, "Re: Shire Limited Account Nos. 301021 and 108017," 9 September 1970.

84. Robert Hilburn, "Fogerty goes from Creedence to one-man band," *Chicago Sun-Times*, 9 April 1973, p. 38.

85. However, it was Tom Fogerty who first left the group in 1971. State of California, Court of Appeal, First Appellate District, *Douglas Clifford, et al., v. Edward J. Arnold, et al.*, Appellants' Opening Brief, 1st Civil No. A023627, p. 6.

    When Tom departed there was an important change in the manner in which the money was handled. The elaborate King David-Shalom-Shire entity was no longer thought necessary by the Kanter people, and Argosy-Venture sent the royalties directly to the trustee at Castle Bank, which held the funds in something called the EJ Clearing Account until they were dispersed on instructions. Ibid., p. 12.

86. Ibid., p. 15.

87. Ibid., p. 17.

88. *Centre Daily Times*, "Newsmakers," 1987.

89. Laurence Peters to Lawrence G. Becker, Esq., Office of Regional Counsel, I.R.S., San Francisco, "Re: *John C. and Martha Fogerty*," 13 December 1979.

90. Author's interviews with Attorneys Scott Pratt, Long Beach, California, and Nelson Barry, San Francisco, California, June 1986.

91. State of California, Superior Court in and for the County of Santa Barbara, *John Fogerty and Martha Ann Fogerty v. Burton W. Kanter, et al.*, No. 121771, 21 March 1978.

92. State of California, Court of Appeal, p. 24.

93. Jonathan Dahl, "IRS Claims Profit Of 'Cuckoo's Nest' Has Flown the Coop," *Wall Street Journal*, 18 February 1987.

94. Author's Interview with I.R.S. investigators, August, 1986, and subsequently.

95. John Fogerty, "VANZ KANT DANZ," (Wenaha Music Company ASCAP, 1984).

96. Statement of Harry Margolis in Nicholas J. Bartolone, "Audit Division, Report of Visit," 6–11 August 1973, p. 5.

10

Conclusions: Cuckoo's Nest to Cocaine

Research that covers a fairly extended period of time always needs a final check to see what may have changed over the course of the investigation itself. So in this final chapter I discuss certain individual and institutional alterations of major players prominently mentioned in the preceding chapters, review what remains of the continuing Castle saga, comment on The Bahamas' vexing problem of drug trafficking, and finally add a remark or two about the "serious crime community."

Some organizations, for instance, have been quite drastically transformed. Resorts International is one. Once the center of Tradewinds' attention, its fortunes ebbed almost more quickly than those of its intelligence division foes. Jim Crosby died in 1986 and Resorts plunged downhill. For a short while it entered the domain of Donald Trump, who purchased the casinos in New Jersey and The Bahamas, and other property from Crosby's estate. By December, 1987, Trump announced he was "inclined" to resign as chairman of Resorts International unless the New Jersey Casino Commission approved some legislation Trump wanted. He pointed out that Resorts was "a sick child"—Wall Street had lost confidence in Resorts Management under the poor investment leadership of Crosby—needing his help if ever it was to regain financial health. What Trump wanted, of course, was to raise capital for what was then called "the next Resorts casino hotel in Atlantic City, the $923 million Taj Mahal."[1]

Whether or not Trump originally wanted to drain and dump

Resorts in favor of his new pleasure palace, he did claim both the future profitability and stability of Resorts depended on the successful completion and opening of the much larger and more lavish Taj Mahal. Writing about Resorts under Trump's management, *New York Times* reporter Donald Janson noted "What was once a relatively debt-free company is now a highly leveraged one."[2]

But help for Trump was soon on its way in the person of multimillionaire entertainer Merv Griffin. For whatever reason, Griffin decided to buy the debt-ridden Resorts International from Trump, presumably confident he could turn the deteriorating properties around. By the summer of 1989, it was reported that Griffin's investments were "losing money at a rapidly accelerating pace, with a staggering second-quarter loss of $27.9 million."[3] Every second they were open, it was reported, Griffin's casinos were losing over three and a half dollars.[4] Last November a Reuters dispatch carried in the *San Francisco Chronicle* revealed a bankruptcy petition by Resorts International was probably going to be filed in the very near future, almost on the "anniversary of Griffin's leveraged buyout of Resorts, after a battle with New York real estate investor Donald Trump."[5] The only certain thing about Resorts International now is that it hardly resembles the dynamic company which captivated Operation Tradewinds for so many years.

Castle Bank is like the proverbial bad penny; it turns up somewhere almost all the time. Past issues are reprised, new ones surface. Over time there emerged and has now long endured a hardy group of survivors known unflatteringly by some as "Castle groupies." These are the true believers, convinced one day the abstraction "justice" will prevail and the Castle question will be honestly resolved. They will know this day, because it will begin with Burt Kanter indicted for perjury, based upon his many false statements under oath at one official court proceeding after another. And so this loosely structured group keeps its eyes open for any news on Castle cases or Castle rebirths. Remarkable as it may seem, the latter appeared to have happened on 22 May 1983 when a small advertisement (briefly mentioned earlier) titled OFFSHORE FINANCE SERVICE was published in *The Miami Herald*'s business classifieds.

The text read, "A strictly confidential service for Florida residents: Trust information; worldwide company formation and subsequent management, investment holding & nominee services: Contact Castle Trust Co. Ltd., PO Box 226, St. Peter Port, Guernsey, Channel Islands, Europe."[6] The announcement was surrounded by others for real estate purchases, "principals seeking qualified Mobile Home Parks," condo apartments on golf course locations, and a group looking for "50 Million To Invest." Within a couple of weeks the Castle followers were alerted, and wondered whether or not, as one stalwart phrased it, "this was going to be a resurrection of Castle Trust with Kanter participation."[7] While little effort was actually made to check out the Channel Islands' Castle, there was reason to suspect it was the old enemy.

Credit for information which fueled this speculation must be given once again to the indefatigable Sally. She located a statement made by Anthony J. T. Gooding under examination by Bahamian attorney Anthony Thompson, which was placed in the "Common Law File No. 19 of 1979, Equity Side, Supreme Court of the Commonwealth of the Bahamas." In this statement taken over some legal issue, Gooding averred that he lived in the Channel Islands. In fact, he said "I physically removed myself in May, 1973 to [sic] Channel Islands." He admitted being "retained as a Director by Castle but never performed as such." Aside from pleading appalling ignorance about Castle affairs in The Bahamas, Caymans, and Panama, Gooding affirmed in this statement that Mrs. Florence Curry was the Treasurer from about 1975 to 1976; that "she and Mr. Wolstencroft kept the books."[8] Gooding, it turned out, lived in St. Peter Port, Guernsey. This surely may reflect nothing more than coincidence. However, a British financial reporter recently declared to me in a private communication that it was his firm opinion, after checking with sources in the Channel Islands, that Guernsey Castle was indeed a resurrection of the Caribbean ones. Beside his contention, though, he could offer no concrete proof. The tantalizing possibility remains, nonetheless.

The Channel watch settled into a familiar frustrating pattern, until other events involving a Castle personality having a Channel connection unfolded. This time it was not Jim Gooding, but rather attorney Lawrence A. Freeman who had been a Castle vice-president and secretary in 1970 and 1971. Freeman's Castle jobs were directly related to the retirement of the "ghostly" Greek Alipranti, mentioned several times in earlier chapters. In an interview with Freeman on 18 September 1987, he asserted the usual ignorance of Castle affairs, but did state that he had "influence" with a top Department of Justice official directly connected with the Castle investigation. He said this official also knew Joel Mallin and Burt Kanter quite well, even describing them as "pals." Freeman's friendship was evident, he added, when in just a few private minutes with this individual Freeman was able to have him call off a Grand Jury appearance for a client deeply involved in the Moran affair.[9]

Freeman's luck ran out when he was indicted in Florida in 1985 for "laundering drug profits for convicted drug dealer Jack DeVoe."[10] Most of the laundering apparently took place in Jersey, the Channel Islands' other favored tax haven. It turns out that Freeman, working through a Castle-type institution known as Compendium Trust, laundered over a million and a half pounds for smuggler DeVoe.[11] This was only the tip of Freeman's problems in the latter 1980s, which increasingly placed him squarely in the nation's current Savings and Loan nightmare. *Houston Post* reporters investigating one of the key real estate deals that caused the collapse of several important Texas Savings and Loans (S & L), found Freeman in the thick of the affair. For instance, it was reported that Freeman represented an important shell company for one of the alleged major S & L swindlers and that "some of the drug money from Freeman and DeVoe was deposited in the Bank Cantrade Switzerland (CI) Limited, which also received" millions drained from S & L depositors through the shell company and others equally fraudulent.[12]

The Florida Department of Law Enforcement's first report on the Freeman money laundering scheme was dated 14 September 1984, and came after an interrogation of DeVoe. Several subsequent interviews with other members of this smuggling group eventually led to Freeman's arrest in 1985. After securing a search warrant the police found documentation of numerous Freeman deals ranging from the establishment of shell companies in The Netherlands Antilles, suspicious accounts in Cayman Island banks, investments probably for smugglers in airplanes, real estate trans-actions for foreign citizens in Florida shopping centers, and par-ticularly the use of Bahamian trust accounts in order, it was speculated, to add the final touch of complexity to his criminal machinations. It was also most interesting to note that one of Burt Kanter's attorneys who represented him in some of the Cas-tle actions also worked for DeVoe. One of the Florida witnesses stated Kanter's attorney helped DeVoe work out two methods of "getting money back into the United States."[13] This same witness noted that Freeman moved the main headquarters of his money laundering operation from The Bahamas to the Channel Islands in 1983 when he set up two trusts—Oka International (the name Dr. Robert Oka was one of DeVoe's aliases), and the Nepal Trust Company. One trust owned the other and DeVoe was the sole beneficiary, he added. Interestingly enough, this action was around the time the Castle item appeared in the *Miami Herald*.

Larry Freeman's troubles would hardly be worth mentioning if they didn't add to the speculation of Castle reborn, and if Freeman didn't turn out to be a key witness in the Zaentz tax case, which is still not quite settled as I write this on the first day of spring 1990. This case started when Jimmy Carter was running for Pres-ident, and though it seemed at long last to have reached closure this past autumn, it still lingers with pit bull tenacity.

Fought in the obscurity of the U.S. Tax Court, the suit (noted in the preceding chapter) by the Internal Revenue Service charges Saul Zaentz and others with hiding the profits from the academy award winning film *One Flew Over The Cuckoo's Nest*, and thus evading substantial taxes due the government. The government's theory from the beginning, although buttressed over time as new facts and witnesses emerged, held that Burt Kanter, certain mem-bers of his law firm, and the Castle Bank crowd engineered this scam. Using their sophisticated expertise in evading taxes, Kanter and the others put together the always complicated foreign com-panies and trusts in such a way that "*all* Cuckoo's Nest profits" made their way back to Zaentz and the other investors "thinly disguised as 'loans.' "[14]

Because of Kanter's central position in the government's con-tentions of tax evasion, there was a great deal of emphasis over the years on Kanter's relationship to Castle Bank. In the recent past, however, the Judge in the Zaentz case has appeared increasingly hostile to the government's position that proving Kanter owned (or partially owned) Castle was either important or germane. That followed a line developed by one of the petitioners' attorneys, Marvin J. Garbis, during a phase of the trial held at the Federal Courthouse in San Francisco, 18 July 1988. Garbis remarked the government was fixated upon Kanter and Castle Bank and added: "I could stipulate that Mr. Kanter owned the Castle Bank and Trust Company, . . . and it wouldn't make a damn bit of difference." The reason, Garbis held, was this: "It is not relevant. The question is did these people, these taxpayers, own the Castle Bank, which they did not."[15] From the winter of 1989 on, the Judge was more and more inclined to agree with the petitioners' position. Finally, in the first week of January 1989, the Court stated "that one of the reasons for the lack of effective settlement dialogue is 'respondent's singular focus on the *sham theory*, which he has vigorously pursued in over two weeks of trial time to the exclusion of the other theories outlined in his trial memorandum.' "[16] The sham theory referred to the position that Kanter owned Castle and thus the scheme was a sham from the start.

The I.R.S. counsel answered the Court, maintaining Kanter's ownership of Castle was clearly significant for several reasons, including perhaps the most elementary one: the funds to produce the movie came from Castle trusts (ironically from money earned by the Creedence Clearwater Revival's exceptional success, most of which went into Zaentz trusts set up by Kanter, etc.), and were routed through one of Castle's Netherlands Antilles' conduits, the already infamous Inversiones Mixtas.[17] Even though the Judge's patience with this issue was waning, I.R.S. counsel Eugene H. Ciranni nevertheless ploughed ahead.

An important part of Ciranni's strategy of proving Kanter (and the late Helliwell) owned Castle, and that the bank's purpose had always been fraudulent and a vehicle for tax evasion, was to establish that both George Bebas and A. Alipranti[18] were nonexistent. On this same subject, Attorney Garbis had earlier stated that even if this was so, it would mean nothing as far as his clients' guilt was concerned.[19] But Ciranni thought otherwise. Indeed, in his response to the Judge's displeasure with the government's alleged Castle fixation in January 1989, Ciranni and his very able assistant, Attorney Debra K. Estrem, wrote that despite the implications of the Zaentz attorneys, the government's "sham theory does not depend on respondent conclusively proving that George Bebas and A. Alipranti were fictitious people, or that Burton Kanter owned any part of Castle Bank, or even that the petitioners completely controlled every entity involved in this tax plan."[20] Instead, Ciranni and Estrem argued these important facts support the government's "sham argument, which is that a good hard look at the entire circular transaction reveals a complete lack of any real economic purpose, beyond tax avoidance."[21]

The absolute bottom line that the government wished to establish was this:

> Castle Bank and CIBC [Canadian Imperial Bank of Commerce, which took over many Castle accounts when Castle had to fade from the Bahamian and Caymanian scenes], . . . were not independent in any respect. . . . Castle basically served as an arm of the LKB&L Chicago office, and even had a Chicago bank account for which Burton Kanter had signatory authority. *Whether or not the Court believes the evidence in the record concerning Castle's technical ownership, it is clear from the events . . . it did whatever it was supposed to do to achieve the expected result in Kanter's tax plans. It performed no independent trustee functions other than keeping track of what LKB&L and Helliwell attorneys put in and took out of its accounts. Castle's employees were no more than window dressing and did whatever the attorney for a tax plan client asked them to do. It is clear from the record that Castle or CIBC never negotiated a single transaction with a LKB&L attorney or client. Its job was to carry out Kanter's tax plans. (My emphasis)*[22]

Bebas and Alipranti were centrally significant, but in supporting roles. And that is where Larry Freeman turned up in this case. He was called as a witness by the Zaentz forces in October 1988 to refute the testimony of Demetrius G. Stampados (discussed earlier), who knew as well as anyone that the Greeks were either fictional or dead and so stated, although slightly obliquely, in 1988. Stampados was questioned by Ciranni in Denver, Colorado (the Court went there as Stampados, who lived in Denver, was ill) about both Alipranti and Bebas. The witness seemed a bit cantankerous in his answers but covered the essential issues. Asked about Alipranti, he first said Helliwell wrongly believed Alipranti won the marathon at the first modern Olympic games held in Athens in 1896. Stampados pointed out the winner was Spirdon Loues, not Alipranti.[23] The point was that Helliwell thought he was cleverly using the long dead marathon winner as one of Castle's owners and officers. It was another display of insider brashness and cleverness.

On the question of the existence of Bebas, which Stampados had earlier denied in a private taped interview, he now affirmed that Helliwell told him Bebas was in fact quite real. Unfortunately for the defense, Stampados then followed this by commenting he watched Helliwell on several occasions sign the names Alipranti and Bebas to various documents.[24] A few minutes later Stampados, on direct examination, angrily added to Helliwell's penchant for using phony Greek names for Castle. Stampados stated he "was very much infuriated when I found out that those names [his mother's maiden name and other family names] had been used by Paul Helliwell on legal documents after I left his law firm."

Stampados finally added that he had gone to Greece sometime after his stint with Helliwell, and there checked the Athens phone directory for Alipranti and Bebas, and found no listing for either man. Without engaging in any deeper investigation as to the existence of these people, he was clearly satisfied they were figments of Helliwell's very fertile imagination.[25]

Although the significance of the existence of Alipranti and Bebas was constantly denied by Zaentz counsel, the Stampados testimony had to be countered, if for no other reason than that the original Bahamian trusts utilized by Zaentz and his partners were formed by Kanter's firm with Trust Settlement "T-5004" dated 1 April 1969. The settlor who executed the document was George Bebas, and the witness was A. Alipranti.[26]

In came the deeply troubled Larry Freeman to help the cause. Freeman testified that he was a lawyer who had worked with Helliwell's Florida firm and then became house counsel for Castle Bank in 1970. This didn't last long and about fourteen months later he was back with the Helliwell firm in Miami. He went on his own in 1972. Once the preliminaries were over Freeman was asked the big question—had he ever met George Bebas. Yes, he said, sometime during the summer or fall of 1964 when he was in Zurich, Switzerland.

It was all very haphazard, unplanned, a chance encounter. Freeman was in Switzerland trying to raise capital for an Arab airline in Egypt when he happened to "go to the office of a businessman from Chicago who was living in Zurich, and as I entered his office, I happened to see by accident, totally unplanned, Mr. Helliwell in an office." Helliwell then introduced him to a man named George Bebas.[27] The office where the meeting took place was that of Philip Barry, the last and most mysterious Castle owner. Freeman remarked that Helliwell and Barry were O.S.S. acquaintances. He added that later in the evening he had dinner with Helliwell and another former O.S.S. officer, William Casey, who was made chief of the C.I.A. by President Reagan.

Freeman was asked whether he ever met Alipranti. His answer was again affirmative—"in the summer of 1971 in Athens." This meeting was arranged by Helliwell while both he and Freeman were again by chance in London. In an off-handed way Freeman told Helliwell he was on his way to Geneva, Athens, and Istanbul on business. Equally casual, Helliwell suggested he should look up some of his Greek friends including Alipranti. And that was that.[28] This was the only positive corroboration of either man's actual existence. It wasn't very much, however. Freeman remembered little about either man, seemed never to have questioned anyone about how it was they became involved in Castle, why neither ever appeared in The Bahamas, and most importantly, why their signatures were forged. The Castle people never had any credible witnesses admit that documents allegedly signed by either man, were really signed by either man. With their physical existence in such doubt, it was enough to have someone affirm the Greeks lived recently enough to take part in Castle affairs. Freeman's function at the Zaentz trial was to verify that simple but quite important fact.

Unfortunately, Freeman's own very difficult criminal justice position, if allowed to enter the case record, would have definitely undermined his credibility. Thus, he and his associates fought strenuously, raising several constitutional issues, hoping to bar questions about his legal problems. In answer to claims that questions about Devoe and money laundering should be out-of-bounds, and also in a complaint to the I.R.S. Chief Counsel's Office, the I.R.S. Assistant Chief Counsel Marlene Gross informed Freeman that his argument against cross-examination on his criminal career, because it might undermine his right to plea bargain, was moot. She pointed out that at the time of his testimony he had already entered into a plea agreement with the Florida Statewide Prosecutor "whereby you [Freeman] will plead no contest to two counts of the twenty count indictment, reserving the right to appeal the constitutionality of the Florida RICO statute, and receive a three year sentence." Moreover, concerning another assertion that maintained that cross-examination about Devoe should be barred because of the attorney-client privilege, Ms. Gross wrote the government has "an affidavit obtained from Jack Devoe or Robert K. Oka . . . which waives the attorney-client privilege."[29] In fact, they had Devoe's affidavit dated 24 January 1989, and a second one from another conspirator in the drug case. This one stated:

> My name is Profulla Mondol. During the early 1980s I worked for Jack R. DeVoe assisting him in some of his illegal smuggling ventures. On several occasions, I portrayed a person by the name of Robert K. Oka. Robert K. Oka was an alias used by Jack DeVoe for the purpose of investing monies without connecting these investment to himself.
>
> It is further my understanding now that a portion of DeVoe's illegal profits were entrusted to attorney Lawrence A. Freeman, in the name of Robert K. Oka. I hereby state that I waive any and all attorney/client privileges which I may have had with Mr. Freeman over any matters.[30]

With Freeman's probity in serious jeopardy, the Zaentz group moved to reach an agreement with the I.R.S. Sometime in the fall those accused of tax evasion agreed to pay somewhere between fourteen and fifteen million dollars. This was substantially less than originally demanded by the I.R.S., but it appeared to some a reasonable offer after so much time and money already had been spent litigating this case. The interested parties were to sign off this past December (1989), but have delayed doing so, wrangling over some apparently important but ancillary issues. Whether the Zaentz tax case has finally reached the end of the line is thus still up in the air, though now it does truly seem close to landing.

While Zaentz and his associates (Kanter included, for he too testified for approximately two and a half days, and once again denied knowing hardly anything of significance about Castle, its ownership and management) wend their way through the tax court on this latest Castle go-round, Dick Jaffe long ago entered another phase of law enforcement. He retired from the I.R.S. in 1979, and was soon hired by the Florida state attorney's office in the Eleventh Judicial Circuit of Florida. Jaffe attended to his new job with the same sense of purpose as before. He was and remains the proverbial straight arrow.

Perhaps his most outstanding contribution in this new position came in the mid–1980s in what was dubbed the "River Cops Case." This concerned about a dozen Miami policemen who formed their own violent drug syndicate. They stole marijuana and cocaine from dealers, dealt it themselves, hired killers to silence potential witnesses against them, and also participated in murders, some of which were carried out by forcing victims to jump into the Miami River and drown—hence, their sobriquet.[31]

Jaffe's work as the state attorney's supervisory investigative accountant came in for heavy praise. One letter came from Jaffe's old employer the Internal Revenue Service. The chief of the Criminal Investigative Division, Ft. Lauderdale District wrote State Attorney Janet Reno about the "invaluable assistance rendered to our office" by Jaffe "during the course of the income tax investigations and subsequent trials of the 'Miami River Cops.' " This letter from Division Chief Dockum was followed by an official certificate of appreciation.[32]

One cannot write about The Bahamas without noting in passing the government's commitment to the international drug trade, which started in the mid–1970s when the traffic in cocaine and marijuana swept into The Bahamas. Drug activity in The Bahamas was constantly expanding, as smugglers established territories and the correct relationships with government and police officials. In 1972, a police seizure of 1,500 pounds of "pot" valued at one million dollars was the largest drug bust in Bahamian history. It stirred misgivings, but was still looked upon as an oddity, nothing very serious, even an occasion for courtroom laughter, and judicial jokes.[33] A few years later the humor was gone. The Bahamas had become a major transshipment point for narcotics between South America and the United States. Additionally, The Bahamas developed a significant internal drug problem as a government-sponsored report published in 1984 established. The nation, it stated, has endured a huge increase in drug-related crime and faces a severe narcotics problem in government corporations, hospitals, banks, hotels, restaurants, industrial corporations at Grand Bahama, government ministries, and so on.[34]

Drug smuggling became the major Bahamian political issue by 1979, dividing the opposition party, the Free National Movement (F.N.M.) from the government. That November, opposition leader Norman S. Solomon argued the government should investigate criminal activities on Norman's Cay, in the Exumas chain, lying 40 miles south of Nassau and 190 miles southeast of Miami. Solomon suspected Norman's Cay housed the most significant drug racketeers in The Bahamas. He was right, and was almost murdered for pointing it out.

With Pindling firmly in power, the government was not about to investigate the smugglers on Norman's Cay. The F.N.M. realized this, but thought it had a slim chance to use this issue as a stepping stone to political power. It demanded elections in 1982. The government agreed, and one way or another won the ensuing election.

By the mid–1980s, The Bahamas was in peril from high-level corruption, which directly expedited the flow of drugs to America.[35] The country itself had been divided by smugglers. About fifteen islands and cays were either totally or partially controlled by drug racketeers. These included the largest islands, such as Andros, Grand Bahama, Abaco, Eleuthera, Cat, Acklins, and Great Inagua Island, fairly close to both Baracoa, Cuba, and Ile de la Tortue, Haiti. The islands were handy storage depots for contraband waiting for the right time and price before being moved. That is why, for example, drug racketeers bought the Darby Islands (Little Darby, Darby, Goat Cay, Guana Cay, and Betty Cay), also located in the Exuma chain, like Norman's Cay. One leader of the Darby criminal syndicate, Tilton Lamar Chester,

Jr., was a former Eastern Airlines pilot. He and his co-conspirators bought the property, using a front company developed by organized crime. They built houses, an aircraft hanger and landing strip.[36]

But it was Norman's Cay which epitomized the absolute nadir of drug racketeering. A small, beautiful island with an inviting anchorage and 3,000 foot airstrip, it was the center of a drug whirlwind. There was sufficient publicity about peculiar occurrences at Norman's Cay by the last week of summer, 1979, to force the government into a kind of slow motion action. It planned a supposedly secret police raid scheduled for the first of September, but this raid was cancelled at the last moment. That provided time for the raid to turn to farce.[37] Rescheduled for 14 September, it was carried out at dawn with exuberance by a team of police commandos. They seized an insignificant cache of weapons and drugs, and arrested 26 people.[38] Charged with violations were fourteen Colombians, two American couples, and a German woman named Margrit Melelinnekogel.[39] An advance warning gave the smugglers ample time to hide hundreds of kilos of cocaine.[40] The confiscated contraband was useless as evidence and the charges were eventually dropped.

A few weeks after the raid, the principal owner of Norman's Cay was identified. He was Carlos Enrique Lehder Rivas (known locally as Joe Lehder, and internationally as Carlos Lehder), described in the local newspapers as a former convict deported from the United States to Colombia in 1975. Just after his forced departure from New York, Lehder was indicted by a Florida Grand Jury for drug-smuggling violations. Lehder was thus a fugitive from U.S. justice for three years when the raid on Norman's Cay took place. Strangely enough, at that time his case file was marked inactive, meaning among other things that he had vanished, that law enforcement could not locate him.[41] But he had not been hiding. On the contrary, Lehder was extremely busy establishing the transport center for what was to become, allegedly, the largest drug syndicate in the world. And because he loved publicity, he granted press interviews numerous times, so that even a mildly alert observer should have had no difficulty finding him.

For example, in the spring of 1979, there was a long feature article about the "mystery man" of Norman's Cay in the Nassau

Tribune. It was reported that he was a 29-year-old millionaire born in Colombia of German descent, who purchased most of the island to develop its marinas and resort potential. The article gushed that Lehder was "very much in love with the Bahamas because it's a place he can come to to get away from everything."[42] It ended extolling Lehder's wealth and civic-mindedness, pointing out he offered the local police force one of his helicopters for patrol.

The publicity about Lehder was extensive, as was the general knowledge of his smuggling activities. Together, this made him appear an attractive, somewhat charismatic individual. Some Bahamians thought him a Robin Hood figure, jousting with the repressive American police. This outlook appeared in print October 1981. It was in the form of a strange letter to Sir Etienne Dupuch, the editor of the Nassau *Tribune*. The letter attacked Dupuch, whose paper had moved from soft feature stories about the Colombians to aggressive reporting on drug racketeering. Dupuch was accused of being a traitor to The Bahamas. "This country is just growing whilst you are dying and you are asking us to turn our country into the hands of the USA," wrote Bahamian Steve Francis who described himself as a young journalist.[43]

Francis was angry over *Tribune* editorials that he felt were directed "against our independence, against our beloved PM, against the young, . . . our music, our education, our art, our islands, our economy." He enumerated a list of 49 questions intending to show Dupuch as a blackguard and Lehder as a hero and benefactor. The questions went like this:

1. Do you know that Joe Carlos Enrique Lehder came to the Bahamas at the age of 26, on January 1st 1976?
2. Do you know that Joe, in trusting the Bahamian investments laws brought US $10,000,000 into the Bahamian economy?
3. Do you know Mr. William Lehder, Joe's father, a Civil Engineer from Germany, has been on the top of the construction industry and development of their city for the last 40 years?
4. Do you know that Joe resides on his 100,000 acre ranch on the Boyaca flats in Colombia, South America?
5. Do you know Norman's Cay is Joe's castle and Garden?
6. Do you know that Joe's only crime is the tremendous concern,

faith and love that he possesses for the Norman's Cay community?

7. Do you know if German-Colombians are black or white?
8. Do you know that the DEA with the assistance of malicious Bahamians such as you began a conspiracy against the Norman's Cay community, and as a result Joe ended up on the Bahamas Government stop list, and Joe had to disappear?

This attack fit in with a more generalized government assault on the editor and his paper. In time the battle worsened, until in 1986 a *Tribune* reporter accused the Pindling government of literally threatening the freedom of the press. The government harassed Dupuch's paper for publishing stories on drug traffickers and public corruption, and for helping foreign journalists covering the same stories. In the minds of *Tribune* people the government had made "a conscious decision to take punitive action against a section of the press that has . . . refused to bend to the iron fist of the Prime Minister and his ministerial puppets, a prime minister who has lost the moral authority to govern.[44] The paper was squeezed so hard by the administration—denied press releases, access to government officials, and work permits for the non-Bahamian staff members—that its current editor and publisher, Sir Etienne's daughter, contemplated closing it in the summer of 1987 and leaving The Bahamas.[45]

Carlos Lehder, on the other hand, had nothing to fear from either Bahamian or U.S. forces for quite some time. Lehder was unafraid of the Bahamian police, unconcerned with either the opposition party or aggressive reporting in the Nassau *Tribune*. He had achieved a degree of sovereignty leading him to object even to the little charades that had to be done once in a while for administration face-saving. Lehder didn't hesitate to bully the Pindling administration after the 1979 symbolic raid, for example. He halted construction reportedly worth $8 million, fired about 100 Bahamian workers, and threatened to move back to his native West Germany (it was incorrectly reported), if the harassment didn't stop. Perhaps Lehder was miffed because several months before the "opera bouffe" attack on Norman's Cay, he told Bahamian authorities "he would not hesitate to pull up stakes and leave the country if he experienced any trouble with regards to his island hideaway."[46]

To make sure his message was clear, Lehder placed prominent ads in Bahamian newspapers stating the Norman's Cay Yacht Club was For Immediate Sale. Along with the club went 165 acres, a marina, clubhouse, manager's house, 10 fully furnished and equipped "Vacation Villas," the airstrip and airport office, four new hangars, staff quarters, mechanic's shop and garage, a laundromat, several trucks, jeeps, vans and station wagons, a house boat, cargo boat, speedboat, five Boston Whalers, and finally two airplanes, an eight-seat Beechcraft and a Cessna 206. All this could be had for $2,932,000; interested buyers were to contact International Dutch Resources Ltd. through the Guardian Trust Company of Nassau. No one dared, however, and neither Lehder nor his company bothered to secure the necessary government permissions required to sell the island.[47]

There really was no reason to sell Norman's Cay, as there was no pressure to halt smuggling. To repeat an earlier point, though Lehder was a fugitive from a U.S. indictment, he was hard to keep quiet, not difficult to find. In fact, the C.I.A. station chief in The Bahamas, Andrew F. Antippas, knew enough about Lehder's activities by 1981 that he approached Prime Minister Pindling about the Lehder-cocaine problem. But all Pindling wanted to know, Antippas said, were his sources of information. Pindling's disinterest in the problem was matched, it appears, by the United States ambassador who told Antippas in 1983 to "find another job."[48]

Lehder's leadership in the Medellin drug cartel ended, of course, with his surprising capture in 1987. But I often wonder what that event really signalled. In the months following Lehder's arrest and American incarceration, Colombian drug racketeers exported more cocaine to the United States than ever before. And Jose Manuel Arias Carrzosa, then Colombia's justice minister, laconically remarked there were many racketeers waiting in the wings to take Lehder's place—"His arrest," the Minister said, "disrupted nothing."[49]

For The Bahamas, however, the Lehder interlude had the potential to bring down the Pindling government. What put that possibility in motion was American television news. A detailed and damning investigative report, put together by producer Ira Silverman and reporter Brian Ross, broadcast by NBC's Nightly

News show on 5 September 1983, forced Pindling into a corner. He simply had to agree an impartial investigation was needed. A Commission of Inquiry, established by the British Governor General, Sir Gerald Christopher Cash, was empaneled on 28 November to inquire into NBC's charges as well as the drug scene in general.[50] Although independent since 1973, the former British colony was a member of the British Commonwealth, which explains Britain's role in the Commission. Evidence from the Commission of Inquiry's public hearings, plus other sources—some inspired by the Commission's efforts and others by its inevitable omissions—revealed massive smuggling operations and political corruption. High Bahamian officials, and/or intimate associates of the prime minister, were found to be crucial to the trade's success. They were the quintessential middlemen, selling protection and a resting place for contraband, permitting transporters for a fee to establish their headquarters on different islands and cays, tipping them off about D.E.A. raids and informants, and bringing together American pilots and Colombian producers.

One example should suffice. F. Nigel Bowe, Pindling's close friend and a long-time defense attorney for the few drug smugglers actually brought before Bahamian courts, was one of the most corrupt. Reporters, taking their cue from narcotics enforcers in the United States described Bowe as "so thoroughly steeped in the drug trade that his name has become synonymous with it."[51] He was among the boldest of the Bahamian criminals. Bowe served cocaine producers and smugglers by introducing one to the other, and then offering sanctuary in The Bahamas. In one instance, Bowe accompanied smuggler Jack DeVoe (whose financial angel we have seen was attorney Larry Freeman) to Cartagena, Colombia, bringing him to drug baron Jose "Pepi" Cabrera Sarmiento. Considered a pioneer in the cocaine trade, Cabrera was charged in 1985 by American authorities with smuggling over 17,000 pounds to the United States during his career.[52] DeVoe flew Cabrera's cocaine into The Bahamas, and subsequently to the United States earning about $10 million in nine months. He kicked back 10 percent ($1 million) to Bowe, who was also being paid by "Pepi."

In 1985, Bowe was indicted in the United States for his part in this enterprise. Bahamian authorities even went so far as to arrest him to ease the international pressure, though he was immediately released from custody on bond. So far, Bowe waits comfortably in Nassau for the outcome of a United States extradition request. In all the many years since the indictment, there has been little constructive American pressure on Bahamian authorities to turn Bowe over. Indeed, the strongest note came three years after the indictment when the State Department commented the Bowe proceedings were progressing very slowly, and added that Bowe was "a personal friend of the prime minister."[53] The unexpressed meaning of that conjunction was clear.

The 1984 Commission of Inquiry provided details of Pindling's corruption in general, which, however, turned out to be relatively unimportant. The key issue, understood perfectly by Pindling and his supporters at home and in the United States, was drug corruption. It was politically imperative to deny the prime minister had anything to do with drug corruption, even if it meant arguing stupefying ignorance of all things around him. The strategy was successful; the Commission of Inquiry concluded there was insufficient evidence to find Pindling in the chain of narcotics trafficking. There was a minority view that sensibly argued "the real question is whether it can be plausibly inferred from the circumstances that any of the payments [to Pindling] were drug related."[54] Furthermore, it continued, the prime minister did not take care to "preclude the possibility of drug-related funds reaching his bank account or being applied for his benefit."

Although the record constructed by the 1984 Commission of Inquiry was overwhelming, it was not finally overpowering. The evidence was insufficient to unseat Pindling and the P.L.P. The opposition party again relied upon winning a national election, which it demanded and got in the summer of 1987. But as in 1982, it couldn't break through. Naturally Pindling characterized the election as one for national independence from the United States, which was tyrannizing Bahamians through the D.E.A. He succeeded to a greater degree than most thought possible. This, despite the fact that Bahamians had a very clear idea of governmental culpability in the drug trade. Indeed, in the fall of 1986, the essence of the problem was summarized for all to see in the headline of a Bahamian tabloid called *The Torch*. "The Country Wants to Know," it read, "Is The Chief Still A Thief?"[55] It was a fair question in 1986, made even more important in 1987 as voters went to the polls.

Until the election, it was believed Pindling was vulnerable, that the P.L.P. was in crisis. This perception was partially derived from several serious defections, the most significant of which occurred in May 1987 when the deputy prime minister resigned to protest Pindling's failure to deal with the issue of corruption.[56] Many of the racketeers thought their run was finally over. It turned out they were poor prognosticators. What threatened to be a close fight was instead a walk-over for the old guard. Pindling and the P.L.P. easily won in 1987 and kept to their steady course.

Among the many reasons for this triumph, one was certainly election corruption. Even though a few American "watchers" were invited to oversee the electoral process, there was no chance for them or anyone else to mitigate fraud and coercion. They did parenthetically note that the Bahamian election seemed cleaner than the one Ferdinand Marcos had just won in the Philippines. Of course that fraudulent victory touched off the peaceful "Snap" revolution which brought Mrs. Acquino to power. In The Bahamas, however, there was no Acquino, no revolutionary fervor, no martyred man. There was only an opposition party calling for moral reform. One of the F.N.M.'s important handicaps was that its leadership was too Caucasian to suit most Bahamians. The opposition brought back bitter memories of racism and colonialism, especially through the skillful electioneering of the P.L.P. Independence from British colonial rule brought about under Pindling was an experience shared by almost all the voters. Moreover, corruption by the 1980s was endemic; criminality had entered the general population where thousands found work and money in the smuggling milieu. For them the P.L.P. represented stability and opportunity. What could the opposition offer but a drastic drop in income for many?

When the Commission of Inquiry proved that The Bahamas was a racket, it was assumed something would happen, although no one was certain what. Some speculated all the P.L.P. leadership would go to jail, without reflecting that it surely wouldn't be a Bahamian jail. The missing part of the optimistic vision heralding the end of P.L.P. power, was the force necessary to carry out the reformation. The opposition always lacked the strength to overcome government criminality, let alone crime so deeply embedded on vertical and horizontal planes—up the political ladder and across a wide zone of the population. After the 1987 election, the reflections of doubt about the future of the P.L.P. turned out to be the workings of either guilty consciences, or the articulated hopes of the truly unsophisticated.

The United States was the only entity truly able to pressure and police The Bahamas. But America was trapped in an ambiguous policy tarnished by more than a few unholy relationships. The ambivalence is clearly evident in the March 1988 State Department's *International Narcotics Control Strategy Report* section on The Bahamas. The *Report* states the Bahamian government "has demonstrated its willingness to cooperate with the United States on narcotics matters," yet announces it is "estimated that 50 to 60 percent of all the cocaine and marijuana that enters the U.S. either transits Bahamian territory or is transshipped in The Bahamas."[57] On the following page it is held that "Despite the very positive operational relationship and official climate of cooperation, narcotics-related corruption continues to be a problem in The Bahamas."[58] And although there are some operational accomplishments enumerated, they are clearly insufficient to allow for optimism.

One last element from the 1988 *Report*, which displays the equivocation at the heart of American-Bahamian relations, concerns banking. On the one hand it is stated that "banking regulations have made money laundering more difficult in The Bahamas," and on the other "absence of control over laundering money . . . makes it difficult to measure accurately the extent of money laundering in the country."[59]

This finally brings us back to the crux of the matter: despite all opinions and bits of puffed evidence to the contrary, international organized crime—the "serious crime community"—thrives in The Bahamas (as it does elsewhere) because it is a home, a haven for the subterranean economy. The serious crime community colonized The Bahamas in thirty years as resolutely as the British had for centuries. The desire to accumulate capital by whatever means (from artistic productions to pure criminality), and to keep that capital outside the vision of revenue agents is what *Masters of Paradise* is about. In the minds of those working in the subterranean economy, capital is always private, having no actual intrinsic or important relationship with the public order. This means that rules and regulations, which might in some fashion restrain capital accumulation, or even worse, recognize that some capital is surplus and that the public weal is better served when a portion of that surplus is distributed to aid those with comparatively little, are to be resolutely resisted.

There is a passion at the center of this phenomenon splendidly described in a lyric by Tim Rice for the Contemporary opera *Evita*.[60] In the final section of the song, *And the Money Kept Rolling In (And Out)*, the lust is most clear:

> If the money keeps rolling in what's a girl to do?
> Cream a little off the top for expenses—wouldn't you?
> But where on earth can people hide their little piece of
>   Heaven?
> Thank God for Switzerland
> Where a girl and a guy with a little petty cash between them
> Can be sure when they deposit no one's seen them
> Oh what bliss to sign your checks as
>   three-o-one-two-seven
> Never been accounts in the name of Eva Peron!

Notes

1. Donald Janson, "Trump to Quit Resorts Post if Pact is Denied," *New York Times*, 6 December 1987.
2. Donald Janson, "$550 Million to Complete Taj Mahal, Trump Says," *New York Times*, 18 October 1987.
3. David Johnston, "Major Losses at Resorts: Gaming License is seen at risk," *Philadelphia Inquirer*, 15 August 1989, p. A–1.
4. Ibid.
5. Reuters, "Resorts May Be Bounced Into Bankruptcy," *San Francisco Chronicle*, 11 November 1989.
6. See *Miami Herald*, 22 May 1983, p. 4–F.
7. Steadman S. Stahl, Jr., Esq, to Mr. Richard E. Jaffe, "Letter" 10 June 1983.
8. Shorthand transcription of a combination of typed and handwritten statement which was copied by "Sarah Jane Woodruff . . . on Monday, the Second day of February, 1981." Sally's sworn statement as to the accuracy of her transcription of Gooding's statement was

attested by two witnesses and sealed by Notary Public Janet Bostwick on 24 February 1981.

9. Author's interview with Lawrence E. Freeman, 18 September 1987.

10. Pete Brewton and Gregory Seay, "Links to mob figures, suspect offshore companies abound" *Houston Post*, 4 December 1988, p. A–10.

11. "Banks hand over documents in alleged money laundering case," *Jersey Evening Post*, 23 January 1988. Also see John Hamshire, "Jersey court silences U.S. lawyer," London *Daily Mail*, 23 January 1988, p. 9. Reporter Hamshire noted the case involved the release of certain Jersey bank documents hotly contested by Freeman, who was then out on bail in Miami facing charges for laundering cocaine money for convicted smuggler DeVoe, "who masterminded the smuggling into America of millions of dollars worth of cocaine from Colombia."

12. Pete Brewton, "International connections in land deal," *Houston Post*, 30 January 1989, p. A–8.

13. See Florida Department of Law Enforcement "Freeman Report #2" based on interviews with James Malone on 5 and 6 May 1985.

14. United States Tax Court, *Saul Zaentz and Lynda Zaentz, et al., Petitioners, v. Commissioner of Internal Revenue, Respondent*, Docket Nos. 3273–86; 4372–86; 5836–86; 6584–86, 38046–86, *Respondent's Memorandum of Law*, 7 April 1989, p. 2. (Hereafter cited "Cuckoo's Nest").

15. Cuckoo's Nest, *Trial*, 18 July 1988, pp. 50–51.

16. Cuckoo's Nest, p. 2.

17. Ibid., p. 29.

18. Throughout almost all the Castle material including court testimony in various cases, Alipranti is spelled with a last "i." However, in the latest transcripts from the Cuckoo's Nest case, it appears the preferred spelling is "Aliprante." Given his nonexistence, it would seem unimportant how the name is spelled; for consistencies sake I'll stick with "Alipranti."

19. Cuckoo's Nest, *Trial*, 18 July 1988, pp. 50–51.

20. Cuckoo's Nest, p. 43.

21. Ibid., p. 44.

22. Ibid., p. 87.

23. Cuckoo's Nest *Trial*, Denver, Colorado, 11 October 1988, p. 764.

24. Ibid., pp. 766–67.

25. Ibid., pp. 771–73.

26. Cuckoo's Nest, p. 13.

27. Cuckoo's Nest *Trial*, Denver, Colorado, 11 October 1988, p. 856.

28. Ibid., pp. 857–60.

29. Department of the Treasury, Internal Revenue Service, Office of the Chief Counsel, Marlene Gross, Assistant Chief Counsel (Tax

Litigation), "Letter to Lawrence A. Freeman, Esq., In re: *Zaentz v. Commissioner*," 14 February 1989.

30. Cuckoo's Nest, Peter K. Scott, Acting Chief Counsel, Internal Revenue Service, Amendment to Respondent's Motion to Resume *Cross-Examination of Larry Freeman*, 24 January 1989, with attached copies of affidavits from Proffula Mondol (Exhibit A) and Jack R. DeVoe (Exhibit B).

31. See United States District Court, Southern District of Florida, *United States of America v. Armando Estrada, et al.*, *INDICTMENT* No. 86–511–Cr–RYSKAMP (s) (s) (s); and *USA v. Estrada, et al.*, Michael P. Sullivan, Assistant United States Attorney, Senior Litigation Counsel, "Government's Motion for Sentencing Hearing and Incorporated *Memorandum of Law*." Among the many news stories on this sordid affair, which as one U.S. Attorney put it, you had drug smugglers moonlighting as cops, see Joan Fleischman, "River Cops sentenced to 30 years," *Miami Herald*, 13 February 1988, p. 1.

32. See Daniel M. Dockum, Chief Criminal Investigation Division, "Letter" to Janet Reno, State Attorney, Eleventh Judicial Circuit of Florida; also Office of the State Attorney, "Inter-Office Memorandum from Janet Reno to Dick Jaffe," 9 October 1988.

33. Lionel Dorsett, "Police Fears Bahamas Fast Becoming Narcotic Center," Nassau *Guardian*, 21 October 1972.

34. See the London *Sunday Times*, "Insight Section," 29 September 1985.

35. *Miami Herald*, special supplement on drugs and The Bahamas, 1984, p. 1.

36. U.S. District Court for the Northern District of Georgia, *USA v. Tilton Lamar Chester et al.*, *Indictment*, 4 October 1983.

37. London *Sunday Times*, 29 September 1985.

38. Nassau *Tribune*, 15 September 1979.

39. Ibid., 18 September 1979.

40. London *Sunday Times*, 29 September 1985.

41. *Miami Herald*, 24 October 1979.

42. Nassau *Tribune*, 28 April 1979.

43. Nassau *Guardian*, 8 October 1981.

44. Nassau *Tribune*, 23 July 1986.

45. Author's interviews with Eileen Carron, Summer 1986 and 1987.

46. Nassau *Guardian*, 5 October 1979.

47. Nassau *Tribune*, 17 January 1980.

48. "I tried to alert Pindling to illegal activity, testifies State Department official," *Miami Herald*, 13 April 1988.

59. Alan Riding, "Colombia Effort Against Drugs Hits Dead End," *New York Times*, 15 August 1987.

50. Bahamas Commission of Inquiry, Appointed to Inquire into the

Illegal Use of The Bahamas for the Transshipment of Dangerous Drugs Destined for the United States of America, p. 6.
51. Ibid.
52. "The World's Deadliest Criminals: The Medellin Cartel," Part 1, *Miami Herald*, 8 February 1987.
53. Reference to the State Department's report in U.S. House of Representatives, *Congressional Record*, 134 (42), 30 March 1988, p. 2.
54. Ibid., p. 408.
55. *Miami Herald*, 14 December 1986, p. 1–A.
56. Don Bohning, "Allegations put pressure on Bahamas leaders," *Miami Herald*, 3 May 1987.
57. United States Department of State, Bureau of International Narcotics matters, *International Narcotics Control Strategy Report* (March 1988), p. 150.
58. Ibid., p. 151.
59. Ibid., p. 150.
60. Tim Rice and Andrew Lloyd Webber, "and the Money Kept Rolling in (And Out)," *Evita* (Evita Music Limited, 1976).

Index